FLASH™: THE FUTURE
Pocket PC | DVD | ITV | Video | Game Consoles | Wireless

FLASH™: THE FUTURE

POCKET PC | DVD | ITV | VIDEO | GAME CONSOLES | WIRELESS

160101

Jon Warren Lentz, Bill Turner, and Ian Chia

NO STARCH PRESS

San Francisco

⊕ Printed in the United States of America on recycled paper

1 2 3 4 5 6 7 8 9 10–05 04 03 02

Trademarked names are used throughout this book. Rather than use a trademark symbol with every occurrence of a trademarked name, we are using the names only in an editorial fashion and to the benefit of the trademark owner, with no intention of infringement of the trademark.

Publisher: William Pollock
Editorial Director: Karol Jurado
Cover and Interior Design: Octopod Studios
Composition: 1106 Design, LLC
Technical Reviewer: Tom King
Copyeditor: Carol Lombardi
Proofreader: Stephanie Provines
Indexer: Broccoli Information Management

Distributed to the book trade in the United States by Publishers Group West, 1700 Fourth Street, Berkeley, CA 94710; phone: 800-788-3123; fax: 510-658-1834.

Distributed to the book trade in Canada by Jacqueline Gross & Associates, Inc., One Atlantic Avenue, Suite 105, Toronto, Ontario M6K 3E7 Canada; phone: 416-531-6737; fax 416-531-4259.

For information on translations or book distributors outside the United States and Canada, please contact No Starch Press, Inc. directly:

No Starch Press, Inc.
555 De Haro Street, Suite 250, San Francisco, CA 94107
phone: 415-863-9900; fax: 415-863-9950; info@nostarch.com; http://www.nostarch.com

The information in this book is distributed on an "As Is" basis, without warranty. While every precaution has been taken in the preparation of this work, neither the author nor No Starch Press, Inc. shall have any liability to any person or entity with respect to any loss or damage caused or alleged to be caused directly or indirectly by the information contained in it.

Library of Congress Cataloguing-in-Publication Data

Lentz, Jon Warren.
        Flash : the future / Jon Warren Lentz, Bill Turner, and Ian Chia.
                p. cm.
        Includes index.
        ISBN 1-886411-96-4 (pbk.)
            1. Computer animation. 2. Web sites--Design 3. Interactive multimedia--Authoring
programs. 4. Flash (Computer file)   I. Turner, Bill. II. Chia, Ian. III. Title.
TR897.7 .L46 2002
006.6'96--dc21

                                                                                20020012370

DEDICATIONS

I dedicate my efforts on this book to my son, Rob. You are the best buddy I've ever had.
   —Jon Warren Lentz

To my 7th grade electrical shop teacher Mr. Crabb, for giving a final exam with instructions saying: "Put your name at top of exam paper then sit quietly and do nothing for the hour." Everyone else in the class diligently answered the questions but me. They all failed. I received an A+. I learned a valuable life lesson: Always read directions.
   —Bill Turner

Dem höchsten Gott allein zu Ehren
Dem Nächsten, draus sich zu belehren

imago Dei in quolibet homine inveniartur
http://www.imagodei.com/mp3

And to my wife, my sweet Carrie. We can do anything together, but I certainly could never have done this without you. Thank you for your enduring love, support and faith. Your name is also printed with magic invisible ink on the spine. It's our secret.
   —Ian Chia

ACKNOWLEDGMENTS

I want to thank all the authors and contributors who pitched in to make this book—especially Ian Chia, for developing advanced techniques for running Flash on the PPC, and also to Chris Pelsor, for his ongoing support. I also want to thank Bill Pollock, publisher of No Starch Press, and Karol Jurado, for giving this book a home when our original publisher went down the drain. Thanks to Dorian Nisinson (www.nisinson.com) for the cover tag line and ongoing inspiration.

I also want to thank my wife, Roanne, for standing by me through this seemingly interminable endeavor—darling, you are truly my dearest friend.

—Jon Warren Lentz

First off I want to sincerely thank Jon, Ian, and all the contributors for their hard work and without whom there wouldn't be a book at all. Special thanks to Jim Cheal for supplying the photography used in the chapter on Video Formats. Jim is a great photographer, having worked for *Time*, *People*, and *US* magazines. His can be found on the Web at www.foto-graf-efx.biz.

My wife Julia deserves abundant thanks for putting up with all the rants I bestow upon her and for being a good sport about it all. Thanks also to Rachelle for handing out the "Mints" when I really needed them.

—Bill Turner

Thanks firstly to Jon Warren Lentz for shepherding this project through an extraordinary process. Though we were beset on all sides, you came through for us again and again, far beyond the call of duty. Thank you—for without you, this book would have died many times. To all my co-authors, thank you for contributing all your insights and expertise to such a comprehensive and gnarly subject. You've made this far more than the sum of its parts. And to you, dear reader—I hope this book empowers you to create useful and great things for others.

—Ian Chia

CONTRIBUTORS

Jon Warren Lentz
Bill Turner
Ian Chia
Erik Bianchi
Larry Drolet
Brett Jackson
Doug Loftus
Chris Pelsor
Jeroen Steenbeek
Bill Williams

BRIEF CONTENTS

CONTENTS IN DETAIL

2

DESIGNING FOR POCKET PCS

Bill Turner

3

GETTING USER INPUT FROM DEVICE KEYS

Doug Loftus

4

DEVELOPING GAMES TO GO

Erik Bianchi and Bill Turner

5

FLASH APPLICATION DEVELOPMENT

Ian Chia

6

STANDALONE POCKET PC FLASH APPLICATIONS

Ian Chia

7

FLASH FOR THE ENTERPRISE

Ian Chia

8

GENERATOR AND FLASH

Larry Drolet

PART TWO:
FLASH ON VIDEO, DVD, TV, INTERACTIVE TV, AND BEYOND

9

VIDEO PLAYBACK DEVICES AND FORMATS

Bill Williams and Bill Turner

10

PREPARING FLASH ANIMATION FOR VIDEO

Bill Turner

11

FLASH ANIMATIONS TO DVD

Bill Turner

12

DEVELOPING FOR INTERACTIVE TV

Brett Jackson

13

AUTHORING FOR THE NOKIA 9200
COMMUNICATOR SERIES

Chris Pelsor, Ian Chia, and Doug Loftus

14

AUTHORING FLASH CONTENT FOR UBIQUITY

Ian Chia

15

EPILOGUE: FUTURE FLASH

APPENDICES

1

THE TRUTH ABOUT 12-BIT COLOR DISPLAYS

Ian Chia and Doug Loftus

2

XML OR LOADVARIABLES?
FROM THE PERSPECTIVE OF A WIRELESS DEVELOPER

Chris Pelsor

3

FLASH FOR C++ DEVELOPERS—AN OVERVIEW

Jeroen Steenbeek

Index
371

PREFACE:
LOOKING FORWARD

How Far We've Come . . .

Since joining Macromedia in August 1999, I have watched the progression as the Macromedia Flash Player developed from a player to a ubiquitous standard. I have been a witness to an amazingly rapid evolution of the technology: In 1999, there was no concept for the deployment of the Flash Player to mainstream devices such as Personal Digital Assistants (PDAs) and Smartphones. But now, upon reflection, it appears so inevitable.

One defining instance was the bundling of Macromedia Flash Player with Netscape Navigator browsers and Microsoft Windows 95, and Windows 98 (1998), which prompted the creation of Flash content as well as Macromedia Flash Player adoption.

Today Macromedia Flash Player is the Standard Rich Client for internet content and applications such as: the ability to create rich presentations, compelling user interfaces, interactive experiences, and applications (online bank, reservation systems, digital dashboards). It is also extensively utilized for navigation control in hybrid Flash/HTML applications.

Some examples of the utilization of Macromedia Flash Player are as follows:

- At Broadmoor (www.broadmoor.com), Macromedia Flash is being used for the interface to the reservation system, leveraging its rich media capabilities.
- General Motors (www.gm.com) uses Macromedia Flash for their dynamic menu systems.
- USABrancShares (www.usabranshares.com) created an online banking system that was completely done in Macromedia Flash.

The State of Devices Today

Consumers and enterprises are migrating from desktop to devices enabling the convergence of devices and data.

The delivery of compelling Flash content and applications, on devices, excites consumers. For instance, the main challenge for hardware manufacturers and service operators, to become successful in the device space, is convincing consumers they need to adopt new technology. This is why content plays a critical role in the creation of the value proposition for these new markets.

You as Flash developers can deliver and already are delivering the content that motivates consumers to promote platform adoption.

Twenty percent of Flash developers plan to work on the development of devices such as PDAs and smart phones in the next year. Will you be next?

Devices in the Future

"The Web is about connecting people to computers through browsers to information. Two new waves will surpass the Web: an executable internet (applications) that greatly improves the online experience, and an extended internet that connects the real world." —Forrestor Research

Growth in devices (Smartphones, PDAs, gaming consoles, and other mobile and embedded devices) is expected to outstrip desktop growth by 2004.

These devices will be connected and sufficiently powerful for Macromedia Flash Player. And in many cases, be marketed in contexts where Flash's strengths in design, media, and applications will inevitably make them powerful contenders.

The next wave on the internet will feature rich applications with responsive user experiences. This wave will include both in-browser and out-of-browser applications.

As a Flash developer, these new challenges present you with the opportunity to evolve the web to its next wave.

As Macromedia Flash improves the users' experience and provides rich applications on the internet and devices. The need for more Macromedia Flash developers increases; being in that position enables you to have a great effect on the Internet and devices. You now have the information at hand to create content for Macromedia Flash enabled devices.

— **Troy Evans**
Macromedia Flash Player Product Manager

INTRODUCTION

Why You Need This Book

There's no shortage of predictions of what will be the *Next Big Thing* in publishing, design, broadcasting, or the Web. In fact, when you try to pay attention to all that noise, everyone gets to feeling, well, a bit like Mr. Murky. But one thing is pretty clear: As it becomes increasingly easy for Everyone.com to design or update their own websites, it makes sense for Web creatives to stay on the bleeding edge of technology and keep one or two steps of ahead of their clients' abilities. Right now, for the ranks of more than one million Flasher developers, the bleeding edge is Flash on devices.

What does all that mean? It means that there is a new wave of opportunity for Flash developers who embrace the opportunities latent within the limitations of the powerful new handheld computers and other devices that are capable (or will soon be capable) of running Flash.

In this book, you will learn how to use Flash for mediums other than the Web—such as Pocket PCs, DVD, video production, TV, and game interfaces—and how to configure your content to display on varied screens, ranging from Pocket PCs to the large screens of HDTVs.

This book will also teach you how to use Flash as a development platform to build a variety of applications—from games and front ends for web services to mobile business applications—and how to deploy these applications on multiple devices. Flash: The Future delivers the core fundamentals for deploying Flash in the broad range of mediums where Flash can be utilized. We also provide troubleshooting techniques, three indispensable appendices, insightful tips and tricks, and unique examples that will help you achieve creative, professional results. Much of the material in this book is cutting edge information which is available nowhere else. (In fact, several of the authors explain how to accomplish feats, such as running Flash content on the PPC—without the browser, which Macromedia claimed to be impossible.)

But there's more to it that just the book, because this is a living book: Each chapter is reinforced with an area within our website at www.flashthefuture.com. Although this is a public website, much of the content will only be available to owners of this book. In these areas we intend to update our information and to offer coverage on new and exciting trends and developments. In addition, we have publicized the email contact information for each of the authors and contributors.

Suddenly, Flash

When the last chapter for the book had been submitted, I sat down to write this introduction. . . . Actually, I stood at my work table, sorting through several small mountains of magazine articles, emails, scrawled notes, and printouts of web pages; sorting, sorting, trying to make sense out of this rapidly changing landscape of Flash on devices. Then I realized that I was looking for something clever, like an acronym, or a Christmas tree, to hang all of these ideas upon. Here's what I came up with: Flash is sudden. S-U-D-D-E-N:

- *Small*—small plugin and compact download size
- *Ubiquitous*—browser and device ubiquity
- *Dynamic*—dynamic database capability
- *Developer-friendly*—developer population of over 1 million
- *Enriched*—enriched, interactive content
- *Neat*—neat design tool. Designers love Flash because it enables neatness: designers retain absolute control over fonts, spacing and layout while providing sound, motion, and interactivity.

Get it? OK, OK. You either love it or you hate it. But even if you don't buy the acronym, you should buy this book because you can still see the logic behind it—which is to say that the points enumerated in SUDDEN really are the reasons behind this book. While there are a lot of books about Flash development and deployment on desktop computers, so far, there hasn't been a book that explains—completely, and in depth—the peculiar details of Flash development for other devices. Yet, all of a SUDDEN, over the last year, there is rapidly growing range of devices that can host Flash content—and the list of these devices is, as I said, growing. All of a SUDDEN, there is a need for a technically oriented guide to this new realm of Flash development. Why? Because there is a future in it!

Until now, application development for embedded devices required the mastery of complex programming languages such as C and C++. Flash has opened up embedded application development to a whole new group of developers. With few exceptions, Flash applications can be just as powerful as applications traditionally written in more complex languages. Consequently, companies are increasingly asking for applications and content for embedded devices. Quite often the perfect platform for the development of these applications and content is—you guessed it—Flash.

Why You Should Care

It's already widely acknowledged that Macromedia Flash has become the standard for delivering rich, interactive web content. In fact, the Flash player is one of the most distributed pieces of software in the history of the Web. This distribution continues unabated as the Flash player is becoming available to many more devices than just web browsers. And, just to sweeten the prognosis, these events are occurring in tandem with a concerted campaign by Macromedia to position Flash as the ideal development tool for PPCs and other devices.

Flash is being used for development on these devices because it facilitates the display of rich, interactive content in addition to ensuring a high return on investment (ROI) due to the fact that Flash makes it possible to author once and deploy to multiple platforms, as well as rapid development and delivery cycles.

But even on the simplest level, Flash makes sense. Assume that you are the hypothetical artist, and that you want to build an custom online portfolio that reflects your personal aesthetic vision. You aren't exactly the starving artist variety, so—in addition to the Web—you're going to want to be able to show your portfolio on your Pocket PC. What are your options? You could find and buy a portfolio program to make your web portfolio (but it wouldn't be so custom) and then maybe you could mangle it to run on the PPC. Or, you could learn C++ and build a portfolio program in C++. Or you could spend a few days learning enough Flash to build your portfolio in Flash and show it—not only on your PPC, but also on your website, your desktop computer, your wireless phone, your DVD, and your Sega, X-Box, or iTV. What's more, in just a few years, it will probably also run on your refrigerator or the dashboard of your automobile. Suddenly, that makes sense, huh?

PPCs Are Taking Over

The Pocket PC (PPC) has overtaken the Palm market by an astounding margin. As of this writing, there are more than 4 million pocket PC's in use. *That's an increase of 2 million in 6 only months!* According to Macromedia, at the end of 2001, more than 135,00 Flash Players had been installed on those devices. By the time you read this, there will be more than 4 million PPCs in use, and downloads of the Flash player will probably have quadrupled.

Every day, there is more news regarding the expanding realm of the PPC and the growing distribution of the Flash player. Microsoft announces plans to release a version of the PPC operating system in Chinese . . . the Pocket PC Phone is rolled out in market after market, around the world . . . successively, Casio, Nokia, and the HP/Compaq announce the standard inclusion of the Flash player on their devices . . . new and exciting uses—ranging from Disney to London's Tate Gallery—are reported for PPC's running applications authored in Flash.

Gaming with Flash on the PPC

Now that air travel includes a longer check in, most passengers (business and otherwise) will have several hours to while away. Maybe they'll have PPCs . . . maybe they'll need something to do with them. How about some Flash entertainment? We say, "Gentlemen, start your Flash game designing engines."

Enterprising PPCs

Pocket PCs are winning in the enterprise arena; according to recent research, most large firms are planning to support Pocket PCs by 2003 while only a handful plan to support Palm.

The reasons for this shift include: branding, total cost of ownership and expandability options. The perception is that Pocket PCs are enterprise products. Palms are for individuals. The current Palm platform doesn't support rich media, sounds, etc, the way a pocket PC can. (We do expect the Palm to evolve, and—when it does—we expect Macromedia to support it with a Flash player.) According to one Macromedia product manager, "We are aggressively pursuing mobile device manufacturers to support the Flash platform regardless of the type of processor and/or Operating System they might choose. And that's 'great' news for Flash developers."

In addition to the intrinsic strength of the devices themselves, there's another reason that many Enterprises may be turning to the PPC. This is something that most seasoned Flash developers already know: There's good ROI, or return on investment, when a firm chooses to develop their applications in Flash as opposed to another development platform. There is a standing army of Flash developers who are fully equipped to build the application in Flash—and they can build it better, cheaper, faster, and it will run on more systems with lower cost to test, maintain or revise.

Other Devices

By other devices, we mean any device other than a desktop/laptop computer or a Pocket PC, where Flash content can be displayed—either with or without a Flash player. Although roughly two thirds of the book is dedicated to the development of Flash content for the Pocket PC, don't be fooled—a great deal of the principles outlined in our discussion of Flash on the PPC is either relevant or the substantial basis for understanding our discussion of Flash development for other devices and platforms. In this section we dedicate three chapters to the coverage of Flash output to Video, DVD, and iTV. We follow this with a chapter that discusses optimal workflow when authoring singular content for deployment on multiple devices. The final chapter is a look at the future of Flash on devices, based on our observation of the developments of the last few months.

How to Use This Book

You will find that a great deal of the content in this book is cumulative—which means that key concepts that may be required for understanding later chapters is presented in earlier chapters. More advanced developers may find that they can jump in anywhere and grok the content. But for less savvy developers, such a tact may prove more difficult. So, if you dive in at Chapter 7 and find that you don't understand it, that probably means that you will want to reset your sights and start at Chapter 1.

This is an advanced book, targeted at serious developers. Although you need not be an advanced developer to use this book, you *do* need to either be familiar with the general concepts and concerns of Pocket PC's running PPC 2002—as pertains to both software and hardware—or you must be willing to do the work, by consulting the wealth of resources that will be suggested in the chapters, or which may be found in the chapter-related areas of our website, at **www.flashthefuture.com.**

—Jon Warren Lentz
Carlsbad, California

**PART ONE
FLASH ON THE POCKET PC**

1

FLASH ON THE POCKET PC

Jon Warren Lentz

In a relatively short period of time, Pocket PCs have become an important facet of the ongoing digital evolution, and Flash has emerged as the most viable platform for developing media-rich content and applications for these handy devices. Consequently, developing content for Pocket PCs is one of the most lively new growth areas in Flash development.

This chapter will introduce you to the most popular Pocket PCs, and the terminology this book will use to describe the operations of the Pocket PC (PPC) operating system (OS). This will be followed by the basic information required for any intermediate Flash developer to author and display a simple Flash page on the PPC—beginning with an introduction to basic issues of screen size, resolution, and orientation (since handheld devices are easily rotated). The focus will then shift to the relevant specs and idiosyncrasies of writing an HTML wrapper (the code needed to support the Flash player within Pocket Internet Explorer, or PIE) to present Flash content in the browser of the latest PPC operating system, Microsoft Pocket PC 2002.

The Current Handheld Lineup

Nearly a dozen major providers sell handheld devices that run the Pocket PC 2002 OS, including Audiovox, Casio, Compaq, Hewlett-Packard, Intermec, NEC, PC-EPhone, Sharp, Symbol, Toshiba, and UR There. Table 1.1 lists these developers and their devices.

Table 1.1: Major providers of handheld devices that run PPC 2002

Manufacturer	Device Name	URL
Audiovox	Maestro PDA1032C	www.audiovox.com
Casio	Cassiopeia	www.casio.com/personalpcs/
Compaq	iPAQ	www.compaq.com/products/iPAQ/
HP	Jornada	www.hp.com/jornada/
Intermec	700 Series	www.intermec.com
NEC	MobilePro	www.neccomp.com
PC-EPhone	PC-EPhone	www.pc-ephone.com
Sharp	Zaurus SL-5500	www.sharpusa.com
Symbol	PPT and PDT	www.symbol.com/products/mobile_computers/
Toshiba	e570	www.pda.toshiba.com/
UR There	@migo	www.urthere.com

If you haven't already purchased a PPC, then you may want to pay a visit to Microsoft's web page which offers a handy side-by-side hardware comparison of available devices: www.microsoft.com/mobile/pocketpc/hardware/compare_devices_americas.asp.

NOTE *When choosing a target device for enterprise development, you may want to contact the manufacturer first to ensure that you will get adequate support and attention. Otherwise, you may find your project unnecessarily delayed.*

The Hewlett-Packard Jornada and the Compaq iPAQ, shown in Figures 1.1 and 1.2 respectively, are two of the most popular Pocket PCs. Although this may change with the merger of these two companies, both units are still widely available and are likely to remain in the distribution channel for quite some time.

Figure 1.1: The Hewlett-Packard Jornada.

HP's Jornada is arguably the most attractive and, with its flip case, the most durable of the current lineup of PPCs. Too, its removable battery and built-in CompactFlash (CF) card slot make it one of the least bulky and most useful offerings.

Figure 1.2: The Compaq iPAQ.

When we began writing this book the iPAQ was, without a doubt, the most powerful and popular PPC available. As a result, we chose it as the target device for many of the examples in this book, but most of the information you'll find here will apply to all PPCs.

PPC 2002: Common Specs and Features

In October 2001, Microsoft released the latest version of Windows CE (WinCE), version 3.0, now commonly referred to as the PPC 2002 OS.

NOTE *If you have an older unit and haven't upgraded to PPC 2002, we strongly advise you to spend the dime and upgrade your OS. The new OS is more stable, offers significant usability improvements, and supports the higher-end tricks that are detailed in this book.*

The latest PPCs run PPC 2002. Fortunately, the hardware specification for the PPC 2002 platform has become more consistent, and devices that meet its specifications must all include, at a minimum, an Intel 206MHz StrongARM SA-110 processor, 32MB of ROM, a minimum of 32MB of RAM, and rechargeable lithium polymer batteries. The best of the PPCs have the maximum 64MB of RAM and support 6,356 colors on an active-matrix screen.

With the possible exception of the PC-EPhone, all of these units sport a screen that's 240 pixels wide × 320 pixels high. User-replaceable batteries are an attractive feature that's available only on some models, such as the HP. Similarly, some manufacturers provide support for expansion cards native to the device, which means that bulky expansion sleeves are not required.

Support for the following cards is most desirable: the SD (Secure Digital) card, the CF-II (CompactFlash II) card, and PCMCIA II cards. The more robust of these devices support dual slots to accommodate simultaneous CF-II and SD cards, which means that users can access extended RAM and have wireless connectivity at the same time.

Wireless

Ideally, wireless should be built into the PPC device, preferably with support for Bluetooth, a hardware specification that ensures communication compatibility worldwide. It is touted as a low-cost, low-power solution with industry-wide support that has the potential to enable links between mobile computers, mobile phones, portable handheld devices, and the Internet. (For more information, visit www.bluetooth.com.)

Rather than go into further detail about each device (which could take pages and pages and would be outdated quickly), we encourage you to visit the following sites for the latest reviews and comparisons:

- www.microsoft.com/mobile/pocketpc/hardware/compare_devices_americas.asp
- www.flashthefuture.com/1
- www.flashenabled.com/mobile

- www.devbuzz.com
- www.pocketpcflash.net
- www.cewindows.net
- www.infosync.no
- www.davescompaqipaq.com
- www.pocketpcmag.com
- www.pencomputing.com
- www.brighthand.com

The Flash Player

In order to display content properly on different devices, you need the correct device-specific Flash player for your PPC. That's because Pocket PCs have proprietary leeway in the hardware design, and those differences may alter the implementation of the operating system—and, more importantly, the Flash player—from device to device. As a result, one Flash player *may not* function properly on all devices (or at least, that was the theory behind the licensing of the player to each manufacturer). Therefore, it's important that you know which version of the player you are working with, and which player is appropriate for your target device.

NOTE *To obtain the latest Flash player, users should contact the manufacturer of their particular device for the appropriate device-specific version. Links for the major versions will also be posted at www.flashthefuture.com/1.*

Player Versions

So how do you find out which version of the player you have? As shown in Figure 1.3, you can find the version information on your desktop PC. Using Windows Explorer, you can determine the version number for a specific player by right-clicking the file, selecting Properties from the context menu, and then clicking the Version tab of the swflash.dll Properties dialog box. The file name for the Flash 5 Player for PPC is swflash.dll.

You can also check on the device itself, from within any Flash movie that uses the ActionScript command trace(getVersion());. A sample Flash app (ActionScript_Platform_Detection.fla) that you can run on your device and does this for you is included on the CD-ROM in the Chapter 5 folder. See Chapter 5 for more details.

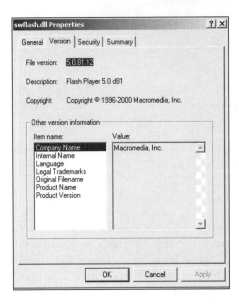

Figure 1.3: The version number of the final beta for the Compaq iPAQ player appears on the Version tab of the swflash.dll Properties dialog box.

According to Macromedia, we learned that manufacturers who have licensed the Flash Player SDK will version their device-specific port, and Macromedia will verify this version number in their certification process prior to release. Players will version by incrementing the rightmost digit of the version string. So, if the base version is 5.0.82.0, Compaq's version of the player for their particular device might, for example, be 5.0.82.1. Check our website at www.flashthefuture.com/1 for current details on the versioning process as well as the Flash Player SDK reference guide.

Other Devices that Use Flash

In addition to the devices described above, two classes of devices are similar enough to the PPC to deserve mention here. These are touch-screen tablets, or Tablet PCs, and PPC enabled phones, which include both the Smartphone (you may recognize it by its code name, Stinger) and the Pocket PC Phone.

Tablet PCs

Microsoft is driving an initiative for a new Tablet PC, which they describe as "the next generation of Windows PC." Also referred to as Web Pads, these are light, slender, wireless, Web-connected devices with touch screens that are about the size of a clipboard. Web Pads and Tablet PCs are primarily envisioned as enterprise devices, deployed within a wireless network at factories, hospitals, and warehouse facilities. Properly outfitted, they could be used to streamline outside sales forces or delivery services—much like the devices that UPS and Federal Express drivers use, but with broader functionality and ease of application development because they support Flash. Executives may also find them useful as satellite devices to keep them connected when they are away from their desks, whether at meetings, in the hallways, or lounging at the water cooler.

Some Tablet PCs are already available, while others are expected to ship soon. For more information about the Tablet PC's manufacturers and specifications—and a glimpse of the prototypes—visit www.microsoft.com/windowsxp/tabletpc/. Acer, Compaq, Fujitsu, Sceptre, Siemens, Tatung, Toshiba, ViewSonic and others have either unveiled or announced plans to deliver Tablet PCs in the near future. Some of these tablets run WinCE 3.0; others run Windows 2000, or even Windows XP. Regardless of the different specifications, these devices will likely be a Flash destination, which would make it even easier for developers to create custom applications for unique and specific uses. Please see www.flashthe-future.com/1 for an update on these exciting devices.

Following is a brief listing of some of these manufacturers and their websites. (If the link has changed, run a search at the site—these devices are in constant flux.)

Manufacturer	Device Name	URL
Compaq	Compaq Tablet PC	www.compaq.com/newsroom/presspaq/tabletpc/index.html
Fujitsu	Stylistic LT P-600	www.fujitsupc.com/pentablets
Sceptre	X-Pad 1000	www.sceptre.com
Siemens	SIMpad SL4	www.siemens-mobile.de/mobile
Tatung	Tangy 440	www.tatung.com/tabletpc/
ViewSonic	ViewPad 1000	www.viewsonic.com/products/viewpad1000.htm

Smartphones and Pocket PC Phones

By their very nature, mobile devices are personal tools. Some people prefer to conduct most of their business in realtime, with a phone. Others prefer the asynchronous freedom of email and data management that the PPC offers. But many others want one device for both.

For the Smartphone to be effective, it must be small enough to be carried easily, yet have a usable screen and comfortable input options. Microsoft's Stinger initiative—or Smartphone—targets this market with a version of Windows CE that is optimized for mobile phones. According to Microsoft, the Smartphone will surf the Web, access email, allow you to use Instant Messenger to chat with friends and, of course, to communicate via voice. As these products have recently begun to emerge, the Smartphone appears to be a smaller device—essentially a cell phone with PPC capabilities—while the Pocket PC Phone is larger and resembles a PPC with with cell phone capabilities. In either configuration, we believe that these wireless devices are the untethered frontier of the PPC. And, because they are built around the PPC, they will support Flash.

Here are a couple of early Smartphone/PPC Phone debuts:

mmO2	XDA Pocket PC Phone	www.mmo2.com/
Mitsubishi Electric	Mondo	www.mitsubishi-telecom.com/

Handheld Terminology

The following section explains the terminology that will be used consistently throughout this book. (For a detailed reference to the PPC 2002 OS, consider getting a copy of *The Unauthorized Guide to Pocket PC*, by Michael Morrison [ISBN 0789724723], which we used as a reference in the early stages of our work with this technology.

The Interface Defined

You can customize the default interface of a PPC 2002 to display a personal image or company logo using the Today Screen Image tool, which is part of the Microsoft Power Toys collection (free in the downloads area at www.microsoft.com/mobile/pocketpc/).

As shown in Figure 1.4, the Today screen has a Navigation Bar at the top and a Command Bar at the bottom, with the Application Screen in the middle.

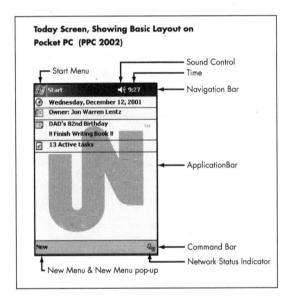

Figure 1.4: The Today screen, showing the PPC 2002's basic layout.

If you've just purchased a PPC, you may be wondering how to navigate it—specifically, how to reach the menus and how to get to the File Explorer. That's easy: Click the Start Menu with the stylus to open a drop-down menu. Depending on the configuration of your device, you should be able to navigate this drop-down menu directly to launch the File Explorer. Or, choose Start • Programs • File Explorer.

File Explorer

The functions and menus in the Command Bar of the File Explorer are shown in Figure 1.5.

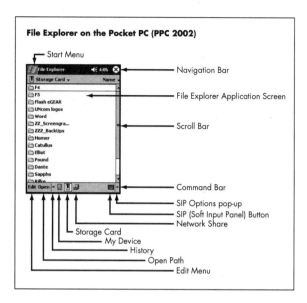

Figure 1.5: The File Explorer on the PPC 2002.

The SIP Options pop-up, shown in Figure 1.6, gives users a choice between the Keyboard and the Letter Recognizer, as well as options for tuning the behavior and appearance of both. (We'll feature the Soft Input Panel (SIP) Options pop-up and the general use of the SIP Keyboard in subsequent chapters.)

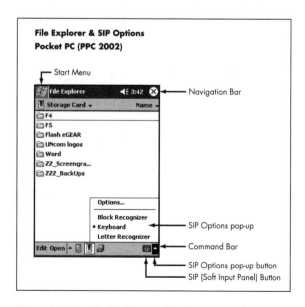

Figure 1.6: The File Explorer and SIP Options on the PPC 2002.

Click the SIP button to invoke either the Keyboard (Figure 1.7) or the Letter Recognizer, depending on which option you selected in the Options pop-up. Subsequent chapters will assume you're using the stylus and the SIP Keyboard to input text and commands and to otherwise control the device.

Figure 1.7: The File Explorer and SIP Keyboard on the PPC 2002.

PIE Defined

On most devices, navigating from the Start Menu will also lead you to Pocket Internet Explorer (PIE). As shown in Figure 1.8, PIE's menus, controls, and options are also found on the Command Bar. (Note the now-familiar SIP controls.)

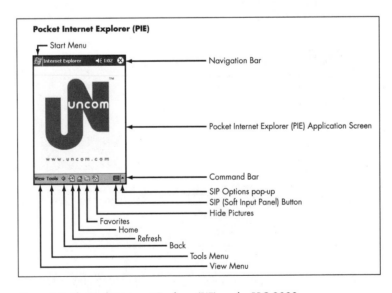

Figure 1.8: The Pocket Internet Explorer (PIE) on the PPC 2002.

The Address Bar, usually enabled by default, is largely unnecessary and gobbles up precious screen real estate, so we strongly advise that you turn it off—and keep it turned off. To do so, open the View Menu at the far left of the Command Bar and deselect the Address Bar option.

Landscape Versus Portrait

There are two basic orientations for viewing Flash content on the PPC: Portrait and Landscape, as shown in Figures 1.9 and 1.10.

Figure 1.9: Flash displayed in Portrait orientation on the PPC 2002.

Designing Flash content for display on the PPC in Portrait orientation is, due to the orientation of the buttons below the screen, literally straightforward. Similarly, as shown in Figure 1.10, displaying content in Landscape orientation seems to make good sense. The buttons can still be accessed on the right edge of the screen, and the screen space is, in many ways, more inviting and—depending upon the application—possibly easier to design for.

Figure 1.10: Flash displayed in Landscape orientation on the PPC 2002.

However, before you jump into Flash and start designing, here's an important caveat to remember when designing content for display in Landscape orientation: The design must be turned sideways *within* the Flash authoring environment, as shown in Figure 1.11.

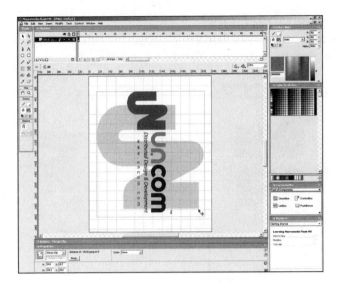

Figure 1.11: Working sideways in the Flash authoring environment to display in Landscape orientation on the PPC.

Furthermore, as shown in Figure 1.12, the results may not be as impressive as you want them to be. As you will learn in later chapters, you cannot disable the contextual menus in PIE, and, consequently, any content delivered in Landscape orientation will suffer the disconcerting (and unprofessional-looking) liability of sideways contextual menus.

The next section discusses one solution to this problem.

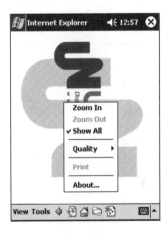

Figure 1.12: Flash displayed in Landscape orientation on the PPC 2002, yet the menu remains in Portrait orientation.

Jimmying Landscape

A couple of programs help avoid the awkwardness of combining Landscape content with Portrait menus: They turn the entire PPC interface sideways. One of these, Jimmy Software's JS Landscape (www.jimmysoftware.com), also allows a developer to set the device resolution to 240 × 480, 360 × 480, or 480 × 640. Upgraded for PPC 2002, JS Landscape is included in JS PowerToys X Series, which now supports all models of Pocket PC 2002 with 16-bit displays.

Figure 1.13 shows the logo shown in Figure 1.12 (which was authored normally within the Flash environment) as displayed in PIE on a PPC with its screen reset using Jimmy's Landscape to obtain 360 × 480 resolution in Landscape orientation. This looks and feels much better, doesn't it?

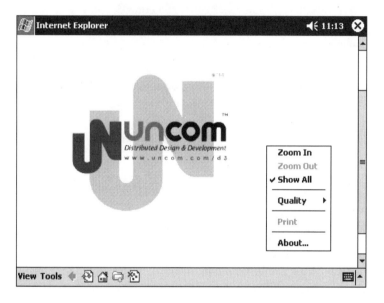

Figure 1.13: Flash content, loaded with JS Landscape, is displayed in Landscape orientation on the PPC 2002.

NOTE *Developing content to display without scrollbars, yet with an altered resolution, can be problematic. It might require a considerable amount of trial and error and could lead to undesirable results if the intention is to switch back and forth between resolutions. Once the resolution and orientation of your unit has been reset, you should realign your screen, using the screen-alignment utility found in the Programs directory of the device (it is part of the OS). Otherwise, you may find it difficult to navigate menus and access the control bar at the bottom of PIE.*

Jimmy's Landscape is also available to developers as the JS API, which delivers control of the orientation, resolution, touch screen, and keyboard from within the developer's program.

Chapter 6 will show you Ian Chia's method for building advanced Flash apps that deliver Flash in the following customized resolutions: 240 × 268 (full-size PIE but without scrollbars), 240 × 294 (without the menu bar and SIP), 240 × 320 (full screen and in Landscape orientation, if you want).

Usable Screen Area

The absolute pixel dimensions of most PPCs are 240 × 320. But our testing would seem to indicate that, without invoking scrollbars, the absolute usable pixel dimensions within PIE on a PPC running PPC 2002 are 240 pixels wide × 263 pixels high. Furthermore, we did notice that, from device to device, there were variations. Sometimes 240 × 263 content will display without scrollbars, but too often the usable screen area (which will display without scrollbars) is even smaller.

We also determined that a screen that is out of alignment can have an adverse impact on the usable screen area. To realign the screen on your PPC, use the Screen application in the System tab of the Settings dialog box.

Phillip Torrone, lead coauthor of *Flash Enabled* (ISBN 0735711771), and the foremost evangelist for the deployment of Flash on PPCs and handhelds (and many other devices, including watches and scooters), conducted an informal survey of people who download content for deployment on the PPC. He found that most users have the address bar on, and that if they turn it off, they usually don't refresh the content. Consequently, for the general public, or for most implementations (other than kiosk mode), the usable screen area is 240 × 240 pixels.

We agree. The best setting for Flash in PIE is 240 pixels × 240 pixels. These dimensions presume that no scrollbars are desired and that the address bar will always be visible. If you create content that exceeds these dimensions, chances are that you will inadvertently surrender a large area of your user's screen to the scrollbars.

But, because the tolerances are so extremely unforgiving, in some situations these conservative dimensions of 240 × 240 will *still* invoke the appearance of scrollbars. (For example, the inclusion of the ALIGN=middle tag in the HTML wrapper for the Shockwave Flash [SWF] file displayed in Figure 1.8 caused a vertical scrollbar to appear.) So it might be safer to work with slightly smaller dimensions, somewhere between 239 × 239 and 235 × 235; otherwise, you will need to test exhaustively to confirm that the scrollbars will be consistently suppressed.

Remember, just a single pixel beyond the maximum dimensions will invoke screen-gobbling scrollbars on your user's PPC—which is not a user-friendly situation!

To assist you in determining how to size your content, Table 1.2 lists the four interface elements that may, depending on how your content is used, impinge on the available screen area. For example, if you expect the user to have the Navigation bar enabled on their PPC, then you must deduct 27 pixels from the vertical dimensions of your usable screen area. (However, if you are deploying an application in kiosk mode—which is when the developer takes control of the device and either limits or turns off most or all user controls—then you can disable any or all of these elements and expect that you will have the entire 240×263 to work with.)

Table 1.2: The vertical dimension of interface elements

Interface Element	Height in Pixels
Navigation bar	= 26–27 pixels
Address bar	= 23 pixels
Command bar	= 26 pixels
SIP Keyboard	= 80 pixels

HTML Wrapper Code to Display Flash on the PPC 2002

In order for Flash to display within the desktop browser, it must be accompanied by an HTML file, which is often referred to as the HTML wrapper. Similarly, an HTML wrapper is required for Flash content to be displayed within the PIE browser on the PPC. However, a few adjustments and edits are necessary for optimal display within PIE on the PPC. The following code, together with subsequent notes, will assist you in your own PPC development.

When developing SWF content for deployment in PIE on the PPC 2002, you must modify the code generated by the Publish feature of the Flash authoring environment. Some modifications—regarding the dimension of your SWFs and the reasoning behind them—were discussed in the previous section. More minor points are addressed in the notes that follow. (The HTML code in Listing 1.1 was used to deploy the SWF in Figure 1.8.) Note that code in this example with a line through it is default code that Flash normally generates, but is not needed for PIE.

NOTE *You'll find this code in the Chapter 1 folder of the CD-ROM, as a Publishing Template, complete with instructions for installation.*

Listing 1.1: Specimen HTML code for wrapping SWFs in PIE on the PPC 2002.

```
<HTML>
<HEAD>
<TITLE>UNcom</TITLE>
</HEAD>
<BODY bgcolor="#FFFFFF" TOPMARGIN=0 LEFTMARGIN=0>
<OBJECT classid="clsid:D27CDB6E-AE6D-11cf-96B8-444553540000"
codebase="http://download.macromedia.com/pub/shockwave/cabs/
flash/swflash.cab#version=5,0,0,0"
  ID=PPC
  WIDTH=220 HEIGHT=235 ALIGN="middle">
 <PARAM NAME=movie VALUE="UNcom_01.swf">
```

(continued on next page)

```
<PARAM NAME=quality VALUE=high>
<PARAM NAME=bgcolor VALUE=#FFFFFF>
<PARAM NAME=scale VALUE=exactfit>
</OBJECT>
</BODY>
</HTML>
```

Here are a few notes regarding this file:

- If you are adept with HTML, you will note that this file is missing a number of "normal" tags. Of course, those are the <EMBED> tags, which are only necessary where the Netscape browser must be supported. Obviously, the Netscape browser is not included in the PPC 2002 system. (On the other hand, if you are authoring for deployment on the desktop browser in addition to the PPC, it may be advisable to edit this file to make your own custom Publishing Template that will include the Netscape tags in addition to the PPC tags.)

- <MARGIN WIDTH> and <MARGIN HEIGHT> tags are not meaningful to PIE.

- TOPMARGIN=0 and LEFTMARGIN=0 are necessary within the <BODY> tag to maximize screen usage. If you exclude them, a blank space is introduced at the top left by PIE's default.

- The HTML wrapper must have the <OBJECT> tag or the SWF will not display in PIE. However, the codebase attribute, which is normally provided by the Flash Publish feature, is unnecessary because PIE does not have the ActiveX controls to take advantage of it.

- The SWF to be displayed is specified within the tag that begins <PARAM NAME=movie.

- EXACTFIT causes the SWF to scale according to the specified WIDTH and HEIGHT, while preserving the aspect ratio.

- Dimensions that appear within the <OBJECT> tag must be specified in pixels, not as percentages.

- The ID attribute, which can occur anywhere within the <OBJECT> tag, must be present for the Flash content to display in PIE on the PPC. But it can be set to anything. (This applies not only to PIE, but also to any ActiveX client that is intended to display Flash content on the PPC.) The default Flash Publish feature does not generate this tag.

- The ID attribute can have any string value, or name. To display multiple instances of Flash on the same page, give each instance a unique name. (You can use these unique tags to set movie properties from JavaScript.)

- PIE 2002, unlike PIE 2000, is case-sensitive for JavaScript. This can lead to the existence of applications that run on one version of PIE, yet break on the other. To author efficiently for display on multiple platforms, including desktops and other devices, observe normal IE and JavaScript conventions.

- PIE 2000 does not support DHTML, but PIE 2002 supports the following (very limited) usage of DHTML: for <DIV> and <SPAN> tags, the innerHTML and innerText can be scripted. This allows for some DHTML effects in your web pages.

Summary

Armed with this brief introduction to Flash on the Pocket PC, you're ready to dig into the following chapters and mine the many tips, tricks, and methods that we have developed for you as you enter the brave new world of authoring Flash content for the most popular pocket computers. In Chapter 2, Bill Turner will introduce you to the fundamental concerns that govern Flash development for the Pocket PC.

2

DESIGNING FOR POCKET PCS
Bill Turner

Chances are that the Flash animations you created for a desktop PC will not run properly on the Pocket PC as is.

This chapter addresses concerns you must consider when designing for the screen of the diminutive Pocket PC. It will touch on the visual concerns by dissecting the optimization techniques used to transform a rather complex animation created for desktops and video to a PPC. This chapter will also discuss screen orientation, color space, sound, and button design. The explanation of the optimization process will use a fully animated cartoon that was initially created for video and DVD (and that is used in the Part II chapters covering video, DVD, and TV as well). This animation now plays quite well on the Pocket PC. We've included Magic revealed, the final optimized FLA (wastepipe_ppc.fla), on the accompanying CD-ROM for your inspection.

Workflow Considerations

Let's first look at how to get the Flash art, or SWF files, and Hypertext Markup Language (HTML) files onto the PPC. The methods we'll use to get our Flash art over to the PPC are fairly basic and apply to all PPCs. (The only exception is the coverage that follows for getting Flash art from the Mac to the PPC.) All PPCs will work via the CompactFlash card method, though, and that's a good thing.

On a PC Running Windows

Dealing with the PPC from a PC is fairly straightforward because both the desktop and PPC operating systems can communicate with each other via Windows' ActiveSync. To enable the communication, install ActiveSync and follow the instructions. Once you've made a connection between the two devices, place the PPC in its sync cradle, and the desktop will be able to communicate with it.

ActiveSync lets you move files and install applications between your desktop Windows OS and your PPC. All the Windows developer needs to do, therefore, is to create Flash content and move the SWF files, along with the all-important HTML file, to the PPC for display and testing in Pocket Internet Explorer.

NOTE *We won't deal with troubleshooting ActiveSync problems here, but you can find discussions on these issues at www.cewindows.net/.*

At this point, PC users may want to skip ahead to the "Colorspace and Screen Dimensions" section, because using ActiveSync on your platform is fairly standard. However, you may find the discussion of the CF card method for quickly transferring files to the PPC (on page 23) useful.

On a Mac

The Macintosh involves much more hocus-pocus than the PC. (Yes, go ahead and chuckle, PC folks, you're entitled this time.)

Okay, Mac users, you might think that the Pocket PC is a Windows-only system; that's quite true, but it's never stopped Mac users from developing for other platforms before. For example, even though this book is about Flash, long-time Macromedia Director users will recognize the fact that Director was available for the Mac a good many years before it was developed for Windows. Still, Mac developers always had to keep a sharp eye on their work (mostly interactive CD-ROMs) to make sure it ran smoothly on the dominant Windows platform.

Well, times have changed and both Flash and Director are cross-platform, but the PPC is not. Oh well, too bad for us Mac users . . . but maybe not! You can just as easily develop for the PPC everything you can dream up for the Mac, such as Flash animation, games, interfaces, and applications—and you might not even need a real PC to do so! Yes, Mac users, those wonderful little PPCs are within your development reach as well. Surprised? Read on.

Transferring Mac Files the Hard Way

As we've discussed, ActiveSync is a Windows application that you run to synchronize your PPC with your desktop. That's all fine and dandy for Windows users, but it seems to leave Mac users out in the cold, which is true for a lot of this type of work.

If you're a Mac user, it's rather unlikely that you are able to keep all that information (such as address books and so on) inside Virtual PC, the Windows emulator that runs on a Mac. But we have other plans for Flash authoring. In fact, even PC users might want to use this technique to eliminate tedious transfers.

As of this writing, Information Appliance Associates has just released an application called PocketMac (www.pocketmac.net) that allows Entourage and Outlook to synch data with the PPC. Initial tests and reports from our associates indicate that this application is a real winner.

The standard way for Mac users to get their Flash work to the PPC is to (1) connect with a Windows PC running ActiveSync, (2) transfer the files to the PC, and then (3) transfer the files to the PPC. Another way is to use a removable drive, such as an Iomega Zip disk formatted for the PC, to shuttle files between the Mac and PC. Neither method is ideal, for sure, and if you don't have a real hardware PC, you're completely out of luck.

But wait; we said we'd be helpful, and we promise you won't need a PC at all.

CompactFlash Memory Cards

CompactFlash (CF) cards offer a much better solution. You know, the little wafers of plastic and silicon that, at this writing, can hold upward of a gigabyte? You might even be using the cards right now for your digital camera. With a PPC that has a native CF slot, or with an iPAQ and the CF Sleeve attached, you can simply plug a CF card into the slot and *bang!* A gigabyte of RAM! Pretty slick. You can even take the cards from your digital camera and view the photos on many PPCs directly.

So, what if you could take other data to the PPC using a CF card? You can, via a CF card reader/writer, sometimes referred to as a digital film reader. These devices are fairly inexpensive; for about $50, you can buy a FireWire CF card reader and writer that will act just like a hard drive on your Mac. Pop in the CF card, and *voilà!* A new volume mounts on the desktop that you can use just like any other hard drive. And you can copy pretty much anything cross-platform you want to it, including videos, MP3s, photos, HTML, and, oh yeah, Flash SWF animation and game files too!

Most CF card reader/writers are made for USB, which is fine—unless, if like most people, you have a bazillion things hanging off every USB hub. We prefer a version made by Lexar Media (www.lexarmedia.com) that uses FireWire. Because FireWire is much faster than USB, deciding which bus to use is a no-brainer. The one we're using doesn't even need a power plug; it derives power from the FireWire bus directly on a G4. How cool is that?

By using the CF reader/writer setup shown in Figure 2.1, you can simply copy any Flash SWF and related HTML files to the CF card. Eject the card (they are hot-swappable), slide the card into your PPC of choice, crank up Pocket Internet Explorer, and let the fun begin. You've just created a direct workflow link between the Mac and the other world known as PPC. (This should impress your boss or clients, too.)

Using this method, Macs are no longer locked out of the Flash-on-PPC revolution.

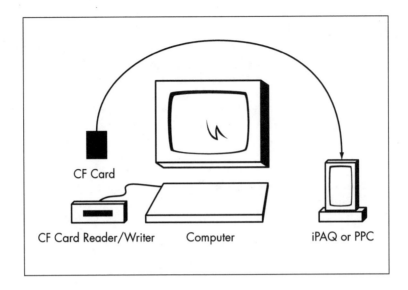

Figure 2.1: A simple CF card reader workflow for a Mac or PC.

NOTE *If you create folders on the CF cards, their files will be readable on the Mac via the Finder, but any links that depend on naming, such as the HTML file linking to the SWF, might not work. One solution is to never use folders on the CF card, but the best solution is to create all the folders in Windows CE on the PPC using the File Explorer. Then, once your CF card is set up with folders, you can copy them from the Mac to those folders via the Finder without the filename mangling problem that would occur otherwise.*

Installing Applications and Managing PPC Files from the Mac

The one big problem with using the PPC with the Macintosh is that you're working with two obviously different operating systems. Although the CF card technique described above works well for moving Flash files and HTML pages, it will not work for installing applications on the PPC.

However, with a little help from Connectix and its Virtual PC (VPC) application, you can install applications and manage file structures on your PPC. Using Virtual PC with at least Windows 98 installed, you can synch to the PPC. Here's how.

First, you'll need some inexpensive hardware. (As of this writing, the USB connection cradle of the iPAQ will not work; you'll need to purchase Compaq's serial version. Hang on to the USB cradle, though–who knows what the future might bring?) You'll also need the Keyspan USB PDA serial adapter USA-19 (about $40) if you don't already have one. This adapter has a DB9 male serial port on one end and a USB connection on the other, which mates perfectly with the DB9 female serial connection of the iPAQ's serial cradle. The Keyspan PDA adapter comes with software drivers you can install on the Mac.

NOTE *You will not be installing drivers in Windows on the VPC side of things; VPC and the Mac system will handle this. Once you launch VPC, you will set the PC via the PC settings (of VPC) to recognize the Keyspan PDA adapter as COM1 Port, as shown in Figure 2.2*

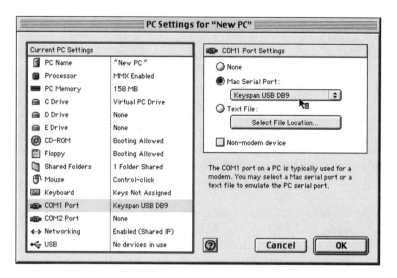

Figure 2.2: The settings that allow Virtual PC to recognize the new hardware.

Once you have the hardware in place, it's time to connect to the iPAQ from your Mac:

1. Once you've set the VPC preferences, proceed to the Windows environment (Windows 98 in our example).

2. Using the iPAQ's CD-ROM installer, follow the directions to install ActiveSync.

3. With your iPAQ out of its cradle, go to the Settings area and tap the Connection tab at the bottom. You'll find the PC connection settings here.

4. Tap the PC Settings area to open the preferences and leave Automatically Synchronize checked. Next, tap the pop-up menu underneath it, select 57600 Default, then tap OK in the top left corner. (Do not return the iPAQ to its cradle just yet; if you do, it will attempt to connect and fail.)

5. Return to Windows and run ActiveSync, then select File • Get Connected. You will be presented with a dialog box that has a Next button at the bottom.

6. Return the iPAQ to its cradle and click Next in ActiveSync to begin the connection process. If the process is successful, you will hear a happy blipping tone from the iPAQ and, moments later, your Mac/VPC will emit a response tone. The Connecting progress bar will play out, and you'll be connected to the iPAQ.

7. You can now explore the iPAQ's files on your desktop computer or even install applications. Frankly, you can do all the things you could do on a PC.

A Few Caveats

This setup is a good bit slower than a USB connection because the Keyspan PDA adapter is really a serial port. Therefore, copying large files via ActiveSync will require a long wait: It's the equivalent of using a dial-up modem for transfers.

If you're transferring large files, use the CF card technique described on page 23. But, when you need to install applications and manage files on the iPAQ (and you will), the Virtual PC technique will work just fine if you don't have access to a hardware PC.

Be careful, too, when removing and replacing the iPAQ from the cradle because it might not re-synch with VPC. If it does not re-synch automatically, you'll have to quit ActiveSync and start over again (with Step 4). (You're a pioneer here; this is not really supposed to work, but we've had it working just fine for many hours of testing.)

Our and Connectix's hopes are to have the USB issues on VPC worked out by time you read this. Check the Connectix website at www.connectix.com regularly.

Graphics Optimization

Well, now that we've made it seem so easy to get your work from the desktop to the PPC, life is a breeze. Whoops, not so fast. These little computers may be a marvel of modern technology, but they have their problems: They're small and slow.

These limitations can be overcome with a little insight. Flash is an astounding application, and its tiny, scalable files have changed the face of the Internet. Unfortunately, some of the vector artwork can be processor-intensive to render on the fly, the way Flash likes to do things.

With any full-screen motion vector animation, the same rule applies whether your target is a desktop or a PPC: The larger the animation, the more horsepower it needs to play smoothly. The screen is certainly smaller on a PPC, but this apparent advantage is diluted because the PPC processor is much less powerful than any new desktop. Let's have a look at how to optimize our Flash applications for the PPC.

Colorspace and Screen Dimensions

The newer PPCs have 16-bit color displays; the older ones were 12-bit. Generally speaking, 16-bit color affords close-to-photo quality, with very little dithering. When using 16-bit color, you don't often need to massage images, but you'll have some work to do when your target is a 12-bit display.

Banding

A 12-bit color screen displays only 4,096 different colors. This limitation can cause banding within smooth gradients from one color to another, such as when yellow fades to red. Instead of displaying a nice smooth transition of color, the 12-bit PPC will show the image in steps, or bands, as shown in Figure 2.3. Banding can be quite undesirable in certain situations and not so bad in others. It's up to you to decide what's acceptable in a given graphic or animation.

Figure 2.3: A smooth gray gradient showing 12-bit banding.

One way to overcome banding is to add a little noise to any photo or gradient you might use in a Flash animation to create a forced pseudo-dither. The trade-off is that this noise will reduce the efficiency of the JPG compression used in Flash when exporting a SWF, resulting in slightly larger files. The choice is ultimately up to you: larger files, or sub-par image display.

12-Bit Color

Whereas the iPAQ displays only 12-bit color (4,096 colors), it operates internally on 16-bit color (65,335 colors) and converts to 12-bit on the fly. However, it does not seem to do any dithering to make this conversion—probably because that would be processor-intensive and slow things down considerably. So the iPAQ seems to make a best guess, which can lead to blocky and banded areas.

Figure 2.4 shows the same two photos before and after the 24-to-12-bit conversion (discussed in the next section) that removes colors from an image while maintaining the image quality. (It may be difficult to tell the difference on this printed page, so we've included the original color image on the CD, together with the FLA phototest.fla and the SWF phototest.swf. Play them on a PPC to see for yourself.)

Figure 2.4: How the iPAQ displays 12-bit color: The 24-bit untouched photos are on the left; on the right are the photos after 24-to-12-bit conversion in Photoshop.

Notice that the busier photo at the top, a New York City street scene, seems little different in either 24- or 12-bit color. That's because our eyes have a hard time distinguishing all the details, so our brain tends to blur them together. The less-busy photo of a building, on the other hand, reveals the banding, particularly on the white wall. (Again, this may be hard to see on the printed page.) Without as much detail to confuse the eye, the banding becomes more apparent and pixelated.

This tells us that we can probably get away without using the 24-to-12-bit conversion method on our busier photos, but that images with smooth gradients, such as a close-up portrait, may require it.

Creating Pseudo 12-Bit Color in Photoshop

To create a pseudo 12-bit color photo from a 24-bit standard RGB photo in Photoshop:

1. Begin with the photo sized exactly as you intend to display it in the final SWF, then separate the three RGB (Red, Green, Blue) channels into three 8-bit files using the Channels palette drop-down menu's Split Channels command (see Figure 2.5).

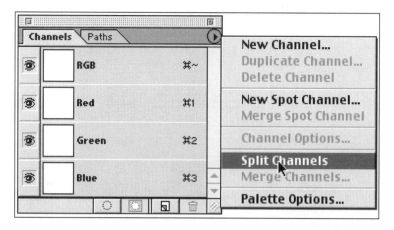

Figure 2.5: The Channels palette drop-down menu's Split Channels command.

2. Convert the three files back to individual RBG color files by proceding from the Main Photoshop Menu and choosing Image • Mode • RGB (even though they are grayscale).

3. Convert the three files to indexed colors using a custom 16-gray-level palette (included on the Chapter 2 folder on the accompanying CD-ROM and seen in Figure 2.6) and set Dithering to Diffusion.

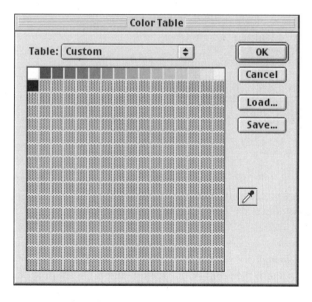

Figure 2.6: Photoshop's Indexed color dialog box showing a custom palette.

4. Once the indexing process is complete, convert all three files to grayscale. (It will seem as though nothing has changed.)

5. Use the Channels palette drop-down menu to select Merge Channels. Click OK in the resulting dialog box and confirm that RGB appears in the Mode box and 3 in the Channels box, as shown in Figure 2.7.

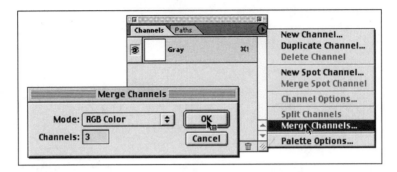

Figure 2.7: The Channels palette drop-down menu and the Merge Channels dialog box.

6. The next dialog box (Figure 2.8) asks you which files you want to merge. These files should be the only open ones in Photoshop, assuming you're working with only one original photo at a time (which we recommend). The Merge RGB Channels dialog box will assume you want to merge these files and will list them under Specify Channels. Press OK, and you should be left with a single RGB file that very closely fakes 12-bit color.

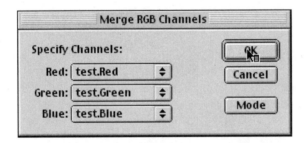

Figure 2.8: Merging the open files into channels to create a 12-bit RGB image.

7. Save this file as the file you'll import into Flash.

NOTE Do not *resize this photo in Flash or it will ruin the 12-bit dithering achieved in Photoshop. Although JPG compression in Flash can pollute the dithering achieved in Photoshop, the end result (the SWF) is far superior to the banding that's sure to result from doing nothing to the original 24-bit photo.*

And here's some more good news: If you're concerned about creating this transformation manually, you'll be pleased to know that a Photoshop action can do all this automatically. It's located at www.pocketpcpassion.com/General/RickJ/colordepth.htm.

Custom Color Picker for Flash

The Photoshop technique just described works fine on photos, but what do you do with art you've created in Flash itself?

Flash's standard palette is rather confining because it uses 216 Web-safe colors. Even though the iPAQ cannot display 24-bit (or millions) of colors, it can render 4,096—obviously many more than the standard palette.

You can create a Flash color set via the Swatches panel using the Add Colors command (under the panel's drop-down menu) and pointing it to a known 12-color bitmap document to read in the colors. Although this will certainly work (as it will with any color set you'd like to create in Flash), the colors will be in completely mixed-up order, as seen in Figure 2.9. You will have greens next to reds next to blacks—all in complete chaos. (That's probably not what you'll want to deal with; even artists like a little order every now and then.)

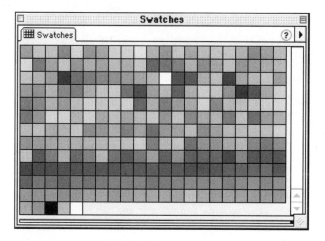

Figure 2.9: The chaos of the Flash Color Picker.

Sort By Color command (on the same drop-down menu as Add Colors) yields a better, but still rather chaotic, ordering of color, so we don't suggest that either. Instead, in this chapter's folder on the CD-ROM, we've supplied you with a bitmap file named 12bitcolorpicker.png that looks very much like a color gamut picker in any other graphics application. To use this file, import it into Flash and place it on a layer in the timeline that will be available throughout your animation, game, or other project. (You can position it off the stage if you like, so that it doesn't intrude on the art space.) Then obtain the Line or Fill eyedropper (by popping up the built-in color swatches for the respective tools, as shown in Figure 2.10), and drag this eyedropper to the imported bitmap placed earlier to choose a color that's restricted to the 12-bit colorspace. If you start out with an empty Flash color set, you may add the colors you use repeatedly to it and save as you would any other color set for later use.

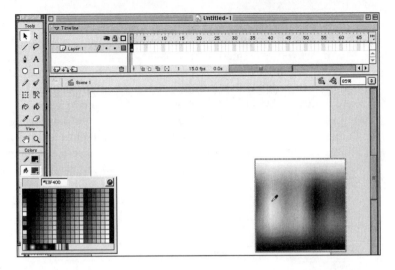

Figure 2.10: Using the 12-bit Color Picker in Flash.

To research the mechanics behind 12-bit colorspace, see Appendix 1, which delves into the numbers and reasoning involved in the colorspace. Warning: This stuff can make your head hurt.

Pocket Internet Explorer (PIE) Steals Precious Real Estate

The PPC's most noticeable and desirable feature is its small screen. While at 240 pixels × 320 pixels, it's not going to replace 21-inch monitors anytime soon, then again you can't carry your 21-inch monitor in your pocket.

Although exact specs are unavailable for the PPC screen's dpi (dots per inch, or as some call it, pixels per inch [ppi]), it equates to just over 100 dpi. That's somewhat higher than the native resolution on a desktop monitor (72 dpi on a Macintosh and 96 dpi on Windows systems). This means that What You See Is Not What You Get, dimensionally speaking, on a PPC.

Here's why: The 72-dpi screen on the Macintosh matches the pica/point measuring system used in publishing. Each dot on the screen equals one point, and 72 points equal 1 inch. Simple. When the monitor is set to its native resolution (not overdriven to show more desktop space) and you use the onscreen ruler to draw a 1-inch square on the screen at 100 percent, you can hold a ruler to the screen and the square will measure exactly 1 inch. In this case, What You See Is What You Get.

However, on the PPC, that same square will measure only about 11/16 of an inch, as shown in Figure 2.11. This means that the same 240 × 320 pixels on your Mac or Windows desktop will be smaller on the PPC, and that spatial difference could affect how you design art for display on the PPC screen. (Of course, the best thing to do when in doubt as to how your art will look on any PPC is to actually view the art on the target device.)

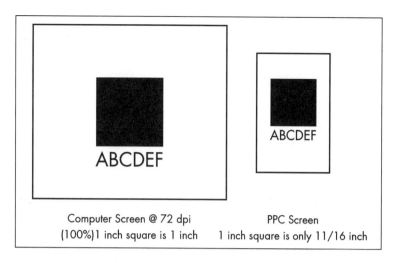

Figure 2.11: The 1-inch square on a 72-dpi screen is no longer 1 inch on the PPC screen.

Less than You Expect

But wait, there's more (or should we say even less) lurking in the shadows. As of this writing, Flash plays on the PPC only via PIE. This means that you don't get the full 240 × 320 screen to play around in without trickery. If you use Flash in the standard way (as a part of HTML and PIE), you get far less screen to work with. So you must be absolutely certain the HTML page you create to display the Flash SWF is no more than 240 × 263 and that the borders are set to 0. (Of course, if you want the user to scroll, then you can go larger.)

Assuming that you will keep the address bar in PIE closed (the default setup), you have only 240 wide × 263 tall and that's it! One pixel over in either direction, and you're doomed to the scrollbar asylum. And the dreaded scrollbars honk down another significant amount of space: Even if only the bottom scrollbar pops up, it invokes the side scrollbar to join in the fray as well.

Limits of the Pocket Internet Explorer Emulator

Doug Loftus

In this chapter's folder on the CD-ROM, you'll find a folder named pie_emu, which contains a Flash movie made to emulate several behaviors of Pocket Internet Explorer (PIE), shown running in an iPAQ. This emulator can aid those who don't have a device, but nonetheless want to create movies for the PPC platform. Following are the main features of the emulator, followed by discussion of a few problems you might run into.

Address Bar

To load a Flash movie into the emulator, type the movie's file name into the address field (next to the Go button), then supply the path of the movie relative to the directory that you are running the emulator from. Click Go to load the movie. (The address bar also maintains a history.)

You can toggle the address bar's visibility by clicking View in the command bar at the bottom of PIE. (In the "real" PIE, this action opens a menu with Address Bar as a choice that, when selected, toggles the bar's visibility.) When the address bar is toggled, the movie's position and scroll status are updated.

Scrollbar

The vertical and horizontal scrollbars are functional and are invoked as they are in PIE. A movie that is 240 pixels wide × 240 pixels high will display with no scrollbars, regardless of whether the address bar is toggled. Several factors determine when scrollbars are invoked, as discussed in the readme.txt file accompanying this emulator.

Soft Input Panel

You can toggle the visibility of the SIP (pop-up QWERTY keyboard) using the SIP options menu button. The SIP is not functional in the emulator, because you can use your computer's keyboard for input, but it's included in the emulator to show how it behaves.

One unfortunate behavior of PIE isn't replicated here: If a movie is loaded that doesn't require scrolling, and the SIP is invoked and then dismissed, scrollbars could remain on the screen until the page is reloaded. So the best procedure is to A, then B.

Refresh Button

The Refresh button can used to reload a movie.

Special Properties Panel

When testing the emulator, you'll notice that using the button labeled P on the iPAQ brings up a dialog box that allows you to resize your movie and see how the exactfit attribute (of the Object tag that embeds the Flash player in the page) works. You can also change the margins and background color of the simulated HTML page holding your movie.

Although the emulator will give you a good idea of how PIE behaves and how your movie will look in general, you won't have an accurate sense of color or performance until you actually run your movie on a PPC. The emulator can also be a good tool for marketing or demonstration purposes. The source (FLA) is included on the CD-ROM if you're interested in seeing how the emulator is coded. (The documentation in the pie_emu file lists additional issues to consider when displaying movies in the emulator.)

Surprise! Use Bitmaps

When creating Flash for the desktop, you will want to save file size and speed downloads, and the rule is to use bitmaps only when there's no other way to express the graphic. This applies in particular to the use of photographs or airbrush-style illustrations in Flash; vectors just cannot replace a photo's quality.

Tracing bitmaps using Flash or Adobe Streamline became a way to use certain (albeit much lower-quality) photos in the pure vector world, but the resulting vectors of such photo conversions can be hard for the processor to render. This becomes obvious when you need to animate those complicated vectors: The process is extremely slow and, on a PPC, it might halt the animation completely.

Bitmaps Can Improve Performance

It may surprise you then to learn that bitmaps are often preferred when developing for the PPC, particularly where photos are concerned. The PPC has a much easier time displaying a bitmap image rather than trying to render the complicated graphic of vectors that results from tracing.

The bitmap files you'll be using in a SWF for the PPC will mostly fall within the screen dimensions of 240×260 (the viewable area in PIE without scrollbars or the address bar). Therefore, they most likely will be smaller in file size than a photo-to-vector tracing conversion of any detail and will play much faster as well as look better.

Your best bet is to resize any bitmaps to exactly the dimensions you want displayed via the SWF before you import them into Flash. If you simply import a larger-than-needed (let's say 640×480) file into Flash and scale it down inside Flash, the entire photo will be included at its original file size and scaled down. This will not save file size and will not display the image optimally.

Even when using a simply gradient created in Flash you may want to opt for a bitmap gradient with a bit of noise added. Want to know why? Figure 2.12 shows a comparison of the banding that occurs when using a smooth Flash gradient next to the same gradient that's been treated with the Add Noise filter in Photoshop.

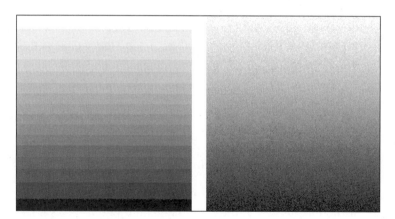

Figure 2.12: A comparison example of banding.

Bitmaps can also be useful when used with the 24-to-12-bit conversion process (explained on pages 28–30) to make gradients for backgrounds and interface parts. The gradients created directly in Flash will band badly (as shown in Figure 2.12) and will not be very attractive. In these cases, a prepared bitmap of the needed gradient can do the trick.

To avoid going through the 24-to-12-bit process, you can simply add some noise to the gradient file in Photoshop. Experiment with various levels of noise to see which one gives satisfactory results. Start with about 2 percent (in the Add Noise filter) applied to the gradient areas of the graphic and export to a format Flash understands, such as PNG or PICT.

Adding noise also works on photos, but is not as reliable as the 24-to-12-bit conversion. Adding the noise to bitmaps forces the PPC display to pseudo-dither and actually makes the bitmap appear smoother on the PPC's screen, compared with the blocks and banding that result from really smooth 24-bit images.

Yes, we know—this is just the opposite of what you've probably been doing with images all your computer life, but keep in mind that the PPC is a very different display device. Experimentation is always a good thing when using bitmaps. What works for one image might not work for another, so you'll need to consider each case individually.

Optimization Techniques

Let's say that you have a Flash animation that plays just fine on desktops, and you'd like to run it on a PPC. As a good Flash artist you've optimized it the best you could, but it still won't play properly on a PPC without long pauses and hiccups. You think you'll just have to start all over again . . . but you don't.

The art of optimizing Flash animations gives whole new meaning to the PPC. The best way to give you some insight is to take a fully animated Flash cartoon meant for desktop and video viewing and dissect it with an eye toward extreme optimization.

NOTE *We initially created this FLA for video and DVD to be played on powerful desktop computers. When targeting such output, we put a premium on the look and sound of the animation, rather than on its optimization. Because we gave no thought to accommodating the lowest common denominator processor, it was really challenging to make this play smoothly on a PPC.*

The goal of this sample optimization is not to force the PPC's processor to do the unthinkable, but to allow the PPC version to provide the same look and feel experience as does the desktop version. To do so, we'll need not only to optimize vectors but sometimes even delete entire objects that can slow down the little computers.

The secret is to remove things selectively, without anyone noticing. The small screen is actually our friend here. Because the screen is so small, lots of details that are visible on the desktop screen and video can be removed without disrupting the flow of the entertainment or graphics. We'll do that first.

Next we'll follow the procedures of graphics optimization used on the Weber cartoon titled "Waste Pipe" (see Figure 2.13).

First, View the Desktop Version

To get a better sense of what the process, first view the animation as it was originally intended, on your desktop. On the CD-ROM, inside the FLAs folder for this chapter, you'll find a folder named "wastepipe desktop." Use the supplied

HTML, wastepipe.html, to display the cartoon in your browser of choice. After watching this version of the cartoon, play the PPC version (in the folder named "wastepipe ipaq") using the supplied HTML, wastepipe_ppc.html. If you can, transfer it and play it from a PPC. If not, play it from your desktop computer—but be sure to use the supplied HTML to launch it. (It's important to use the HTML files to launch the SWF because they constrain the displayed dimensions and other factors.)

Figure 2.13: The opening scene of the sample animation.

Now that you've watched the cartoon, other than size, what's the difference? We're glad you asked. Read on to find out.

Major Performance Enhancers

> **NOTE** *"Quality level" does not refer to the quality of your art or animation, but to the quality of anti-aliasing that the Flash player performs in realtime during playback. Most people use the default High Quality setting because it produces the best-looking results but, as you'll learn next, this might not be the wisest choice for playback on the PPC.*

The first thing we did was to find out exactly where in our animation the problems lay. To do so, we simply used the desktop version and created an HTML file that would instigate the show's playback in PIE on the PPC at the proper dimensions. It played terribly: Long pauses, stuttering frames, and a loss of sound synching seemed to be everywhere. In fact, at one point it seemed to kill the entire system. We smelled plastic melting—not a good sign.

We then ran a test by simply changing the HTML parameters to display at the Medium Quality setting instead of High Quality. What a difference!

Use Medium Quality Mode

The number-one performance offender was running our animation in the High Quality display mode. Remember that High Quality is the default for *desktop* animations, but Flash 5 offers the Medium Quality mode, which is perfect for the PPC's screen. Medium Quality's lower anti-aliasing mode takes a serious strain off the PPC's processor and looks nearly as good as High Quality, as shown in Figure 2.14.

The fact that the screen is so small works in our favor here because you simply cannot tell much difference between the two quality modes without straining your eyes. Medium Quality mode also makes smaller text (which would otherwise require anti-aliasing) more readable because it tends to blur the text far less.

NOTE *Medium Quality mode may cause unwanted reformatting of text, particularly where line wraps are important. Be sure to watch for these problems.*

Figure 2.14: The right side is set on Medium Quality; the left on High Quality. As you can see, it's difficult to spot any differences.

Even though using Medium Quality mode helped tremendously, we still had a long way to go. We found that certain areas would play fine, while others would not. Those areas that dragged the processor down were most likely dragging because of using Flash created gradients.

Remove Gradients

Gradients, or the blending of one color smoothly to the next, gives your art an airbrushed look that is often quite useful. Unfortunately, gradients also eat up processor cycles in order to render in the Flash player. If you have a large number of gradients in your project, consider removing some so that your animation will play smoothly on the PPC.

In our sample animation, one area of heavy gradient use occurs during the underwater fish scene. This section would still freeze and stutter pretty badly, even on the Medium Quality setting. As you can see in Figure 2.15, we solved this problem by removing the gradients that make the water go from a darker to a lighter shade of blue.

Besides producing the banding effect (discussed earlier), gradients adversely affect motion around and in front of them. We therefore chose to replace every gradient with a solid. This may be a hard decision artistically, but it's one you must make in order to have smooth playback. If you absolutely must use a gradient, use a bitmap (as discussed earlier) and try not to motion-tween it around much, if at all.

Figure 2.15: The before (left side) and after of the gradient removal.

Replace Art with Symbols

Another task to perform is to replace any art that can be repeated with symbols. In a linear animation, that means using graphic symbols. Until movie-clip symbols can be viewed in motion on the main timeline while scrubbing (dragging the playback head) the sections you want to view with the playback head, you must use graphic symbols, not movie-clip symbols. This is not really a bad thing—you can change any symbol on the stage to any method (movie-clip or graphic symbol) you need via the Instance panel. You both save file space and improve performance by doing this.

NOTE *Movie-clip symbols—although quite useful in advanced interactive projects such as games and interfaces—have little to no use in a linear animation such as a cartoon. The same is true for sounds with the Synch set to Event. Event sounds do not force the animation to drop frames, as the Streaming synch does. This dropping of frames to keep up with the soundtrack is extremely important in a linear cartoon, especially with lip-synch. The same approach is also used in digital video (such as QuickTime) on slower computers that cannot keep up the frame rate.*

Fortunately, we had already used graphic symbols throughout the original animation, making our task a little easier. Unfortunately, we found that some of our symbols could benefit from a sub, or nested, symbol.

Take the swimming fish (all the fish facing left) in Figure 2.16, for example: They consist of a three-frame animation of a fish with its fins moving about and its belly contracting and expanding. Every now and then, the eyes blink. In the rush to make the original, we had duplicated the three frames on the symbol's timeline and did not take advantage of symbols. This alone is not really a problem—the problem comes when you duplicate the fish many times on the main timeline, as we had done. Once we consolidated this three-frame animation into a graphic symbol, the school of fish played considerably better.

Figure 2.16: The entire school of fish (except the one talking) is really just three individual drawings instanced many times on the stage.

Full-Screen Tweens? Think Again

Trying to move around full screens of action quickly is also a serious processor killer, and it is crucial to determine what really has to move at any given time. Of course, during a section of lip-synching or other important parts of the animation, you'll want to avoid at all costs having a full-screen pan, or dolly, going on. Doing so would kill all the hard work you put into the lip art and everyone will notice.

You can motion-tween full screens of animation, as long as you watch for frame dropping or stuttering. Although lowering the frame rate is helpful, it results in the serious problem of synching with your soundtrack. This is a viable solution if there's no soundtrack synch, but keep in mind that your animation will play back slower *everywhere*, not just during the tween. (This is probably not what you want.)

You can shorten the time a full-screen motion-tween exists, as long as you remember that, depending on content, it will stutter. Is this stutter acceptable?

Only you or your client can be the judge of that. You might also ask yourself whether that full-screen motion-tween is really necessary. In many cases, you'll find that it is not. Try designing motion and scene changes without it. If you must have it, then try eliminating peripheral objects in the scene, such as text on objects and other unneeded processor hogs.

Flatten Grouped Objects

If you've used Flash to create artwork, you've surely used grouping. Grouping helps to protect certain areas of art while you work on other details. For instance, suppose a character's face is one group and the eyes are another group on top of the face group. This arrangement is very useful while you're creating the art, but it taxes the processor unnecessarily upon playback. Grouped objects can hide many unneeded vectors for the processor to deal with, so consider trying to eliminate all possibly useless vectors for playback on the PPC.

For example, the bathroom scene in the cartoon (shown in Figure 2.17) shows all sorts of objects while we dolly in the room. We originally left these objects grouped so we could edit them in the future, which meant that what you saw was being rendered while everything behind the scenes was also taking up processor time.

Optimizing this scene required that we save it with the grouped objects intact as a different reference file (in case we wanted to edit objects later). Then, by ungrouping everything in the art and deselecting the resulting art, we forced the art behind objects to be clipped, or erased, and in essence flattened the image to a single graphic of the entire bathroom. We then optimized the remaining vectors (over 50 percent of the vector points were removed), and thus helped the dolly shot motion-tween dramatically better.

Figure 2.17: The before (left side) and after of the bathroom dolly, or zoom-in, scene. Massive optimization was needed to achieve acceptable movement.

This bathroom dolly shot is critical to the story line. In it you see the various wastes, such as Hair Lard and Xylene, that the character plans to dispose of through his newly built waste pipe. These features would be difficult to read on the small screen without the dolly tween shot, which gives you a closer look at the items before getting into the scene.

As you can see, sometimes you must accept a little lack of smoothness to get your message across. In our case, we decided that having a few frames drop was not as bad as losing a significant part of the message. We also thought it was important to keep the animation as consistent with the desktop version as we could.

More Performance Enhancers

At this point, we now have a mostly playable animation, but let's do a little more—actually, a little less. After watching your animation play many times, you'll begin to notice some less significant details that can be removed. We did.

Focus on What's Really Important

Sometimes you can add too much detail to an animation. Although this won't cause much problem with the desktop player (particularly on faster computers), the PPC may balk. The trick is to be frugal without being Scrooge.

The job of editing your scenes is certainly an art form, and one that you'll get better at with practice. For example, here's how we reduced the detail in the scene with the swimming fish (which turned out to be one of our most troublesome performance scenes):

- We reduced the amount of information in the bubbles. We optimized the bubbles by removing their transparency, and we also reduced the number of bubbles the fish emit. By reducing the bubble rate from 7 to 3, we significantly optimized the scene while retaining its original feeling.

- We optimized the surroundings by removing every unneeded point from elements. For example, we made the sea grass nearly angular, which is hardly noticeable on the small screen.

- Wherever we used a brush stroke, we reduced that stroke to a minimum without disrupting its flow. For instance, there's a scene where the man, Mr. Murky, is tugging on a monkey wrench in his quest to build the waste pipe. Whenever he would strain, a little scribble of stress cloud would appear above his head. Although this added to the subconscious communication and humor, it was not really needed—so we discarded it.

- We also severely curtailed the motion line trails from the swinging of the monkey wrench. By deleting over half of the motion line trails and leaving only the most prevalent strokes, we saved more processor time for other things.

Optimize Strokes and Lines

Because nearly all of the artwork you create in Flash will consist of strokes (using the Brush tool) and lines (using the Pencil, Rectangle, and Oval tools), it makes sense to look closely at these techniques when enhancing performance. The lines you draw should be as optimal as possible without diluting your style of drawing. Optimize too little and you have a performance problem; optimize too much and you end up with art so simple and angular looking it will no longer resemble your original art.

The scene in Figure 2.18, in which the character beats on the pipe, was a real performance problem, requiring an overall optimization of the character's lines. Once we completed that optimization, we selectively optimized even further, and here's how:

To optimize the repeating graphic symbol of Mr. Murky working and beating on the pipe, we first selected all the art, and then chose Modify • Optimize. In the resulting dialog box, we moved the slider to about a fourth of the way from the left, which reduced the redundant vector points by about 20 percent. This produced a smoother Mr. Murky, and this step should be a standard one with any Flash animation.

We then went through each frame of the Mr. Murky symbol and used the Lasso tool to select areas we felt did not need as much detail, such as his shoes, his legs, and his belly. Areas such as the face and hands were left alone, because they carry more information. To reduce the information in the selected areas, we cranked the slider up to about three-fourths from the left and ran the Optimize function again on only the selected areas. We estimate that this netted us another 15 to 20 percent reduction in vector points. The bottom line is that on the small PPC screen, it still looks the same.

Figure 2.18: This character required overall optimization of vectors as well as selective area optimization. Before (the bottom half) shows far more lines coming from the monkey wrench.

Even the Little Stuff Adds Up

Developing animation for the PPC is such a balancing act that everything counts. When you're drawing, using the Paint Brush instead of the Pencil can double the number of vector points for each stroke, as shown in Figure 2.19. This might not mean much when you're using only a few strokes, but when you're drawing complicated graphics, and hundreds of them, the number of points needed can add up quite quickly. Add to this the fact that the thick and thin quality of the Paint Brush strokes is not terribly apparent on the PPC small screen, and it's clear why the extra detail can be left out.

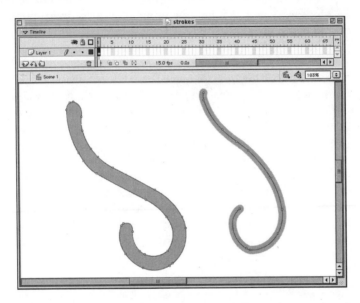

Figure 2.19: The difference in vector points needed to render a Brush stroke (on the left) opposed to a Pencil stroke.

In short, use the Pencil or similar single-vector lines as much as possible. Avoid completely the urge to use line styles such as stipple, dotted, and dashed because they will adversely effect on playback on both the desktop and PPC.

Also, avoid using transparent colors except when absolutely necessary—for a car or house window, for example. As in the case of the bubbles in our fish example, transparency adds little to the finished animation and is barely noticeable on the small screen.

Sound Issues

Fortunately, sound is not as much of an issue on the Flash 5 Player as it was on version 4, which didn't allow you to use MP3. You could use the ADPCM with version 4, but doing so strained the processor, and some passages would simply halt while the animation decompressed and played. The only other alternative was to use RAW uncompressed audio—which sounds great, but is not less filling. In fact, when you used RAW audio, the file size was huge (multiple megabytes for a few minutes of sound or music). Not exactly a desirable thing for a computer with limited installed RAM.

The Flash 5 Player brings to the table probably one of the most important advances of all: the ability to use MP3 compression on the audio portions of your animations, your games, and to some degree, your applications.

Avoid Stereo, if Possible

We found during the optimization of the cartoon that the sound needed little attention. We always import sound into Flash at its most pristine, uncompressed format of 16-bit 44.1-kHz stereo. When exporting for the PPC, though, we did find that it was best not to use stereo playback. Although using mono may seem prehistoric, most PPC users won't be viewing your cartoon or playing your game with headphones or while connected to a home stereo amplifier. Most will be listening through the tiny little speaker on the front of the PPC, which is adequate for most uses. If your goal is to create MP3s that play in stereo at a higher fidelity and bit rate, consider lowering the bar on the animations involved. You can only shove so much data through the little PPC guy.

Usability

So far, we've focused on optimizing linear animations, but good designers also consider other components of usability: buttons, menus, text, and user feedback.

Buttons Without the Over State

Unfortunately, with the PPC you have to think differently about on-screen buttons. Because all on-screen buttons are activated by tapping a stylus, there is no more Over state. The computer has no idea where you might be hovering your stylus until you tap the screen. This, of course, renders useless any button you design with an Over state. In fact, if you do use an Over state, you may confuse the software into showing the Over state frame or nested movie clip momentarily before going to the Down state.

On the desktop player, you can have a button that will play a short movie clip while the mouse pointer is in the Over state. On the PPC, however, a complicated button with a movie clip might attempt to play the clip before going to the Down state, which can ruin the user experience. So PPC designers must say goodbye to these types of buttons. (However, the other three states—Down, Up, and Hit—still work just fine.)

Size and Legibility

On the small screen, there's not much space and no Over state available to explain what a button does (in other words, no ToolTips). This makes it tricky to design buttons that explain themselves. Design too many large buttons, and there's no screen left for the content. Make your buttons too small, and users may have difficulty tapping them. See Figure 2.20 for an example.

Figure 2.20: The bargain between size and legibility in the buttons that control a game. Notice the Restart button is well away from the main controls (the arrows).

Button Placement

The placement of your buttons demands closer attention than usual, too. Consider this scenario: Your game requires that the user tap the screen to move about. You also have a Restart button that resets the game in case the player gets hopelessly lost. It's not a good idea to place these buttons close to each other, because the chances of a player slipping with the stylus are fairly high. If the Restart button is within slipping distance of the most-used navigation button (see Figure 2.21), the player might accidentally restart the game, which would make a player on the verge of a high score quite unhappy.

If you do need to place critical buttons, such as a Restart, close to the common tapping area, consider adding insurance in the form of a "Are You Sure?" button (as shown in Figure 2.22). Better yet, simply isolate the doomsday button elsewhere on the screen.

Figure 2.21: The Restart button is much too close to the navigation buttons.

Figure 2.22: The "Are You Sure?" button alleviates this design problem.

Remember too that simply touching the screen with your fingers triggers a button as well. To guard against this, include an "Are You Sure?" button—and make certain the OK button is not in the same place as the button that took the user there. If it is, users could actually hit the Restart and OK buttons simultaneously with either the stylus or their fingers.

Drop-Down or Pop-Up Menus

To support multiple functions, design buttons with drop-down or pop-up menus. By using these methods, you can give your users access to many functions that will disappear from the screen once they've made a choice.

Using a second screen of button or menu choice graphics can work in some situations, such as when you're displaying the rules of a game. In this method, a single small button in the corner takes the user to a new screen of options, as in the slot machine game discussed in Chapter 4. Your application will determine whether you can take advantage of pop-up or drop-down menus.

Text

Make sure that your text is legible and that the font you choose is readable. Avoid fancy fonts with lots of details and choose bitmap fonts over fonts that will anti-alias with their surroundings; bitmapped fonts seem to work better at smaller sizes. Although a font such as Snell Roundhand might be very attractive, plain old Helvetica will be far more readable at a small size.

Feedback

The lack of an Over state for buttons (discussed above) can make it harder to give feedback to your users (for instance, to tell them that the command they've requested has been accepted by the device). The Down state (your only alternative) is not really the place to add animated movie clips, because users will seldom tap and hold. Though they can be taught to tap and hold a button to, say, bring up an instruction screen that displays as long as they hold down the button, the first time through, they'll most likely simply tap the button and wait for something to happen. (You might label your tap-and-hold buttons "Hold" if space permits.)

About the only way you can inform the user that a button has been tapped is to have a sound go off in the Down state. Along with this, you might want to change the graphic of the Down state to show the change in the button's state. But don't be too subtle here, or you can thwart the purpose. Use a sound as well as a distinct color or graphic change to communicate that a button has been pressed and that the computer will now perform the requested function. (You will find a good example of this usability in the slot machine game included on the CD-ROM and discussed in Chapter 4.)

Summary

You should now have a better understanding of what it takes to create Flash animations for the PPC. You also know that deciding what to leave in and what to take out is a balancing act. Perhaps most of your immediate projects will be converting desktop Flash to PPC Flash—but, as the PPC gains popularity, you might find more projects strictly for the little computer that could.

Now that you are familiar with the basic issues confronting Flash designers who target the PPC, Chapter 3 will consider a slightly more complex issue: how to build Flash content that accepts user input from the device keys, the hardware buttons commonly found beneath the screen of the PPC.

3

GETTING USER INPUT FROM DEVICE KEYS

Doug Loftus

Anyone familiar with Flash development knows that the ubiquity of Flash on the desktop PC has led to an increased awareness of the need for Flash content to be highly usable. The challenge of designing for usability extends to devices as well, where a detailed familiarity with user input schemes can help developers exploit the strengths of a given device and avoid its weaknesses, to create interfaces that are easier to use and less error-prone.

This chapter will focus on taking user input from the dedicated navigation button found on a PPC (or keys that can be remapped by the user to perform traditional QWERTY keyboard roles) and consider how such input schemes can contribute to the usability and performance of Flash applications for the PPC.

An interface that relies mainly on keypresses to accomplish a variety of user tasks can be useful for building a variety of applications, including games. Here, we'll cover one approach to coding an interface of this type. We'll use buttons, movie clips, and ActionScript to construct a Softkeys object, which dynamically assigns actions (function calls) to keypresses. A game (P*NG, similar to the more familiar PONG) will serve as a simple example of how to implement this interface.

The Five-Way Button

Take the iPAQ's control button (shown in Figure 3.1) as an example of a navigation button. This large, joystick-like button, referred to as the Up/Down control, is one of the iPAQ's most distinguishing features. It is "joystick-like" in that it looks and feels as though it might behave like a joystick, but it's really a five-way button with discrete states for Right, Left, Up, Down, and Enter.

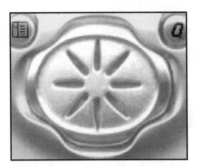

Figure 3.1: A view of the iPAQ five-way navigation button.

What Else Can That Button Do?

The shape of the Up/Down control ("control button" hereafter) suggests that it behaves like a set of arrow keys. Although it lacks the arrowhead markings found on most arrow keys, its shape suggests four major compass points, corresponding to a standard arrow direction.

This is indeed the case; however, other cues as to its function are either lacking or misleading. The fifth position isn't really indicated: pressing the middle of the control button is equivalent to pressing Enter. Both the radial pattern on the face of the control button and the button's behavior when pressed around its perimeter suggest that it might behave like a game controller, but only *one* of its five states can be engaged at any time—there's no "in-between."

NOTE *Many of the newer PPC devices now offer a five-way button that is multi-capable. However, devices with their limited mono five-way buttons remain on the market and are still in wide use. Consequently, this distinction remains relevant. Too, some PPCs permit the user to remap keys that by default are dedicated to launching applications. The HP Jornada is one such device; it has a dedicated Game Buttons control panel for managing user-created button profiles. If you have such a device, remapping options are typically found on the Windows CE Start Menu (select Start • Settings • Buttons). For updates and developments on this topic, see www.flashthefuture.com/3.*

While researching this chapter, I circulated a SWF to a few of this book's coauthors under the guise of testing the arrow functions of the control button. When I later revealed that the real subject of the test was the Enter function (which we'll cover on page 52), one of the authors replied that he didn't know there was an Enter button! I mention this to illustrate that a PPC can be used for many tasks without ever touching the control button, and it's fair to assume that most users won't be as familiar with this button as you'll be when you finish this chapter.

Designing for the Button

In the context of Flash authoring, these observations boil down to the following recommendations when you're developing for the PPC:

- **Inform the user**—If you're designing an interface for key-based input, tell users how to use the five-way control button.

- **Avoid designs that require simultaneous keypresses**—Because many navigation control buttons can be in only one of five discrete states, an activity such as "moving forward with the Up arrow while pressing Enter to fire" can't play out on the earlier PPCs. As this example suggests, the discrete mono behavior of the control button might have a greater impact on games than on other applications.

- **Specify the target device(s)**—Given that some devices have both mono and five-way control buttons, offer users a strategy for using their application on both, or exclude some devices.

Key Event Handling

Of course Flash can recognize the key events that fire when the five-way control button is used. For example, Table 3.1 shows a mapping of the key events in Flash using the iPAQ as a target platform.

The ActionScript side of handling key events is like the desktop environment, except that only five key code constants are relevant in this case: Key.UP, Key.DOWN, Key.LEFT, Key.RIGHT, and Key.ENTER. (If handling key events is new to you, relax: Code examples will be presented on page 54, following an overview of the control button's firing behavior.)

The firing rates in Table 3.1 were timed using a Flash movie and represent average times measured for more than 100 events. (Note that pressing Enter produces both a keyDown and a keyUp event—but only upon release.)

NOTE *You can also trap events fired when the Soft Input Panel (SIP), the on-screen QWERTY keyboard, is in use. However, because of its intrusive presence on the display, the SIP isn't likely to be useful as a means of user input for tasks other than text entry.*

Table 3.1: Key events in Flash on the Compaq iPAQ

Control Button Gesture	Key Constant (Code)	Button on(keyPress StringId):	Repeats	Default Interval	Fastest Interval
Up	Key.UP (38)	"<UP>"	Yes	~120 ms	34 ms
Right	Key.RIGHT(39)	"<RIGHT>"	Yes	~120 ms	34 ms
Down	Key.DOWN (40)	"<DOWN>"	Yes	~120 ms	34 ms
Left	Key.LEFT (37)	"<LEFT>"	Yes	~120 ms	34 ms
Enter	Key.ENTER (13)	"<ENTER>"	No	–	–

Event Handling by Movie Clips

Movie clips can intercept the messages that fire when a key is pressed (in ActionScript, a keyDown event) or released (a keyUp event). For these messages to reach a Flash movie hosted in a web page, the movie must be given focus—typically when the user clicks on it.

To code movie clips to respond to these events, use the syntax onClipEvent(event), where event is either keyUp or keyDown. Upon detection of a key event, the Key object's getCode() method will determine which key was pressed. Another method, Key.isDown(keyCodeConstant) (where keyCodeConstant can be any of the constants Key.UP, Key.DOWN, and so forth), returns true if the key supplied as an argument is being held down at the time of the query.

Event Handling by Arrow-Key Gestures

To handle events from arrow-key gestures on a PPC, you can use keyDown and keyUp without a hitch—these events fire when the key is pressed and when it is released, respectively. And, again for arrow presses, Key.isDown() can be used reliably to detect a pressed key.

As you might have guessed, the control button's Enter function has a different event-firing pattern. A keyDown event is only registered in Flash when the middle of the control button is *released*, not when it is pressed. At the moment of release, a keyUp event also registers, so either event can be used to detect an Enter press, although keyUp more accurately reflects the button's state and, for the sake of coding clarity, should be used. Too, Enter doesn't fire continuously, and Key.isDown(Key.ENTER) does not return true while the button is depressed in the "Enter" position.

NOTE *On most desktop keyboards, Enter behaves like any other key, producing distinct keyDown and keyUp events and firing repetitively.*

Events are handled by button instances in a manner consistent with this scheme. For example, trapping an Up arrow press with on(keyPress "<UP>") will execute the handling code when the key is first pressed and repeatedly thereafter as long as the button is held down. However, when using on(keyPress "<ENTER>"), the handling code is executed only once, after the control button is released.

Movie clips and buttons also differ in a crucial way with respect to event handling. An invisible movie clip (that is, a clip with its _visible property set to false) will continue to process key events; however, a button within an invisible movie clip will no longer capture events (see Figure 3.2).

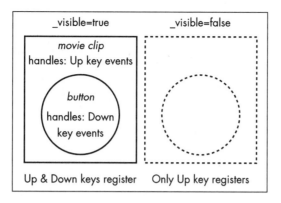

Figure 3.2: The effect of a movie clip's _visible property on event handling.

Event Firing Rates

As we have just seen, arrow-key events fire continuously while the control button is depressed. As shown in Figure 3.3, the rate at which these events fire (as well as the initial delay) is a user-adjustable setting, accessible via the WinCE Start Menu (Start • Settings • Buttons).

Figure 3.3 shows the default setting for the repeat rate (at maximum), which is set with a slider. As shown in Table 3.1, the maximum repeat rate corresponds to an interval of roughly 120 milliseconds (ms). However, if you crank the repeat rate to 11, the interval is a blazing 34 ms and quite stable. That's pretty fast—in Flash terms, that corresponds to a frame rate of roughly 30 fps, which exceeds the currently recommended maximum (18 fps) for the desktop Flash 5 Player.

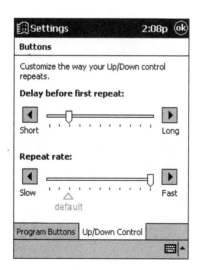

Figure 3.3: The WinCE Buttons Settings control panel on an iPAQ, showing the user-adjustable settings for the control button.

With a high repeat rate, a Flash movie's frame rate can be set to a typical level (12 to 18 fps), and the control button can be used to scroll text or menus with greater speed than possible at those frame rates. Although you can do this by handling events with a button (or by trapping keyDown events with a movie clip) and using updateAfterEvent() to ensure that the stage is redrawn at the rate of events, rather than at the movie's frame rate (as shown in Listing 3.1, below), you can't assume that the user has hiked his or her control button's repeat rate. Therefore, it's generally better to use enterFrame events to control user-driven continuous motions, such as scrolling or maneuvering game objects. (However, for enterprise-wide deployment or for games, it's not difficult to imagine circumstances in which a need for very smooth, continuous action, coupled with a reasonable frame rate, might make it appropriate to direct users to alter their Up/Down control settings.)

Listing 3.1: Example code that illustrates how to detect key presses using either a button or a movie clip.

```
// button instance
on(keyPress "<UP>") {

    // This code executes once every time an event fires
    // from the control button, regardless of the
    // movie's frame rate.

}

// movie clip - simple event trap
onClipEvent(keyDown) {

//Key.UP is a constant property of the Key Object
//Key.UP = 38, and Key.getCode() returns this value
//when the control button fires in its "Up" state

    if (key.getCode() == Key.UP) {
        // this code will execute at the rate of
        // events, but the stage will only be updated
        // at the movie's frame rate unless...
    }
    // unless you include the following statement

    updateAfterEvent();

    // The above statement forces an update
    // of the stage after each event
}
```

```
// checking for a depressed key
onClipEvent(enterFrame) {

    if (Key.isDown(Key.UP) {

    //This code will execute at the movie's
    //frame rate, independent of the event
    //firing rate, as long as the key
    //remains depressed.

    }
}
```

If you have an iPAQ, test the scrolling yourself with the sample movie menu_study.swf, (in the Chapter 3 folder on the CD-ROM). Try it with your control button's repeat rate set to different speeds, because the sample SWF uses key events handled by buttons, rather than enterFrame events, to control the rate of scrolling.

NOTE *To view a movie on the PPC, transfer both its SWF file and the corresponding HTML file (menu_study.html in this case) to your PPC.*

Limitations and Potential Problems

The fact that the control button doesn't behave exactly like a game controller isn't really an issue, but its inability to fire events from two or more keys simultaneously could restrict some designs.

Inadvertent Enter Gestures

Another aspect of the control button's design brings us back to the "test" alluded to on page 50. This test movie (key_test.swf, included in the Chapter 3 folder on the CD-ROM) requires the user to do nothing more than move a ball around the screen using arrow-key gestures. However, in addition to measuring the elapsed time, the movie also tracks the number of Enter presses (in this situation, such presses are, by definition, errors) and displays this number with no label—a stealth test of inadvertent Enter presses. Three people were given the test movie, and each reported that the number increased to at least 1 within 45 seconds. Those who subjected the control button to a game play–style workout made many more inadvertent Enter presses along the way.

This suggests that, because earlier iPAQs lacked a distinct Enter button, users are more likely to make inadvertent Enter gestures while using the arrow functions of the control button. This might make a designer reconsider using the common user interface (UI) scheme that makes use of arrow keys for navigating fields or lists and then requires the user to hit Enter to take action on an item. Although usability testing is always the best idea, we recommend that any UI of this type targeted for this iPAQ should be user-tested with specific regard to the frequency of errors caused by inadvertent Enter presses.

User Input and Interface Usability

Despite the control button's shortcomings as an input mechanism, dedicated navigation keys on a PPC are a smart touch. These keys can help to alleviate some of the usability problems introduced by the touch-screen UI of PPCs.

Advantages of the Touch Screen

Touch-screen UIs are typically easier to use than mouse-driven ones because they offer direct access to screen objects without a mouse interfering with a user's intentions. Still, touch screens have their own drawbacks, some of which are exacerbated as screen size is decreased.

Watch Your Step

As mentioned in Chapter 2, touch screens don't track the stylus (or your finger) as it hovers above the display, so there is no way to convey the equivalent of a "mouse-over" state for screen objects to the user. Therefore, tasks that require the user to select from a group of closely spaced items, such as lists and navigation menus, can be more error-prone because the user isn't being told which object will have focus once the stylus touches the screen's surface. Both parallax (users' inability to judge position precisely based on the angle from which they view the screen) and this lack of positional feedback can contribute to such selection errors.

NOTE *Parallax is an optical phenomenon that results in erroneous judgment about the relative positions of two objects. A familiar example is in reading your car's fuel gauge. From the driver's vantage point, the needle rests on the "one-quarter full" mark; from the passenger's seat, however, it might appear to be only slightly above Empty.*

A Place for Everything

Mouse-based GUIs have given us a familiar set of conventions that don't always translate well to a touch screen. When a mouse is the input device, it's typically safe to ignore whether a user is right-handed or left-handed when considering where to place objects on the screen. However, when using a touch screen, the user's hand will often obscure some part of the display, as shown in Figure 3.4.

Small touch screens can introduce unique UI design problems. As you can see in the left and middle panels in the figure, right-handed and left-handed users of the scrollbar experience this interface differently. Although right-handed individuals can easily use the scrollbar and scan the content as it moves by, left-handed users would find it difficult to use the scrollbar without obscuring their view of the text. (This does not necessarily mark a particular bias against left-handed people, by the way; it's not hard to imagine similar conflicts arising just as easily for right-handed users, depending on the design.)

Although the control button may make it easier to scroll the content in this example, reliance upon the control button to resolve too many design issues would be likely to result in an unwieldy UI.

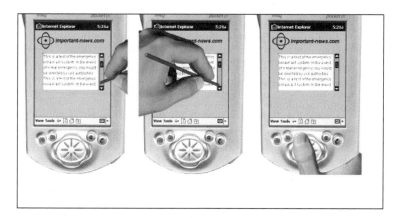

Figure 3.4: A small touch-screen example: The right-handed user manipulating the scrollbar (left panel) does not obscure the screen, but the left-handed user does (middle panel). The right panel shows how the control button can make scrolling easier for all users.

Why Hardware Keys Matter

These represent a subset of the concerns that you should address when designing Flash interfaces for small touch screens. Designs that minimize the user's exposure to the drawbacks of small touch screens are likely to perform better by resulting in fewer user errors. Although nearly every application is associated with a unique set of design problems that you must solve, you can address some common interface problems by using the hardware keys as UI controls.

Hardware buttons are not a panacea for all of the interface ills that might befall an application running on a small touch screen and, clearly, nothing can be said of a given design's usability until it has been tested. The remainder of this section, however, will propose one possible solution to some of the problems we've considered—a solution that involves using the control button. This example will also tie together a lot of the material covered in this chapter so far.

Example: A Scrollable Menu Using the Control Button

As suggested in Figure 3.4, the use of the control button to scroll a text field addresses the inability of some users to scroll the text and maintain an unobstructed view of the content. Here we'll tackle a more involved UI scheme, involving menu navigation and selection, to see how the control button can figure into an interface design.

The UI scheme described below is common to numerous real-world desktop and web applications. The requirements for our hypothetical UI are as follows:

1. The user must be able to select items from a menu of variable length.

2. A description or preview of content associated with the selected item must be displayed.

3. An additional action on this item by the user must result in retrieval of the actual content.

4. An area at least 220 pixels wide × 80 pixels high must always be present on the screen to hold various content.

Because the first three requirements describe such a commonly encountered motif, I'll leave it to you to think about how to implement this scheme as a touch-screen (only) UI. You might try building this yourself now, and then comparing your UI with the one we'll analyze in the next section. But rather than examine alternative approaches to the problem let's jump straight to the proposed key-based UI.

Figure 3.5 shows a screen from the movie menu_study.swf (included in the Chapter 3 folder of the CD-ROM). It's a hypothetical interface for content previewing and retrieval, meant to be navigated using the control button, or arrow keys, depending on the device. The Up and Down arrows move the selection highlight in the menu and automatically scroll the list when necessary to keep items in view. A Right arrow gesture displays preview information for the highlighted item. The scroll indicator, between the Menu and Info fields, is only a visual indicator of scrolling progress and not a control.

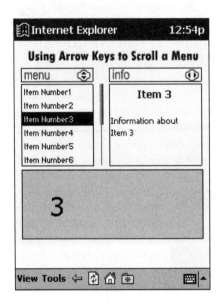

Figure 3.5: A hypothetical interface for content previewing and retrieval, meant to be navigated using the control button or arrow keys.

You can try this UI out for yourself on a PPC. The layout provides the screen items called for in our list of requirements: a menu, a preview area, and a large reserved block of space. Items are selected from the menu on the left, and a press of the Right arrow key displays information in the Info panel at the right. Though not implemented in this sample movie, an additional Right arrow press could retrieve content, perhaps displaying it in a new screen. A Left arrow press from this position would return the user to the screen in Figure 3.5, and one more Left arrow press would clear the Info panel.

Meeting the Requirements of the UI

We can break this interface down further by examining how the control button is used to meet the requirements of the UI, and how well its incorporation into the design addresses anticipated UI problems. To do so, we'll look at a few particular functions—focus, select, preview, and retrieve.

Focus

A startup screen, which appears prior to the one shown in Figure 3.5, provides instructions for navigation and prompts the user with a "tap screen to continue" message. Tapping this screen brings up the screen shown in Figure 3.5.

 Problems addressed or raised: This next step helps to ensure that the Flash movie has focus (when the page loads, the movie does not—by default—have focus), enabling the Flash player to register keypresses. However, the movie can lose focus anytime the user accesses another part of the browser or OS (such as the Start Menu). Because keypresses are used exclusively beyond this point, obstruction of screen items by the user's hand won't be an issue.

Select

The control button's Up and Down keys are used to navigate the menu. When one of these keys is used, the next or previous menu item is highlighted, providing a visual cue that the item has focus. In addition, these keys will automatically scroll the list to keep the selected item in view. Because this design permits (in principle) menus of any length to be used and provides a means of selecting menu items, our first UI requirement is met.

 Problems addressed or raised: Errors of selection involving small targets (such as menu items) should be more difficult to commit because no screen taps are involved. Because menu items don't have to be directly selected, they can be set in a small, aliased font that is readable and that permits more information to be displayed in a small space. Using the control button to scroll the menu frees up some screen space, because it eliminates the need for a scrollbar large enough to be easily manipulated. Visual feedback of scrolling progress is provided in the form of an indicator (which is not a functional scrolling control), placed to the right of the menu where, for better or worse, people are accustomed to seeing it. This scheme could have problems if many menu items are involved—navigating the menu could be cumbersome, and the approach would need to be rethought.

Preview and Retrieve

The Right arrow key is used to expand content, and the Left arrow key collapses content or reverses the user's progress through the interface. Previewing of content is implemented and Requirement 2 is met. The third requirement is not met because retrieval isn't actually implemented but, as proposed earlier, another Right arrow press would take care of this task.

Problems addressed or raised: Acting on items using the Right and Left arrow keys (rather than an Enter press) avoids errors caused by inadvertent use of Enter. The overall layout preserves a left-to-right model of information flow common to cultures whose languages read from left to right, and the model is reinforced by the use of Left and Right arrows to control the display of information. The preview information is not automatically displayed as items are selected in the menu list. Doing so could save the user a step if this information is available for rapid display—however, it might not be desirable to have content flickering in the Info panel as the list is navigated. A classic designer's choice between functionality and usability.

Testing Usability

You can design an interface with usability in mind, but it won't be "usable" until testing confirms that it performs well. Thus it remains to be seen whether the interface we just examined would really contribute to a better, more error-free experience for the user. As any UI design text will suggest, early, iterative testing and building is critical to arriving at an interface that truly keeps the user's needs in focus. One of the advantages of Flash is that it can be used to rapidly prototype an application or interface scheme. Compared with the typical level of effort involved in designing and developing compiled, standalone applications, developing with Flash makes it easier to obtain information quickly about what works and what doesn't in a given design.

Another matter highlighted by this example is that an application that is navigable by keypresses might need to rely on a small number of keys to perform a wide variety of tasks. Device keys that work this way are sometimes referred to as soft keys, and they are the focus of the next section, where we'll examine a strategy for using soft keys in an interface.

Using ActionScript to Manage Soft Keys

Soft keys are hardware keys that perform different functions, depending on the context within a given application or among different applications. (The term apparently refers to the notion that the key functions are not hard-wired, as they are for a power on/off button, for example.) Soft keys are commonly used on automated teller machines (ATMs): The keys that form a column on one or both sides of the display screen usually have different meanings on each successive screen, as shown in Figure 3.6. On the first screen, the topmost key might be used to select for English language; on a later screen, the same key might initiate a cash withdrawal, or specify a dollar amount, and so on.

NOTE *In this section there are three variations on the term "Soft keys." These are not interchangeable, but have specific meanings, which are:*

- *soft keys – which refers to hardware keys that have multiple functions that change according to context within the application.*

- *Softkeys – the name of a specially coded movie clip (or smart clip, in F5 parlance).*

- *softkeys – the instance name of the above Softkeys movie clip, when it is used within a Flash movie.*

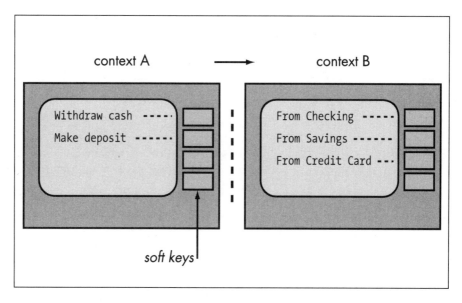

Figure 3.6: As shown, the soft keys of an automated teller machine perform context-dependent functions.

Arrow keys on portable devices can also be soft keys; because Flash can receive events from the control button, it's also possible to create Flash-based applications that can be navigated almost entirely using only keypresses. Whether a given Flash application would benefit from such an interface will depend on the tasks in the application, end-user needs, and so on—but many applications would likely benefit from a sensible blend of touch-based and key-based gestures that balances efficiency, ease of use, and reduction of user error.

Whether an interface is partly or entirely controlled by soft keys, it is useful to have a strategy for managing key behavior throughout a movie. The remainder of this chapter will focus on exactly that: an ActionScript-based approach to managing the functions associated with keypresses in different contexts of an application.

Overview

Figure 3.7 highlights the different contexts that arise in a hypothetical application. In each context, soft keys are used to complete tasks and move about the application, and the commands or functions that must be executed in ActionScript might vary from one context to the next.

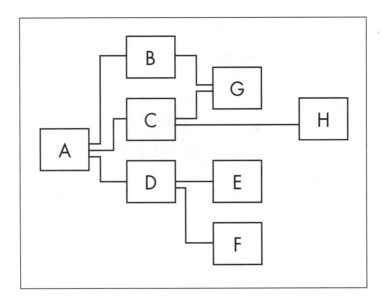

Figure 3.7: A UI scheme that shows all of the different functions performed by soft keys in a hypothetical application.

When an application that uses soft keys has numerous contexts, it can be a challenge to design an interface that is not only easily grasped by the user but is easy for you to comprehend and maintain as well. The basic problem arises from our need to declare event handlers for keypresses that occur in every context of the movie. In Flash terms, using movie clips to handle key events means that each and every context needs a movie clip prepared to associate key events with the appropriate responses. There are several general approaches to authoring a movie like this; we'll consider a few representative approaches in the sections that follow.

Multiple Clips

One approach is to code multiple movie clips, one per context; put them on labeled frames of a master clip; and then send the Playhead to the appropriate frame, as shown in Figure 3.8. One drawback of this method is that it can become cumbersome to manage several contexts, because it involves drilling into the master clip and accessing a child clip's Actions panel each time a change is made. However, for a simple interface it's a fine approach.

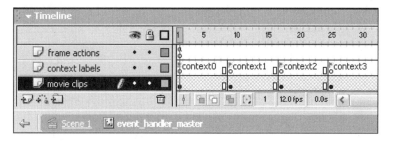

Figure 3.8: The Flash 5 authoring environment, showing the timeline of a "master event handler" movie clip. On each labeled keyframe, a movie clip is present to direct keypresses to perform actions appropriate to that context.

One Clip, Many Decisions

Another way to assign key events to context-appropriate actions is to have a single movie clip on the stage that handles events at any point in the application and is coded to use conditional statements to decide what should happen—perhaps using a global variable to hold the name of the current context. As shown in Listing 3.2, if only a few contexts exist, this approach has the advantage of centralizing the code and making it easier to make sense of what is happening—at a glance. However, if an application is sufficiently complex, you could end up with a tangle of nested if statements and, quite possibly, performance lags will result.

Listing 3.2: Example event-handling code that uses conditional statements to call the correct function for a given keypress.

```
// this movie clip handles all events
// based on the value of the global
// variable 'current_context', keypresses result
// in execution of the appropriate code

onClipEvent(keyDown) {
 var c = _root.current_context; //get the context
 var k = key.getCode(); //get the code for the key

   if (k == key.UP) {
      if(c == "Context0") {
         doSomethingUp();
      }
      else if (c == "Context1") {
         doSomethingElseUp()
      }
   }
   if (k == key.DOWN) {
      if(c == "Context0") {
         doSomethingDown();
      }
```

(continued on next page)

```
        else if (c == "Context1") {
            doSomethingElseDown()
        }
    }
}
// and so on... if right and left arrows and enter are needed

    updateAfterEvent(); // refresh the stage after each event

}
```

One Clip, Few Decisions

This approach uses a movie clip (or set of buttons) nested within a container clip to handle and manage key events. The container clip is coded so that it has its own internal methods for associating a given keypress with the appropriate function call. This container clip is, of course, a MovieClip instance—although if we write a set of custom methods for this clip to enable it to manage soft keys, then for convenience, we can also refer to the container as a Softkeys object. This approach can allow you to flexibly manage key events. In this case, the event-handling code for keypresses, when applied to a movie clip, might look like the code in Listing 3.3.

Listing 3.3: Example key event handling within a Softkeys object—a movie clip coded specifically to handle and manage key events in ActionScript.

```
// this movie clip is nested within a Softkeys parent
onClipEvent (keyDown) {

// get the code of the key that was pressed
 var k = Key.getCode();

//doSoftkey is a method of Softkeys
    if (k == Key.UP) _parent.doSoftkey(1);
    else if (k == Key.RIGHT) _parent.doSoftkey(2);
    else if (k == Key.DOWN) _parent.doSoftkey(3);
    else if (k == Key.LEFT) _parent.doSoftkey(4);
    else if (k == Key.ENTER) _parent.doSoftkey(5);

    updateAferEvent(); // refresh the stage
}
```

The Softkeys Approach

As Listing 3.3 shows, when we use the Softkeys object to handle events, each of the five different key events results in a call to a single function, doSoftkey(key_num), where key_num is an integer. The same function is called whenever a key is pressed, regardless of the context. We'll be digging into the Softkeys object to see exactly how it works internally, but right now we'll step back and consider why the Softkeys object is useful.

The power of the Softkeys object lies in its ability to pair keypresses with function calls on the fly. It does this based on instructions (in ActionScript) that it receives at runtime. This approach makes it easier to manage complex UI schemes that potentially involve many contexts. To see how easy it is to use this construct, take the example of the movie shown in Figure 3.9. Each square represents a movie clip, with child movie clips shown inside their parent clips. The names of functions defined in those movie clips are listed within boxes; the instance name of the clip is in a black box. The Softkeys object (movie clip), also on the stage, is named "Softkeys." Listing 3.4 shows how to send the Softkeys object in this movie (instantiated as the movie clip softkeys) a set of functions to be called in response to a keypress.

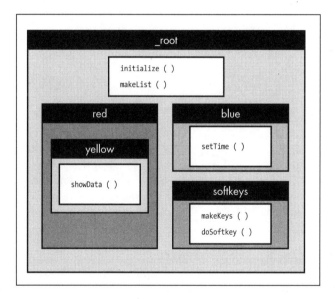

Figure 3.9: A schematically depicted Flash movie that uses a Softkeys object to manage the handling of key events.

**Listing 3.4: Sample code for using the Softkeys object—calling the makeKeys()
method to programmatically assign function calls to keypresses.**

```
// first, an array is declared

var commands = new Array();

// command strings, in the form
// "movieclip_instancename.method_name"
// are assigned to elements of the commands array
// array elements 0-4 assigned the command strings for the
// Up, Right, Down, Left, and Enter keys, respectively.
// null is assigned if no action should be associated
// with that key

commands[0] = "green.makeList"; // associated with Up key
commands[1] = null; // Right key
commands[2] = "blue.setTime"; // Down key
commands[3] = commands[4] = null; // Left and Enter keys

// the array of command strings is passed as an argument
// to the makeKeys method of Softkeys

softkeys.makeKeys(commands);

// that's it - when this code executes, the Softkeys object will
// take care of linking the commands to keypresses
```

Using the Softkeys object has two huge advantages: We can avoid using a
multitude of individually coded movie clips, and we don't need to create
baroque schemes of condition testing in the event-handling code. At the same
time, we centralize all key event management, making the code more generic,
which means that it is easier to maintain and easier to reuse.

Authoring with the Softkeys Smart Clip

Now that you've seen how to send commands to the Softkeys object (in Listing
3.4), you can begin using it right out of the box—simply find the movie
softkeys.fla (in the Chapter 3 folder on the CD), which contains the Softkeys
smart clip. Copy the clip to your own movie and give it an instance name—"softkeys" is a good choice. Right-click (or Command-click) the clip to display the
Clip Parameters panel, as shown in Figure 3.10. The parameter num_keys can be
set to the number of keys that you want to manage. For most purposes, this
number will be set to 5 if you are using arrow and Enter presses. On the other
hand, if you know that you only want to use the Up and Down arrows, you
would set num_keys to 3, because we can't skip keys in our numbering scheme
(see Listing 3.4). In this example, you'd need to assign "null" to the Right key,
but you wouldn't have to do any unnecessary typing for the Left and Enter keys.

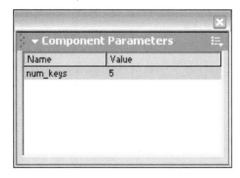

Figure 3.10: The Clip Parameters panel of the Softkeys movie clip.

Coding the Softkeys Object

You don't need to know exactly how the Softkeys object works to use it, but of course we're going to go over how it's coded. After you see how this object works, you might have some ideas of your own about how to extend its functionality and customize it for your own needs.

Custom Object or Smart Clip?

We could set about coding Softkeys as a true custom object—that is, we could use a constructor to create a new object or class, as in function Softkeys(), and then define properties and methods of the class. To use the object, we would instantiate it using my_softkeys = new Softkeys(), where my_softkeys is a variable name of our choosing.

However, it's unlikely that we'd ever need to instantiate more than one Softkeys object, so it makes more sense in this case to simply add the code, along with the buttons or movie clips needed to recognize key events, to a container movie clip, so that we end up with a reusable little package in the form of a smart clip. So again, reference to this package as a "Softkeys object" should be regarded as a convenient way of saying "a movie clip coded with custom methods for managing soft-key events and function calls."

Coding Strategy

The core strategy for coding Softkeys relies on dynamic function calls, or code that can execute a function whose name isn't known until runtime. So, to start off with, we need to figure out how to do that. ActionScript provides various ways to accomplish this, but this approach is more straightforward. The code in Listing 3.5 defines a function that has just one job to do—execute another function—using the eval() method of ActionScript.

Listing 3.5: The definition of a function that can execute another function whose name is passed as an argument.

```
// functionNameString is a string variable that
// specifies the name of the function to call.
// references to functions use dot syntax,
// and are relative to _root. SO -
// if the function is defined on the main timeline
// only the function name is used ("_root" is omitted)

function doSoftkey(functionNameString) {

// eval is used to resolve the string to a function name
// followed by the function operator '()'
// which tells the interpreter
// that what follows is a function

    eval("_root." + functionNameString)();

}
```

This approach to executing functions dynamically will work pretty well for most needs. But, as you can see, this code includes no provision for passing arguments to the function functionNameString. We can get around this easily by making sure that any user keypresses call only functions that don't need arguments, which isn't terribly limiting. Now we can get on to coding the rest of the Softkeys object.

Preparing for Soft-Key Input

To keep things relatively simple, we'll implement a few extra touches but focus on giving you a core that you can then modify and build on if desired.

My preference for handling key events is to put the handlers in buttons, because I sometimes like to have a clickable set of buttons on screen as well as keyboard input. For the iPAQ control button, I've made a set of five movie clips, one for each available key gesture. The buttons are nested in movie clips in case we want to do anything with them graphically: They can be addressed by instance name and processed by the Color object, or they can have any structure for displaying different states. Figure 3.11 shows the Library for the movie soft-keys.fla. The code placed on the "invisible" (with only its hit state defined) button within the movie clip softkey1_UP is shown in Listing 3.6. The argument passed to doSoftkey() is an integer used by the Softkeys object to assign the correct function call to the keypress. As indicated in Listing 3.4, keys were arbitrarily numbered 1 through 5 starting clockwise with the Up arrow, ending with Enter at number 5.

Figure 3.11: The Library for the movie file softkeys.fla, showing the symbols used.

Listing 3.6: The code for the button that captures an event fired by the Up arrow key, nested within the symbol "softkey1_UP".

```
on(press) {

  _parent.doSoftkey(1);

}

on(keyPress "<UP>") {

  _parent.doSoftkey(1);
}
```

The code shown in Listing 3.6 is the minimum necessary, and it can be altered based on the needs for a given interface. If some other event—for example, a sound—should always accompany a keypress, you might add that to the handling code, as well as any code necessary to change a graphic state if you are using the buttons on the interface. Once things are set for a given interface, you probably won't need to deal with these five clips again. Though not shown, the remaining four keys are coded as shown in Listing 3.6 for the Up arrow.

Inside Softkeys

The Softkeys object itself consists of the five movie clips on one layer and, on a frame in the layer above, an #include directive references a file named softkeys.as, which includes all the code for the Softkeys object. You've seen some hints as to what kind of functions Softkeys needs—a doSoftkey() method, for example, to dynamically call other functions. However, we first need a way to accept the set of command strings that will be associated with keypresses to invoke a new context in the application.

A more concrete look at what we need to do, at a minimum, to make Softkeys work is shown as pseudo-code in Listing 3.7.

Listing 3.7: A pseudo-code (plain-language) overview of the role played by the Softkeys object.

```
PSEUDO-CODE FOR SOFTKEYS OBJECT

Create a container (array) to hold command strings;
name it commands_array
   --commands_array will have a length equal to the number of
     softkeys specified.

Create a method for accepting an array of command strings
   --name the method makeKeys
   --assign each element of received array received to elements
     of commands_array.

Create a method to dynamically execute one of the command strings
in response to a keypress.
   --name the method doSoftkey
   --doSoftkey accepts as an argument an integer used to access an element
     of commands_array, using a predetermined numbering scheme
   --the function referred to by the commands_array element is executed.
```

Now that we have used pseudo-code to organize our coding strategy, we can proceed with a full listing (Listing 3.8) of the code behind the Softkeys methods. I've thrown in a few useful amenities.

Listing 3.8: Code for the Softkeys object.

```
/* ==================================================================
ActionScript Source File
FILENAME: softkeys.as
COMMENT: Softkeys methods; include as frame code in softkeys mc
        callable methods:
        makeKeys, killkeys, recallKeys
================================================================== */
```

```
// This version of Softkeys saves the last
// context's commands, making them available
// for recall. This might be extended to build up
// a history of contexts as the user progresses
// through the app, so that their steps can be retraced.

// the current context's commands
var commands_array = new Array();
//last context's commands
var saved_commands = new Array();

//initialize these array elements each to null
//length of array is established by
// 'num_keys'- the number of softkeys -
// which is set in the Clip Parameters panel
for (var i = 0; i < num_keys ; i++) {

    commands_array[i] = null;
    saved_commands[i] = null;

}


// this version of makeKeys stores the current set of
// commands in saved_commands array, then takes the
// new context's commands passed in arg_array
// and assigns them to commands_array (the active commands)

function makeKeys(arg_array) {

    for (i = 0; i < num_keys; i++) {

        saved_commands[i] = commands_array[i];
        commands_array[i] = arg_array[i];

    }
}


// doSoftkey is passed an integer (num)
// keys are 1-indexed by our choice, so
// num-1 is used to access array element


function doSoftkey(num) {

    var i = num - 1;
```

(continued on next page)

```
    if(commands_array[i] != null)  {
      eval("_root." + commands_array[i])();

}


// restore saved commands


function recallKeys() {

  for (var i = 0; i < num_keys; i++) {

    commands_array[i] = saved_commands[i];

  }
}

// set all to null - no action on keypress

function killKeys() {

  for (var i = 0; i < num_keys; i++) {

    commands_array[i] = null;
    saved_commands[i] = null;

  }
}
```

Implementing Soft Keys—Just for Fun

Let's face it: "User input" is a pretty dry topic—necessary, yes, but short on excitement. If you're interested in programming games in Flash for the PPC (covered in detail in Chapter 4), however, there's no dispensing with the knowledge of input controls needed to make the gaming experience more satisfying. So we'll take a look at those elements relevant to key input using an example that implements the Softkeys object and uses keypresses to control a game of P*NG. The movie png_ipaq.swf, with its corresponding FLA file and all related code, is included in the Chapter 3 folder on the accompanying CD-ROM.

NOTE *This Softkeys P*NG game was coded to demonstrate what is possible within the limitations of the earlier models of the iPAQ. At the time that we were in the final preparations of sending this book to press, we obtained a newer iPAQ (a 3765) and discovered that the keypresses no longer control the game paddles–although they do correctly navigate the game menus. Such are the delights of development when devices have a "flavor of the month" frequency! Please refer to the chapter-specific area of our website, www.flashthefuture.com/3, for an update on this game and the related code.*

The notion of directly manipulating files, scrollbars, and other UI controls by touching the screen really can be appealing, but for controlling games it's a different story. Although some games (tic-tac-toe) would be just fine using touch, other games are likely to feel odd if game pieces are moved about by touch. (Imagine a racing game that required you to drag the car around the track with your stylus or finger.) The presence of arrow keys on the iPAQ, despite the aforementioned drawbacks of the control button, can enhance the device's appeal as a gaming platform.

Controlling P*NG

Figure 3.12 shows the P*NG game's two primary contexts: an Options screen that allows the player to choose the difficulty and style of play, and the game screen itself, in which the player moves a paddle vertically on the screen. Keypresses control all nearly all aspects of the game, with just a few screen taps thrown in to ensure that the movie has focus.

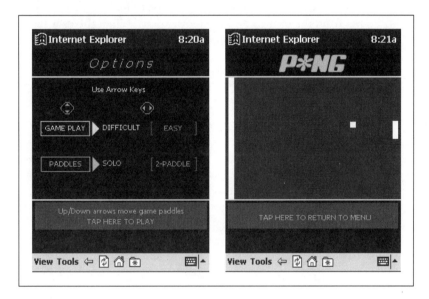

Figure 3.12: The primary contexts in P*NG.

We'll assume that all game functions have been written and everything's ready to go, so all we need to do is create a way to manage keypresses. The interface uses only three keys: Up, Down, and Right (num_keys in the Clip Parameters panel of softkeys is set to 3). This simple game has only two well-defined contexts, so we can make two arrays that hold the commands needed in each context. These arrays are defined on the main timeline and are shown in Listing 3.9.

Listing 3.9: As shown, the commands associated with keypresses in the two main contexts of the P*NG game are stored in arrays on the main timeline.

```
var menu_commands = new Array("_menu.toggleMenuItem",
                             "_menu.toggleOption",
                             "_menu.toggleMenuItem");

var game_commands = new Array();

game_commands[0] = "_pong.paddleUp"
game_commands[1] = null
game_commands[2] = "_pong.paddleDown";
```

Establishing Contexts

The game's splash screen appears prior to its Options screen, which requires a tap from the user to give the movie focus. When the user taps the screen, a function on the main timeline named showMenu() is called. This function is shown in Listing 3.10.

Listing 3.10: The showMenu() function from P*NG, which tells the Softkeys object to create the soft keys for the game's Options menu.

```
function showMenu() {

// hide the splash screen
   splash._visible = false;

// stop game
   pong.gotoAndStop("standby");

//call a function in the _menu clip
   menu.initialize();

// make sure the menu is visible
   menu._visible = true;

// create a set of soft keys to control menu item
// and option selection
   _softkeys.makeKeys(menu_commands);

}
```

On the Options screen of the game (shown in Figure 3.12), you'll notice that a good-sized button is placed below the menu and can be tapped with a finger to continue. This avoids using Enter to proceed, and once again ensures that the movie has focus just prior to the appearance of the game screen. When this button is tapped, it calls the function startGame() on the main timeline, which, like showMenu() above, calls the Softkeys method makeKeys() to establish key control for the game play context.

Controlling Game Play

When game play starts, there's only one thing to do: Move the paddles up or down. We'd like to use enterFrame events to control paddle movement, so the functions paddleUp() and paddleDown(), defined in the movie clip named _Pong, are going to act simply as switches that turn on, or off, a "paddle engine" that moves the paddles according to the movie's frame rate. When the user presses the Up key during play, pong.paddleUp() is called, which tells the movie clip paddle_engine to go to a frame labeled "up." The paddle engine's structure is shown in Figure 3.13. When the Playhead is sent to the "up" frame, a clip in that frame moves the paddles in response to enterFrame events. This code is shown in Listing 3.11.

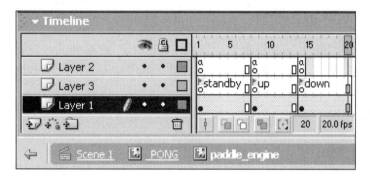

Figure 3.13: Paddle engine structure for P*NG.

Listing 3.11: The code for a P*NG "paddle engine," which is switched on and off by keypresses.

```
onClipEvent(enterFrame) {

// every time an enterFrame event fires,
// see if the Up key is being held down
// if it is, move the paddles accordingly
// if it isn't, move the playhead off this frame
// to avoid executing code unnecessarily

  if(Key.isDown(Key.UP)) {

    //paddle movement code

  }
```

(continued on next page)

```
      else _parent.gotoAndStop("standby");


}
```

Now that we've shown you how to code a simple P*NG game, and once you've examined the updates at www.flashthefuture.com/3, you'll be ready to start creating your own Soft key games and applications—and you'll be ready to deal with the ongoing challenge of changing hardware specification in this fast moving device arena.

Summary

This chapter showed how to handle key-driven user input in Flash applications for the Pocket PC. Clearly, there are plenty of good uses for the PPC's five-way button and, in using it to obtain input, you will be able to make applications perform better for users. Of course, the prospect of coding an entire interface to be navigated using keys can be challenging. But some aspect of every application will likely benefit from such a "touch." Every interface has individual needs and must be treated accordingly.

This chapter used P*NG as a working example of how to implement a key-driven UI and as a preview of the next chapter: an in-depth look at creating games for Flash on the PPC.

4

DEVELOPING GAMES TO GO

Erik Bianchi and Bill Turner

So you want to learn to make miniature games for the Pocket PC? You might want to consider the following chapter before rushing into it.

In this chapter, we delve into game development for portable devices, using Compaq's iPAQ as our target platform. To illuminate the challenges and limitations of developing portable games, we have split the chapter along two naturally occurring lines: art and graphics, and the scripting of the graphics that makes the game work.

First, we'll discuss the PPC platform itself as it pertains to game creation and Flash. Then, we'll introduce a slot machine game example, which we've included on the accompanying CD-ROM so you can follow along. By viewing the authoring FLA files used to create the slot machine, you'll better understand the reasoning behind the working game and its components.

Know Your Platform

If you assume that your game will run the same on every device and machine, it might perform poorly or, worse yet, not at all on different platforms. Your particular target platform will deterimine how you will build your game.

The following sections discuss some key platform-specific factors, which you should consider before you begin any game development for a target device. We will also discuss some of the weaknesses and strengths that play an integral role in development for your chosen device.

Target Device

NOTE *Before creating our game, we need to choose a target device. The nature and characteristics of our game will depend on the device's system resources. For example, most PPCs have no dedicated hard drive, sound chips, or graphics chips; this means that every computation (including processing, graphics, and sound) is done through the main CPU, and all of the data (including the programs and plug-ins, the application itself, and all temporary information) is stored in memory. Memory too is limited to anywhere from 16MB to a maximum (at this writing) of 64MB of RAM, and from 16MB to 32MB of ROM.*

Strengths

One great thing about developing for the PPC is that, because the units are mostly indentical, playback will be consistent on each device. You know exactly what you're developing for, and there is no need for guesswork about processor speed, available memory, sound capabilities or quality, or performance. If you have a particular device, like an iPAQ, and you are developing for an iPAQ, you know what your user will see and hear.

Weaknesses

The iPAQ's CPU is a workhorse. It's only 206MHz, yet it does everything from computations to sound to graphics. And it's one of the most powerful PPCs currently available on the market.

Developing content for high-end desktop systems is far more forgiving than developing for the PPC, however. When developing for a desktop system, you can develop with multiple tweens, alpha channels, bitmaps, ActionScript, music, and sound effects and have them all playing and executing simultaneously. When developing for the PPC you need to limit the amount of concurrent activity and consider carefully how you will use each Flash function, or whether you will use them at all.

Memory is another area of concern. Most iPAQs, for example, have 16MB of ROM, where the OS and other preinstalled applications reside. Without a CompactFlash (CF) card, the RAM (which is either 32 or 64MB) is used to store all additional applications and files that the user chooses to install or create, including Word documents, Excel spreadsheets, MP3 audio, and so on. Consequently, it is imperative that you streamline your Flash files by limiting simultaneous actions and events and also by using good memory-management techniques.

User Input (Interfacing) Is Critical

The PPC's UI is another area that requires considerable attention. On a PC, we can use the mouse or keyboard, and we can also detect different states of the mouse (Roll Over/Off, Drag Over/Off, Press, and Release). On the PPC, we have the comparatively limited resources of a stylus, the SIP keyboard, and a five-way button, as discussed in Chapter 3.

The stylus interacts with the screen much like a mouse and has nearly the same detection available to it as well. Bear in mind, however, that the majority of interactions with the screen are performed by pointing and clicking (pressing and releasing). The available rollover/off states would require users to drag their stylus across the screen, which wouldn't be very intuitive on a device like the iPAQ, whose primary interactions are point and click.

Although a developer could design to allow users to drag objects, it can be difficult to maintain consistent screen pressure, which makes it too easy to inadvertently drop something that's being dragged. Plus, dragging might prove to be too much wear and tear on the screen.

The SIP displayed on the screen is essentially a keyboard emulated by the PPC's OS. Although it can be used much like a traditional keyboard, the SIP has a major disadvantage: It consumes almost half of the screen.

The IPAQ's control button (with a speaker built in) is ideal for controlling a character's movement, for moving a paddle across the screen in a "PONG-like" game, or for scrolling text. (For more information regarding the control button and other forms of user input with an in-depth technical overview, including programming actions for the button, refer to Chapter 3.)

When developing a UI design scheme, consider the PPC's particular strengths and weaknesses to determine the type of input that will be the most intuitive for you game. For example, games like Tetris or Pac-Man should probably use the control button, whereas games that require a selection, such as a trivia game, are better off using the stylus.

Consumer Information (Knowing Your Audience)

No matter how great your game, if you overlook the nature of your demographic, you could be headed down the wrong path.

So what do we know about our audience? Well, for one, we know that PPCs aren't cheap: Fully equipped, some cost nearly as much as a decent laptop. And we know that most PPCs are not purchased primarily to play video games. The majority of PPC owners are businesspeople who use it to keep themselves organized and up-to-date on the latest news and events for their local city, or for a city they might be visiting. With access to the Internet, email, directions, contacts, appointments, and Word and Excel files, a well-outfitted PPC offers users nearly all the essentials of a laptop.

We also know that PPCs are for the most part easy to use and maintain, and they are much smaller and lighter than a laptop–they can fit easily into pockets, purses, or briefcases.

This tells us that our potential audience, at its most basic level:

- Will mostly consist of on-the-go executives who are over the age of 25 (because most businesspeople are past college age).
- Will prefer a fun, fast, simple game rather than a long, involved, role-playing game because they're probably fitting in game playing time between their work.

Of course, this is a very basic analysis, and you should thoroughly analyze your intended market before you proceed. Still, armed with this fundamental information and with this basic audience profile in mind, let's set out to design a fun, fast, simple game that doesn't require a lot of groundwork. For our example we'll design a casino game, such as a slot machine or poker. (However, don't let this stop you from targeting the PPC with the next *Mario Bros.* or *Zelda*. If the Internet has proven anything, it's that there is a niche for everything.)

Delivery

If your audience doesn't know how to find and install your game, they won't be able to play it. While you could program a custom installer (if you know your way around C++) we'll consider the following two simple options for deploying your game:

Wireless access—Create a PIE compatible website and allow users to surf your site and play your games at their leisure.

ActiveSync—Allow users to download a zipped file of your game to their desktop and have them extract its contents to a folder on the PPC via ActiveSync so they can store and then launch and play your game.

Before deciding which way will work best for you, consider the advantages and disadvantages of each. The first one requires you to create a PIE-compatible website. This isn't too bad considering that PIE is not much different than Internet Explorer, with some subtle differences. (For a design reference for PIE, see Appendix 2 for a listing of URLs.) The advantage of this approach is that it lets anyone who visits the site play the game immediately. The disadvantage is that the user will be required to download and play while being connected—and most wireless ISPs charge by the minute, by the amount of information downloaded (per kilobyte), or sometimes both, so playing online can get expensive.

The second option requires the user to download the game to a desktop machine and then transfer the files to the PPC. One obvious advantage of this approach is that users are not required to be online while playing the game; instead, they can transfer the game and play it whenever they want. Of course, the disadvantage is that users must download and transfer the files themselves, which can lead to errors and frustrations, especially if they are not too Internet savvy or good with installing programs.

The best approach is to offer both options and allow users to decide which works best for them. Barring that, it's a judgment call, and your choice will depend on the nature of your game and how you want to structure the user experience.

Why a Slot Machine?

As mentioned earlier, we're going to build a slot machine game, like the ones that eat your money in Las Vegas, except that ours will be free! (Which also means that you won't be winning any money either.)

Why a slot machine? As you'll learn in this chapter, the subject of game design can be very involved. Certainly, it's well beyond the scope of a single chapter in a book. The purpose here is to reveal some of the procedures and techniques that you must understand when creating games for the PPC. We've chosen to design a very basic game, a slot machine, that nearly everyone understands how to play.

As much as we'd love to have created a 3-D perspective shoot-'em-up, or a drive-like-mad race, or our own version of role-playing endeavors in vast 3-D worlds, we could not. But that's one of the first points of this chapter: These devices have significant limitations that require you to realize what you cannot do. From there, you can proceed to examine what *is* possible. Among other things, you can create viable puzzle and board games and snappy gambling machines that will play on the PPC quite well.

NOTE *As we develop our sample game, keep the game's Flash authoring file open as you read. You can find this file on the accompanying CD-ROM, Chapter 4, slot.fla.*

Graphics

Our first step in designing the slot machine was to decide how it would look. We wanted a nice chrome-and-wood look with flashy colors.

We could have created the basic art in Flash or FreeHand, but achieving the chrome look would have required many blends and gradients. Knowing that this type of vector art really slows things down on the PPC, we chose to use a rendered bitmap–we wanted to save the speed for executing the scripting and the spinners (the windows that display the fruits or gold bars). This does not mean you should use only squares and circles in your games. Try to strike a balance between speed *and* looks.

When designing the graphics for any game, keep your graphics as streamlined and fast moving as possible. This is especially important when designing for a machine with limitations like the PPC, and when working with Flash; the vectors used to create graphics can take time to render on the fly. Bitmap images, such as photos and airbrushed graphics, fit this bill and actually work better in Flash than elaborate vector-created graphics on the PPC.

Creating Our 3-D Machine

The first step is to get a suitable rendered bitmap out of your 3-D application and into Flash. We created our basic slot machine in a 3-D modeling and rendering program, as shown in Figure 4.1. Use any modern 3-D application, such as Swift 3D, which has the additional strength of a direct linkage to Flash. (You could use other popular applications, such as LightWave or even Maya, but those applications seem like overkill for such a small graphic.)

Figure 4.1: The base graphic of the slot machine.

We wanted our player to be able to pull the slot machine lever down to initiate the spinners, just like they would on a real slot machine. To do this, we chose to render several graphics of each lever position. But, unlike with the usual 3-D animation, we were heavily constrained by file size. To make our game perform well on the PPC, we needed the final product to be as "byte svelte" as possible.

To accomplish our goal and to keep the graphics sleek, we:

1. Rendered the base of the machine without the lever by hiding it during the first rendering pass. Then we hid the base and made three separate renderings of the lever only: one in the up position, one tilted toward you 20 degrees, and another in the fully pulled down position.

2. Saved the renderings of each element with an alpha channel for manipulation in Photoshop. (The alpha channel masks out the background, leaving only the item that is being rendered–in our case, the machine and three positions of the lever. If your 3-D program can't calculate an alpha channel during rendering–most, if not all, can–you will have to use Photoshop's Path and Selection tools to build an alpha channel for each element.)

3. We next brought these masked elements into a single Photoshop file, each precisely aligned on a separate layer. We saved this file (with layers intact) as our master file, as shown in Figure 4.2.

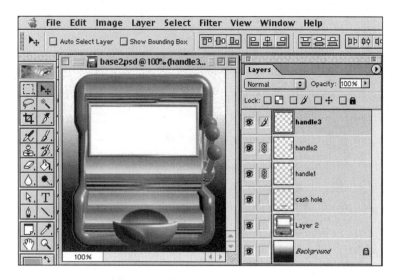

Figure 4.2: The Photoshop Layers file showing the various slot machine game parts.

NOTE *If you're using PICT files on the Mac, only the first alpha (channel #1) will be saved because PICT does not support multiple alphas in a file. Also, when using PICT be sure to save as 32-bit with no compression. PICT files with compression delete the alpha you want to maintain when importing into Flash.*

4. Working from this file, we successively deleted layers and saved our isolated elements (as PNG or PICT files) as four separate files, ready for import into Flash. (The big trick here is to be sure to have the elements aligned and to export the alpha channels.)

5. Once we saved out the separate files–in either PNG or PICT format–we reopened the lever images in Photoshop and cropped them as closely as possible to reduce file size in the finished product. (Crop out the blank space, but be sure to leave a margin of about 5 to 10 pixels around each image for anti-aliasing purposes in Flash).

6. Next, we imported these lever files and the base slot machine into Flash and aligned as needed.

The base slot machine is used as the background layer, while the levers are assembled into an animated sequence within a movie clip (see Figure 4.3) and placed accordingly. This construction provides a clip to be played (via a button or script) whenever we need to make the machine's lever appear to be pulled forward, as it would in the real world.

Figure 4.3: Compression vs. Appearance.

While file size is very important when creating bitmaps for the PPC, so too is the look. If you compress the images with too much JPEG compression (when exporting from Flash to SWF), details you want and need might be lost. But if you don't use enough compression, the file size can become too large for a pleasant download experience, which is to say nothing of how poorly the game might perform within the limitations of the PPC. While most people will wait a little longer for a cool game to download than they will for other media, they won't wait forever.

We've used a slot machine as an example, but certainly this information can apply to any game project you have in mind where you want a killer look. In almost any circumstance, bitmap images look far better than vector graphics. They are particularly useful as backgrounds or environments where you want to really shine the look of your game.

Optimizing Bitmaps

Optimizing the bitmaps of a Flash animation is an art unto itself. In Chapter 2, we described two different tricks for obtaining optimal image display on a PPC: the addition of noise and pseudo 12-bit dithering of 24-bit images.

But adding noise or dithering can cause JPEG compression to be less efficient, so we have a dilemma. The noise and dithering make the image look better, but it also makes the file size larger. One thing in our favor is the fact that the images measure only 240 by 263 pixels (which is also the maximum size you can view SWFs in PIE). Furthermore, we use only one at full screen size, because the levers are cropped (remember, that's why we cropped them closely earlier in Photoshop).

To optimize our bitmaps, we chose to apply JPEG compression to each of the slot machine's individual elements by double-clicking the element in the Library window and then choosing the level of compression, from 0 to 100% Quality. With 100% the image is left virtually untouched quality wise but produces a larger file as opposed to 0% which makes a tiny file that will most likely be gibberish and unusable. Different photos/graphics can produce different results so testing is needed to find the sweet spot between file size and image quality. A good starting point is at 50 to 60%.

After a little fiddling, we found that our best solution was to compress the sections showing the lever in motion the most (because they are seen for only split seconds) and to use less compression on the image of the idle lever (which is seen for much, much longer). That was the balance we struck between what looks good and what is most file efficient.

To determine which setting will work best for you, try different levels then use the Test button to preview the results as shown in Figure 4.4 to see what works.

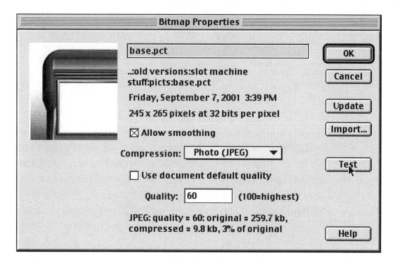

Figure 4.4: Applying different levels of JPEG compression in Flash.

Each of your projects will have different needs, so there's no universal formula to guide you as to the most optimal compression to use; you must consider each project on its own terms. That said, as a general rule, items of less significance and those that appear on screen for only a brief instance should be compressed the most, while those on which the user's eyes will dwell should be compressed much less.

Animating the Tumblers

The tumblers, or the fruit icons, that spin when the game is played are drawings. They are contained in movie clips that are animated programmatically so that they can be displayed in whatever order they are needed.

The art was developed from simple drawings that originated in Flash and then exported as bitmaps. We opened the drawings in Photoshop and blurred them using the standard Motion Blur filter, then, imported the results back into

Flash and used them to build the spinning effect that is seen in the movie clips. You can see the before and after images in Figure 4.5.

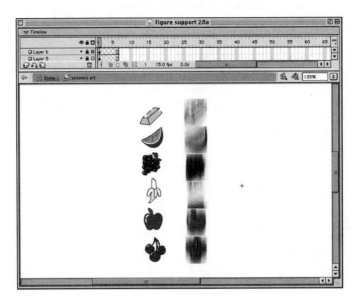

Figure 4.5: Here we have the original art drawn in Flash (on the left) and the results after processing in Photoshop (on the right).

This blurring technique allowed us to create a feeling of speed that would be very difficult, if not impossible, to do any other way. Although the tumblers are not spinning quickly (which would be very processor intensive), we create the illusion that they are. This is a very old trick in the world of animation, and is derived from a photographic film technique, where a slow shutter speed causes the moving object to leave blur lines on the film.

While your game might not use tumbling fruit (obviously), you can use this blurring technique to good effect with items such as speedy space aliens, bullets, missiles, or any number of fast-moving objects. By using the blurring technique, you can trick the player into thinking things are moving much faster than they really are—a sleight of hand that is crucial to creating the right sensation of speed in certain games. PPCs just do not play complicated Flash games at high speed, so sometimes trickery is a very welcome friend indeed.

Introduction Screen

The inclusion of an introduction screen is not only a professional touch but also a functional one. It's a good place for you to put the title of the game that is about to be played, as well as credits and copyright information, and a time for the game to load everything into RAM.

The intro screen should last about three to four seconds; anything else will just seem too long. If you think your intro screen needs more time than that, consider reducing the amount of information presented, and move the excess to another screen that users can bring up if they wish. (Although often necessary, legal disclaimers and such can be very boring, so try not to force the user to sit through too many seconds of gobbledygook.)

Even if you're making a game that tests the player's psychic abilities, you will need an intro screen to force *focus* on the game window. Because PPCs have no application windows, it's easy to forget that the Flash SWF file may not have focus, and that's a potential problem that can lead to bewildering and odd results upon first play (the hardware buttons won't work properly, for example). When we speak of focus, we mean bringing the application running the game to the front and making it active, much like on a desktop computer.

To ensure that the game has focus, savvy developers offer an intro screen with a button that the player must tap to initiate the game. The button moves the game to the first play screen and, in so doing, ensures that the player has tapped the screen and thus given focus to the Flash SWF, as shown in Figure 4.6. By creating a button on a stopped frame in your intro screen and having it set to simply play after the user taps it, you've created a device that forces the user to give Flash focus before attempting to play the game itself.

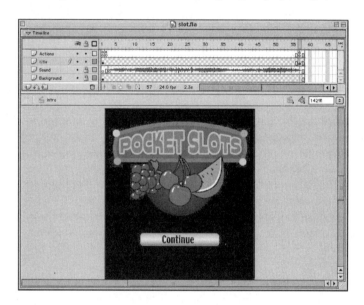

Figure 4.6: Here we see the all-important introduction screen with the Continue button that forces focus on the game window.

Where Do We Put the Rules?

Graphically integrating the rules into your game can present a problem, but one that's easily solved. The main problem we face is the PPC's small screen. Because we want the game to take up the entire screen, where do we put the rules and a way to restart the game?

In a pop-up menu, of course. By placing things like rules and seldom-used (but necessary) items in a pop-up menu, we can make the pop-up menu take over the entire screen and make the information readable, and all we need to add is a little button which won't take up much space at all. Too, by leaving the pop-up menu background slightly transparent or by allowing the game to be seen behind the rules screen, as shown in Figure 4.7, we let players know that they have not left the game.

Figure 4.7: The rules screen before (on the left) and after activation (on the right).

The other advantage in make the rules always available to the player without their having to leave a game in progress is that it allows us to maintain the user's enthusiasm for playing. If players have to stop the game to reread an important rule, they might become frustrated, and they may stop playing.

Always design games with rules that are simple and to the point. Let's face it–players don't want to read; they want to *play*–and they'll probably want to do so without reading the rules first.

Of course, once the players are stumped by some aspect of your game, they'll probably read the rules. And, if it's a complicated game, they will eventually need to read those rules in order to play at all. So give players easy access to the rules and make it easy for them to do so without stopping the game in progress.

Sounds

As a general rule, sounds can make or break a game–but they can also bloat file size significantly. This brings us to another dilemma: Although the Flash 5 player's support for MP3 compression is a useful improvement over the Flash 4 Player, developers still need to be careful about the number and quality of the sounds in a game or animation.

Here's what we suggest:

- Unless absolutely necessary, use mono instead of stereo MP3. Mono is half the file size and works just fine for bleeps, boings, and crashes in a game.

- If you must have music, it might sound better to use mono at a higher bit rate than to use stereo at a lower resolution, especially if the file size is the same in both cases. Give it a try and see.

Payoff Animation

Every game must have a payoff animation; if not, what's the sense in beating it? So when designing your game's payoff animation, you must be very clever and balance entertainment with file sizes. Things such as a cool short burst of sound effects accompanied by a variety of "Congratulations, you did it!" screens with limited animation goes a long way and is a good starting point. Always, always be very judicious and take advantage of all the tricks discussed in Chapter 2 and elsewhere in this book to optimize the payoff animation as much as possible.

Wouldn't it be nice if, once a player wins the slot game, the Radio City Rockettes sing and dance a musical extravaganza? Well, no dice. Large productions will contribute to bloated file size, and we cannot afford that. If the game consumes too much of the PPC's limited internal RAM, users probably won't keep it on their machine for any length of time. (Of course, this point is moot if they use CF memory cards, but we cannot depend on that.)

Because optimizing Flash on the PPC is all about working with tiny files, we opted for a nice little jingle of coins dumping into the reward dish (shown in Figure 4.8) to congratulate our players on their fabulous luck.

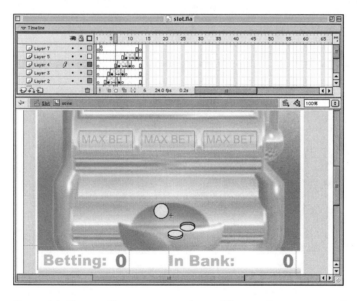

Figure 4.8: The payoff animation must be small but satisfying.

Building the Game

Although the game you see on the screen is the only thing most players will think about, Flash game developers are interested in what makes the game tick. So it's time to put aside the artist's beret for now and dive into the other side of Flash: ActionScript; the programming side.

In the flow of most Flash game development, there's the "concept and art" end and the "scripting (or programming) and implementation" end. This is seldom handled by only one person. Users who excel in creating graphics rarely excel in programming, and vice versa. The need for teamwork becomes obvious in any Flash game of complexity.

A corollary of this is that, when designing your game, you should keep the concept flexible to make it easier to deal with the shortcomings of not only Flash but the target platform as well. For example, while our first notion of a slot machine game seemed simple enough, to make it work on the PPC we had to trim out some of the high concept pieces. Such as nice to look at but unnecessary animations, for example; lights twinkling and chasing each other around the machine.

No matter how cool your graphics are, their ability to perform on the target platform will dictate your game's direction. And you will know which direction to take only after programming the graphics as they are to be played; that's when you'll discover the hurdles you'll face.

Figure 4.9 shows the initial parts of our sample project with all of our graphic elements completed and ready to go.

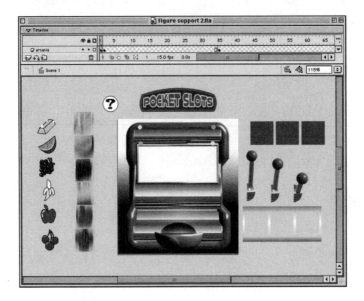

Figure 4.9: All graphics, but not a game yet.

With our graphic elements in place it's time to move into making the game work by writing the scripts that will tell the graphics how and what to perform during the game play.

Considerations

But before we go any further, let's ask ourselves some critical questions before we write a single line of code or set a delivery date:

Feasibility—Will it be possible to develop your game? Do you have the technical and design ability to do so? Is it within the project scope and budget?

Fun factor—Is your game fun? Does it match your demographic? Why will users want to play your game? And, once they've started why would they continue playing? Will they play again?

Game-play flaws—Can you play your game in your mind? Does it make sense? Are the rules confusing or do they contradict each other? Do the controls feel like second nature? Is the UI intuitive?

Demographic—Will your target audience enjoy this kind of game? Do they have the time to play it and learn its controls? Is it familiar to them?

Business factors—Do you have enough time, resources, and budget to follow this project through to completion? Do the clients clearly understand what they will be getting? Will it accomplish the goals or deliver the message as it was originally intended to do?

Platform-Specific Game Design

Once you have a general understanding of all the factors and variables we've discussed so far, you need to determine what type of game will be suitable for that combination of platform, delivery, UI, and demographic.

When designing a platform-specific game you design the game to play solely on one platform or device. Because Flash is mostly platform independent and plays pretty much the same regardless of the device, OS, or browser, Flash developers don't face the challenges that a C++ programmer would encounter when making a game for the PC that could later be ported over to a Macintosh, Playstation 2, Microsoft Xbox, or Nintendo GameCube console.

However, though we don't need to design a platform-specific game per se when designing for the PPC, the PPC's particulars (such as screen size, resolution, processor speed, and overall system performance) do place constraints on our game design, as we have discussed. We have to be realistic. We're just not going to be making the next Quake. (Making the next Quake for a high-end desktop machine isn't really all that feasible, either. That would require a team of more than 30 highly experienced programmers working for over a year, and a multimillion-dollar budget.)

Game-Play Mechanics 101

Solid game play requires balance, consideration, and preplanning. Game-play mechanics involves determining, before the game is built, how a game is going to be played, why it will be fun, and how everything will work. In its simplest form, game-play mechanics involves playing out the game in your mind. By visualizing the entire game, from controls to look and feel, you'll be able to address many issues, such as game-play design flaws or overall design flaws, before beginning production. Game-play flaws, like not providing reverse in a driving simulator or creating a boxing game in which the opponents cannot block, can kill a game.

Game-play flaws differ from design flaws. Design flaws can take players out of the game and introduce new elements that fit awkwardly with the game's design or overall theme. A feature or function that has been overlooked is also a design flaw.

Real-world examples of design flaws are a car without room for an engine, or a screen door on a submarine. A real world example of game play flaw would be a baseball bat with slippery oil on it's handle. The bat is designed well but the slippery oil was introduced that makes it difficult to use.

When making a game, try not to reinvent the wheel. Use what works and what people are accustomed to seeing. When building your first few games, consider taking a familiar concept and improving its design by adding value. If you hit a wall and can't brainstorm your way around a game-play or design flaw, it may be time to move on to another idea.

Of course, other key considerations are the fun factor, playability, and replay value. No one wants to play a game that's boring or tedious–that's why we don't see too many Tax Filing Simulation video games. Not many users in our demographic will want to play a game that requires five hours to get up to speed. And nobody wants to play the same game repeatedly unless the reward for doing so increases or the goals change; otherwise, it's just boring. Savvy developers ensure that their game can sustain expectations of challenge, entertainment, and reward.

One good way to determine what kind of game to make (also known as its genre) is to study the market to see what people are buying and what is selling. For our particular demographic and target device, we decided that any casino game would be a safe bet (no pun intended). We chose to build a slot machine because it requires little groundwork; the rules and game play are probably already familiar to the player and we figured they'd be able to jump right in and start playing. (This also works out great for the developer because there's not much need to post the rules, which leaves more time for coding.)

UI Design Limitations

Remember, our PPC has specific UI limitations. But what's great about designing a slot machine game is that user interfacing is limited to touching the screen to place a bet and spin the tumblers. The slot machine's relatively simple interface makes it easy for the user to get into the game.

Playback Performance

Another benefit of creating the simple slot machine game is that it requires no complex animations or calculations. As you will learn later in this chapter, it's fairly easy to break up all the required routines so that each line of code can execute before any animation occurs. This leaves less opportunity for a conflict between animation and code that might hinder performance.

Because more advanced games require complex collision-detection routines, sound effects, controls, and other features in addition to the animation, they are difficult (if not impossible) to develop for the PPC. By sticking with less complex games, you can easily avoid playback issues.

NOTE *For more information on playback optimization, refer to Chapters 2 and 5.*

Cross-Platform Game Design

It is sometimes beneficial to make a game that can be played on multiple plat-forms and devices. You can use several different approaches, such as direct ports or spin-off titles. Although a detailed discussion of this topic is beyond the scope of this book, here are a few pointers.

Direct Ports

When you direct port a game you copy it from one device to another. But some Flash games are too difficult to port due to time or budget constraints, limita-tions of the target platform (such as processing power), or because the Flash player is unsupported.

The best way to design a truly cross-platform game is to use Flash 4 syntax in the Flash 5 authoring environment. This way, the game will be playable on both players with no additional tweaking.

Unfortunately, limiting development to Flash 4 syntax means that we lose timesaving Flash 5 features, such as arrays and functions.

Some games can port over from the PC to the PPC with little headache or hair removal, however. Simple games, like slot machines or Tetris-style games, usually port without a hitch.

Porting from the PPC to the desktop is typically not much of an issue, though a few enhancements might be desirable to suit the hardware's larger screen, faster processor, sound capabilities, and such. Most of these enhance-ments are mostly cosmetic and will require little effort and few if any modifica-tions of code.

Spin-offs/Promotional Titles

Sometimes, for technical or aesthetic reasons, direct ports are not feasible. In such cases, a spin-off of an existing desktop game might be a good development path. For example, an adventure game like *Zelda*, which features top-down per-spective and requires many bitmaps, would be impossible to port to the PPC. So, instead of redoing the entire game for the PPC–which would require the user to download and store all levels, sounds, and animations–a suitable spin-off would be to make a minigame using the same design theme as in the primary title, but limited to a simple 2-D fishing or shooting gallery.

A spin-off can help to brand a game across multiple platforms, broaden its audience, and result in still more unique titles. To add value, you might also consider using the spin-off as a promotion by bundling it with the primary title.

Know Your Code

We've discussed the importance of understanding your target device and target audience, and we've looked at some basic game design principles and how they will affect your game's code. We'll turn now to the logic and concepts of building a working game for use on the PPC. We'll consider performance and playback issues, as well as how to code around device limitations.

Write Pseudo-Code

Pseudo-code is simply the logic and structure of how your code will work, written in plain English as a series of steps, which can be read from top to bottom. You can write pseudo-code anywhere; if you're sitting in a restaurant and inspiration strikes, you can write it on your napkin. Listing 4.1 contains a real-world example of pseudo-code and the logic applied to opening a door.

Listing 4.1: Simple pseudo-code showing how one might enter a door.

```
//Open Door
Check if door is locked
If door locked:
      Use key

Turn doorknob
Push door open
```

The line starting with // is a comment that the computer would ignore if this were real code. In this case, it's the title of the algorithm used to check whether a door is open. The second line is a conditional statement, which means that, if the door is locked the code uses a key to unlock the door; if it is unlocked, the code skips down and turns the doorknob. The final line resolves either condition and pushes the door open.

Pseudo-code allows you to focus on the logic and flow of the game, which will help you to spot logical errors before writing a single line of ActionScript. Writing pseudocode for you game can save you hours of development time by creating the rough programming logic for your game and refining its logic.

Use pseudo-code to avoid logic errors and to map your game's logic. Writing pseudo-code is a vital step in the development process, especially when you're working with deadlines and budgets. It can save you hours of reprogramming to fix a logic error that could have been prevented simply by drafting the logic first.

Later in this chapter, in the section "Code: Project Slot Machine," we will take a look at the source code for a Flash slot machine designed specifically to run on the PPC. But before we move on, let's take a quick look at some Flash 5 features and concepts that we used extensively throughout the slot machine project.

Coding Basics

When designing for the PPC, it is critical that you optimize your code and reuse the same code as much as possible. Using functions, loops, arrays, and variables will help cut back on file size and make your code more manageable because you can program in little chunks.

Functions

C and C++ programs aren't written in timelines; they are written in blocks of code to define scope and functions. Functions give us the ability to make any given character on the screen walk: Instead of having ten walk routines for ten different characters, we could have one routine used by all ten. Another benefit of functions is that local variables and arrays defined using the keyword var expire at the end of execution, meaning they are taken out of memory.

Loops

Using do and for loops allows us to target multiple objects or change multiple values using one line of code instead of having to manually rewrite each line of code for each object, which helps to cut down file size. However, some loops can become very process intensive. To increase speed, try removing the loop and replacing it by manually targeting each object. You might also try setting properties using Flash 4's slash syntax. Although this approach will increase file size, it can also speed up performance.

Variables

Variables are used to dynamically store objects or movie clip names or paths. They can also hold mathematic values and operations, and can be used for counts. Variable counts are usually represented by a single letter, such as $i, j, k,$ or sometimes n.

Arrays

Arrays can store multiple values or objects. We can use an array to make a dynamic data list for storing and tracking names, paths, or prize amounts. Arrays also enable us to use array notation. For more information on array notation, see the section "Evaluation (Using Array Notations)," later in this chapter.

Code: Project Slot Machine

Before writing any pseudo-code, determine some key goals for your code and how you can accomplish them. Given the PPCs limitations, your primary goals should be speed, file size, and memory management.

With that in mind, let's get our hands dirty and start with the logic of the slot machine. We'll keep things simple by creating a three-tumbler slot machine that matches up only three positions.

The most common elements found on such a slot machine are:

- Tumblers with various icons
- Lever (also known as the "One-Arm Bandit") for spinning tumblers
- A button to spin tumblers
- A button for betting

- A button for betting the maximum amount
- A coin drop

The pseudo-code to interact with the machine would look something like Listing 4.2.

Listing 4.2: Simple pseudo-code.

```
//Slot Machine Basic Interactions
Bet Coin(s)
Spin Tumblers
Check if Tumblers Match
If they Match:
    Winner
Else
    Loser
```

With this pseudo-code beginning, you have a solid foundation on which to build your game. Each segment will need to be further defined and refined, of course, and more algorithms and processes will need to be thought of and implemented, but you've begun drawing your map.

Expanding the Pseudo-Code

Beginning with the slot machine's basic interactions, start at the top and work your way down, writing out each line in pseudo-code as little function blocks. For example, beginning with Bet Coin(s), you can define the function blocks shown in Listing 4.3.

Listing 4.3: Defining functions blocks.

```
//Place Bet
Button 1 = Bet One
Button 2 = Bet Max
Button 3 = Spin

//Button 1 Routine
Check if Bet One is placed
If placed
    //Adds 1 to the total of Bet (Bet = Bet + 1)
        Bet += 1
Else
    Button = off

//Button 2 Routine
Check if Max Bet is Placed
```

```
If placed
     Button Off
Else
     Bet = Max

//Button 3 Routine
Check if Bet is great then 0
If Bet > 0
     Spin tumblers
Else
     Button = off
```

Keep digging deeper from here and move onto the next function and then the next. For example, you'll find that, in order to make the tumblers spin, you must write more logic, and that logic will require yet more logic.

Once you get the hang of it, you should be able to write out the entire game in about an hour. Eventually, you'll find better ways to accomplish a task and determine that the logic you have currently is no longer suitable. Ideally, you'll write the same game three or four times and then combine different sections from the various versions.

NOTE *Always complete your pseudo-code from the beginning interface programming to end sequence functionality. If you only do the first 80 percent of the pseudo-code, you'll have no way of knowing how, or even if, it will work with the last 20 percent of the game. Also, remember to take into account possible updates and functionality you might want to add and how you can plan now to make these future changes easier.*

Overview: The Source

In this section, we will focus on some key functions in the source code and explain why some things are done in particular ways. You'll find the source file for the slot machine in the Chapter 4 folder. When you open the FLA, you'll see a number of layers and two scenes. The first scene is a simple intro scene. The next scene named "Slot" is where the main scripting takes place. Go to the scene "Slot", be sure your Actions Panel is open, and select the first frame of the Scripts layer so that you can review the source while we point out some key areas of interest.

NOTE *Once you start to work on a game always, always finish it. Never assume that you could do it if you really needed to. If you've never taken a game from start to finish 100 percent, then how could you possibly know what to expect when working on other titles? How can you give accurate time estimations, create a decent project plan, or plan for the unknown?*

With the Actions panel open, you will see a lot of functions. In fact, the game's engine consists of a series of functions, and all these functions can be found on this single frame. This was done intentionally for the following reasons:

- It closely resembles the way games are structured in other programming languages.
- It will save us from having to search for code on objects, Smart Clips, movie clips, objects embedded in movie clips, movie clips embedded in movie clips frames, frames in movie clips, and so on.
- It allows us to see much more clearly how a change in one function might affect another function.
- It lets us create a shell made up of empty functions. This is a trick that fleshes out the makeup of our engine, enables us to work on functions one at a time, and allows us to test each of the functions as we go which makes tracking logical errors easier (in case anything was overlooked in the pseudo-code). To do this, add a trace() function that returns the function name and the variables that are being used inside it. If you see a function with variables that have incorrect values–such as NAN or undefined–or if the function doesn't get traced at all, you've found a good starting point to begin debugging.

The int() function

The initialize function (int()) keeps the variables consistent with the rest of the structure of our game by initializing all global variables and objects within itself. It can also be called later in the game, however, and it can be used as a soft reset as well.

NOTE *It is good programming practice to always initialize global variables and array values despite the fact that Flash will do this for you automatically. A variable is essentially a naming convention for an allocated space in memory. In other programming languages, such as C and C++, if you do not initialize a variable with a starting value, that variable will receive whatever value was left in that memory location by a previous program.*

Flags and Buttons and More, Oh My!

When you examine the code in the source file, you will notice a number of flags, such as the one used for the tumblers found on lines 5 through 8, which are shown in Listing 4.4. These flags are used to hold two values, either "On" or "Off"–or sometimes 0 or 1. Flash uses these flags like light switches. If something should be on but it's not, Flash will turn it on. Similarly, if something is on but it needs to be off, Flash will turn it off.

Listing 4.4: On/Off Flags.

```
function ini () {
    // Hide Menu
    menu._visible = 0;
    menuState = "Off";
```

Instead of On/Off, we could use the equivalent 0 or 1, but this is less efficient because Flash's interpreter will convert it to a true or false statement when it's compiled. Using On/Off is also consistent with the button states, which are tracked as being On or Off, and which correspond to frame labels found in each button (as opposed to referencing frame numbers). This naming convention provides simplicity when passing the On/Off arguments, and makes it easier to understand the coding in development, since button On or Off is more intuitive than button 0 or 1.

The three buttons SPIN, BET ONE, and BET MAX, are instances of the same genericButton movie clip in the library. As shown in Listing 4.5, the Initialize Buttons sequence under the ini() function found on line 2 sets the individual names and values that are passed by each instance.

Listing 4.5: The Initialize Buttons sequence.

```
// Initialize
ini();
// .................................................................
// Initialize Function
function ini () {
    // Hide Menu
    menu._visible = 0;
    menuState = "Off";
    // Initialize Global Variables
    cash.num = 50;
    bet.num = 0;
    betMax = 3;
    sign.cfall = 0;
    sign.cdrop = 0;
    // checkWin count
    k = 0;
    // Tumbler Count
    j = 0;
    // Flag for Tumbler
    spinning = "Off";
    // Flag for Sign
    lights = "On";
    sign.play();
    // Initialize Buttons
    var nameArray = [null, "BET MAX", "BET ONE", "SPIN"];
    // Sets up Button names and action
    for (var i = 1; i<4; i++) {
        set ("button"+i+".name", nameArray[i]);
        set ("button"+i+".a", i);
    }
    // Sets Bandits Action
    bandit.a = i;
    // Initialize Button States
    buttons("On", "On", "Off");
```

A Few Words About Arrays

As shown in Listing 4.5, nameArray is preceded by the keyword var. This means that it will be discarded from memory as soon as the ini() function has finished executing, which enables us to recycle that memory space for something else.

When you plan your coding structure, determine whether you'll be changing the values of an array frequently. If so, it's advisable to declare the array as a global array outside the function. Otherwise, every time you call the function it makes a new array object, which is processor intensive. It is far less processor intensive to change the values of an array than to repeatedly create new arrays with new values and then delete them.

Because arrays are 0 based, the first element of an array is array [0]. To specify an element that will never have any value associated with it, use the keyword null. This allows you to make the array consistent with more normal naming conventions for objects on stage. For example, because there is no button 0, the first element of the array is assigned nameArray [0] = null. Consequently, the first button is button1 rather than button0.

Loops

The second part of the initialization button routine highlighted in Listing 4.5, a loop, is useful because it eliminates the need to manually set each button and its variable. The local variable i maintains the count. When the loop starts, the value of i is set to 1 to correspond with button1. The value of i is incremented with every pass until the loop stops after its third pass.

We've used a for loop because bench tests show it to be consistently faster than any other loop on the PPC. In addition to providing speed, a for loop is also easier to read and manage than a while or do loop.

The ensuing line of code within the loop utilizes array notation, which is explained in detail in the "Evaluation (Using Array Notations)" section later in this chapter. Finally, in the last line of the loop, the a variable passes arguments when calling the buttons' action(a) function.

Button Logic

The buttons themselves are used only to call the function action(a) and then pass along their values, which were set in the a variable when they were initialized. This occurs in the following line of code:

```
bandit.a = i;
```

By having one centralized button function, we can reuse a single generic button movie clip and place the logic outside the button.

Button On/Off Controller

The final line of code in Listing 4.5, the Button Controller (buttons (state1,state2,state3)) function, uses array notation to dynamically pass its button On/Off states.

NOTE *We did not use the keyword var in front of valueArray because, as explained previously, by redeclaring arrays using var in a function, you create and delete a new array every time the function cycles, which creates extra work for the CPU.*

A Word on Smart Clips

Although we could have used Smart Clips to set up the buttons on the stage, it wouldn't have been consistent with the structure of the rest of the code and would have increased file size.

TIP *Here's a tip if you ever need to get a little performance boost out of your functions. Instead of using loops to set values of objects, try manually setting each object individually using Flash 4's slash syntax.*

Evaluation (Using Array Notations)

Array notation is a technique for referencing values in arrays. It is especially useful when coding for the PPC because it replaces the processor-intensive eval() function. To target a dynamic value stored in a variable, you would normally have to write:

```
name1 = "Dave";
firstName = eval ("name" + 1);
```

Without the eval() statement, *firstName* would return "name1". Using too many eval() functions can cause your program to come to a crawl. As shown here, array notation is a very effective workaround:

```
nameArray = [null, "Dave", "Steve", "Mark"];
firstName = nameArray [i];
```

In this example, nameArray stores three names (excluding null, of course). Here's how it works: If *i* is equal to 1, then the variable *firstName* looks at the value in nameArray[1], which is "Dave". (Remember, Flash arrays are 0 based, so the first element is in position 0, while the second is in position 1, and so on.) Because accessing an array is just like accessing a variable, we deliver the same result that we would get using eval()–but without the overhead.

Flash 5 Dynamic Targeting

Macromedia's official recommendation is to refrain from using the tellTarget command in Flash 5 because tellTarget has been deprecated and replaced by the with() function. As shown here, however, the with() function won't allow you to target objects or movie clips dynamically without using the eval() function:

```
i = 1;
with (eval ("button" + i)){
     gotoAndStop (2);
}
```

Furthermore, the with() function is a processor-intensive command. Adding eval() to the with() function and having these together in a loop can be overly processor intensive for the PPC.

The best alternative is to use the array access operator []. The [] operator allows us to manipulate arrays and also properties of an object; and, because movie clips are considered properties of objects, we can also target them using []:

```
i = 1;
this["button" + i].gotoAndStop(bValue [i]);
```

This snippet of code targets button1 of the main timeline. The keyword this specifies the location of the object on the main timeline.

The randomizer() Function

To maximize the game's response time, the random-number generation (randomizer()) for all three tumblers is handled before any animation is played. The variable *odds* represents the frames in the icon animation and is set in the ini() function odds = 12.

As with arrays, the random() function is 0 based. While random (odds) would ordinarily choose a number between 0 and 11 (12 numbers counting 0), because there is no frame 0 in our icon movie clip, we specify random (odds) + 1. Thus, if the random return is 0, 0 + 1 = 1 and 11 + 1 =12.

The spin() Function

At first check, the spin() function determines whether the value of the global variable *j* is greater than 3. If *j* is 3 or less, then it sets the spin flag (spinning) to "On", increments *j* by 1, and then targets the icon inside the first tumbler to go to the first randomly selected frame that the randomizer() chose. It then plays the spin animation.

On the Scripts layer of the main timeline, at line 199 of the frame action, a variable called *target* is created that dynamically stores the path of the tumbler that needs to be modified. Every time that the variable *target* is used, it simply references the path of the targeted object or movie clip, which is more efficient than redetermining the path to the target multiple times.

The spin() function is invoked three times. By using the variable *target*, we get the path to the object only three times instead of six, which saves processing power and increases speed.

Unfortunately, ActionScript has no way to loop for an extended period of time without causing an error. So, to make the other two tumblers have a delayed spin, we use frame-based function calls. On the third frame of the tumbler movie clip, we have the frame action _root.spin(1). Each time that spin() is invoked, the variable *j* is increased by 1. Because each tumbler is the same object, the spin() function will be called four times, and each time it will target a new tumbler to play, as specified by "tumbler" + j. However, the last call will be ignored (because j = 4) and the value will be reset to j = 0.

The checkWin() function

On the last frame of the scripts layer of the tumbler movie clip we call a checkWin(k) function. Here, k counts much like j in the spin() function. In this case, the Win condition is only checked after the last tumbler has made the function call (if ($k > 2$)). If no Win is detected (and if there is still money in the bank), the buttons will reset, allowing the user to continue play. But if a Win is detected (the tumbler icons all match), then the lights and sound animation will play, money will be added to cash.num, and the screen will be updated via the updateScreen() function.

The reward is correlated to values set in the icon movie clip, because every frame in the icon movie clip has a *val* that corresponds to an element position in the reward array, as shown here:

```
reward = [null, apples,bananas,grapes,melons,cherrys,gold];
var bonus = reward [tum1.icon.val]*bet.num;
```

Prototyping and Testing

If you haven't already played this game, now would be a good time to give it a spin. As you can see on playback, we've hit the mark and accomplished what we originally set out to do. Our code is small (3KB) and fast, and the playback is fast and fun.

Testing and prototyping were an indispensable part of the process that led to this success. We spent days researching and developing prototype engines, beginning with the button logic. The button logic was crucial to ensure that the buttons would react quickly enough on the PPC.

Another crucial prototype was the randomizer, which was originally a part of the spin() function. Early performance tests showed almost double the speed when the two functions were separated. Consequently, the game was built around this observation, which could only have been obtained through early prototyping, before construction of the game was actually begun.

Red Flags (Extremely Processor-Intensive Commands)

You will find a compressive database of red-flagged functions in the area for this chapter at www.flashthefuture.com/4. Check there for our most recent findings.

Do-It-Yourself Flash Benchmarks

To see how fast your snippets of code might run, see the Flash benchmark FLA, in the Chapter 4 folder.

Main Code

For your convenience, in Listing 4.6 we've extracted the main code of the game from the frame action of frame 1 of the Scripts layer of the main timeline. In addition to this main block of code, other bits of code are attached to objects that are referred to from the main code. To better understand the game in its entirety, open the source file slot.fla in the Chapter 4 folder.

Listing 4.6: The overall code.

```
// player commands
fscommand ("allowscale", "false");
// Initialize
ini();
// ...........................................................
// Initialize Function
function ini () {
    // Hide Menu
    menu._visible = 0;
    menuState = "Off";
    // Initialize Global Variables
    cash.num = 50;
    bet.num = 0;
    betMax = 3;
    sign.cfall = 0;
    sign.cdrop = 0;
    // checkWin count
    k = 0;
    // Tumbler Count
    j = 0;
    // Flag for Tumbler
    spinning = "Off";
    // Flag for Sign
    lights = "On";
    sign.play();
    // Initialize Buttons
    var nameArray = [null, "BET MAX", "BET ONE", "SPIN"];
    // Sets up Button names and action
    for (var i = 1; i<4; i++) {
        set ("button"+i+".name", nameArray[i]);
        set ("button"+i+".a", i);
    }
    // Sets Bandits Action
    bandit.a = i;
    // Initialize Button States
    buttons("On", "On", "Off");
    // Initialize Tumbler Values
    tumValue = [0];
    // Initialize Screen
    updateScreen();
    // Icon Positions
    odds = 12;
    // Bonus amount for getting 3 in a row
    apples = 10;
```

```
        bananas = 20;
        grapes = 30;
        melons = 40;
        cherries = 50;
        gold = 100;
        // Stores order of icons and their related bonus found in each tumbler
        reward = [null, apples, bananas, grapes, melons, cherries, gold];
}
// .................................................................
// Button Actions
function action (a) {
        // Turns Sign Off
        if (lights == "On") {
                sign.gotoAndStop(1);
                payOut.stop("win");
                lights = "Off";
        }
        // Bet Max
        if (a == 1) {
                beep.start();
                var amount = betMax-bet.num;
                if (amount>cash.num) {
                        amount = cash.num;
                }
                cash.num -= amount;
                bet.num += amount;
                updateScreen();
                checkBet();
                // Bet One
        } else if (a == 2) {
                if (bet.num<betMax) {
                        beep.start();
                        ++bet.num;
                        --cash.num;
                        updateScreen();
                        checkBet();
                }
                // Button Spin
        } else if (a == 3) {
                beep.start();
                if (bet.num>0) {
                        buttons("Off", "Off", "Off");
                        randomizer();
                }
```

(continued on next page)

```
                        // Bandits Spin
            } else if (bet.num>0 && spinning == "Off") {
                    buttons("Off", "Off", "Off");
                    bandit.play();
            }
    }
    // ....................................................................
    // Update Screen
    function updateScreen () {
            // Adds "$" to Screen
            cash.out = "$"+cash.num;
            bet.out = bet.num;
    }
    // ............................................................
    // Check if Bets need to be closed
    function checkBet () {
            if (bet.num == betMax || cash.num == 0) {
                    buttons("Off", "Off", "On");
            } else {
                    buttons("On", "On", "On");
            }
    }
    // ............................................................
    // Button Controller
    function buttons (state1, state2, state3) {
            // Button States
            bValue = [null, state1, state2, state3];
            // Changes Button current state
            for (var i = 1; i<4; i++) {
                    this["button"+i].gotoAndStop(bValue[i]);
            }
    }
    // ............................................................
    // Random Number Generator
    function randomizer () {
            for (var i = 1; i<4; i++) {
                    rnum = random(odds)+1;
                    tumValue[i] = rnum;
            }
            // Invokes Spin
            spin(1);
    }
    // ............................................................
    // Spin
    function spin (n) {
            if (j<3) {
```

```
                spinning = "On";
                j += n;
                var target = this["tum"+j];
                target.icon.gotoAndStop(tumValue[j]);
                target.play();
        } else {
                j = 0;
        }
}
// ........................................................
// CheckWin
function checkWin (n) {
        k += n;
        if (k>2) {
                if (tum1.icon.val == tum2.icon.val && tum2.icon.val == tum3.icon.val) {
                        var bonus = reward[tum1.icon.val]*bet.num;
                        lights = "On";
                        cash.num += bonus;
                        sign.cfall = 0;
                        sign.cdrop = bonus/10;
                        playWin(sign.cdrop/2);
                        sign.play();
                }
                k = 0;
                // Resets Slot
                if (cash.num>0) {
                        buttons("On", "On", "Off");
                }
                bandit.gotoAndStop(1);
                bet.num = 0;
                updateScreen();
                spinning = "Off";
        }
}
// Play Win sound effects
function playWin (loop) {
        payOut.start(0, loop);
}
```

Summary

With its small screen, slower-than-desktop processor, and no hard drive, the PPC introduces serious challenges for game development. You must tackle these issues for your game to be a success.

By now you should be familiar with the process of porting a game from the desktop to the PPC. But what we are really helping you to learn is how to port your design and development skills so that you can deploy effective content on the PPC. So far, our examples have been games. But games are merely applications that are designed for FUN. In the next few chapters we will turn our focus to developing more businesslike applications. As we progress from Chapter 5 through Chapter 7, these applications will become increasingly more advanced, and more capable of communicating with the PPC's operating system.

5

FLASH APPLICATION DEVELOPMENT

Ian Chia

Moving from smaller entertainment content to large business applications also means learning a different worldview. This chapter presents a crash course in advanced Flash application development and identifies valuable survival skills for Pocket PC Flash programming.

Developing Flash applications for devices poses many unique advantages and challenges. This chapter will cover the strengths that Flash brings as an application development platform for Pocket PCs and compare its performance with other popular development platforms. It will also examine the formal application development process and why it's a likely model for the majority of PPC Flash content. The milestones in this process cover many aspects of development, and we'll discuss what developers—from both ends of the spectrum, whether a designer coming to program, or a C++ programmer learning Flash—need to consider within the Flash application mindset.

Flash developers are generally self-taught, and each has unique skills in blending multimedia with programming. This chapter will serve as a map and guide to integrating those Flash skills within a wider perspective in order to create sophisticated Flash content for devices. It will also cover intensively the many technical issues involved in optimizing Flash applications for Pocket PCs.

Finally, we'll also discuss an extensive range of development techniques particular to Pocket PC content, with a detailed look into the issues and workarounds.

Flash Applications Overview

Creating Flash applications for devices is a unique challenge. The competency of developers can range from visual designers who need more control and interactive power for their content to software engineers who use Flash because of its multimedia abilities, ubiquity across multiple platforms, small memory footprint, and strong basis in the ECMAScript international standard (upon which current JavaScript and JScript are based: see details at www.ecma.ch/). In addition, handheld computing tends to represent a different paradigm, because a handheld device is more readily configured to act as a portable node within a large, distributed web application.

What then is the best way to develop these types of sophisticated Flash content? Dive in and code like crazy to keep afloat? This may work with small pieces of interactive content built by a one-person shop, but device applications usually involve larger teams, with specialist skills in content design and creation, application development, network and database connectivity to middleware, as well as quality assurance of the overall product. In such an environment, a Flash movie on the device is only a component in the grand scheme of things.

What Is an Application?

We've all used applications. Anything that runs on your computer on top of your operating system is considered an application, ranging from the largest programs, such as integrated office suites, to small single-task programs, such as a solitaire card game or a notepad. Applications can function by themselves (as in the case of a calculator), or they can be interconnected (as is a spreadsheet table pasted within a word processing document). In fact, even your operating system is an application that serves as an overall container and provider of hardware services for the myriad other programs on your system.

Applications can also be connected from computer to computer over a network and, increasingly, this is the standard model for our connected world. The web browser on your machine retrieves Flash movies to be displayed locally, and it may send encrypted transactional data back to the webserver for further e-commerce processing. Peer-to-peer applications exchange data directly with a massive network of interconnected machines and leverage the individual strengths of each single machine into a coherent distributed application, where the nodes (the individual machines) cooperate to form a greater whole (the distributed application). Much like a telephone is useless when only one telephone exists, a network becomes a complex ecosystem only where many levels of applications exist.

What Does This Have to Do with Flash?

Imagine a Flash-based application on a Pocket PC that communicates wirelessly to a sporting venue. The Flash movie is able to tell you where you're located within the venue's map; you're able to order refreshments, pay online, and have the food delivered personally to you. You can view the seating plan from various points in the stadium. You can pull up recent plays and access statistics and graphics accompanying the action. In fact, an application along these lines has already been developed for the Staples Center sporting venue by ICEWRX, Inc. (www.icewrx.com).

Or, imagine a 3-D molecule viewer that can retrieve an extensive range of chemical structures from a range of public online databases and store them locally in a database on your Pocket PC, which enables you to access them later for further study. The molecules are searchable from within the Flash viewer, and the 3-D models can be rotated and zoomed for analysis. Such an application can be built using Flash in conjunction with a middleware layer and integrated within a custom eMbedded Visual Basic or eMbedded Visual C++ application accessing a Pocket Access database. Some of these techniques will be discussed in this and the next two chapters.

Or, imagine a college music classroom where students are learning music theory on their individual handheld devices. The class has a tutor available to offer personal assistance, but students progress at their own pace through the interactive material, guided by the music notation, audio playback in their head-phones, and text coursework on their handhelds' LCD displays. At the end of the class, students walk up to the classroom's desktop computer and beam results and progress via infrared, to be stored and later retrieved by the lecturer, evaluated, and then returned to students. Total cost of ownership and minimum OS requirements are lower for the college's music lab, and more machines are available to students because of the machines' smaller size. Again, this handheld application is a natural fit for Flash because of its multimedia abilities and capable scripting language.

Characteristics of the Flash Platform on Handheld Devices

Flash has been used to build applications since its early days. Typical applications that use this platform include the following:

- Glorified PowerPoint presentations
- Online product demos
- Marketing media (movie sites/viral e-cards/simple promotional games)
- Self-contained calculator/converters without backend transactional services
- Training applications (CD-ROMs, courseware, technical support guides)

An even more recent trend is the use of Flash as a front end to intranets and web applications. Significant usability advantages can be leveraged from using Flash to custom design every aspect of the user interface, to lower band-width usage, and to graph business data dynamically.

When Should I Use Flash on a Pocket PC?

On the Pocket PC, Flash runs as an ActiveX control within Pocket Internet Explorer (PIE) or within an HTML window embedded into a custom eMbedded Visual C++ or eMbedded Visual Basic application.

If your application requires rich media with a shorter development cycle (versus C++, Visual Basic, or Java), then Flash is a natural fit. If you need to deploy an application across multiple platforms—including desktop machines running Windows, Macintosh, and Unix—and Pocket PCs, then Flash offers significant advantages because of its principle of identical playback across all platforms. Although Java may appear to deliver some of these goals, using Java to develop a Flash-like application often results in a heftier file size than the optimized SWF file of a comparable Flash application. Furthermore, additional Java classes would likely be necessary to match the strong media abilities of Flash, which would result in the additional disadvantage of large downloads for users. Compared with Flash, Java's graphic ability is slow when displaying full screen graphics. Because Java-based graphics are bitmap-based, they're not easily scalable compared with Flash's strengths in vector animation.

In addition to these esoteric geeky considerations, Flash offers real bottom-line advantages that any CFO would love. See the sidebar on this page for return-on-investment advantages that Flash development provides.

Business Advantages of Developing Applications in Flash

If your application is an appropriate fit for Flash technology, then you'll have some distinct return-on-investment (ROI) advantages compared with other technologies. Flash applications offer benefits in both short- and long-term development costs.

Short-term cost savings during development include the following advantages:

- Debugging code, such as client-side validation, is simple compared with supporting multiple platforms for web browser–based applications, because Flash's virtual machine executes applications identically across multiple platforms.

- Flash offers stronger control over visual layouts compared with HTML style sheets or Java. The user interfaces (UIs) for your applications will be developed faster and with more consistency.

- Building a quality UI in Java, eVC, or eVB is time intensive. "Reskinning" an interface is even more difficult in Java, but easily accomplished in Flash. Because Flash is also a strong visual design environment, graphic designers can develop the UI without holding up the code development process of ActionScript programmers.

- The Flash visual engine features optimized anti-aliased vector graphics, bitmap graphics, and a highly capable font management system. The availability of highly responsive, quality user interfaces empowers corporate end users to get on with their jobs without the business application getting in the way.

- Quality ActionScript programmers are generally less expensive than Java programmers.

Longer term, once the application is developed, maintenance and deployment of a Flash application also brings cost savings. Benefits reported by companies include:

- Significantly higher performance and lower costs. Specific statistical ROI information is available from Macromedia at www.macromedia.com/software/flash/special/inspiration/.

- Unlike HTML, Flash applications do not require page refreshes when data is retrieved from corporate databases. Therefore, server load and bandwidth is significantly decreased. End users receive faster response times, improved user experience, and better usability.

- Flash content is streamed from the server, offering an immediate experience without having to wait for the entire application to download.

- Maintenance costs are decreased. Flash applications can be easily designed to be modular in nature, enabling easier upgrades than other technologies, such as Java or DHTML, can offer.

- Developing quality user interfaces can significantly reduce customer service calls.

- The standard hardware and operating system requirements are decreased.

- Flash can deliver business data with dynamic, live graphing, enabling useful views of business activity. Applications like this are very hard to do with gif/jpeg assets using other technologies.

- Customers find it easy to install an application. The application can be browser-based or run locally as an executable. Flash applications don't require a huge download (as does the Java Virtual Machine, which Microsoft no longer supports or includes on their operating systems).

Flash Limitations: When to Go Elsewhere

Flash is not the be-all and end-all. If your application requires high-speed performance and low-level access to the operating system, then C++ is more appropriate for the task. You may need to display complex HTML along with your UI, in which case C++ or Visual Basic is far more appropriate. Or you may need to access standard network protocols, such as ftp or telnet. These services are beyond the scope of Flash's multimedia-focused featureset.

Flash on a Pocket PC device exhibits some distinct differences from the desktop players. Let's take the HP iPAQ models as an example.

- Both the StrongARM SA-1110 and the newer XScale ARM PXA250 processors run ActionScript roughly 10 (or more) times slower than on a low-end Pentium III processor.

- The iPAQ 3600/3700 series has only 4,096 colors available on its LCD screen. Some photographic images will dither badly unless adjusted during development. The later models incorporate a 16-bit color LCD display.

- Unless the device is sharing the desktop's Internet connection via Pocket PC 2002 or via Wi-Fi, it's likely to be only semi-connected, or infrequently connected, to the Internet. Content may have to be transferred via ActiveSync from the desktop host or, if the device is connected via a cell phone instead of a landline, online access may be limited to the 9.6–14.4 Kbps transfer rate of cellular devices.

- Compared with the desktop, keyboard entry is laborious because users rely on writing recognition or a virtual keyboard.

- Without headphones connected, an iPAQ merges the left and right stereo audio channels to mono through its single speaker.

Being aware of the ground rules enables you to create more effective content. The "Application Development" section that begins on page 119 offers an extensive range of development techniques and insights to help you create better applications for your device.

Building Advanced Handheld Flash Applications: The Big Picture

Knowing how to build something and knowing how to build it well are two different things. Flash developers come from many backgrounds and can bring multidisciplinary skills to a PPC project. However, these strengths can also be a weakness if combined with a lack of exposure to implementation and systems integration of large business applications. This section introduces the big picture for developers from all ends of the um to promote a better understanding of what's involved in advanced application development.

Necessary Skills

What do I need to know if I'm a designer who is moving into programming? Developers of sophisticated content for handheld devices typically see Flash as only one component of a greater whole, so the first thing to consider is how to view the big picture.

NOTE *If you're a software developer, you might like to proceed to "The Flash Pocket PC Platform Versus Other Popular Languages" on page 115 for a more technical analysis of the strengths of Flash.*

Software engineering consists of steps that many self-taught Flash developers consider automatically, but that business software development teams will formally break into separate components. These include, briefly,

- Identifying requirements and problem analysis
- Design of a solution
- Gathering raw assets for content
- Coding development/debugging
- System integration
- Testing or quality assurance
- Deployment

Recognizing each development step as a distinct task helps you to identify goals and focus your effort where it's needed most. Once the task is completed satisfactorily, moving on to the next step is simplified because basic requirements have been met beforehand. You can imagine the issues that would arise in testing if the problem were inadequately analyzed: The solution could be inherently flawed and ill-met for the requirements of the job.

If you're new to Flash application development, you'll also find a thriving online community with many resources to assist you. The Flash developer community is remarkably generous. With an appropriate amount of grounding, you'll soon begin to find your own ActionScripting feet.

The Flash Pocket PC Platform Versus Other Popular Languages

From its simpler origins as an animation tool, Flash has steadily moved toward becoming a rapid application development (RAD) platform. What? This animation tool is a RAD environment? Putting our preconceptions aside for a moment, consider how long, compared with Flash, it would take to build a simple calculator in Microsoft's eMbedded Visual Tools (eVC or eVB). Add some requirements to the specification—such as the ability to animate the numbers or handle alpha transparency or reskin the calculator—and you can see how rapidly the points stack up in favor of Flash.

From a software engineering perspective, Flash could be considered a RAD platform with a robust visual integrated development environment (IDE) where one can drag and drop user interface widgets and other visual and audio assets with minimal effort. Flash is far stronger as a visual presentation system than other IDEs, such as Visual C++ or Visual Basic. Coupled with these multimedia strengths is an implementation of the ECMA-262 Script standard with modifications that tie the scripting language back into the multimedia framework and legacy of prior versions of Flash: ActionScript.

Furthermore, Flash offers good interfaces to backend web technologies, so that developers can communicate with application servers using http and https calls, and pass data using GET and POST. Data can also be exchanged using standard URL-encoded variables or XML. Socket connections can be established at any port higher than 1023, and data can be exchanged as a raw stream or XML.

Libraries to handle multimedia functionality are already built into the playback engine, so technologies—such as MP3 playback, font embedding, network access, dynamic loading of assets, and garbage collection of memory—are handled transparently by the host Flash Player engine.

Best of all, the Flash Player is a virtual machine that renders content and scripting identically across multiple operating systems and platforms, enabling the write-once, run-anywhere dream of Java. All this makes a persuasive argument for Flash as a platform for the rapid development of media-rich thin clients—that is, small applications that are deployed on client side computers reaching back to server side resources, but that can still provide a compelling experience.

Flash as an OOP Tool

Flash also has a well-developed document object model (DOM) and enables development of applications using object oriented programming (OOP). The discussion of Flash as an OOP tool is beyond the scope of this chapter, but the following resources provide excellent material:

- *The ActionScript Definitive Guide,* Colin Moock (www.moock.org/asdg)
- *Building Object-Oriented Applications in Flash 5,* Robin Debreuil (http://www.debreuil.com/docs)
- Object-Oriented ActionScript tutorials by David Yang (http://www.quantumwave.com/)
- The incomparable Flashcoders-l list, focused solely on advanced Flash scripting (http://chattyfig.figleaf.com)
- *ActionScripting in Flash,* Phillip Kerman: Perhaps the most accessible book on ActionScript; ideal for beginners (www.phillipkerman.com/actionscripting)
- Java programmers familiar with the functionality provided by AWT and Swing can adopt J:ACK, an advanced Flash 5 object-oriented visual component infrastructure, designed to match the hierachies provided by the Java classes (chattyfig.figleaf.com/jack). Care should be taken when implementing a J:ACK based implementation as the framework can consume considerable CPU resources on a Pocket PC.

How Do I Build It Well?

Aside from the satisfaction of delivering an outstanding product, we all ultimately want to know how to save our businesses and ourselves time, money, and stress.

Each of the seven development milestones mentioned on page 114 requires strategies and tools to manage the development process and, although these tools include Flash, it isn't the only tool. Just as we're trying to view Flash as a component of a wider application process, we should also consider integrating other tools with Flash development.

Project management strategies should play an important part of the process. Whether it means writing out the goals and schedules on paper or creating a project with software that tracks the progress, planning always avoids many headaches later on. Following, in no particular order, are other strategies that will smooth the development process:

Make It Portable

During the development phase, consider separating application logic from presentation. In plain English, this means attempting to write ActionScript that is portable (to a large degree) from your visual system. Usually, this means creating generic software engines that can be reused for a number of visual interfaces. Using this approach, development and debugging of software logic and the visuals can proceed separately and be done by different team members. Many benefits are derived from this approach, which is common in traditional software development, but has only recently become popular within the Flash development community.

For a good ActionScript basis in this technology, consult the "FLEM—the FLash Event Model" (http://chattyfig.figleaf.com/flem/) and "ACK!— ActionScript Component Kit" libraries by Branden Hall (http://chattyfig. figleaf.com/ack/). Flash MX provides new Flash Components and new listener classes in Flash 6 ActionScript. Unfortunately, Pocket PCs as well as other devices are currently limited to Flash 5 functionality so, until the next generation of devices adopts the next generation of Flash technologies, we're limited to using technologies such as FLEM. However, consideration must be given to the performance overhead imposed by using these event and component models, as ActionScript performs much slower on a Pocket PC. There will be situations where responsive interfaces can be provided by direct coding compared to a generic event engine solution.

Do the Homework

Because ActionScript is such a close cousin to JavaScript, it pays to do research with a search engine before embarking on the task of writing code. The number of publicly accessible JavaScript libraries is staggering, and you may avoid the effort of reinventing the wheel by finding JavaScript routines that can be ported to ActionScript with minimal effort.

Keep Track I

Version control has not been given much heed in Flash development, but given the ambitious projects being developed using the Flash 5 featureset, the need for adequate version control becomes apparent. *Version control* is the ability to record successive builds of an application and roll back to an earlier revision if a problem arises in the code of a subsequent build. In its simplest form, version control means successive backups with distinct file names and directory structures so a logical record is kept of the project's development. More sophisticated forms enable source code to be "diffed"—that is, the differences in source are highlighted rapidly, so changes can be spotted quickly. Because version control software does not readily handle binary format files such as FLA, the use of ActionScript includes files (.as) is encouraged, because these plain text files are readily accepted by version control software, and the check-in/check-out process with accompanying developer notes becomes possible. Quirks of working with .as files are presented in the sidebar nearby. (Version control is covered in depth in Chapter 14, "Authoring for Ubiquity.")

The use of ActionScript includes as a standardized approach in software development will encourage the creation of components or modules so that several developers can work on a Flash project simultaneously. Even if you work by yourself, using AS includes will enable version control software to integrate with your Flash development workflow and provide benefits that aren't possible using only FLAs.

Some important tips:

1. Don't use a semicolon! Contrary to the original Flash 5 documentation, you must not use a semicolon after the include statement, because it will generate errors and will not work. This is a mistake in the documentation.

The correct syntax is #include "mylibrary.as"
This syntax will *not* work: #include "mylibrary.as";

2. Cross-platform developers should use backslashes for paths. When working with Macintosh and Windows machines across a network and if the AS file doesn't exist in the same folder as the FLA, use the backslash as the directory delimiter. Even though backslash is normally a Windows directory delimiter, Flash interprets this as the cross-platform character—not the Unix or web forward slash or the Macintosh colon character.

The correct syntax is #include "includesfolder\mylibrary.as"

Keep Track II

Documentation and code commenting are obvious steps, yet one that many developers avoid (including this writer). Implementing these steps will prove to be an incredible asset and will save time and time and time. (Did I mention time?) Aside from the obvious benefits it provides in a team project, personally going back over old code that is well commented will help you pick up quickly where you last left the project. Plus, it will save you time. (Did I mention that?)

Smarter Testing

Debugging and testing are important and related tasks. On the current Pocket PC platform, you have the disadvantage of not being able to integrate the Flash debugger with the client platform, because they reside on separate machines. Hence, debugging tools using custom Flash solutions become necessary. The ioLib library (http://www.shovemedia.com/ioLib) provides an excellent mechanism for comprehensive viewing of a project's variables while they're running inside the SWF. You will need to resize it for the limited display size of the Pocket PC, but it's still a valuable tool.

Simpler strategies, such as placing a debug layer in your movie with dynamic text fields set to appropriate variables, are also useful. When you've finished testing, alter the layer to a guide layer rather than delete it. That way you can return to it later if needed, but the debugging assets won't be exported as part of your SWF.

Application Development: The Little Picture
(or, The Devil's in the Details)

Because creating a Flash application is on the bleeding edge of handheld development, it's not likely that you'll find answers to all the important issues of targeting Flash for Pocket PC in the official Flash manuals, the Pocket PC Authoring Kit from Macromedia, or the official macromedia.flash.handhelds newsgroup at forums.macromedia.com—although these resources offer good starting points. What's often missing is an in-depth coverage of the minutiae that can be potential deal breakers for your project and their corresponding workarounds, or real-world coding strategies that will allow you to design your Flash application for Pocket PC and other platforms from the ground up. The rest of this chapter is a comprehensive reference guide to the numerous development issues specific to Pocket PC development. They are arranged in four major sections: general topics, scripting, networking, and hardware.

First, however, you must decide on your authoring platform.

Flash 5 or Flash MX?

With the release of the Flash MX authoring tool and the accompanying Flash 6 Player, it's important to remember that Flash 5 remains the most advanced player released so far for Pocket PCs. Flash 6 capability is not yet available for devices, given that the processors used in most handheld devices struggle with the featureset of Flash 5, let alone the more complex tasks (such as streaming video and on-the-fly vector drawing) available under Flash 6.

So should you use Flash 5 and ignore the Flash MX authoring tool? If you own Flash MX, then the enhancements made to the new authoring environment will make development much easier. Just be careful to always target your Pocket PC content for Flash 5 compatibility. If you own only the Flash 5 authoring tool, then you're still set for Pocket PC development, albeit minus some useful templates and authoring tool enhancements.

General Topics

Improving Movie Performance

At the time of this writing, the majority of Pocket PCs on the market are powered by the Intel StrongARM SA-1110, which runs at 206MHz. This processor handles all computation with the Pocket PC device. This includes running the operating system, managing the memory shared among all active and background applications, networking, rendering graphics, playing audio, and processing all computations required by the Flash Player and the SWF's ActionScript.

Because we're relying on a single processor to do all the work within the device, you'll obtain best results if the CPU is focused on executing your Flash application, and not on a range of unrelated tasks. If you're distributing a Flash application to end users, a readme file—that requests users to click Settings • System • Memory • Running Program List • Close All before launching the HTML file—will help to free up memory that a graphically intensive Flash movie may require.

A third-party utility, JS Overclock, will overclock a 206MHz StrongARM Pocket PC, but this product is officially unsupported by the device developers, so you accept the risk of damaging your Pocket PC when running this application. Hence, although the performance benefits of overclocking may be appropriate for your own Pocket PC, don't expect your target clients to adopt this strategy.

As of July 2002, a number of Pocket PC manufacturers, including HP, Toshiba, and Fujitsu, have started to release Pocket PCs based on Intel's new XScale enhanced StrongARM processors. Compared with the older StrongARM, which runs at 200 MIPS (millions of instructions per second), the 400MHz XScale processor performs at 500 MIPS using less battery consumption. Although the XScale processor has a faster clock speed on paper, Windows CE 3.0 and the standard Pocket PC 2002 applications aren't optimized for newer instruction set. Hence performance on a 400MHz XScale Pocket PC isn't necessary faster than the older 206MHz StrongARM processor. In terms of Flash movie performance, some tasks perform faster, but certain operations can actually be much slower. Care should be taken to test on XScale devices if aspects of your Flash movie depend on speed critical operations. The XScale processor has been designed with a specially optimized RISC instruction set to handle multimedia functionality with greater efficiency, with the microarchitecture allowing complex data to be processed over both the wired and wireless Internet. Macromedia has publicly announced support for XScale optimizations in a future Flash Player, so we can look forward to a generation of the Flash Player that will take advantage of these speed improvements. But until then, supporting XScale devices will require careful planning and testing, as the performance differences between XScale and StrongARM processors can lead to some unexpected development issues.

Improving Visuals

Currently, the leading range of Pocket PCs uses 12-bit or 16-bit LCD screens powered by the 206MHz StrongARM processor. Flash developers accustomed to the current generation of Pentium IIIs and 4s or Macintosh G3/G4 desktop machines will be shocked at the slow rendering speed of handheld devices. Because the Flash Player uses a software renderer, the relative sluggishness of Pocket PC CPUs determines how effectively your animations will play.

Strategies that have been discussed in Chapter 2 to boost performance include using bitmaps instead of vectors where appropriate. As a caveat, intensive use of bitmaps can increase memory consumption, which will lead to other issues covered in the "Red Box Problem" section (pages 151–152). Authoring effective visual content on Pocket PCs requires a careful juggling act to balance the need to boost animation speeds with minimal memory resources.

The anti-aliasing quality of your movie can dramatically affect rendering speeds as well. Desktop Flash content generally defaults the overall display quality to high, but on the Pocket PC, you should consider adjusting the _quality setting throughout your movie as the content changes. Where static screens occur, use _quality="high" to achieve displays similar to other ClearType-enabled Pocket PC applications. Where rapid animation occurs, consider switching to _quality="low" or _quality="medium". Being able to dynamically alter the quality setting on the fly means that you can choose to present your best side at all times.

To avoid unpleasant dithering artifacts on popular 12-bit LCD devices such as the Compaq iPAQ 3600/3700 series, remember to use the 4,096 safe color palette. This topic is covered exhaustively in Appendix 1, "The Truth About 12-Bit Color Screen Displays."

Full-Screen Flash Projector on Pocket PC

Macromedia provides only a browser-based Flash Player on Pocket PC, but a range of methods enables you to obtain full Flash Projector capabilities. (Chapter 6 will guide you through the process of creating your own full-screen Flash applications for Pocket PC.) In addition, several third-party solutions are available for differing purposes, which we'll cover on page 122.

The capabilities of a Flash Projector are:

- Full-screen display, which enables portrait or landscape presentations on a device;

- Access to any domains for ActionScript's loadMovie and XML methods, without the security restrictions encountered when running Flash in a browser; and

- Special fscommands that include launching external files or disabling the drop-down menu.

Matching the capabilities on a custom Pocket PC solution can be achieved with the following strategies.

- Zooming the browser full screen is accomplished by using eMbedded Visual Basic or C++. It is unfortunate that PIE doesn't possess a standard kiosk mode like its desktop siblings, but Chapter 6 will detail simple projects that enable full-screen capability.

- Removing the domain security restrictions is also easily accomplished and is covered in the ActionScript topics (discussed on page 127).

- Although fscommand is not implemented in the Pocket PC Flash Player, you can achieve many results with the getURL's JavaScript commands, or by setting appropriate parameters within your <OBJECT> tag in HTML. These topics are covered in the "JavaScript (JScript) Communication with ActionScript" section (page 128). With the exception of quit and trapallkeys, all the standard Flash Projector fscommand functionality is easily implemented for the Pocket PC using standard ActionScript and HTML techniques. Quit and trapallkey commands require the use of eVB or eVC, which is covered in detail in Chapter 6.

For handheld kiosk Flash applications, Phillip Torrone (http://www.flashen-abled.com) has developed a commercial solution. The application remaps the hardware system buttons to the ASCII values 1 to 5 so that Flash content is able to use these buttons within the movie (and usefully prohibits the user from switching to another application). Note that Calendar alerts will affect the full-screen mode and force the kiosk application's title bar to appear, enabling users to kill the kiosk application. As well, GigaBar users will have the application appear in the title area above the kiosk, unless they disable the GigaBar application before launching the kiosk. These are very minor caveats, though, because typical deployment of standalone kiosk devices wouldn't involve calendars or the GigaBar add-on. By design, there is no programmatic way to terminate the kiosk application, which is an advantage within a commercial deployment environment. The only way it can be killed is via a soft reset of the device. Finally, the Soft Input Panel (SIP) is not available (because the content covers the whole screen area), so custom movieclips for alphanumeric entry have to be designed in order for users to enter keystroke data.

Flash Assist from Ant Mobile (http://www.antmobile.com/) is a freeware solution for personal use that allows launching of HTML and accompanying SWF files to various screen sizes. Anthony Armenta, the developer, has a commercial Pro version for purchase, which allows custom development in eVC by using a wizard driver interface. Flash Assist Pro is covered in more detail in Chapter 6.

Finally, MultiIE (http://www.peterepeat.com) adds a full-screen mode to Pocket IE. Used in conjunction with Flash-based web pages, it allows much of the same full-screen functionality but remains within the typical Pocket IE context.

Hiding the Context Menu

The Flash Player's context menu appears whenever you tap and hold over any Flash movie. To hide the contents of the context menu without the showmenu fscommand, include the following param tag after the <OBJECT> tag within the HTML page:

```
<PARAM NAME="menu" VALUE="false">
```

Authoring for Standard Pocket PC Fonts

Microsoft has specified the Pocket PC platform to include only two standard system fonts: Tahoma (normal and bold weights) and Courier New are available on all devices. These TrueType fonts are identical to font versions of the same name that are found on contemporary desktop Windows operating systems. If the Microsoft Reader is installed, the fonts Frutiger Linotype and Berling Antiqua (in normal, bold, and italic weights) as well as the dingbat Bookdings will be present. However, if your project uses any of these latter three fonts, it's advisable to embed the font within the SWF rather than relying on the Pocket PC to have those fonts preinstalled. For example, an iPAQ upgraded to Pocket PC 2002, but without the Microsoft Reader installed, will have only the Tahoma and Courier New fonts in place.

If you discover a Pocket PC font that you want to use in Flash authoring, you will be puzzled when navigating to the \Windows\Fonts directory on your device, because it's likely to be empty. Fonts are normally stored in the \Windows directory and have the normal .ttf suffix. Using Windows Explorer via ActiveSync, you'll be able to see the TrueType files within the \Windows directory—but only if the Show hidden files and folders option is enabled within Explorer.

My HTML Page Loads, but No Flash Movie Appears

If you find that your Flash movie is viewable on a desktop browser but inexplicably disappears on your Pocket PC, then the most likely issues are:

- HTML is incorrect.
- The SWF is in the wrong directory.
- The SWF is in the root "\" directory of the Pocket PC.
- The SWFs disappear when using the developer release of the Flash 4 Player.

In these circumstances, you'll see the HTML page, but nothing will appear where your Flash movie should be.

The most common HTML mistake is the missing ID attribute within the <OBJECT> tag. The correct syntax for the ID attribute is ID="myname" where the myname string variable can be any value. Normally, it's not important, unless you're targeting the Flash movie with JavaScript commands. However, because of a quirk of Pocket Internet Explorer, you must include an ID attribute in order for an ActiveX control to be created on the page, unlike its desktop IE counterparts.

NOTE *When authoring in the Flash MX environment, publishing with the official Pocket PC 2002 template will insert the correct ID attribute into the HTML. In fact, the official Pocket PC 2002 HTML template file (written by this author) also contains a number of useful comments about compatibility on various browsers, so make sure you read the HTML at least once. However, the official Pocket PC template FLA is incorrectly sized at 240 × 250 pixels. To fix the template and add a number of other useful screen sizes, install the files in the Flash_MX_templates folder on the CD-ROM's Chapter 5 directory.*

If the SWF can't be located by the HTML, then a similarly empty web page appears. These can be diagnosed with a tap-and-hold over the blank area where the Flash content should be, which pops up Flash's drop-down menu. However, the menu will have a grayed-out "Movie not loaded" message at the top. Although this can be caused by a misplaced SWF, it's important to note that a bug in the Pocket PC Flash Player will also cause this error if the SWF is located in the root "\" directory of your device.

If you're using the developer release of Flash 4 instead of the official Flash 5 Player on your device, you should note that a Flash 4–specific bug causes SWFs to be deleted once they're opened by the Player. The standard workaround is to mark the SWFs as read-only using Windows Explorer before transferring them from the desktop machine to the Pocket PC.

Even though the Netscape <EMBED> tag isn't used by Pocket Internet Explorer to create the Flash movie on the HTML page, it's generally useful to include this tag along with all its parameters in the HTML. You might use the same HTML page as a pop-up window on your site to demonstrate the Flash application, and you'll need the <EMBED> tag for Netscape browsers or Macintosh Internet Explorer to view this content. Leaving the <EMBED> tag nested between the opening and closing <OBJECT> tags per standard Macromedia HTML conventions will not affect the performance of your handheld Flash content. If your online content is designed for both desktop and Pocket PC browsers, then it's also wise to include the CODEBASE attributes, which, although unnecessary on the Pocket PC, will force a desktop IE browser to automatically download the Flash Player if it's not already installed.

loadMovie from Storage Card Halts the Movie

If you plan to store your application on a storage card media such as CompactFlash, then you should structure your movie so that any background loading of assets won't interrupt the visual animations. This behavior is very different from the desktop, where a loadMovie action of a large SWF will result in no discernible interruption of the Flash visuals.

Perform a loadMovie from the main device's memory will cause a slight hiccup in any animations on screen while Flash and the Windows CE operating system cooperate to load in the SWF. However, loadMovie operations from a storage card are much slower, because they read data from a slower type of memory, such as CompactFlash or perhaps even a Microdisc drive. Table 5.1 shows a range of average times to execute a loadMovie action for assets taken from main memory and from a CompactFlash storage card.

Note that the hiccup halts only visual animations, and not audio playback. If you need to initiate loadMovie actions for files that may take a second or more to load, then a short audio loop with a loading message screen is a useful strategy to improve the user experience during the delay. If you would like to test how your device performs with a range of storage media, a testbed movie is provided in the folder named loadMovie_compactflash_delays on the CD-ROM's Chapter 5 directory.

Table 5.1: Time in milliseconds to load SWFs from main memory and CompactFlash

File Size	Main Memory	Storage Card
100KB SWF	69ms	254ms
470KB SWF	155ms	966ms
1MB SWF	308ms	2139ms

Scripting

Warning the User if Flash Is Not Installed

If you're offering content to be distributed widely, your application should be able to warn the user if the Flash Player is not installed. The JScript page in Listing 5.1 will test for the presence of the Flash 5 Player on the device and redirect the user to an f5notinstalled.htm or success.htm page accordingly. Because the following script relies on a timed delay if the player isn't installed, the code has been tested for content loaded from the speedier main memory as well as slower memory off CompactFlash media.

Listing 5.1: Code to check whether the Flash 5 Player for Pocket PC is installed.

```
<html>
<head>
<script language="javascript">

// create JScript object manually by referencing the
// Flash 5 Active X Control by name and major version number
var swflash = new ActiveXObject("ShockwaveFlash.ShockwaveFlash.5");

// if a Flash object was successfully created, then redirect to
// the Flash content page
if (typeof(swflash)=="object") location.href="success.htm";

</script>

<!-- if the above JScript code doesn't find a Flash 5 ActiveX
     control installed on the Pocket PC, redirect after
     two seconds to an error page to notify the user       -->
<meta http-equiv="refresh" content="2;url=f5notinstalled.htm">

</head>
</html>
```

The script will allow only a device with the Flash 5 player installed to proceed to success.htm. If the user has installed the older Flash 4 Developer Release that was publicly available, it will redirect to the f5notinstalled.htm page. Make sure your error message explicitly states that the most current version of Flash is required, because it may not be obvious to the end user. A sample project is included in the F5_PPC_detection folder on the CD-ROM's Chapter 5 directory.

Faking fscommands on the Flash Player for Pocket PC

Although Macromedia hasn't implemented the fscommand action in the Flash Player for Pocket PC, almost all the functionality can be matched using various techniques. Table 5.2 lists the six fscommands available on the desktop Flash Projector and the corresponding workarounds for the Pocket PC Flash Player.

Table 5.2: Techniques for matching fscommand functionality on Pocket PC

Command	Purpose	Pocket PC Technique
"showmenu"	Enables or disables the full set of context menu items.	Use the Menu parameter within the HTML <OBJECT> tag to turn off. the content menu. Note that the 'About Macromedia Flash Player' menu option will still appear, even when showmenu is set to false. See the Hiding the Context Menu technique (page 122) for full details.
"exec"	Executes an application from within the projector.	Although the "exec" command is not available, simply calling a getURL action with the correct path to a file will cause the application to automatically launch and load the file. For example, to load a Pocket Word file located in the folder \My Documents\Business\Expenses.pxl, use the following ActionScript command:* getURL("file:///My%20Documents/Business/Expenses.pxl");
"quit"	Terminates the Flash Projector.	This command is not easily replicated on the Pocket PC. If your Flash content is running within a "wrapper" application, a useful strategy is to use the native IHttpNegotiate::BeginningTransaction interface provided by the Pocket PC API. This will intercept a HTTP request before it is sent over the network. If the URL of the request matches a unique string, such as quitProjector instead of the usual http://, https:// or file:// URLs, it will terminate your wrapper application.
"allowscale"	On a desktop projector, prevents the Flash movie from shrinking and growing in relation to the Projector's window size.	On the Pocket PC, this command is unnecessary because windows are not resizable on this platform.
"fullscreen"	Enables a Flash Projector to zoom full screen.	Using a wrapper application that initiates a full-screen instance of Pocket IE will create a Flash movie that utilizes the full 240 × 320 pixels. Consult Chapter 6 for more details.
"trapallkeys"	Causes all keystrokes, including keyboard shortcuts, to be sent to the Flash movie.	No workaround on the Pocket PC, but largely unnecessary if using a wrapper application, because it won't respond to a CTRL-Q command to quit—as will Pocket IE or the desktop's Flash Projector.

* Note that the file path uses all forward slashes within Flash, and the way to reach a file located on the local device file system is by using the file:// protocol. Because the path starts with an opening slash as the root directory, the three forward slashes as in file:///My Documents/ or file:///Program Files/ are correct. You must correctly URL-encode all characters, such as spaces, with corresponding HTML entities. If you wish to launch nonstandard file types and applications, then additions to the operating system's registry are required and detailed at: http://www.microsoft.com/mobile/developer/technicalarticles/. Remember that your Flash application will continue to run in the background after launching the external application. Try to conserve CPU cycles by launching the external application within a keyframe that is not visually, aurally, or ActionScript intensive, or the Pocket PC's performance will be very sluggish because it will multitask both Flash and other running applications. For more information on URL encoding, visit www.macromedia.com/support/flash.

For Flash movies playing in a web browser, fscommand can also be used to send messages from the movie to the browser. See "JavaScript (JScript) Communication with ActionScript" (page 128) for more detailed information.

Removing Domain Security Restrictions on XML and loadVariable

One of the main advantages of content running within the Flash Projector instead of within a browser is that the security restrictions that prevent ActionScript from accessing multiple domains is removed. The rationale is that if you, the user, are running an installed application rather than an online web page, then the application must be from a trusted source and not designed to retrieve or send any confidential information without your permission. Therefore, loadVariable and the load, send, and connect methods for XML and XMLSocket may be used freely to access a range of data stores, both online and locally.

The popular belief that SWF content within a browser has a security restriction that locks these data access methods the originating domain is not strictly true. In fact, the security model for Flash checks whether the movie requesting access is loaded from the local file system. If the protocol to load a SWF file begins with http:// or https://, it's presumed that the file is online and the standard domain security sandbox is in place. However, if a SWF is loaded with the file:// protocol, then the security model mirrors that of a Projector, and access is freely permitted.

This is excellent news for Pocket PC Flash developers, because any local SWF content is permitted full access to any domain, even when running within Pocket IE or another wrapper application, so long the URL to launch the HTML page begins with file://. In fact, this is true even when launching HTML pages from File Explorer. (You'll note that the location bar shows the URL beginning with the file:// protocol.) Chapters 6 and 7 will cover the correct syntax, in depth, for loading HTML and SWF content within wrapper applications and advanced XML content.

NOTE *Using the file:// protocol also removes the domain security restrictions for the Flash Player running in a browser on the desktop operating systems.*

File Paths Under Pocket PC

The Windows CE operating system underlying Pocket PC devices has a unique way of addressing the local file system. Windows CE regards the internal memory of the device to be addressed off a backslash (\\) root level directory, and any additional storage is considered a Storage Card by the operating system, whether the media resides on CompactFlash, Microdrives, MultiMediaCards, or Secure Digital cards. Unlike its desktop counterparts, the PPC operating system does not use drive letters.

NOTE *A backslash (\\) translates as the root of the device, and not the root of the storage memory.*

All fully qualified file names (those containing a full directory path to the file) begin with the backslash character under JScript or eMbedded Visual Basic and eMbedded Visual C++. Under Flash ActionScript, the Windows CE backslash is translated to the normal forward slash found in URLs. It's important to remember the difference, because file paths defined with the \\ character within ActionScript are invalid.

Here are some examples of the correct ActionScript syntax to access typical directories and files:

- `loadMovie("/Program%20Files/mygame/credits.swf");`
- `loadMovie("/Storage%20Card/Flash%20game/stage2.swf");`
- `myxml.load("/Windows/flashapp_prefs.xml");`
- `loadVariables("/My%Documents/FlashExpenses/help.txt");`

Chapter 6 will discuss advanced techniques for discovering the SWF's current directory using both JScript and eVB solutions.

JavaScript (JScript) Communication with ActionScript

ActionScript can execute JavaScript (Microsoft's JScript), and JavaScript can control the timeline and retrieve ActionScript variables. This enables many sophisticated techniques (covered further in Chapter 6). However, because of the quirky nature of JavaScript/ActionScript integration, this section will survey all the issues now in order to help you to avoid them in your projects.

In order for JavaScript to be aware of the Flash movie, the ID attribute (for Internet Explorer) or Name attribute (for Netscape) must have a valid JavaScript string in the Object and Embed tags respectively. This ID or Name will be used by JavaScript to reference the SWF object (also known as an instance of the Flash ActiveX control or plug-in). Secondly, when referencing the SWF, the correct hierarchy within the HTML document's document object model (DOM) must be specified, or JavaScript won't find a valid SWF object. Pocket IE has an additional quirk in that its DOM requires the path of the instance to be specified similar to the syntax window.mySWFobject, whereas desktop IE 4+ is happy with either window.mySWFobject or with Netscape's window.document.mySWFobject syntax. The JavaScript property navigator.appName is usually used to catch these minor but vital differences, but Microsoft decided to rename the appName property on Pocket PC Microsoft

Pocket Internet Explorer instead of the usual Microsoft Internet Explorer. The HTML in Listing 5.2 demonstrates a methodical approach that covers all these quirks.

Listing 5.2: HTML/JavaScript and ActionScript integration.

```
<HTML>
<HEAD>
<TITLE>JavaScript and ActionScript communication</TITLE>
</HEAD>
<BODY BGCOLOR="#FFFFFF" LEFTMARGIN="2" TOPMARGIN="2" MARGINWIDTH="2"
MARGINHEIGHT="2">

<!-- Although the CODEBASE attribute is unnecessary for Pocket IE,
this demo will work on desktop IEs and Netscapes as well as Pocket PC.
Therefore, you should include the CODEBASE attribute to ensure correct
downloading of the Flash Player for desktop IE if required. -->
<OBJECT CLASSID="clsid:D27CDB6E-AE6D-11cf-96B8-444553540000"

CODEBASE="http://download.macromedia.com/pub/shockwave/cabs/flash/swflash.cab#versio
n=5,0,0,0"
        ID="myswf" WIDTH="200" HEIGHT="170">
        <PARAM NAME=movie VALUE="js2swf.swf">
        <PARAM NAME=quality VALUE=high>

        <!-- The SWLIVECONNECT attribute is a Netscape-only attribute and enables
        JavaScript to ActionScript access for Netscape 3.01 to 4.x. It does not
        work for Netscape 6.x or Mozilla. -->
<EMBED SRC="js2swf.swf"
        QUALITY="high"
        WIDTH="200" HEIGHT="170"
        SWLIVECONNECT="true" name="myswf"
        TYPE="application/x-shockwave-flash"

PLUGINSPAGE="http://www.macromedia.com/shockwave/download/index.cgi?P1_Prod_Version=
ShockwaveFlash">
        </EMBED>
</OBJECT>

<SCRIPT LANGUAGE="JavaScript">
// Define the correct path to reach the SWF instance within
// the HTML's pages document object model. Pocket IE has a different
// heirachy of referencing the Flash object on the HTML page, and
// *MUST* require window.mySWF type syntax. Desktop IE 4+ can
```

(continued on next page)

(continued on next page)

```
// cope with window.document.mySWF type syntax, which is what
// Netscape uses, but for the sake of correctness, we'll bundle
// the IE and PIE DOMs together. We need to define the DOM path here,
// and *not before* the OBJECT/EMBED statements, because the SWF instance
// won't have been created earlier, causing these paths to fail.
if (navigator.appName == "Microsoft Internet Explorer"
        || "Microsoft Pocket Internet Explorer") {
            mySWFobject = window.myswf;
}
if (navigator.appName == "Netscape") {
    mySWFobject = window.document.myswf;
}


// demonstrate that calling a JavaScript function from getURL
// can pass multiple parameters
function myfunction(mystring,mygetTimer){
    alert("String passed from ActionScript is: "+mystring);
    alert("The SWF has been playing for "+mygetTimer+" milliseconds.");
}

</SCRIPT>

<BR><BR><FONT FACE="Tahoma" SIZE="2"><B>Use JavaScript</B> to
<a href="javascript:alert('Using Flash\'s GetVariable JavaScript method, the
textfield is: '
+mySWFobject.GetVariable('mytextfield'))">retrieve the variable</a><br>
from the SWF's text field.<br><br>
Click the following links to alter the text field<BR>
inside Flash by <B>using JavaScript.</B><BR> 
<a href='javascript:mySWFobject.SetVariable("mytextfield","FOO")'>FOO</a> |
<a href='javascript:mySWFobject.SetVariable("mytextfield","MAN")'>MAN</a> |
<a href='javascript:mySWFobject.SetVariable("mytextfield","CHU")'>CHU</a><br>
</FONT>
</BODY>
</HTML>
```

Although the above code is quite long, most of the length comes from the comments that were inserted to explain the rationale of each subsection. Stripped of comments, JavaScript integration can be performed quite simply.

Persuading ActionScript to execute JavaScript is also very simple. Like its desktop counterparts, JavaScript can be called by using the familiar getURL("javascript:myfunction(param)") syntax.

Multiple arguments can be passed to JavaScript with getURL. Remember to enclose strings with single or double quotes, whereas numbers may be passed as is. Also, because the URL parameter for the getURL action should be a single string, to avoid confusion, it's best to construct JavaScript calls in ActionScript syntax similar to the following:

```
on (release){
    jsparams = "'" + mytextfield + "'," + getTimer();
    jsCommand = "javascript:myfunction(" + jsparams + ")";
    getURL(jsCommand);
}
```

Because of a limitation of the getURL action, you're limited to a single getURL call per frame within Flash. If you need to execute multiple JavaScript calls from ActionScript, you must either create a two-frame loop so that multiple getURL calls are spread out over the frames, or you must roll your multiple JavaScript calls into a new discrete function that can be reached with a single getURL action.

To see a demonstration file covering all of the above points, consult the javascript_actionscript_integration folder in the CD-ROM's Chapter 5 directory.

JScript Differences Between Pocket IE 2000 and 2002

Pocket Internet Explorer 2000 was a simple animal. There were no DHTML abilities, and the JScript engine was case-insensitive. But the Pocket PC 2002 release includes a number of enhancements to Pocket IE that can trip up the unwary developer.

One of the most important changes is that JScript is now case-sensitive. This can mean that content that previously worked under PPC 2000 will appear to fail inexplicably under PPC 2002. But if you enable JScript Error Alerts (as explained in the next section), the alert dialogs can aid the debugging process.

The JScript engine has been upgraded to the JavaScript 1.2 standard, although regular expression matching with the standard RegExp object is not supported. However, useful functionality, such as the switch statement, will perform as expected. Pocket IE 2002 also adds some limited DHTML support. For <DIV> and <SPAN> tags, the innerHTML and innerText can be scripted, allowing for some limited DHTML effects in web pages. Event support for ActiveX controls integrated within Pocket IE 2002 has also been added. An ActiveX control can now fire an event to trigger custom JScript code attached to the event. This opens up some interesting possibilities with applications such as hardware barcode scanners interfaced to a Pocket PC via custom ActiveX controls and custom Flash applications.

Displaying JScript Error Alerts in Pocket Internet Explorer

By default, scripting error alerts are turned off in Pocket IE. Debugging syntax errors, objects, or incorrectly performing JScript code is thus extremely difficult—because you don't know what part of your JScript is failing. You can enable JScript error alerts by using a free powertoy—The Microsoft Internet Explorer Tools for Pocket PCs—that allows one to easily toggle the JavaScript error alerts on or off as well as set the browser's cache size. (Download this gem from www.microsoft.com/mobile/pocketpc/downloads/powertoys.asp) Alternatively, you can manually switch the settings by adding the following registry changes to Windows CE. We provide these instructions so the interested developer can see what is going under the hood of the operating system. A number of other operating system tweaks to the Windows registry can be useful for the developer, and you'll find a database of registry changes for the Pocket PC at www.phm.lu/PocketPC/RegTweaks/.

CAUTION *As always, manually editing your Windows CE registry should only be done if you're familiar with the process of editing a system registry, and even then only after you've backed up critical data. If incorrect steps are taken, you take the risk of locking up your Pocket PC, or losing information. Although extreme care has been taken to ensure the accuracy and clarity of the following information, we accept no responsibility for your use of the following instructions.*

Under the registry key [HKEY_CURRENT_USER\Software\Microsoft\Internet Explorer\Main], create a New DWORD Value that says

```
Value name: ShowScriptErrors
Value data: 1
```

The registry editor will inform you that the Value type is REG_DWORD. To revert to the default state, alter the registry key's value data to 0 (zero).

The value can be in any base, such as decimal, binary, or hex. To simplify your effort to manually edit your registry—and remaining mindful of the preceding cautionary note—you can use the Pocket PC PHM RegEdit application (included in the PHM_RegEdit folder on the CD-ROM's Chapter 5 directory) to edit your Pocket PC's registry.

Once you've enabled JScript error alerts, sooner or later you will notice that, under Pocket IE 2002, the line numbers reported can be extremely confusing. That's because, unlike the desktop Internet Explorers, the JScript engine under PIE 2002 always assumes line 1 to be the line containing the opening script tag `<SCRIPT LANGUAGE="JavaScript">`, regardless of its actual line position within the HTML page. More confusingly, if you have multiple `<SCRIPT></SCRIPT>` sections, each corresponding opening `<SCRIPT>` tag is regarded as line 1 if an error is reported. Therefore, it's actually possible to have JScript report a syntax error in line 2 when in fact the error may be located at any other line number, as demonstrated in Listing 5.3. To avoid nightmares of debugging complex JScript/ActionScript projects, it's best to debug small sections of code before integrating them into larger structures.

Listing 5.3: Example of incorrect syntax errors reported by Pocket IE.

```
<HTML>
<HEAD>
<TITLE>Incorrect Line Numbers Reported by PIE</TITLE>
</HEAD>
<BODY>
<P>Hello World!</P>

<!--

Let's imagine a large section containing the
Flash movie starts here, and continues for about 20 lines
-->

<!-- This is the <SCRIPT> section of the HTML page --->
<SCRIPT LANGUAGE="JavaScript">
// the next line is line 35
alert("I am line 35"); // deliberately generate a syntax error
// PIE will report that the error is on line 3
</SCRIPT>
</BODY>
</HTML>
```

Debugging Flash ActionScript Without the Flash Debugger

Macromedia doesn't provide a debug build of the Flash Player for Pocket PC, which makes communication with the authoring tool's debugger impossible. Although this is inconvenient, you can still implement a range of strategies to produce debugging information on your device. In fact, you can produce a log file saved onto the Pocket PC during the SWF's execution that actually surpasses the usual debugging techniques available on the desktop.

The most immediate feedback you can provide about simple variables is to trigger a JScript alert within PIE. By passing a small group of variables and some basic labeling to PIE, the browser can pop up an alert dialog window above your running Flash movie—an especially useful feature, given such limited screen sizes. As shown in Figure 5.1, you can debug an internal Flash variable with a custom JavaScript dialog box.

Figure 5.1: Pocket Internet Explorer alert displaying Flash variables.

This technique is most easily implemented by inserting a simple prototyped method, as shown in Listing 5.4, into the basic Object. This method will be inherited by all other ActionScript objects, thereby giving you access to the JScript alert anywhere within your code.

Listing 5.4: Adding the JavaScript alert() Method to ActionScript objects.

```
// Place this prototype definition at the start of your movie
Object.prototype.alert = function (debug) {
getURL ("javascript:alert('" + debug + "');");
}
// now the alert() method will be accessible from anywhere within your movie
alert( "This Pocket PC is running Flash " + getVersion() );
```

However, if you have a range of variables that you want to constantly monitor, then a pop-up alert window can get annoying. In this case, it's better to create some dynamic text fields that match your variable names so that the fields will be updated in realtime as your variables change. And here's a trick: If you intentionally place all of your debug text fields on the same layer in your movie, then you need perform only one step—switching that layer to a guide layer—to hide the debug information when you have completing debugging. (A more sophisticated extension of this technique is to use Jon Williams's ioLIB 2.0 library at http://www.shovemedia.com/. However, some work is required to alter the library to fit within the Pocket PC's limited screen size.)

Saving Persistent Data Between Flash Sessions

One aspect of Flash 5 ActionScript that is missing on the PPC is Flash's ability to save and recall data external to the SWF. The concept of persistent data is important for many applications, including saving user preferences, state of progress, high scores, usernames, and passwords. Fortunately, two different strategies allow Flash to use external technologies to save and recall data at will. With one strategy, Flash can interface with JavaScript to control standard browser cookies (which are small text files usually sent by servers). The other strategy (discussed in Chapters 6 and 7) is to integrate the Flash movie within a standalone eMbedded Visual Basic or eMbedded Visual C++ application and use the capabilities of these host languages to save and load text files, Pocket Access databases, system registry keys, and more. This section will examine Flash and browser cookie integration.

Although the power provided by integration with eVB/eVC is impressive, situations occur where a developer might instead choose cookies as a data store. Cookies offer several advantages, one of which is that they are readily available to any browser without the need to install additional software. As well, custom eVB/eVC applications are only playable on the Pocket PC platform. If your application is deployed to both desktop and Pocket PC devices, then the only local storage common to all these platforms are browser-based cookies. But cookies also have some disadvantages. The data isn't write-protected, and the user could inadvertently wipe out all cookie data simply by tapping the Clear Cookies command in Pocket Internet Explorer. Another disadvantage is that some users, fearing privacy violations, may have the feature disabled. Furthermore, cookies are unsuited for storing large amounts of data, because there is a physical limit on the size and number of cookies allowed per domain. Bearing in mind the uses and caveats of integration with cookies, Listing 5.5 shows a sample JavaScript that demonstrates saving and retrieving simple text data within a cookie.

Listing 5.5: JavaScript cookie code compatible with pocket and desktop Internet Explorer and Netscape browsers.

```
<HTML>
<HEAD>Cross-browser Cookie Demonstration</HEAD>
<BODY>
<SCRIPT LANGUAGE="JavaScript">
function setcookie(name,value,expires,path,domain,secure){
    var curcookie = name + "=" + escape(value) +
        ((expires) ? "; expires=" + expires.toGMTString() : "") +
        ((path) ? "; path=" + path : "") +
        ((domain) ? "; domain=" + domain : "") +
        ((secure) ? "; secure": "")
    document.cookie = curcookie;
}

function getcookie(name) {
```

(continued on next page)

```
            var search = name + "=";
        if (document.cookie.length > 0) { // if there are any cookies
            offset = document.cookie.indexOf(search) ;
            if (offset != -1) { // if cookie exists
                offset += search.length ;
                // set index of beginning of value
                end = document.cookie.indexOf(";", offset) ;
                // set index of end of cookie value
                if (end == -1)
                    end = document.cookie.length;
                return unescape(document.cookie.substring(offset, end));
            }
        }
    }


// check if cookies are enabled at all in this browser
if (document.cookie.length == 0) {
    // if there are no cookies present, set one and check if it's been added
    // to the cookie jar
    setcookie('testcookie','1');
    if (document.cookie.length > 0){
        // cookies are enabled, so remove our test cookie by
        // setting its date in the past.
        document.cookie="testcookie=CLEAR; expires=Sun, 09-Nov-99 01:00:00 GMT";
    } else {
        // warn user that cookies are required for this application
        alert ("Sorry, but in order to save your preferences, "
                +"we'll need to use cookies within your browser. "
                +"Please enable the cookies feature within your browser.")
    }
}


var cookiecolor = getcookie('customcookie');
document.write("The cookie is :" + cookiecolor + "<BR>");
function myset(cookievalue){
    // set the expiry date of this cookie to 365 days from today
    var expiry = new Date(new Date().getTime() + 365 * 24 * 60 * 60 * 1000);
    setcookie('customcookie',cookievalue,expiry);
    // refresh this HTML page so the user can see the change reflected
    location.href = location.href;
}
</SCRIPT>
<A HREF="javascript:myset('red')">cookie is red</A><br>
<A HREF="javascript:myset('blue')">cookie is blue</A><br>
<A HREF="javascript:myset('green')">cookie is green</A><br>
</BODY>
</HTML>
```

You'll notice the setcookie() function accepts the parameters name, value, expires, path, domain, and secure. These are standard arguments that a cookie may possess. The mandatory requirements are, of course, a cookie name and the value of the cookie.

The optional expires value dictates the date on which the browser will automatically purge the cookie and is in JavaScript GMT format. We suggest specifying a date far into the future when you save the cookie: The data will persist until the date is reached, and you'll be sure that the function is available whenever you need it. In Listing 5.5, the expiration date is set one year into the future for the persistent data. Conversely, you'll notice that we also check whether cookies are enabled within the browser by writing and immediately checking for the presence of cookies, and the removal of the cookie is accomplished by setting the date into the past.

The optional path value is normally used to set directory permissions of a cookie (that is, whether it's accessible across a root directory or only at certain child levels). When the Pocket PC is used locally by JavaScript, leaving the path parameter blank allows a cookie name to be used for each directory, without the values conflicting with other identically named cookies. For example, two cookies both named highscore may be saved from an HTML page within \My Documents\Pong and another HTML file located in \Program Files\SpacePong. Although the cookies' names are identical, they will be treated as distinct cookies by the browser, because the parent HTML page's file path is different.

The domain and secure parameters have no value when used locally on the Pocket PC, because they pertain to server-delivered cookies with http:// or https:// URLs, rather than a file://-based URL.

When integrating JavaScript cookies with Flash, use getURL JavaScript: calls to execute the appropriate setcookie or getcookie functions. If you have multiple variables, the solution is either to pass a long URL-encoded string or to save an individual cookie per each ActionScript variable.

My ActionScript Slows the Movie Down Dramatically

In addition to affecting the rendering of visuals, the relative slowness of a Pocket PC processor affects ActionScript performance. For optimal performance from scripts, the following points should be considered when designing applications:

1. Deliberately segment intensive scripting over multiple frames to avoid Flash's script alerts.
2. Balance data management time versus data parsing speed.
3. Optimize XML performance.
4. Consider older Flash 4 tellTarget syntax instead of Flash 5 dot syntax.
5. Optimize Flash byte code with Flasm (a Flash byte code assembler).

Each of these points is explained in great detail in the following sections.

Segmenting Intensive Scripting

When computationally intensive ActionScript runs for an extended period, it may eventually appear that the computer has crashed. That's because all available CPU cycles are being consumed in calculation and, as a consequence, the interface becomes unresponsive to normal user input. To avoid confusing the user, Macromedia has implemented an alert dialog that lets the user decide whether to abort script execution within a Flash movie. This dialog is shown in Figure 5.2.

Figure 5.2: The Flash Player's abort ActionScript alert.

The alert will occur after 20 seconds of ActionScript if the playback head does not proceed to another frame on the timeline. Note that this is a change from standard Flash 5 behavior on the desktop, where the time limit is normally 15 seconds.

You can bypass this scary-looking alert box by designing your scripts to execute over multiple frames, instead of in a single-frame ActionScript loop. By executing over more than one frame within Flash's timeline, the ActionScript interpreter gives continuous access back to other housekeeping functions for the Flash Player and its wrapper application—in our case, PIE and, by extension, the operating system. Doing this will enable animations to continue executing, receive stylus and button events, and allow normal application control—such as closing or switching to another application under Windows CE—to occur.

As an example for segmenting a normal ActionScript function over more than one frame of the timeline, consider the simple prime number–finding function shown in Listing 5.6. This function can found in the folder named pseudo_thread in the CD-ROM's Chapter 5 directory. The code has been written to work within a single frame. Although this function takes only approximately 6 seconds on a Pentium III 500MHz PC, on the iPAQ it will take approximately 60 seconds, resulting in the dreaded script alert box.

Listing 5.6: A single-frame implementation of the prime number algorithm.

```
// Prime_SingleFrame.FLA
// Simple ActionScript port of the "Sieve of Eratosthenes"
// Invented by the Greek mathematician Eratosthenes in about 200 B.C.
// Original public JavaScript version by Tom Way at:
// http://www.eecis.udel.edu/~way/prime.html

function findLowestPrime (max) {
    var i, j;
    var sieve = new Array();
    // coerce the array to our max length, by forcing an
    // undefined into the last index.
    // even though all the other values in the array are
    // still equal to undefined, manually defining the last
    // array index will coerce the length to our max number.
    sieve[max-1] = undefined;

    var sqrtmax = Math.round(Math.sqrt(parseInt(max, 10)+1));
    var last = 2;
    // perform cross-off
    for (i=2; i<=sqrtmax; i++) {
        if (sieve[i] == undefined) {
            for (j=last*i; j<max; j += i) {
                sieve[j] = 1;
            }
            last = i;
        }
    }
    // return highest below max
    for (i=max-1; i>0; i--) {
        if (sieve[i] == undefined) {
            return i;
        }
    }
    return 1;
}

var starttime = parseInt(getTimer());

// find the highest prime number below 20,000
// and report the time taken for the calculation
var input = 20000;
var maxPrime = findLowestPrime(input);
var elapsed = (getTimer() - starttime)/1000 + " seconds";
```

(continued on next page)

```
trace("The highest prime below "+input+" is "+maxPrime);
trace("Elapsed time for calculation= "+elapsed);
stop();
```

By creating a pseudo-thread approach where the overall calculation is broken into discrete time-slices, the code enables Flash to multitask animations over the timeline, as well as to avoid locking up the CPU because it's consumed in executing only your ActionScript. This approach, as shown in Listing 5.7, avoids the script alert box altogether.

Listing 5.7: A pseudo-threaded implementation of the prime number algorithm.

```
// a thread controller movieclip has this script over the clip:
onClipEvent( enterFrame ) {
     frameEvent();
}


// Constructor for thread object

threadObject = function(max,callbackRef) {
     this.allowedTime = 1000 / (20); //SET FRAMERATE HERE!

     // sample defaults for properties on instantiation
     this.i = 2;
     this.j = 0;
     this.max = max;
     this.sqrtmax = Math.round(Math.sqrt(parseInt(this.max, 10)+1));
     this.last = 2;

     // initialize the "Sieve of Eratosthenes" array
     this.sieve = new Array();
     this.sieve[max-1] = undefined;

     // register the first callback
     threadclip.obj = this;
     threadclip.frameEvent = function() { this.obj.threadCalc(); }
     // register the final callback
     this.mycallback = callbackRef;

}
// the function that is threaded to calculate the highest prime number
threadObject.prototype.threadCalc = function() {

     //determine when to stop the parsing.
     this.stopTime = getTimer() + this.allowedTime;

     // perform cross-off
```

```
while (this.i<=this.sqrtmax) {

    if (this.sieve[this.i] == undefined) {

        //if we've run out of time in this frame, setup call for next frame
        if ( getTimer() > this.stopTime ) {
            //Create a reference to this object in the "parser" mc
            threadclip.obj = this;
            //Make parser's frameEvent call this function
            threadclip.frameEvent = function() { this.obj.threadCalc(); }

            trace("one cycle");

            //and return to wait for next frame
            return;
        }

        //while there is time in this frame, perform calculation
        this.j=this.last*this.i;

        while (this.j<this.max){
            this.sieve[this.j] = 1;
            this.j += this.i;
        }
        this.last = this.i;

    }
this.i++;
}

// return highest below max
var flag=false;
for (var prime=this.max-1; prime>0; prime--) {
    if (this.sieve[prime] == undefined) {
        flag=true;
        this.mycallback(prime);
        break;
    }
}
if (!flag) this.mycallback(1);

// after all execution is done for this particular thread,
// clean up and unbind the frame event.
delete this.i;
delete this.max;
delete this.stopTime;
```

(continued on next page)

```
        _root.threadclip.frameEvent = null;

}

function complete(prime){
    trace ("highest prime is "+ prime);
    var elapsed = (getTimer() - starttime)/1000 + " seconds";

    trace("Elapsed time = "+elapsed);
}


// start thread:
// find the highest prime below 50000
// and when complete, callback the function "complete()"
foo = new threadObject(50000,_root.complete);

stop();
```

Using this approach, we have to construct a custom ActionScript object called threadObject. When the threadObject is first instantiated (created), we dynamically remap a function called frameEvent to a custom method within our threadObject: in this case threadCalc(), which allows the processing of the overall algorithm only within strictly allotted time-slices. When the time-slice has elapsed, control is passed back to the normal Flash timeline in order for other animation and processing to occur—hence the pseudo-thread concept. We make sure that frameEvent() is called regularly by placing it within an onClipEvent(enterFrame) handler within a blank controller movieclip.

This object oriented approach allows us to store all the intermediate values of our calculations within a single object without having to maintain external variables that may be corrupted by the execution of other ActionScript.

Balance Data Management Time Versus Data Parsing Speed

Because ActionScript performance is considerably slower on a Pocket PC, normal approaches to data exchange using loadVariables or XML with middleware servers should be reconsidered, because the client-side performance hit can be significantly different. Each technique has its strengths.

For some speed-critical applications on Pocket PC, loadVariables parsing may be the only recourse—even if XML is the native data format stored by the backend. In these cases, it would be worthwhile to develop a custom server-side technique to translate your XML data into a flat format data stream (meaning a format that the client-side Flash movie can retrieve with loadVariables). Usually, that will mean a standard URL-encoded file. For a detailed comparison of the performance differences using loadVariables versus XML techniques on the Pocket PC, consult Appendix 2.

Overall, remember to consider both client-side and server-side requirements when designing distributed web applications with Pocket PC clients. Because performance speed is tied to the hardware limitations of handheld processors, sometimes it's better to use server-side resources to massage data for optimal client-side processing, which reverses the general trend (which is favorable on desktop machines) of using client-side calculations to lighten the load on server resources.

Optimizing XML Performance

The speed of XML parsing has been one of the main complaints about the Flash 5 featureset, so it comes as no surprise that it's even more of a concern on the slower processors of Pocket PCs. You can improve overall XML performance in four ways:

1. Replace the standard XML parser with the XMLnitro library.
2. Use the XMLq library to pseudo-thread XML parsing.
3. Place data in attributes instead of conventional nodes.
4. Use an SAX (simple API for XML) parsing approach instead of the conventional DOM (document object model).

Use the XMLnitro Library

XMLnitro is an ActionScript library developed by Branden Hall (http://chatty-fig.figleaf.com/~bhall/killastuff/XMLnitro.as) to override the standard XML Object's parser. By using an undocumented Flash 5 function called ASNative, this library provides increases of 70 to 120 percent over the performance of the native Flash XML parser. It can be seamlessly implemented within your applications by adding the following magic line before calling any XML ActionScript:

```
#include "XMLnitro.as"
```

Use XMLq

XMLq (developed by John Wehr) is an enhanced version of XMLnitro. It's perfect for XML projects on handheld devices because it's designed as a pseudo-threading parser, able to parse XML files over a number of frames. Hence, animation and other user interface aspects continue to function normally, while XML content is parsed transparently in a background process. John Wehr provides a demo and free .as library for XMLq at http://www.alabamasubs.com/541am/xmlq/. For projects that use the FLEM event model discussed earlier, a similar FLEM-based implementation is available at http://chattyfig.figleaf.com/flem/xmlflem.zip.

Place Data in Attributes

Although data for XML is more often contained within XML nodes, there are significant advantages to placing it within XML tag attributes instead. Consider the following simple XML document. Using XMLnitro instead of the standard XML object to parse the document reduced the time required for execution by approximately 75 percent.

```
<SHOE><MATERIAL>LEATHER</MATERIAL></SHOE>
```

However, when the node's data is condensed into an attribute, the performance increase is even more radical. In the following example, "Leather" has been changed into an attribute:

```
<SHOE MATERIAL="LEATHER"></SHOE>
```

This condensation provides even greater processing benefits, taking only 50 percent of the original time with the standard XML parser, and 38 percent of the original using the XMLnitro parser.

Generally, the more complex the XML document, the greater the incentive to use attributes, instead of nodes, as wrappers for your data. Consider the following XML documents:

```
<DRESS><MATERIAL>Cotton</MATERIAL><SEASON>Summer</SEASON>DEFAULT</DRESS>
<DRESS MATERIAL="Cotton" SEASON="Summer" VALUE="DEFAULT"></DRESS>
```

Here, XMLnitro takes 80 percent of the original time to parse the document. However, parsing the data as attributes instead of nodes offers us the most radical improvements. Parsing the attributes format, the standard XML Object's parser reduces the time taken to 27 percent of the original. XMLnitro requires only 23 percent of the original parse duration!

Use a SAX Approach

Finally, if all of these strategies still don't eke out the speed increases or memory usage you're after, you should consider using a SAX approach to parsing XML instead of the tree-based DOM model employed natively by Flash. SAX stands for Simple API for XML, which was originally a Java-only API. It became the first widely adopted API for XML in Java and is a de facto standard with a wide cross-language implementation today. Neeld Tanksley has written an ActionScript implementation entitled SimpleSax (http://www.xfactorstudio.com). For further information about SAX, visit the official site at http://sax.sourceforge.net/.

Normally, at parsing time, an XML text document is converted to a document object model with branches of nodes. The whole document is created in memory and, because of that, any node can be randomly accessed at a later stage. However, SAX parsing uses a streaming model, which is similar to the streaming media model that we're familiar with for online video or audio. Thus, SAX data is pulled from a source and placed into a small buffer. The data in the buffer is dealt with and replaced continually by new data coming down the stream until the contents of the entire file are exhausted. Using the SAX strategy, an XML document's nodes are streamed node by node in a continuous data stream and, rather than processing the nodes elsewhere in your code, you must handle each event as they're called back to you. This may seem very strange compared with the DOM mode, but it creates considerable speed improvements, even over XMLNitro. Additionally, memory usage is far more frugal than when loading a large XML tree into memory—considering the limited memory available on devices, this is a considerable advantage.

Flash 4 tellTarget Syntax Versus Flash 5 Dot Syntax

With the release of Flash 5, Macromedia introduced object oriented dot syntax, streamlining the addressing of objects and properties for developers. Unfortunately, the optimizations under the hood were not implemented to match the execution speed of the older Flash 4 slash syntax. Consequently, the deprecated tellTarget command results in code that runs faster than dot syntax. Although you should carefully consider whether your project might be deprecated by a future version of Flash on the Pocket PC, the immediate benefit of faster speed might outweigh the future what-ifs, especially because performance is more critical on this platform than on desktop machines. If you opt for the faster code solution, be sure to comment your code heavily and clearly in order to facilitate reworking your scripts, should the need arise to rework your deprecated slash syntax and tellTargets.

Wouter Van Brock has an extensive ActionScript Performance Test Framework comparing syntactical and performance differences between Flash 4 and Flash 5 ActionScript. You'll find these open-source FLAs at http://www.addith.com/actionscript/code_depot/as_performance.html. Because these benchmarks were designed for the desktop Flash Player, some editing of the source is required for them to cope with the Pocket PC's screen size and slower CPU in order to prevent the abort ActionScript alert dialog.

Flash Byte Code Optimizations with Flasm

Flasm is a Flash assembler/disassembler that reduces ActionScript into the byte code instruction set that Flash's virtual machine executes.

Code optimizations can also be obtained by working with Flasm, but Flasm may not be worth approaching. The value of using deprecated (but faster) code is this: Coding with certain Flash 4 syntax, such as setProperty, in mind will increase the performance of your projects without forcing you to learn Flasm's pseudocode.

However, if you have code that can't be optimized satisfactorily by pseudo-threading or other standard forms of optimizations, then it may be worth the investment to learn Flasm (http://flasm.sourceforget.net).

By hand-optimizing the instructions, one can perform miraculous performance increases over already optimized ActionScript code (cases of 200 percent speed increases have been observed). After you've rewritten your ActionScript using Flash byte code, Flasm then reassembles the instructions into a SWF. Your host movie can use loadMovie to load the optimized Flasm SWF and call the optimized functions using normal ActionScript in the parent movie.

Note that this is unsupported by Macromedia, and Flasm code carries the risk of breaking in future versions of Flash (a rather unlikely event, given that this approach executes native code within the SWF format publicly published by Macromedia). Flash movies that have been optimized with Flasm exhibit the same performance increases on the Pocket PC Flash 5 Player as they do on the desktop players, and tests with the Flash 6 Player (although not exhaustive) show that they remain compatible with the newer playback engine at the time of this writing.

Networking

How to Determine Whether the Pocket PC Is Connected Online

Because of its extremely portable nature, a Pocket PC may not be connected to the Internet at any given time. If your Flash application has features that require Net connectivity, you'll need a reliable way to check whether there is a working Internet connection available.

A basic request/response type Net request (like a Flash version of ping) is to initiate a loadVariables command to a simple server-side script. If you are going to do this, initiate a timer so that you can cancel from the loadVariables request, rather than lock the user into waiting if the device is not connected. If you place the code into a controller movieclip, you'll be able to utilize the onClipEvent load and enterFrame events to make an online request, wait for a server-side response, and then check to see if the allotted response time has elapsed, without adversely affecting your movie's overall execution. Listing 5.8 demonstrates the type of script you would place on a controller movieclip instance to accomplish this. You'll also find a full example that pings www.flashthefuture.com in the test_network_connectivity folder in the CD-ROM's Chapter 5 directory.

Listing 5.8: Code to check whether the Pocket PC is connected online.

```
onClipEvent(load){
    // number of milliseconds before timing out and returning an error
    timeOutInterval = 15 * 1000; // 15 seconds
    this.endTime = getTimer() + timeOutInterval;

    // URL to load "ping" file from to detect network connectivity
    // the "ping.txt" file is just a simple URL-encoded file with the contents:
    //    ping=true;
    pingURL="http://www.flashthefuture.com/5/ping.txt";

    // Initiate "ping" by loading the file from an online location.
    //
    // We add a nocache variable based on the local time in milliseconds
    // to prevent the variable from caching -- therefore, if the device
    // is disconnected from the network at some further stage, but the
    // ping.txt file was cached, this will force it to reload, making
    // sure the test is fresh every time instead of returning bogus
```

```
        // cached results.
this.loadVariables(pingURL + "?nocache=" + new Date().valueOf());
}


onClipEvent(enterFrame){
    if (getTimer() > this.endTime){
        // we've timed out without a response online
        // move the parent movie to the error message
        _parent.gotoAndPlay("error");
    }
    timeRemaining = parseInt( (this.endTime-getTimer( ) )/1000)+1;
    _parent.status="Checking ...\nplease wait\nfor "+timeRemaining+" sec.";
}


onClipEvent(data){
    // Success! We've been able to reach an online file
    _parent.gotoAndPlay("success");
}
```

HTTP-GET and HTTP-POST Requests

The Macromedia engineers have built a mechanism to enable HTTP-POST requests independent of the browser under Windows CE, because Pocket IE supports only "GET" requests and not "POST" requests. Unlike Flash's performance on Macintosh Internet Explorer 4.5 (and earlier versions), where "POST" was not available because of browser limitations, both HTTP-GET and HTTP-POST requests are available getURL and XML actions.

Developing Network Content Using Your Cradle and Your Desktop Machine

Having a webserver installed on your desktop machine that is connected to the Pocket PC's cradle can be very handy. Rather than continually copying content over to the Pocket PC, you can browse the published movies on the desktop's directories within Pocket IE. This can reduce the tedium of using a stylus to input URLs.

ActiveSync always installs two distinct IP address for the desktop and Pocket PC client via ActiveSync: The desktop is always 192.168.55.100, and the cradled device is 192.168.55.101. To confirm this, start up the desktop's webserver and make sure that ActiveSync is enabled. Then point Pocket IE to the URL http://192.168.55.100, and you should see the home directory of your webserver. If you have directory listing turned on, you should be able to browse the directories at will. You can then add your Flash development directory as an alias or as root to your webserver and bookmark the directories on the Pocket PC.

If you wish to use host names instead of a distinct IP address, then you'll want to use Pocket Hosts, which is a freeware application by Marc Zimmermann. It's available at http://www.zimac.de/cestuff.htm. This is especially handy because Windows CE does not support a host file, as do its desktop counterparts. Instead, host names have to be manually added to the system registry. Pocket Hosts makes this process easy.

Autodetecting the Pocket PC Platform from a Webserver

Flash 5 ActionScript's getVersion() method will return a string containing the platform and version number of the Flash Player build. The syntax for the string is

```
Platform MajorVersion,MinorVersion,BuildNumber,Patch
e.g. WINCE 5,0,88,0
```

In the string shown above, the platform and version number are delimited by a space, and the version number is delimited into sections by commas. For Pocket PCs, the rightmost digits of the version string (Patch) will be incremented for different ports of the Flash Player by the device manufacturers. The Platform component of the string for Pocket PC devices returns "WINCE," which identifies Windows CE to be the underlying platform. Table 5.3 contains the version numbers of the Flash 5 Pocket PC Players so far officially released.

Table 5.3: Flash 5 Version strings for the Pocket PC.

Device	Version string
Casio Pocket PC 2000 (MIPS processor)	WINCE 5,0,86,17
Casio Pocket PC 2000 and 2002 (StrongARM)	WINCE 5,0,86,2
Microsoft release for all Pocket PC 2002 devices	WINCE 5,0,88,0
HP iPAQ certified release	WINCE 5,0,88,0

(If this situation changes, we will post an update in the relevant area of the book's website at www.flashthefuture.com/5.)

Following are more convenient commands to know:

- To obtain a string for the Platform, use getVersion().split(" ")[0].
- To obtain the partial version numbers, ranging from Minor Version to Patch, use getVersion().split(",")[i], where i is an integer from 1 to 3.
- The Major Version can be retrieved with getVersion().split(" ")[1].charAt(0).

For your convenience, a simple PPC/Flash detection movie is included within the as_platform_detection folder on the CD-ROM's Chapter 5 directory.

More goodies can be mined from a webserver connection. When making a request to a webserver, Pocket Internet Explorer (PIE) on WinCE 3.0 reports numerous facts about its environment (including screen pixel size and user agent). For example, under Pocket PC 2002's PIE, specific device information reported by a HP Jornada in the http header request to a webserver includes the following:

```
HTTP_USER_AGENT - Mozilla/2.0 (compatible; MSIE 3.02; Windows CE; PPC; 240x320)
HTTP_UA_OS - Windows CE (POCKET PC) - Version 3.0
HTTP_UA_LANGUAGE - JavaScript
HTTP_UA_PIXELS - 240x320
HTTP_UA_VOICE - FALSE
HTTP_UA_COLOR - color16
HTTP_UA_CPU - ARM SA1110
```

The more unusual HTTP_UA prefix supplies device-specific information that a server-side script can detect and redirect accordingly. Note that useful information, such as the device's pixel screen size and color depth, is reported as well as the CPU. For example, the XScale-based Toshiba e740 Pocket PC 2002 reports http_ua_cpu as ARM PXA250. Both the standard HTTP_USER_AGENT and the nonstandard HTTP_UA_OS provide additional details about the operating system. The HTTP_USER_AGENT's MSIE 3.02 label will prohibit many contemporary sites (most notably many e-commerce sites) from being accessed by a Pocket PC device, so if you intend to provide services to Pocket PC clients, it will be prudent to detect the HTTP_UA_OS variable in order to redirect users to a more suitable experience. The HTTP_US_VOICE variable is used within Microsoft's Smartphones to indicate voice capability. Additionally, if there aren't already enough options, you can also use the ColdFusion script (available within the cfm_platform_detection folder on the CD-ROM's Chapter 5 directory) to show the full client information that PIE sends to the webserver when making such an http request. This is shown in Listing 5.9.

Listing 5.9: ColdFusion script displaying browser platform and HTTP headers.

```
<!--- This is compatible with ColdFusion 5 and MX --->
<cfset x = GetHttpRequestData()>
<cfoutput>
<table cellpadding = "2" cellspacing = "2">
  <tr>
    <td><b>HTTP Request item</b></td>
    <td><b>Value</b></td>
  </tr>
<cfloop collection = #x.headers# item = "http_item">
  <tr>
    <td>#http_item#</td>
    <td>#StructFind(x.headers, http_item)#</td>
  </tr>
</cfloop>
  <tr>
    <td>request_method</td>
    <td>#x.method#</td>
  </tr>
```

```
  <tr>
    <td>server_protocol</td>
    <td>#x.protocol#</td>
  </tr>
</table>
<b>http_content --- #x.content#</b>
</cfoutput>
```

Or, if you prefer Perl, the CGI script shown in Listing 5.10 (available within the perl_platform_detection folder on the CD-ROM's Chapter 5 directory) can be used to perform a similar function.

Listing 5.10: Perl script displaying browser platform and HTTP headers.

```
#!/usr/local/bin/perl

use CGI ":standard";

print header('text/html');
foreach $key (keys %ENV) {
        print "$key=$ENV{$key}&";
}
```

NOTE *Make sure you edit the shebang (#!) to point to the location of Perl on your server. If you're running ActivePerl locally on your Windows desktop machine for development, the shebang line should read something like #!C:\Perl\bin\Perl.exe.*

Alternately, when your Pocket PC is online, visit www.flashthefuture.com/5/detectpocketpc for a live test. Pocket PC sniffer and redirection scripts for ASP, PHP, and CFMX are also available for download at this URL.

Once you've determined useful client-side headers for your web application to validate, you'll be able to redirect online requests on the server side to appropriately targeted Flash content, based on the client's platform.

Hardware

Aside from the many software related issues discussed previously, the Pocket PC's hardware playing back your Flash content will impose some particular constraints relating to memory, button input, and audio.

The Red Box Problem: Running Out of Memory

Memory is at an absolute premium on Pocket PCs. On desktop machines, operating systems typically use the hard drive as a supplement when physical RAM usage is exceeded by applications. This is termed virtual memory. Pocket PCs contain a fixed amount of RAM, which is shared between stored programs (analogous to hard drive storage on a desktop) and application memory (similar to the RAM that actually executes applications and the OS on a desktop PC). Because hard drives are not standard on PPCs, they have no virtual memory.

Thus if your Pocket PC has 32MB RAM, then the 32MB is split between storage (for programs you have installed and your files) and free memory available for those programs to use when running. Optional storage, such as CompactFlash cards or Microdrives, can help alleviate the limited memory, but not all users have these add-ons installed, which means that you cannot count on additional memory unless you are developing for an enterprise deployment where the configuration of the devices can be specified.

Flash content is deceptive in terms of memory usage. Because the vector-based SWF format is incredibly efficient in terms of file size delivery, one can make the mistake of assuming that the RAM used when rendering visuals is similarly insignificant. But in reality, rendering graphics is a memory-intensive task. The highly compressed JPEG, GIF, and PNG formats used in Flash need to be decompressed into memory before display. For example, a single 200×200 pixel JPEG file compressed to 10KB can occupy around 120KB when decompressed.

On a single-level timeline, separate JPEGs in individual frames are successively decompressed into memory, resulting in increasing RAM usage as each JPEG is displayed. In the Flash Player, this allocated memory is not released (termed garbage collection in other programming languages), so a sequence of bitmap images of moderate length can easily exceed the available memory—resulting in the dreaded red boxes that the Flash Player defaults to when there is no more memory available.

ActionScript provides only a limited range of functionality to release memory when assets that have been loaded into RAM are no longer required. Using loadMovie and unloadMovie and external movieclip assets can free up large sections of memory. But this method can be problematic because it requires that numerous assets must be external movieclips. At this time of writing, unloadMovieClip and unloadMovie do not free memory that has been allocated by programmatically created movieclip instances with attachMovie.

For developers authoring on Windows 2000/XP Professional, the Processes tab of the Windows Task Manager provides a useful means of inspecting memory usage while a Flash movie is executing. To get an accurate reading, you should first open a web browser window or the standalone Flash Player and note the Mem Usage before any SWF content is loaded. Then, as the movie executes while you interact with it, you can track the amount of RAM allocated and released. Macintosh developers on OS 9 can use the memory bar graphs provided under About This Computer, but the information provided is only a visual guide, making accurate estimates more difficult on that platform.

The memory usage of the Flash Player on the Pocket PC is similar to the desktop Player on both Macintosh and Windows, so the results given will be a good rule of thumb to expect on the Pocket PC—although content that uses sizeable amounts of RAM on the desktop should always be checked again on a handheld. For testing critical content, the best solution is to run a memory profiler concurrently with your Flash content on the target device. The next section presents a sample tool to achieve this, along with the eMbedded Visual C++ source project if you wish to customize it further.

Pocket PC Memory Profiler ActiveX for Flash Content

Jeroen Steenbeck and Ian Chia have developed a small ActiveX control designed to profile memory while your Flash movie is executing in order to see how efficiently your Flash content is handling memory management. By displaying accurate measurement of RAM usage as the Flash movie is running within PIE, you can isolate problem areas within your project and develop strategies to avoid the mysterious Red Box visuals that indicate Flash has run out of memory.

The profiler runs as an ActiveX control visible on the HTML page alongside the SWF content. You can find a demo and installation instructions included within the memory_profiler folder on the CD-ROM's Chapter 5 directory.

Simply insert the HTML shown in Listing 5.11 in your page anywhere between the <BODY> tags to create an instance of the profiler on your web page.

Listing 5.11: Paste this HTML within your page source to create the Memory Profiler ActiveX within your web page.

```
<P><OBJECT ID="memProfiler"
CLASSID="CLSID:1271D64B-626F-4EB0-AFE0-3FD8162672AE"
WIDTH="150" HEIGHT="50">
</OBJECT></P>
```

When you launch the HTML page, you'll see the memory profile appear, as shown in Figure 5.3. The profiler has a single form button that will reset the memory usage counter. Press this button when you want to set a reference point to begin calculating successive RAM usage, with positive numbers indicating additional memory usage and negative numbers showing memory freed by the Flash Player. The other numbers displayed indicate the total physical memory and the available physical memory within your Pocket PC.

Figure 5.3: A view of the memory profiler ActiveX within PIE.

You may prefer to view the profiler above or below the SWF in the HTML, depending on the user interface of your Flash movie. It's best if you can have the profiler visible along with your Flash user interface, in order to interact with the SWF and observe memory usage at the same time. However, given the limited screen size of Pocket PCs, scrolling the page up and down is also a workable alternative.

If you are interested in extending the functionality of the memory profiler, the full source code is provided in the same directory on your CD-ROM, as a Microsoft eMbedded Visual C++ 3.0 project.

Keyboard Limitations on iPAQs

Although the iPAQ's 5-way control button resembles a gamepad controller, due to a limitation within the hardware design, multiple keyDown events are not possible on the 3600/3700 series of iPAQs. Fortunately, Compaq altered the hardware on the 3800 series and above to resolve this issue.

Unfortunately, diagonal input from the control buttons relying on a combination of the vertical and horizontal directional arrows is still not accepted, which can pose issues for game developers. As well, the keyUp event is not registered on the virtual keyboard.

Audio Issues on Pocket PC

Flash audio on Pocket PCs suffers some limitations. Scrolling a HTML page with a SWF playback of MP3 audio will also result in involuntary pausing of audio playback. That's because MP3 playback is a CPU-intensive task that requires decompressing and buffering a stream of audio data on the fly. Because of the limited performance of the StrongARM processor under WinCE 3.0, you'll find the Flash Player's audio paused whenever Pocket IE takes over the CPU in order to scroll the HTML page.

So, if you are planning to deploy Flash projects with MP3 audio, be sure to test all of your chosen bit rates with the final Flash Player for Pocket PC before encoding your audio assets. You may also find that encoding the files within Flash may be more reliable than MP3s that are imported already encoded. In this case, to conserve publishing time (because every time you publish, the MP3 assets are re-encoded to a SWF), break out your audio assets into a separate SWF and perform a loadMovie action within the parent file instead of retaining all the sound files within the main FLA.

Two particular issues relate to iPAQ development:

- On a large number of 3600 series iPAQs, the wiring for the left and right channels of the headphone jack is reversed, so stereo content that performs as expected on the desktop will be experienced in reverse on the iPAQ headphones. A useful way to work around this issue is to offer a utility within your user interface to swap left and right channels, if correct stereo orientation is important to your content.

- Another iPAQ audio limitation is the built-in mono speaker. Left and right channels are combined into a single mono signal, which is played through the internal speaker. Any stereo panning effects will be canceled if the user relies on this as their audio feedback. If stereo is a requisite of your application, be sure to warn the user that they will need to connect through the headphone jack.

Summary

Flash application development is a complex affair. Placing Flash applications onto Pocket PC devices adds even more layers of complexity. If we treat Flash application building as nothing more than a designer building another Flash movie, then major problems will occur when the Flash components are required to integrate into sophisticated systems for full-fledged applications.

However, models of development for software engineering can clear some of the murkiness, if we take the time to integrate them into our development process. We need to recognize that Flash application development for handheld devices generally requires a different perspective, and we also need to pay attention to the characteristics and common processes of this model. Yes, many challenges exist on this platform. But the rewards are great—the opportunities to create compelling, media-rich content for a new generation of handheld computing devices are truly exciting. And the possibilities are numerous. For example, Chapter 6 will show you how to move beyond the limitations of PIE by running Flash within a wrapper application written in eVB or eVC.

6

STANDALONE POCKET PC FLASH APPLICATIONS

Ian Chia

By integrating Flash within an eVB and eVC "wrapper," you can customize the look of your application and, unlike content based within Pocket Internet Explorer (PIE), your project will gain usability and performance benefits associated with "normal" Pocket PC applications.

This chapter will incite you to join the revolution and leave behind the user interface and the application limitations of Pocket Internet Explorer by running Flash within an eVB or eVC "wrapper" application. You will learn to customize the screen size and standard elements such as the Navigation Bar, Start button, Command Bar, and Soft Input Panel (SIP). This will enable you to maximize your screen real estate, add standard Pocket PC application features (such as shortcuts in the Start and Program Files menus), and provide an installation procedure just like a "real" application launched from your host Windows desktop computer. Further reference, additional assets, and updates are in the relevant area of our website, www.flashthefuture.com/6.

Leave PIE Behind—Run Flash as a "Real" Standalone Application

Why limit your PPC Flash content to running within a typical browser? By running your Flash content inside an eMbedded Visual Basic (eVB) or eMbedded Visual C++ (eVC) wrapper instead of Pocket Internet Explorer, you gain the benefits of a "real" application.

All the Flash content discussed thus far has been running inside of PIE. Although Macromedia doesn't provide a standalone projector for the Pocket PC platform, we can create a custom application wrapper to display Flash content. Creating your own application wrapper offers a number of benefits, discussed below:

- You have the ability to fully exit your Flash application! The Pocket PC operating system has a quit-like function for applications, but all this does is minimize your application to the background. This isn't an issue for many programs, but if you have an CPU-intensive Flash application, such as an action game, although you may have "closed" it, your minimized program will still continue to run in the background. This will slow your Pocket PC's performance down to a crawl if you attempt to run other applications, because the CPU will be trying to execute multiple programs simultaneously.

- You gain the full available screen size of your Pocket PC. Although the standard pixel dimensions of an official Pocket PC device are 240×320, most applications have only a subset of the full screen size to play with, because the top of the screen is occupied with the Start button and the Navigation Bar, and the bottom edge is taken by the Command Bar and Soft Input Panel (SIP). Building your own wrapper allows you to choose which elements to display and which to exclude, allowing you to maximize the entire screen.

- You gain the ability to lock users to your single application, either until they choose to quit or forever (that is, until they wipe the RAM). Being the only foreground application means that you can hog all the CPU resources and even use the Pocket PC in full-screen landscape mode, flouting standard Pocket PC user interface conventions. Locking the user into a single application, even on reboot or wakeup, is useful for kiosk-type applications, such as museum guides or restaurant ordering systems, where the user shouldn't have access to underlying Pocket PC applications and system settings.

- You can dispense with all the unrelated user interface elements of PIE, such as the Internet Explorer Navigation Bar (name your Flash application with your own custom string!), the URL address bar, and even the View • Tools • Back • Refresh • Home • Favorites options on the Command Bar. Although these options are useful for web browsing, they have no useful function for a dedicated Flash application. Take the next step and omit the browser altogether.

- You have the option of launching your application from the Start Menu or as an icon from the Program folder, just like any other application. Typically, Flash content for Pocket PC has been installed as an HTML document with an accompanying SWF and, to launch the application, users must hunt through their directories with File Explorer to launch the HTML. This is a less-than-professional experience. With a custom application wrapper, you can install normal program shortcuts with customized icons, and your Flash content will appear and launch just like any other installed program on the Pocket PC.

- You can install your Flash content just like any other application: with a custom installer run from your desktop machine accompanied by an uninstaller option under the Pocket PC's standard Remove Programs Control Panel.

Customizing Flash

This chapter will cover the following options for customizing your Flash application:

1. How to use a very simple eMbedded Visual Basic program as a wrapper to run Flash as a standalone application with a custom Navigation Bar, Quit Button, Menu Bar, and Soft Input Panel (SIP) (see Project 1).

2. How to run a standalone application as above, but hide the bottom Command Bar and SIP (see Project 2).

3. How to hide the Start button so that the user can't switch applications, and how to disable the hardware buttons so that users can't switch to another application (see Project 3).

4. How to run the application full-screen by hiding the taskbar and how to add a custom close button and disable hotkeys. This mode also enables the best landscape mode experience (see Project 4).

5. How to set up kiosk mode, including how to add reboot and wakeup capabilities to ensure that the device will always restart in your kiosk application.

6. How to investigate the options available to eMbedded Visual C++ developers who wish to use Flash as an embedded component. Some simple projects include a sample standalone application and Today Screen plug-ins.

7. How to create an installer that provides a typical installation procedure for Pocket PC applications, including the display of a readme document and an end-user licensing agreement (see Project 5).

8. How to provide a custom icon for your application and create shortcuts in system menus such as the Start Menu to launch your application.

Don't worry whether you've never used Microsoft's eMbedded Visual Tools suite (eVB/eVC) before. We'll proceed through the examples slowly, using plenty of screenshots to guide you through the process of building your first eVB applications.

NOTE *Microsoft's eMbedded Visual Tools (eVT) suite is freely available to developers. You can download the whole suite from* http://www.pocketpc.com/ *at any time–although be forewarned that it is a hefty 300MB download. Alternatively, you can order a CD-ROM from Microsoft for a nominal fee. The download page offers ordering instructions for the CD-ROM. Make sure you also download the Pocket PC 2002 SDK, which updates eVT to include changes for the new operating system. At the time of this writing, the SDK can be found at www.microsoft.com/mobile/developer/downloads/ppcsdk2002.asp.*

Flash as a Standalone 240 × 268 Application

The template for a standalone Flash application is the standard user interface for a Pocket PC application. Figure 6.1 shows the typical Pocket PC application interface, with the main Flash content area, the Start button displayed, the Navigation Bar (showing the application's name), a quit button (shown as a circled OK in eVB applications), and the Command Bar at the bottom of the screen displaying the Soft Input Panel (SIP).

Figure 6.1: A basic Flash standalone application with typical Pocket PC user interface.

The maximum Flash stage size for this configuration is 240 × 268 pixels. Looking carefully at Figure 6.1, you'll notice that the SWF bleeds to the upper edge of the content area, with the bottom of the Navigation Bar butting against the SWF. However, at the bottom is a one-pixel horizontal line that divides the SWF from the SIP Command Bar. This dividing black line cannot be removed, because it's a feature of the Command Bar. (There is a matching black line below the Command Bar area–which seems silly, considering this is a whole wasted line of pixels–but if you do a screenshot and transfer the image to your desktop, you'll see the extra black line on the very bottom row of the image to make up the full 240 × 320 screen area. See the sidebar nearby for more details.)

At any rate, a complete Command Bar area has black line above and below the gray area.

In case you've forgotten the details of PPC screen dimensions, the full screen area is 240 × 320 pixels, whereas the usual (limited) maximum height for a SWF is 268 pixels. The Navigation Bar and the Command Bar are each 26 pixels high. Note, however, that those top and bottom black Command Bar lines are included in that 26-pixel height, and that they cannot be removed, unless you turn off the whole Command Bar area.

Furthermore, the Start button is considered part of the Navigation Bar, although it can be removed and leave the Navigation Bar present, producing a non-switchable app (if you also lock off the hardware buttons). The SIP, however, is considered part of the Command Bar area.

Here's that math, from top of screen to bottom:

Navigation Bar	26
Content area	268
Command Bar	26
Total	320

Here are the standard variations:

1. Standard Projector has a content area of 240 × 268 pixels.
2. Projector minus Command Bar has a content area of 240 × 294 (268 + 26) pixels.
3. Projector minus Navigation Bar and Command Bar results in a full screen of 240 × 320 pixels.

This screen size is identical to the maximum dimensions of Pocket Internet Explorer, but you actually end up with more usable screen size. That's because you won't have to worry about whether the address bar is enabled by the user, which will invoke vertical scrollbars. Furthermore, the eVB application has been designed so that 240 × 268 SWFs will be rendered without ugly HTML page scrollbars appearing.

Run the Demo

Before proceeding, you can make sure that you understand exactly how this looks on your Pocket PC by installing a demo Flash application that uses this basic Pocket PC interface. In the Chapter 6 directory of the CD-ROM, you'll find a folder named 240x268_sample. Within this folder, you'll find a Windows installer titled 240x268_setup.exe. With your Pocket PC connected via ActiveSync, you can work directly from the CD—the installer will automatically copy the appropriate files over to your device. If you encounter any dialog boxes asking if you would like to overwrite a system file, answer yes. Once the installation is complete, launch the 240x268_SWF_demo file from your Start Menu.

Because of the way eVB applications are installed, the eVB runtimes (that is, the interpreter for the eMbedded Visual Basic language) need to be installed on the Pocket PC as well as your eVB application (the .VB file). For both Pocket PC 2000 and 2002, Microsoft has released the same version of the eVB runtime, and it's usually bundled with an eVB application's installer just to make sure that the end user's device will execute correctly. However, it's a little quirky: It bundles the runtime files stamped with the time you created the installer, rather than the original creation date from Microsoft, which usually ensures confusion for the end user. You can avoid this by creating applications in eVC covered later in this chapter. However, the learning curve for eVC is considerably steeper, so you should balance ease of development versus a readme note to the end user before installation.

When you launch the 240x268_SWF_demo application, the first screen that will appear is the standard Pocket PC application user interface, and then, a moment later, a Flash movie of Astrogrrrl's face will appear in the middle of the content area. When you drag your stylus within the SWF, ActionScript will report the coordinates of your stylus tip. It will report horizontal values from 0 to 239 and vertical values from 0 to 267, both relative to the top left corner of the Flash movie (which is just like the coordinate system within a normal web browser).

In fact, Pocket PC Flash Projectors are simply dedicated web browsers. The standalone applications throughout this chapter are wrapper applications—that is, they wrap an embedded HTML browser into a custom user interface shell. This embedded browser in turn loads an HTML page containing a Flash movie.

Desktop developers who are used to embedding the Flash ActiveX control directly into a C++ or Visual Basic application might be surprised at the roundabout approach of building an embedded browser. However, the interface for Pocket Internet Explorer is different from its desktop siblings, and it was not possible for Macromedia to engineer the Pocket PC Flash ActiveX control so that it would be compatible with loading into a Web page as well as other environments. Although official licensees of Macromedia's Flash 5 Player SDK do receive a generic Windows CE control that can be embedded directly into other applications, for our purposes, this is unnecessary.

Coordinate Quirks

It's a quirk of Flash on the Pocket PC platform that mouse coordinates will still be reported if you drag the cursor off the SWF's stage area onto the application's Navigation Bar and Command Bars. When you drag the stylus above the SWF, the Y coordinate will continue to be reported, albeit as a negative number. Drag the stylus below the SWF into the Command Bar, and the Y coordinate continues past 267. If you check the Flash movie on a desktop browser, you'll note two major differences between the Pocket PC and the desktop version. In the Windows desktop browser, coordinates are reported only when the mouse is within the SWF. More importantly, coordinates are constantly reported when the mouse is over the SWF, regardless of the condition of the mouse button. On the Pocket PC, because of the usability differences of a stylus, coordinates are reported only when the screen is tapped or the stylus is dragged around.

Performance Worries

The cautious developer might also wonder what performance hits might be suffered because of using a wrapper application in eVB or eVC instead of Pocket IE. Because our wrapper applications use the same HTML View API within the Pocket PC, there are really no distinct differences between the applications. Based on our intensive ActionScript benchmark tests, the performance differences are so negligible as to be considered nonexistent.

JavaScript Access

But things can get much more interesting when we deploy our content in a wrapper. To begin with, consider Flash ActionScript integration with JavaScript. Because we are, in fact, running a custom web browser within our application, we have standard access to JavaScript within our web page. We can perform bidirectional ActionScript-to-JavaScript communication, as discussed in the topic JavaScript (JScript) Communication with ActionScript in Chapter 5. Also, because our wrapper application is loading a local HTML page using the file:// protocol, the normal domain security restrictions within ActionScript are removed, giving us in effect the same access rights as a Flash Projector on the desktop.

The eVB projectors shown in this chapter always look for an index.htm file located within the same directory as the wrapper application. (By editing the eVB code, you can alter the HTML file's name to one of your choice.) Consequently, when you're creating your own projectors, you'll need to spend a little time thinking about where you plan to create the projector's directory on the device, because this will affect the projector's opening of the correct HTML and SWF file. Project 5 explains how to create Pocket PC Shortcuts, so that you can launch your application from a variety of locations on the device.

Although communication with JavaScript within our wrapper is no different from its implementation within PIE, communication between ActionScript and eVB or eVC is more complex, especially because fscommands aren't implemented on this platform. However, we can achieve bidirectional communication for these languages, and this is covered in Chapter 7.

Project 1: Building Your Own 240 × 268 eVB Projector

Now that you know the advantages of creating your own custom projector, it's time to build your own application. Don't be nervous if you've never used the eMbedded Visual Basic environment before. We'll gently lead you through the process here with a step-by-step guide. At the end, you'll have your own custom projector, complete with desktop installer.

The eVB HTML viewer code used in this chapter is based on Alex Yakhnin's article, "Saddling the HTML View Control from eVB," which appeared at www.devbuzz.com, thanks to Derek Mitchell of devbuzz.com, Inc.

Here's the procedure:

1. Copy the Project_1_240x268_Projector directory from the Chapter 6 folder of the CD-ROM to your desktop machine, right-click the folder, and select the Properties option. Uncheck the Read-only attribute so that all files can be saved over. Then, working from either Windows Explorer or My Computer, open flash_standalone_240x268.ebp. (The .ebp suffix stands for eMbedded Visual Basic Project.) This will launch the eMbedded Visual Basic environment (if the eVT suite has been correctly installed on your desktop machine).

2. As shown in Figure 6.2, select the View • Project Explorer menu option, which will open the Project Explorer. The Project Explorer window appears. Expand trees to show Flash_Standalone_application • Forms • flashContainer.

Figure 6.2: Selecting Project Explorer.

3. Right-click the file named "flashContainer (flashContainer.ebf)" and, from the ensuing contextual menu, select View Object. A window will pop up with a box with resizing windows inside. Ignore this. Right-click again on "flashContainer (flashContainer.ebf)" and select Properties from the ensuing contextual menu. Figure 6.3 shows the correct Properties menu selection.

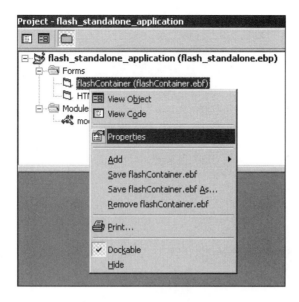

Figure 6.3: Selecting the Properties option.

4. A window labeled "Properties - flashContainer" will appear. In the input fields near the top is a field labeled Caption. This is the name of your application as it appears in the Navigation Bar. Figure 6.4 shows the Caption field selected and about to be edited. Click in the area where it currently says My Application Name and customize it to your preference.

Figure 6.4: Customizing the Caption field.

5. Press CTRL-S to save the Caption change to your flashContainer.

6. Then, as shown in Figure 6.5, select File • Make flash_standalone_standard.vb.

Figure 6.5: First step in saving your eVB projector.

7. Enter the file name of your eVB executable. (You don't have to include the .vb suffix; eVB will add it for you if you forget.) You can make the name anything you want.

8. Close eVB and open your HTML editor.

9. Edit the index.htm file so that the <param name=movie value='test.swf'> tag has the name of your own SWF. Remember that the standard wrapper here accepts SWFs sized to 240 × 268. Save the HTML file.

10. Copy the .vb file from your desktop to the Pocket PC along with the index.htm file and your SWF file. (If you haven't made your SWF yet, just copy the SWF demo file provided in the Project_1_240x268_Projector directory.)

11. Launch the .vb file on your Pocket PC, and you'll see the SWF appear within your custom application. Note that the Navigation Bar has the application's title using the information you entered in the Caption field. The OK button in the top right corner will exit your application. Due to the design of the Pocket PC user interface, this button is labeled "OK" by the operating system instead of the "X" you find in typical Pocket PC applications. Confusing as it may seem, on a Pocket PC 2002 device, OK will dismiss a dialog (in this case our application). Minimizing on this platform is accomplished with a new Pocket PC 2002 "innovation" termed Smart Minimize, which is controlled by an X button. Breaking from its own strict user interface conventions, Microsoft has designed X to minimize any

application on a Pocket PC, unlike the desktop's behavior where X will quit an application. (Needless to say, proponents of usability are confounded by Microsoft's decision.) Also note that the bottom Command Bar is empty, except for the SIP. If everything went according to plan, you should see a Flash Projector application similar to Figure 6.6.

Figure 6.6: The completed projector.

If the application didn't run, that's most likely because it threw up an error dialog that says, "Cannot find extension file pvbDecl.dll. Please run setup to restore this file." If this occurs, it's simply because the eVB runtimes are missing on your machine. To fix this, you will need to run the 240x268_setup.exe installer. It will install the correct runtimes on your Pocket PC, and then you can launch your projector's .vb file again. Project 5 explains how to bundle your eVB project with an eVB runtime installer in order to ensure that the runtime is always installed when you distribute wrapped Flash content.

Although you don't need to work with the code that loads the Flash, it is within the eVB file. If you want to take a look, the specific code that is used to load Flash correctly within the HTML object is heavily commented in the eVB file. You'll note that we create the HTML window larger than the required 240 × 268 pixels in order to prevent scrollbars from appearing. Here's why: It seems that the HTML View control has a bug that will inadvertently display scrollbars, even if the content is sized to the exact dimension available. Although the workaround creates a larger HTML object than required, the effect is a 240 × 268 Flash content area with no scrollbars.

240 × 294 Projector: Hide the Command Bar and Soft Input Panel

The next step is to create a wrapper application that hides the bottom Command Bar and SIP. Many Flash applications don't require alphanumeric entry or, if they do, they often can provide a custom keypad movieclip that can be shown or hidden at will. This enhanced wrapper provides three additional benefits:

- The screen size can be upped to 240 × 294 pixels.

- Custom keypads can aid correct data entry, because unused keys are simply not available.

- The custom keypad can be positioned anywhere within the stage, or it can even be semi-transparent. The standard Pocket PC SIP always appears over the bottom third of the screen, obscuring the content under the SIP. In contrast, a custom movieclip used for input can be positioned at will so that your text fields can be placed anywhere on the stage, including the lower third that you would normally need to avoid.

Project 2 will now guide you through very similar steps to create a Flash Projector with the enhanced screen size.

Project 2: Building a 240 × 294 eVB Projector

All steps to build this projector (except 1 and 9) are very similar to Project 1.

1. Copy the Project_2_240x294_Projector directory from the Chapter 6 folder of the CD-ROM to your desktop machine, then right-click the folder and select the Properties option. Uncheck the Read-only attribute so that all files can be saved over. Then open flash_standalone_240x294.ebp.

2. Open the Project Explorer by selecting View • Project Explorer. Expand trees for Flash_Standalone_application • Forms • flashContainer.

3. Right-click "flashContainer (flashContainer.ebf)" and select View Object. A window will pop up with a box with resizing windows inside. As before, ignore this. Instead, right-click "flashContainer (flashContainer.ebf)" again and select Properties.

4. A window labeled "Properties - flashContainer" appears. Customize the name of your application by editing the field labeled Caption.

5. Use CTRL-S to save the Caption change to your flashContainer.

6. Select File • Make flash_standalone_standard.vb.

7. Enter the file name of your eVB executable. You don't have to include the .vb suffix because eVB will add it for you if you forget. You can make the name anything you want.

8. Close eVB and open your HTML editor.

9. Now, edit the index.htm file so that the <param name=movie value='test.swf'> tag has the name of your own SWF. Remember that this time, the standard wrapper here accepts SWFs sized at 240 × 294. When you are finished, remember to save the HTML file.

10. Copy the .vb file from your desktop to the Pocket PC along with the index.htm file and your SWF file. If you haven't made your own SWF yet, just copy the SWF demo file provided in the Project_2_240x294_Projector directory. (Make sure you create a new directory on the Pocket PC, unless you want to overwrite the index.htm file from Project 1.)

11. Launch the .vb file on your Pocket PC and you'll see the SWF appear within your custom application. You should see a Flash Projector application similar to Figure 6.7. This time, note that the upper Navigation Bar and Start button appear as usual, but that the bottom Command Bar and SIP have disappeared.

Figure 6.7: A typical 240 × 294 Flash Projector.

240 × 294 Projector: Hide Start Button and Disable Hardware Buttons

As mentioned earlier, Flash applications can be very CPU-intensive, particularly for intensive ActionScripting or visuals. Although eVB applications have the OK button that quits the application, a user can still switch to another application by selecting an option on the Start Menu or via the hardware buttons. This has the same effect as minimizing via the X button on other applications. So, here's the problem: If the Flash content is still consuming most of the available CPU cycles while minimized, the Pocket PC's performance will be extremely sluggish if the user attempts to run other applications, which will provide a bad user experience associated with *your* Flash application.

With this scenario in mind, the best strategy is to lock off all user options to switch to another application. By hiding the Start button and disabling the hardware buttons, the only way a user can switch to another application is by quitting your Flash Projector via the top right OK button. This type of projector can be very useful for Flash content that demands a user's full attention, such as a game or a cartoon.

Project 3 will guide you through now-familiar steps.

Project 3: Building a Non-Switchable 240 × 294 eVB Projector

The S309HotKey ActiveX control, a new component that allows an eVB application to remap or lock out access to the hardware buttons, must be added to your system to complete this project. You can ensure success with this seemingly more difficult task by following the first few steps very carefully, after which the rest of the project will cover familiar ground.

1. Install the S309HotKey ActiveX control onto our desktop system. That way, when we open eVB, our project will find the correct ActiveX control installed for compilation. The control is freeware from Software 309, and it is available from http://nsbasic.com/s309/HotKey/S309HotKey_Desktop.zip. You will also need to download the Pocket PC version of this control from http://nsbasic.com/ s309/HotKey/S309HotKey_PocketPC.exe. (Further information about Software 309 is found at http://nsbasic.com/s309/.)

2. Once your downloads are complete, unzip the S309HotKey_Desktop.zip file and copy the S309HotKey.ocx file to your Windows System32 directory. On a Windows 98/ME system, the target folder will be C:\Windows\System32 (or similar). For Windows NT/2000/XP systems, the folder will be C:\WinNT\System32. Following text up to next item goes with above item 2. (Note that your C:\ drive letter may differ if you have a dual boot machine.)

3. Next, click your desktop's Start button and select Run.

4. In the text field marked Open: enter **regsvr32.exe S309HotKey.ocx** and then click OK. The Run dialog box should resemble Figure 6.8. (Note that Windows NT and Windows 2000 systems will require you to log in with Administrator rights before you can register ActiveX controls.)

To log in and out as different users under Windows NT and 2000 systems, open the Task Manager by pressing CTRL+ALT+ENTER, and click the Log Off button. When you log back in, enter the Administrator username and password to gain administrative access.

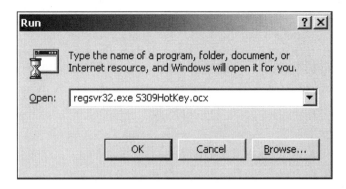

Figure 6.8: Registering the S309HotKey ActiveX control on your desktop.

5. The system should return with a successful message like the one shown in Figure 6.9. Click OK.

Figure 6.9: Successful registration of the control into your operating system.

6. Copy the Project_3_240x294_Projector directory from the Chapter 6 folder of the CD-ROM to your desktop machine, and right-click the folder and select the Properties option. Uncheck the Read-only attribute so that all files can be saved over. Then open flash_nonswitchable_240x294.ebp.

7. Open the Project Explorer by selecting View • Project Explorer. Expand trees for Flash_Standalone_application • Forms • flashContainer.

8. Right-click "flashContainer (flashContainer.ebf)" and select View Object. A window will pop up with a box with resizing windows inside. Ignore this and, as before, right-click again "flashContainer (flashContainer.ebf)" and then select Properties from the ensuing contextual dialog.

9. A window labeled "Properties - flashContainer" appears. Customize the name of your application by editing the field labeled Caption.

10. Use CTRL-S to save the Caption change to your flashContainer.

11. Then, select File • Make flash_standalone_standard.vb.

12. Enter the file name of your eVB executable. You don't have to include the .vb suffix as eVB will add it for you if your forget. You can make the name anything you want.

13. Close eVB and open your HTML editor.

14. Edit the index.htm file so that the <param name=movie value='test.swf'> tag has the name of your own SWF. (The standard wrapper is the same as Project 2 and accepts SWFs sized at 240 × 294.) Save the HTML file.

15. Copy the .vb file from your desktop to the Pocket PC along with the index.htm file and your SWF file. If you haven't made your own SWF yet, just copy the SWF demo file provided in the Project_3_240x294_Projector directory. Create a new directory on the Pocket PC unless you want to overwrite previous files.

16. Before launching the .vb file, it's important to install the S309HotKey control onto your Pocket PC as well. Launch the S309HotKey_PocketPC.exe you downloaded in Step 1, so the installer will copy and register the ActiveX to your Pocket PC.

17. Finally, launch the .vb file on your Pocket PC, and you'll see the SWF appear within your custom application. Visually, the screen will appear very similar to Project 2, with the omission of the Start button. Your hardware buttons are now also disabled until you exit the Flash Projector. You should see a screen similar to Figure 6.10.

Figure 6.10: The non-switchable 240 × 294 Flash Projector.

Full-Screen 240 × 320 Flash Projector

Now, to consolidate all of our success in taking over the Pocket PC with increasingly more dedicated Flash Projectors, we will take over the whole screen. Full-screen projectors with a resolution of 240 × 320 pixels can be used for Flash games or as screensavers. Note that, now, because we're hiding all elements of the Pocket PC interface, a Flash movie can be designed for either normal portrait orientation or a 320 × 240 landscape orientation. Third-party applications like JSLandscape are no longer necessary for switching the screen into landscape mode, because our standalone Flash application can do that all by itself, using a combination of the _rotation property within ActionScript while luxuriating in the novelty of using the entire screen as its display area.

However, because the standard eVB application interface will now become fully hidden, we will need to introduce a small close button that can quit the application. Otherwise, the user would have no way to use other applications on the Pocket PC, short of a soft-reset.

A full-screen visual experience can be very compelling on the Pocket PC, and Project 4 will illustrate this by building a full-screen Flash screensaver. Strickland Consulting's freeware screensaver engine, PocketCandy, (found in the PocketCandy directory in the Chapter 6 folder of the CD-ROM) is a wonderful application that runs in the background and adds the missing screensaver functionality to Windows CE. The most current version of PocketCandy can be found online at http://www16.brinkster.com/motbe/ce/PocketCandy.asp

Project 4: Building a Full-Screen 240 × 320 eVB Projector

The full-screen projector is provided in two versions: one with standard hardware button access, the other without. If you intend to create a projector that locks out hardware buttons, make sure you follow steps 1 to 5 of Project 3 before proceeding with Project 4. Follow the steps in Project 4 carefully, because there are a few minor differences in the procedure.

1. **To create a full-screen projector with standard hardware button access**, copy the Project_4_240x320_Projector directory from the Chapter 6 folder of the CD-ROM to your desktop machine, then right-click the folder and select the Properties option. Next, uncheck the Read-only attribute so that all files can be saved over. Then open flash_standalone_240x320.ebp.

   If you want to create a projector that locks out all hardware buttons, copy the Project_4_240x320_No_Buttons directory instead. Then, right-click the folder and select the Properties option. Next, uncheck the Read-only attribute so that all files can be saved over. Then open flash_standalone_240x320.ebp.

2. Open the Project Explorer by selecting View • Project Explorer. Expand trees for Flash_Standalone_application • Forms • flashContainer.

3. Right-click on "flashContainer (flashContainer.ebf)" and select View Object. A window will pop up with a box with resizing windows inside. As usual, ignore this. Then right-click "flashContainer (flashContainer.ebf)" again and select Properties.

4. A window labeled "Properties - flashContainer" appears. Customize the name of your application by editing the field labeled Caption.

5. Press CTRL-S to save the Caption change to your flashContainer.

6. Select File • Make flash_standalone_standard.vb.

7. This time, enter the file name of your eVB executable as flash_screensaver.vb.

8. Close eVB and open your HTML editor.

9. Edit the index.htm file so that the <param name=movie value='test.swf'> tag has the name of your own SWF. The full-screen projector accepts SWFs sized at 240×320.

   Note that the Pocket PC regards the screen as vertical by default. So, even if your movie is intended for landscape orientation, the dimensions are still entered here as 240×320 and not swapped around to 320×240. Save the HTML file.

10. Copy the .vb file from your desktop to the Pocket PC's \Windows directory along with the index.htm file and your SWF file. If you haven't made your own SWF yet, just copy the SWF demo file provided in the project's directory.

11. Launch the .vb file on your Pocket PC, and you'll see the SWF appear within your custom application. Note that your Flash movie occupies all available screen real estate, except for a small square marked X in the top right corner. You should see a Flash Projector application similar to Figure 6.11. Tap the X, and the projector will quit.

Figure 6.11: A full-screen 240 × 320 Flash Projector.

12. Copy the flash_screensaver.scr file from your desktop directory to the Pocket PC's \Windows directory.

13. Install the PocketCandy screensaver engine by launching the installer PocketCandy.exe from your PocketCandy directory (mentioned on page 171). You may prefer to install just a few of the many bitmap screensavers provided with the package, so you can compare them with the quality of a Flash-based screensaver. After installation, open the PocketCandy control panel via Start • Settings • System • PocketCandy and configure the active screensaver to be the flash_screensaver.scr file, as shown in Figure 6.12.

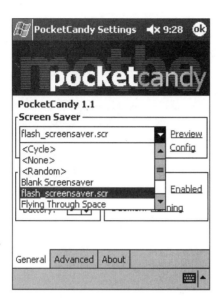

Figure 6.12: Configuring the Flash screensaver.

14. Click Preview to check that the screensaver launches correctly. Then you can click OK to exit the control panel. After the assigned time delay, your Flash screensaver will automatically launch. You can click the small X in the top right corner to exit your screensaver.

Full-Screen Pocket PC Kiosk with Flash

Pocket PC devices make excellent portable, interactive kiosks. In fact, a number of venues—including Disneyland, museums, and sporting arenas—are beginning to deploy Pocket PCs to a variety of valued customers, in order to enhance their experiences within the complex. Building interactive kiosks with Flash technology is one of the most logical approaches, because Flash's visual, audio, and scripting abilities can quickly create a compelling experience that would be difficult to match, both technically and financially, using other solutions.

Building upon the full-screen projector in Project 4, we need to add some simple features for a kiosk, to ensure the Flash application starts every time the device is switched on. The device can return from two different states—wakeup or soft reset—when it is turned on.

From Soft Reset

To trigger the Flash content to start up after a soft reset, place a shortcut to your Flash .vb application in the \Windows\StartUp folder, and this application will be run every time, just after the Pocket PC environment is rebooted.

NOTE *The easiest way to create a Windows CE Shortcut is to use ActiveSync's Explorer window. Locate the application, right-click on the file, and select Create Shortcut from the menu. Then cut and paste the Shortcut to the destination directory.*

From Wakeup

Enabling your Flash content to start after a system wakeup event is a more complicated issue, because you'll need to call the native Pocket PC API CeRunAppAtEvent. Doing this will cause your application to be called every time after wakeup. Because the API is not accessible from within Flash, a small custom eVB/eVC application will need to be created and run before launching your Flash application. It will need to include a call to CeRunAppAtEvent with NOTIFICATION_EVENT_WAKEUP as the second parameter and the path to your executable as the first parameter. The following lines of eVB code demonstrates how to trigger an application after a wakeup event:

```
Public Const NOTIFICATION_EVENT_WAKEUP = 11
Public Declare Function CeRunAppAtEvent Lib "Coredll" (ByVal AppName As String,
ByVal WhichEvent As Long) As Long
CeRunAppAtEvent("\Windows\Start Menu\MyKiosk.vb", NOTIFICATION_EVENT_WAKEUP)
```

Using Flash Within eMbedded Visual C++ Applications

So far, we've covered various projector configurations using eVB. Although eMbedded Visual C++ requires a steeper learning curve, the principles for using it to create Flash application wrappers are exactly the same. We first create a window within our parent wrapper that encapsulates the HTML View control, then we instruct the HTML object to load an HTML page that contains the Flash object.

You should be aware of these issues when developing eVC applications using Flash:

- Using the simpler Pocket PC 2000 API, after you create your HTML View control instance, you need to populate the instance with an HTML string using the DTM_ADDTEXTW message. For the Flash ActiveX control to be able to find the file path to a SWF, the HTML string needs to be an intermediary frameset document, which in turn loads a normal HTML file. Alternatively, the string can be a simple HTML <HEAD> section with a <META-REFRESH> tag to load a second file. This second HTML file will contain the standard <OBJECT> tag to instantiate the Flash control within the HTML View object.

- Pocket PC 2002 devices can use the new DTM_NAVIGATE message in the HTML API to directly load the HTML page without an intermediary frameset.

- By trapping the NM_HOTSPOT message, you can send one-way messages from Flash into eVC via ActionScript's getURL. As an example, a full-screen application can use this application to quit via a button within the Flash interface by sending a getURL message with a unique URL that's interpreted by eVC.

- Bidirectional communication between eVC (or eVB) and ActionScript can be achieved through the use of XMLSockets and a dedicated socket server. This technique will be examined in depth in Chapter 7.

Using the older Pocket PC 2000 API, you'll find a sample project in the STHTMLDialog directory in the Chapter 6 folder of the CD-ROM. This eVC project uses the STHTMLDialog library by Vassili Philippov from http://www.pocketpcdn.com/articles/htmldialog.html. This freeware STHTMLDialog library simplifies the building of HTML View–based eVC applications.

STHTMLDialog as a Flash Wrapper

This sample application creates a standard Flash Projector with a 240×268 display area. The projector works on both Pocket PC 2000 and Pocket PC 2002. Although the original documentation states that JavaScript and HTML frames are unavailable, this is incorrect. The project will load a Flash HTML page from a dynamically generated frameset, and Flash can interact with JavaScript in the HTML document. The disadvantage of this approach is that trapping the NM_HOTSPOT message is unsuccessful, because it seems that separate instances of the browser object are instantiated for each frame and the WM_NOTIFY message doesn't get posted to the parent window from the Flash frame.

A Different Approach: HTMLHost for the Pocket PC 2002

With the release of the Pocket PC 2002 API, fixes to the HTML View control and a new DTM_NAVIGATE message allow an application to load an HTML document based on a URL. By using a file:// protocol–based URL, you can successfully load a local Flash HTML document. This technique overcomes the frameset workaround, and you can successfully trap the NM_HOTSPOT message within this framework. You can find a sample eVC application in the HTMLHost directory within the Chapter 6 folder of the CD-ROM. This is an edited version of the HTMLHost sample available within the Pocket PC 2002 SDK, located under \Windows CE Tools\wce300\Pocket PC 2002\samples\ win32\HTMLHost. Because this technique relies on a new addition to the Pocket PC 2002 API, the application won't work on older 2000 devices.

FlashAssist Pro: Use a Wizard to Create Standalone Flash Players

The commercial FlashAssist Pro from Ant Mobile Software (antmobile.com) is an exceptionally well designed product that allows even a novice eVC developer to create standalone, installable Flash applications for the Pocket PC using a simple wizard-driven interface. With a number of mouse clicks, an entire application's source code is generated that can be quickly compiled into a runtime executable that can run Flash content at a variety of screen sizes. In addition, a number of commands can be triggered via ActionScript, including the ability to quit the application, control the Soft Input Panel and system volume, and save and load from a simple data store on the local file system. For advanced developers who seek a head start in creating their own advanced Flash applications, the eVC source code is fully commented and easily extensible to add functionality specific to different needs. Although the product costs US$200, it's a good investment for the serious eVC developer as it requires substantial hours of research and development to match the features of FlashAssist Pro.

Using Flash as a Pocket PC System Component

Other interesting opportunities for Flash content on your Pocket PC 2002 device are offered by the new HTML-based bubble style Notification API and Today Screen/Dashboard applets. Unfortunately, because of incompatibilities between the Notification API and the Flash 5 ActiveX control for Pocket PC, it's not possible to dynamically populate a notification with HTML that will instruct Flash to find the correct file path to the SWF. The usual workaround of a frameset document within the notification that loads the target SWF also fails, because it seems that the Notification API fails to correctly size the bubble vertically, resulting in a notification bubble of only one text line height, regardless of the target frame's HTML content. You can view the Flash movie, but only if you scroll within the tiny notification area, which is a less-than-satisfactory experience.

The good news is that developing Flash-based Today Screen or Dashboard applets is possible, and Gigabyte Solutions Animated Today Screen product is available at www.gigabytesol.com/at2002.htm. If you're interested in developing your own Today Screen Flash plug-ins, then we suggest that you create your Flash applet using HTML View techniques. In addition, some useful resources are the following:

- http://www.microsoft.com/mobile/developer/technicalarticles/todayapi.asp
- Today Tester, a utility to assist in testing Today plug-ins (includes source) from http://www.scottandmichelle.net/scott/cestuff/testtoday.zip

Java and Flash on the Pocket PC

Although Java isn't able to create a native browser window on the Pocket PC, you can have Java-specific components of an application and integrate them with a Flash-based user interface. By following the techniques of bidirectional communication (that will be covered in Chapter 7), you can create a Java-based socket server that communicates with a Flash user interface hosted within an eVC or eVB wrapper application. With this methodology, the Java socket server will be part of your Java application and communicate with other specific back-end services or data stores via a Java transport of your choice.

Flash Applications Installers

Now that we have learned how to build a professional looking standalone projector for our Flash content, we'll move on to the final aspect of deployment: creating installers that run from the desktop to automagically expand and copy all of your assets into their appropriate locations on the Pocket PC, just like a typical commercial application. Unlike launching Flash content via HTML files loaded within Pocket IE, we can also create unique application icons that are launchable from the Start Menu or, just like a "normal" Pocket PC application, from the Program directory. The installed files can be located in the \Program Files directory similar to typical applications, or the \Windows directory for Flash screensavers, or other appropriate locations, such as the \My Documents or \StorageCard directories.

Installers have several advantages. They present a simplified user interface for the end user and also can automate a range of important tasks, including:

- Creating a shortcut in the Start Menu and/or Program Files menus.

- Providing an uninstall option within ActiveSync so that users can perform a one-click removal of the application.

- Presenting an end-user license agreement that defines and protects the developer and end user's legal responsibilities.

Although commercial Pocket PC installers such as InstallShield (http://www.installshield.com) are available, this chapter will focus on a freeware solution, using a combination of the eVB's Application Install Wizard, Scott Ludwig's EZSetup (http://www.eskimo.com/~scottlu/win/), and OnHiatus's Launch and Pike.

We need to create some essential assets for the installer. Firstly, the most basic component is a .CAB (Microsoft cabinet) file, which is a compressed archive of all your projects assets, including the HTML and SWF files and short-cuts that must be created in order to launch your file. In later stages, we'll add a .EXE launcher with a custom icon, as well as an end-user licensing agreement incorporated into the installer. We'll guide you through this project with step-by-step instructions, so don't worry—it'll be a manageable process.

How Do I Create a Pocket PC Installer for a Mac Desktop?

Although the majority of Pocket PC users own Windows desktop machines, there is also a Mac-based audience who won't be able to run an installer .EXE file from their operating system. However, you'll be glad to know that the solution is simple and doesn't require extra work to support both operating systems. The simplest way to deliver a Mac-friendly installer is to supply the .CAB file of your application. Since you'll have to create a .CAB file in order to complete the final installer .EXE file, you won't be inconvenienced by this step. A Mac user may transfer the .CAB file from the desktop to their Pocket PC using a storage card, downloading a linked file using Pocket Internet Explorer, receiving an email on the Pocket PC with a .CAB file attachment, or using PocketMac to transfer the file via USB or a TCP/IP network. Once the file is on the device, simply tap to launch the .CAB file, and all the assets will automatically copy to the appropropriate locations. The .CAB file will even clean up by deleting itself upon completion!

If you wish to provide downloadable installers from your website, you can provide a link to the .EXE file for Windows users and a .CAB file for Mac users or people browsing your site using Pocket Internet Explorer. To enable PIE to download .CAB files correctly, make sure you create a MIME type that will force PIE to save the file onto the device, rather than attempt to display the .CAB's contents as gibberish text within the browser. You can do this by "inventing" a MIME type for your CAB file, following the guidelines laid out by the Microsoft Cabinet SDK, such as:

MIME type: application/x-cabinet_wince_arm

File suffix: .cab

This technique will also work if you wish to provide Theme Skin Files (.TSK) files (a slightly different .CAB file format) used by the Flash-based Animated Today Screen product. The following MIME type will allow users browsing from their Pocket PC to save .TSK files directly onto their device.

MIME type: application/x-cabinet_wince_arm

File suffix: .tsk

Make sure you remind the user that .TSK files must be saved in the \My Documents directory for Animated Today to use it.

TIP *It may seem a chicken and the egg situation regarding Flash on the Pocket PC for Mac users, because the only official installer is naturally provided by Microsoft for a Windows desktop. Fortunately, we've provided an unofficial installation guide for Mac users at http://www.flashthefuture.com/5/mac_to_ppc.htm.*

Project 5: Building a Flash Application Installer

1. Launch eMbedded Visual Basic and open your completed project. Compile a .vb file by selecting File • Make (your project's name).vb. Use the Options button to enter appropriate application properties, such as version number and information, as shown in Figure 6.13, before clicking the OK button to compile the .vb file.

Figure 6.13: Entering your project's properties.

2. Select Tools • Remote Tools • Application Install Wizard, and you should see the dialog box in Figure 6.14.

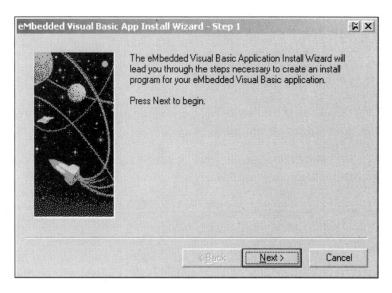

Figure 6.14: The Application Install Wizard.

3. Click the Browse button and locate your eMbedded Basic Project (.ebp) file. Click the Next button.

4. Click the Browse button and locate the .vb file you compiled in Step 1. Click Next.

5. Select a directory where the installer files will be created. You can select an existing directory using the Browse button or create a file path, such as C:\my_flash_installer. If the directory doesn't exist, the Wizard will ask whether you'd like it to create one.

6. The Wizard offers a list of CPUs that to target for your application. (Although Pocket PC 2002 supports only ARM processors, older versions supported the SH3 and MIPS processors as well.) As shown in Figure 6.15, check the Arm 1100 box and click Next.

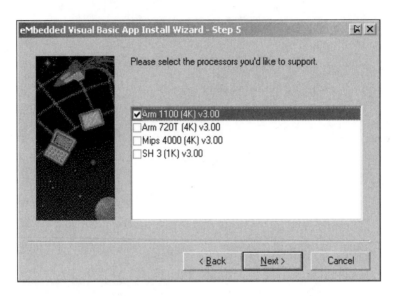

Figure 6.15: Selecting the Arm 1100 processor.

7. The Wizard now offers a range of Microsoft and third-party ActiveX controls installed within the eVB environment. Leave these options unchecked and click Next.

NOTE *Before adding additional files, consider this: Because the Wizard will display the full path to each data file, this can lead to some confusion if your assets are in a deeply nested folder on your hard drive, because all you'll see is a truncated path to your assets and not the actual file name. The trick is to copy all the files to a folder with a short name like "assets" before you reach this step, so your Wizard will look something like Figure 6.16. Because the Application Install Wizard only lets you install the data files into the same Pocket PC directory as the .vb file, it's important to structure your SWFs to load all movies from the same directory and avoid nested directories.*

8. You can now add any additional data files. All the SWF and HTML files for your Flash application are considered data files. Make sure you include *all* of the assets. Every time you add a file, the Wizard will ask you whether it should be installed to the Windows directory as a system file. For normal Flash applications, this is not necessary. By clicking No, you place the SWF/HTML files in the same target directory as the .vb file. Because the

Application Install Wizard only lets you install the data files into the same Pocket PC directory as the .vb file, it's important to structure your SWFs to load all movies from the same directory, and avoid nested directories. Make sure to also check the Include Device Runtimes in CAB file box because the end user's Pocket PC may not contain the eVB runtimes. For example, both Pocket PC 2000 and 2002 on the iPAQ do not contain the eVB runtimes after a hard reset. When you've added all data files, click Next.

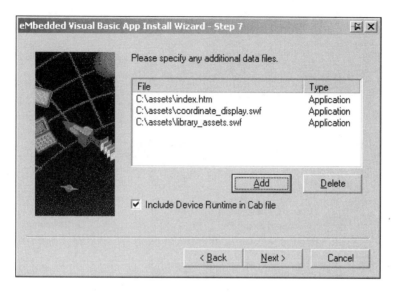

Figure 6.16: Adding your Flash application files as data files.

9. The Wizard will now prompt you for the Default Install Directory as well as the Application Name, Description, and Company Name. Here's what these fields do:

The Default Install Directory is the folder under which the assets are saved to both your desktop machine and the Pocket PC. If you choose to remove and then later reinstall from the Add/Remove Programs option within ActiveSync, the desktop directory is where the .CAB file will be retrieved from. On the Pocket PC, the same directory name contains the original assets, such as the .vb file and HTML and SWF assets.

The Company Name and Application Name fields are combined in an ActiveSync dialog box that will ask a question along these lines: "Install (Your Company Name) (Your Application Name) using the default application install directory?" during installation onto the Pocket PC.

The information entered in the Description field will appear when you select the application within the Add/Remove Programs dialog within ActiveSync.

10. Now click Create Install, and eVB will whir away. A DOS window will temporarily appear while the Cabwiz application runs in the background. After all the files are compiled into a single .CAB file, you'll be able to click Finish to return to the normal eVB environment. When you examine the install directory, you'll find a range of files and folders, similar to what is shown in Figure 6.17.

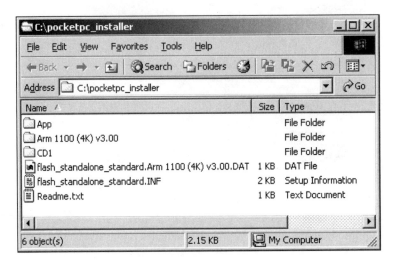

Figure 6.17: The Application Installer Wizard's generated installer files.

11. Open the CD1 directory, and you'll find a simple Setup.exe installer along with a .INI file containing the information you entered in Step 9, as well as a single .CAB file containing all your compressed assets.

NOTE *If you were to run the Setup.exe file now, it would install your Flash application to the Pocket PC, and you'd be able to launch it via the Programs folder on your device. As well, it has automatically entered the correct information into the system registry so that if you were to delete the application in the usual manner (via Start • Settings • Remove Programs), all the correct assets–including the .vb file, HTML and SWF files–would be removed automatically. The same facility is also available under the Add/Remove Programs option within the desktop's ActiveSync application, demonstrating that eVB's Application Install Wizard provides both installation and uninstallation facilities.*

12. If you want your installer to automatically add an entry to the Start Menu instead of the Programs folder, you need to edit the .INF file slightly. Open

the .INF file in your favorite text editor and locate the DestinationDirs section. You'll see a line like this:

```
Shortcuts=,%CE11%
```

Because the installer supports only a single shortcut entry, you will need to edit this line to point to your preference. When .inf files are written for a Pocket PC installation, macro strings represent destination directories within the .inf file. This is important because directories may have different names depending on the language into which the device has been localized. Table 6.1 shows the list of macro strings defined for the Pocket PC. Because %CE17% represents the \WINDOWS\Start Menu directory, change the line to read as follows:

```
Shortcuts=,%CE17%
```

13. If you decided to alter the shortcut's destination, you'll need to rebuild the .CAB file accordingly: Just open the Readme.txt file that was generated by the Application Install Wizard and highlight the lines after "To rebuild the cab files run the following command" so that the highlighted text ends with "Arm 1100 (4K) v3.00." Copy this text then select Start • Run on the desktop and paste the text into the Open: text field. Click OK. You'll see a Console window pop up very briefly, which shows the new .CAB file being generated. Now you can copy the .CAB file in the installer directory back into the CD1 directory. Next, remove the old Pocket PC application via Start • Settings • System • Remove Programs and run the Setup.exe program on the desktop again. Now check on your Pocket PC, and the shortcut will have been correctly added to your Start Menu.

Table 6.1: List of macro strings defining Pocket PC directories

Macro String	Pocket PC Directory
%CE1%	\Program Files
%CE2%	\Windows
%CE4%	\Windows\StartUp
%CE5%	\My Documents
%CE6%	\Program Files\Accessories
%CE7%	\Program Files\Communication
%CE8%	\Program Files\Games
%CE11%	\Windows\Start Menu\Programs
%CE12%	\Windows\Start Menu\Programs\Accessories
%CE13%	\Windows\Start Menu\Programs\Communications
%CE14%	\Windows\Start Menu\Programs\Games
%CE15%	\Windows\Fonts
%CE17%	\Windows\Start Menu

Customizing the Application Icon

You'll notice that all eVB applications come with a generic icon that is non-customizable. In order to place your own stamp of identity on your eVB projectors, you'll want to create a small .exe file that has your own unique icon: That way, any Shortcuts pointing to this .exe file will adopt the icon.

Tony Jones has created the Launch application (found in the Launch directory of the Chapter 6 folder on the CD-ROM), which is a simple .exe launch generator. Follow the instructions in the application's help system to create your own launchers. This excellent freeware application does have an occasional quirk where the .exe files generated sometimes have a semicolon (;) character appended to the end of the file name, which then prohibits it from launching correctly. Simply check within the Explorer window of ActiveSync and rename the file without the offending semicolon. Launch will load standard .ICO files and generate the launcher with these icons. If you like, you can use the accompanying Pike icon generator to create icon files using your Pocket PC. Pike is found in the same directory. Note that these applications are written in a language called PocketC and require the free PocketC runtime to be installed on your device. The PocketC runtime can be found in the same directory, labeled pkcrt_pocketpc.exe.

eVC applications are compiled with custom icons of your own choosing. The icons are imported resources and can be altered within the Resource View of the Workspace pane within eVC. If you have problems, you should consult the eVC documentation for more information.

Providing an End-User Licensing Agreement

Although the standard installer provided by Microsoft does the job, it does lack niceties such as the ability to display an end-user licensing agreement before the application is installed. *End-user license agreements* (EULA) normally define and protect the developers' and end users' legal rights and responsibilities. Fortunately, a freeware installer takes the .CAB and .INI files we've been working with and generates a more professional looking installer application that incorporates EULAs and readmes as well. The EZSetup program by Scott Ludwig is available from http://www.eskimo.com/~scottlu/win/index.html.

Summary

In this chapter, you've learned how to create standalone Flash Projectors for the Pocket PC. These custom applications can render Flash content in a variety of sizes and have many advantages over running Flash content with Pocket Internet Explorer. We've examined strategies for creating such wrapper applications using eVB and eVC and the relative advantages of each language. Finally, we've examined the advantages of creating a professional installer for your Flash application, so that end users receive an optimal experience from the moment they begin to install your application. Chapter 7 will show you how to take your Flash applications to the next level using eVB and eVC applications that communicate with an integrated Flash user interface to create media-rich Flash applications.

7

FLASH FOR THE ENTERPRISE

Ian Chia

This chapter explores how eMbedded Visual Basic (eVB) and eMbedded Visual Basic C++ (eVC) applications can communicate with an integrated Flash user interface to create media-rich Flash applications while retaining the power of eVB or eVC for your enterprise systems.

Because Flash is by nature an interactive visual medium, Flash applications can be more intuitive to use than typical eMbedded Visual Basic (eVB) or eMbedded Visual C++ (eVC) applications. Flash is more than eye candy: It allows sophisticated visual and aural interfaces to be designed rapidly and elegantly. By connecting Flash ActionScript with business application logic in eVB or eVC, you can offer Flash enterprise applications that connect to a complex backend system, enabling media-rich applications that would be enormously difficult to create if they were to implemented with other tools.

No Limits

Most business applications for Pocket PC (PPC) are developed in eMbedded Visual Basic or eMbedded Visual C++, because these languages offer deep integration with Windows CE. That means that they facilitate basic tasks like file system access, connection to a network via a broad range of protocols, direct access to local and networked data stores, and communication with distributed business logic.

Flash lacks many of these abilities, however, because it started as an animation program and then evolved into a browser plug-in. Security issues require that browsers and their component plugins cannot have the same deep system access afforded to eVB or eVC. ActiveX controls embedded in a browser have strict security restrictions to prohibit hackers from sending your private information to undisclosed destinations on the Internet.

Nonetheless, many Flash front-end applications have built that deep system connection by working with middleware and backend services. Traditional business applications—including retail systems, hotel reservations, calendars, floor plan design, banking, and marketing—use Flash instead of HTML or Java because Flash offers end users many advantages, including elegant interfaces, interactive visuals, rich audio, and customized branding.

But what if we could have the best of both worlds—rich Flash interfaces and presentations with the power of eVB or eVC—in the same application? Then, instead of relying on the PPC's ActiveX controls, you could have a fully branded, media-rich application on your device. The answer is that you can. This chapter covers techniques that allow Flash to exchange messages with eVB and eVC to enable powerful, integrated applications. With this solution, business needs—such as dynamic charts, live mapping, illustrations, and animations—can all become the front end of a sophisticated enterprise application.

What Is an "Enterprise?"

The term *enterprise* usually refers to corporate systems or distributed data that's accessible throughout an organization. Planning systems, workgroup applications, factory floor control systems, health care applications, large corporate databases, and mainframe computer applications are all examples of corporate enterprises.

Enterprise applications are specialized by nature and are often designed to work for specific audiences, with only relevant data presented within custom interfaces. Although Windows CE's standard user interface controls are sufficient for many business applications, it's very difficult to use Windows CE to create a strong visual interface because of the amount of coding involved and because of the limited 240 × 320 pixel screen size. Flash, by contrast, offers the ability to create intuitive visual and aural interfaces integrated with the normal application logic and services demanded by eVB and eVC enterprise applications.

Communicating Between eVB/eVC and ActionScript

To build effective Flash-based applications, Flash ActionScript must be able to pass data back and forth to the "host" environment. The basic standalone applications covered in Chapter 6 allow the Flash movie to be displayed only within an HTML page, using basic JScript communication between the page and the SWF movie. Clearly, enterprise applications need far more than we can derive from simple JScript access to browser cookies.

Unfortunately, because of Pocket Internet Explorer's limitations, the Flash Player for PPC hasn't implemented fscommand, which is the way Flash typically sends one-way messages to host applications on the desktop. Fortunately, we can achieve two-way asynchronous communication between Flash and the underlying application logic via an eVB/eVC program.

fscommand: The Old Way of Communicating in ActionScript

Compared with the desktop Flash Player, the Pocket PC Flash Player has a lot of problems, many of which stem from its use of fscommand to enable communication between Flash and the "host" environment. Desktop versions of the Macromedia Flash Player include the fscommand action that can send a one-way message to a JScript or VBScript function within a browser.

Standalone Flash Players are also capable of a range of fscommands that are specific to the needs of a standalone application. (We discussed this capability in Chapter 5, where we showed the workaround for delivering similar functionality on the PPC.) Furthermore, when embedded within a Windows application, Flash can also use fscommand to send messages from the Flash ActiveX control to the C++ or Visual Basic host application.

But in all three circumstances (whether working with the Flash Player in a web page or the standalone player, or when Flash is embedded in a Windows application), messaging between the host and Flash on the Pocket PC is difficult. For one, fscommand isn't implemented. Too, you can't directly embed Flash into an eVB or eVC application.

Because Pocket Internet Explorer (PIE) has a different ActiveX interface than the desktop IE browsers, Macromedia was forced to engineer the browser control portion of the Flash Player for PIE so that it works only when loaded within a HTML page. Consequently, embedding the control directly within eVB and eVC and using the typical techniques for desktop development produce incompatible results. In this scenario, the PPC Flash Player is unable to load any SWFs from the file system. And, without fscommands, Flash has no way to send a message to the host environment outside of PIE and JavaScript.

So, rather than struggle with this mess to develop enterprise applications for deployment on the PPC, we needed a totally different mechanism for transporting messages between Flash and the host application. The light came on when we realized that we could use Flash's TCP/IP socket support to create a new messaging transport outside of the usual fscommand and getURL's JavaScript techniques!

Bidirectional Messaging Using the Flash XMLSocket Object

The Flash ActionScript XMLSocket object offers a convenient, standard way to support bidirectional communication between a Flash movie and an eVB or eVC application. The XMLSocket object creates a persistent TCP/IP socket connection within the Flash application to a simple socket server, running in turn as a component of an eVB or eVC application. Once the connection is made, the XMLSocket object acts as a transmitter and receiver, messaging data to and from eVB/eVC.

NOTE *Although the XMLSocket object is intended for XML-formatted data, it can accept either plain string data or XML.*

The XMLSocket object has two limitations:

- The TCP/IP socket connection must occur on a port greater or equal to 1024. This security restriction is by design and prohibits hackers from creating Flash applications that attack Internet services assigned to officially numbered ports. These so-called "privileged" ports support common services, including http (port 80), ftp (port 21), pop (port 110), smtp (port 25) and others. When using XMLSocket on a PPC, you should avoid ports 5678 and 5679 because these are used by Microsoft's ActiveSync. (ActiveSync also uses ports 990 and 999, but these port numbers are below 1024 and inaccessible to XMLSocket.)

- Data sent and received is terminated by a byte with a zero value (also known as the ASCII null character). Therefore, you cannot send binary data containing zero bytes unless you convert the data to a text-encoded form, such as Base64 or BinHex. (You'll find links to third-party ActionScript libraries for safely encoding binary data at www.flashthefuture.com/7.)

Connecting from Flash ActionScript

Because the XMLSocket object is a native socket client, all you need to do to create a socket connection using Flash 5 is to create an instance and call the connect method. The following two lines show how to create an instance and store it in the mySocketClient variable. Once the XMLSocket instance is created, it executes the connect() method, which attempts to connect to the localhost server on port 5000.

```
mySocketClient = new XMLSocket();
mySocketClient.connect("localhost", 5000 );
```

NOTE Localhost *is a networking term that describes the actual machine that the code is running on, and the localhost domain always has the IP address 127.0.0.1. As discussed in Chapter 5, a PPC stores host entries within the registry, but always has the localhost/127.0.0.1 entry created by default.*

Asynchronous Messages: Doing Other Stuff While Hanging Around

When communicating with another person, we're used to asynchronous dialog, which simply means that both ends can talk at the same time. A telephone is an asynchronous device, because you don't have to wait for the other party to stop before you can say something. Synchronous communication is the opposite—a listener waits until the other end has finished sending its message. Walkie-talkies are an example of synchronous communications; each listener must wait for the closing "Over" phrase to know that the speaker has finished before jumping in with their own message.

Asynchronous communication is vital for our Flash application, because it allows us to execute other items, such as animations or scripting, while waiting on a command from the eVB or eVC host. Without asynchronous communication, the Flash movie would seem unresponsive, locking up until it received a message from the host.

Callbacks

XMLSocket *callbacks* allow our Flash applications to use asynchronous communication. As the name suggests, a callback is a way to interrupt the current flow of thought and force execution down a different track.

ActionScript handles the callback by allowing the programmer to register a function for different events. As the program runs, a background process checks for cues to trigger that event. When the event occurs, the function that's registered for the event is "called back," and the function executes. Once the function has completed, the program continues from where it was interrupted.

The XMLSocket object has a few different callbacks, but the onData callback is the most useful for incoming messages. This callback is triggered when the XMLSocket object receives a string terminated by a zero byte. If the onData callback has been registered when it receives this string, the message (minus the terminator byte) is passed to the callback function as a string argument.

The syntax for onData is simply

```
mySocketObjectInstance.onData = myMessageParserFunction;
```

where myMessageParserFunction is a normal ActionScript function defined earlier in the code. It's important to define this function *before* the onData callback is registered, because ActionScript needs to have an existing function for the callback to refer to—if no function exists, the callback will be ignored.

The Note on page 188 mentioned that the XMLSocket object can send and receive either plain-text or XML messages. Recall the discussion in Chapter 5, where you learned about ActionScript's slow XML performance on the PPC. We can join those two concepts to create a workable method by limiting the bulk of our communication between Flash and the host to simple text strings, thus bypassing any XML parsing and associated performance hits.

In cases where XML has a clear advantage over plain text, we can register the callback "onXML" instead. Instead of being triggered by the reception of a terminated message, this callback will be triggered once the message has been parsed into a XML tree.

The syntax for onXML is very similar to other callbacks, as shown here:

```
mySocketObjectInstance.onXML = myMessageParserFunction;
```

Sending a message is simple. Once an instance of the XMLObject has been created, use the send method to create an outgoing message.

```
mySocketObjectInstance.send(theMessageString);
```

Because the incoming messages are stripped of their zero byte terminators before being passed into the callback functions, the send method doesn't require a zero byte to be manually appended to the message string. Flash automatically adds the closing zero byte as it sends the message over the socket connection. The outgoing message can be a plain-text string, an XML-formatted string, or an XML object with standard nodes and attributes.

Successful Messaging Strategies

Although Flash 5's XML performance isn't optimal, there is a way to obtain fast XML performance in the messaging system.

Because ActionScript is very slow at parsing XML documents, it's faster to *receive* short plain-text messages than it is to receive comparable XML documents. But XML performance in eVB or eVC is *much* faster than with ActionScript, so it's okay to *send* XML from Flash as long as we try to avoid any parsing before sending. Thus, if your needs favor XML over plain text, one solution is to send outgoing messages as an XML-formatted string and to receive incoming messages as plain text—or to manage your XML data by keeping it stored mostly within attributes rather than nodes.

The following code creates a temporary XML object to parse a string into a valid DOM tree before sending—but, unfortunately, with a resultant XML parsing hit:

```
var message = "<command><msg>Sample Message</msg></command>";
var tempXMLMessage = new XML();
tempXMLMessage.parseXML(message);
mySocketInstance.send(message)
```

To avoid the XML parsing bottleneck, send a string formatted as XML. This reduces the outgoing code to the following line, without the performance hit above:

```
mySocketInstance.send("<command><msg>Sample Message</msg></command>");
```

Now, for outgoing code. If you are forced to accept incoming XML messages, follow the XML strategies discussed in Chapter 5's Optimizing XML Performance topic. If you keep nodes to a minimum by encoding information within attributes, you'll keep the XML parsing performance hit to a minimum.

Exchanging Large Datasets Between the Host Wrapper and ActionScript

When a project must use large amounts of XML data to communicate, remember that XML parsing can rapidly consume memory as the parsing process constructs the tree of nodes. Also, the abort script alert may be triggered if parsing takes longer than 20 seconds. To avoid both of these problems, exchange the XML information in sections rather than all at once by creating some form of exchange protocol with the server that allows the server to send a limited range of datasets. By going back and forth and breaking the data exchange into smaller packets, the Flash movie will successively process the data. Once the XML packet is parsed, Flash sends a continue message back to the server, which in turn sends the next block, and so on.

Programming eVB or eVC Socket Server

A thorough discussion of Winsock programming is beyond the scope of this chapter, but you will find detailed information in the PPC SDK in the Microsoft Windows CE • Communications, Networking and Telephony Services • Windows Sockets section. A single-client socket server is not a particularly difficult piece of software engineering, and you'll find further documentation and example source code in the Winsock Sample Applications • TCP Stream Socket Server section of the same documentation directory.

This chapter provides working demonstrations of eVB and eVC socket servers with full source code (available in the Chapter 7 directory of the CD-ROM). Both the eVB and eVC socket servers follow the principles outlined by the Microsoft documentation.

Integration with Java, Python, or Perl

If your projects are built with languages other than eVB or eVC, the XMLSocket approach will work just as well, provided your application can include a socket server. The PPC runs Java, Python, or Perl very successfully, and a socket server written in any of these languages will happily communicate with Flash using all the same principles. The Flash user interface must still be hosted within an eVB or eVC wrapper, because Flash for PPC must be displayed within a HTML page. Flash can, however, communicate with other background applications because the socket communication is language-agnostic, so don't discount the opportunities to use Java, Python, or Perl if your project warrants it. This approach is also worth bearing in mind for future device platforms where the Flash Player may have limited integration with the platform.

Integrating eVB and Flash

Microsoft provides a notoriously buggy Winsock eVB ActiveX control that wraps the Winsock PPC API into a form that eVB can call. Fortunately, Pete Vickers of GUI Innovations (www.gui-innovations.com), a PPC developer and consultant, has created a superior solution called CESockets.

CESockets is a DLL that can be instantiated as an object within eVB. CESockets mirrors the standard Winsock API calls, which means that a socket server can be created very easily. In fact, the socket server example discussed below is a minor adaptation of Pete's chat socket server example that was tweaked to accommodate sending the zero byte terminators that Flash requires.

NOTE *Check out the CESockets folder in the Chapter 7 directory of the CD-ROM for more on the functionality of CESockets (including IRDA capabilities).*

To help you to unravel the integration of eVB and Flash, we've included an example: The bidirectional_eVB_Flash5 folder in the Chapter 7 directory of the CD-ROM contains a Flash client for exchanging messages with an eVB application. If you examine the code, you'll see that Flash can send messages to the eVB server as the contents of a text field. The eVB application sends messages to Flash in a similar fashion, but adds four short text commands that can trigger animation within the Flash movie: .go and .stop will start and stop radio broadcast waves animating; .day and .night will change the background sky color. These messages are received by the onData callback, and some simple ActionScript controls the relevant movie clips in response.

As an example of the integration of eVB and Flash, Figure 7.1 shows the Flash interface of a small planet with radio broadcast towers. A message entered in the text field is sent to eVB by clicking the arrow button. The second text field displays the messages from eVB.

Figure 7.1: The Flash socket client.

Figure 7.2 shows a standard-looking eVB application with text fields and form buttons. The socket server is a component of this application and is called to receive and send any information on the same port number that is shared by the Flash movie.

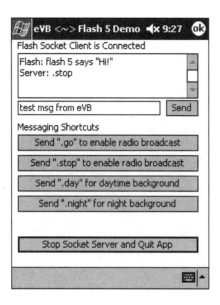

Figure 7.2: The eVB socket server.

The CESockets DLL has one limitation: It pauses all execution of the eVB application while it's waiting for the initial socket to connect. Not only is the eVB application halted while the socket server waits, but any ActiveX controls within the application are also brought to a standstill, including the HTML viewer and the accompanying Flash movie. Therefore, it's not possible to have a single integrated Flash/eVB application using this DLL solution. Fortunately, though, Pete Vickers is (as of this writing) developing an ActiveX version of CESockets that should solve this problem. For updates, you can check the relevant area of our website, www.flashthefuture.com/7.

To run the bidirectional_eVB_Flash5 demo, do the following:

1. Copy the bidirectional_eVB_Flash5 directory into the \My Documents folder of your PPC.

2. Copy the two shortcuts within the above directory into the \Windows\Start Menu folder and the CESockets.dll into the \Windows folder of your device.

3. Launch the socket server by selecting it from the Start Menu icon.

4. Launch the Flash socket client within the Start Menu.

5. Use the Start Menu to exchange messages between the two applications and to switch between them.

6. When you've finished playing, close the socket server by clicking the top right OK button and accepting the CESockets demo registration warning. (It's highly recommended that you close the socket server before the Flash socket client to avoid hanging sockets and finding that you need to perform a soft reset!)

7. Finally, close the Flash socket client by clicking the top right OK button. Even though the CESockets DLL doesn't allow the full integration of Flash into a single eVB program, you can, for the most part, hide the fact that this is a two-application system from the end user by using the CreateProcess API to launch the Flash user interface once the socket server has successfully started. Thus, users don't need to be aware of a background server application; all they need to see is the Flash front end.

Once both applications have completed the task, terminate them with these steps:

1. Detect the eVB Form_OKClick in the Flash socket client.

2. Send a message to the server to terminate the server.

3. Server closes the socket and closes the Flash socket client via the API's TerminateProcess call.

4. Server then quits via eVB's App.End.

NOTE *In order for this approach to work best, the application should be configured to prevent the user from switching applications via the Start menu or via the hardware buttons (see Chapter 6, page XX).*

Integrating eVC and Flash

Our demo eVC server takes a slightly different approach to integrated messaging. Because eVC can easily thread tasks, it's easy to produce integrated Flash applications. And, because this application messages data back and forth and does extensive processing in both ActionScript and eVC to massage the information into the XML we require, it is an excellent example of how comprehensive data exchange can be created in Flash/eVB or eVC applications.

NOTE *The bidirectional_eVC_Flash5 folder in the Chapter 7 directory of the CD-ROM contains a demonstration of a standalone application with full source code from expert Flash and C++ developer Greg Birch. Greg's application uses many techniques discussed in the previous section regarding eVB, but instead of using plain text to communicate, Greg's application uses XML-formatted data to exchange information between Flash and the eVC socket server.*

Figure 7.3 shows Greg's standalone application with the Flash movie embedded (within our now-familiar HTML View object). In this application, the eVC server retrieves the root directory of the PPC and sends the data into Flash. Flash then parses the XML stream using SAX (see Chapter 5) and reformats the XML data into an HTML table displayed within a Flash text field. Directories are hyperlinked using the undocumented ASFunction action, which calls an ActionScript function from hyperlinks within Flash HTML text fields.

The syntax for a text field is similar to the following:

```
<a href="ASFunction:_root.getDir,\My Documents\">
```

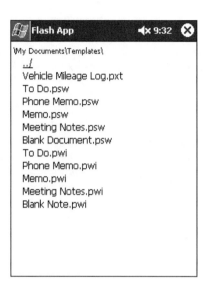

Figure 7.3: Using Flash to browse directories on your PPC.

The demonstration has one (intentional) gotcha, though. Whereas it lets you browse through the directories on your machines as long the information sent by the eVC socket server isn't very complex, the application will hang on directories such as the \Windows folder. Greg suggests that you consider these three key points when creating your applications:

1. Large XML documents are difficult for Flash to process in one hit. If you have an Ethernet connection between your desktop and your PPC, tweak the connect() method so it points to the IP address of your PPC, using syntax similar to the following line. You may need to substitute the IP address for the correct one on your network.

```
test.connect( "192.168.0.1", 5000 );
```

Then run the Flash client on your desktop and the socket server on your PPC. (Rename the HTML or SWF file on your PPC so the integrated Flash movie won't load, or you'll have two clients trying to connect.) On a Pentium III 500MHz desktop, it takes approximately 15 seconds to display the PPC's Windows directory. The 206MHz StrongARM usually requires 10 to 20 times more time to execute the same ActionScript, which will lock up the machine and eventually display the script alert dialog. (You can address this issue with the pseudo-threading technique discussed in Chapter 5, page 140.)

2. The RAM consumed is excessive when parsing the XML generated by the Windows directory—it uses about 13MB of memory before releasing it. This is an issue for low-memory devices such as PPC's. To address this, try to manage the exchange of datasets in smaller blocks. By avoiding large XML structures, you can keep memory usage within acceptable limits.

3. Although this issue isn't as apparent on the desktop, once the XML is parsed, there's a much longer processing time, which is likely to be Flash processing the HTML text field and rendering it onto the screen. This is about two to three times longer than the actual SAX parse. Again, you can improve rendering speeds by using techniques to successively add data into Flash over a number of data exchanges.

NOTE *The demonstration project is clearly commented for the eVC developer to examine, but the socket server is beta quality and should not be relied on in a commercial production setting. For example, there is no clear way to terminate this application—the user has to use an application switcher such as iTask to quit. Greg continues to work on this project, so there should be more stable releases at www.ultrashock.com/tutorials/devices.php, or you can look for updates at www.flashthefuture.com/7. The FlashAssist Pro product, discussed in Chapter 6, provides a localhost XMLSocket server in its data store implementation, which can be customized to different needs. Consult www.antmobile.com for more information.*

Security Issues with a Localhost Socket Server

Running a server from your localhost IP address poses some security issues that should be addressed for any commercial application. Remember the following when designing a real-world application:

- Lock down all but local access to your server. If your PPC is connected to the Internet or intranet during normal use, the simplest way to ensure that all commands originate from the PPC is to allow only connections from the localhost or 127.0.0.1 IP address. For example, if you use the PPC Winsock getpeername method to retrieve the peer address to which a socket is connected, you can dismiss all other socket-connected requests.

- If you're still concerned that your host application can receive messages only from the Flash movie and not other local applications, create some simple authentication between the embedded Flash movie and the server.

- If you're running a local firewall application on the device, open the port up for localhost access. Otherwise, the device's firewall security will prevent Flash-to-host socket communication.

You're highly unlikely to encounter a situation that merits authentication, but you should consider locking down access to the localhost from external IP addresses for any publicly released application, especially if you are unaware of the applications installed on the end user's device.

Summary

Fully integrated Flash and eVB/eVC applications can provide compelling solutions for the enterprise by mixing the best of both Flash and the PPC environment. The strategies discussed enable host applications with Flash visuals and audio in the front end and complex business logic in the underlying eVB/eVC.

It's relatively easy to use Flash's native support for sockets via the XMLSocket object to build a messaging system that can communicate bidirectionally with the host. Messages can be sent in plain text or XML formats, and robust solutions can be designed, as long as you design your code to avoid the common pitfalls on the Pocket PC (such as excessive memory and CPU consumption and possible security issues when running a local socket server).

Now that you've seen how robust a Flash application can be on the PPC, in Chapter 8, we will change gears and consider what can be done to streamline the process of dynamically updating Flash content with server-side products, using tools such as JGenerator MX.

8

GENERATOR AND FLASH

Larry Drolet

Initially released as a separate product (known as the Generator Authoring Templates) for Flash 3, Macromedia Generator has gone through one major revision and two minor upgrades. The last version, Generator version 2, release 3, was released in April 2001.

Built from the JRun platform, Generator is an outstanding Java 2 Enterprise Edition (J2EE) application service for backend and server-side Flash and image creation.

Generator can be indispensable when you're developing Flash content for versions 4 and 5. This chapter will prepare you to deliver content to both PPCs and desktops—dynamically, from the same basic Flash movie.

This chapter introduces Generator and explains what it can do for the development of Flash movies, especially those that target the PPC. Chapter 9 will continue the discussion of Generator as it delves into the development of increasingly more advanced Generator-based applications.

NOTE *Generator technology is not dead. In fact, with the announcement of JGenerator 2.1 in July 2002, Generator took a bold new step. JGenerator version 2.1 MX allows for the dynamic server-side creation of Flash MX files. Much like the deprecated Macromedia Generator, JGenerator is a server-side tool for creating Flash movies through an online and offline mode. JGenerator is compatible with Generator template files (.swt, Flash 5 format) and in some cases will increase performance up to 20 times. JGenerator only outputs SWF files, although the integration with Flash MX, charting tools, dynamic text effects, and use of XML data sources make this product superior to the previous version of JGenerator and Macromedia Generator.*

JGenerator is available from JZox.com in three flavors: Community edition (free), Developer edition ($125), and Enterprise edition ($435). What a difference from Macromedia Generator pricing! The Developer edition can be installed on a desktop and used for development of dynamic Flash files, although the Enterprise edition is needed to run JGenerator on a production server. Also necessary for JGenerator in a production environment is a servlet engine; the JZox.com site goes into detail about the various options. To put it simply, Generator technology is exceptional and JGenerator is going to be an incredible addition to what this technology can offer over the Internet.

What Is Generator?

Generator is an extension of Flash. In fact, Generator is to Flash what middleware, such as JSP, is to HTML. Although Flash excels at the creation of presentations and movies by combining multiple media (text, images, sound, video, and multimedia) into a single Flash movie, it cannot do so on the fly. Generator allows Flash movies to insert content dynamically, without using the LoadMovie or LoadVariables ActionScript methods. Although Generator and several similar products are obtained separately from Flash, they should not necessarily be thought of as separate products.

NOTE *In this chapter, all references to "Generator" imply Macromedia Generator; references to "Generator technology" may include Generator as well as all similar programs that create dynamic Flash movies. The term "dynamic Flash" indicates movies created using Generator objects.*

Think of Generator as a kind of middleware. When an Internet user requests a middleware page from a browser, the webserver finds the web page and processes the server-side script (VBScript or PHP, for example) and delivers the final HTML to the browser. Behind the scenes, the webserver uses an engine to translate the server-side script and perform various functions in order to display the correct data. This translation process occurs after the initial request and before the final result is delivered; the term "middleware" describes this process in the middle.

Many websites today use middleware languages—such as Active Server Pages (ASP), PHP, Java Server Pages (JSP), or Perl—to process information on the fly and deliver dynamic web page designs and content. Creating a middleware page is like creating an HTML page: The coding process is slightly different, reflecting the blocks of code that a webserver will process, but the end result is the same—a web page.

Many developers use HomeSite to create HTML, and you can use this same program (but with a different syntax) to create ASP middleware. Like middleware, Generator content is created by adapting something you are already using. As stated earlier, Generator is an extension of Flash in the same way that JSP is an extension of HTML. In both cases, the final result that's delivered from the script, or code, will be far different from what was written. Like their middleware counterpart, Generator movies will not play unless they are first processed by a server-side (or development) process. When a Generator movie is delivered, either locally or via a browser, it can include more data than it held when it was created, but it is simply a Flash movie, as shown in Figure 8.1.

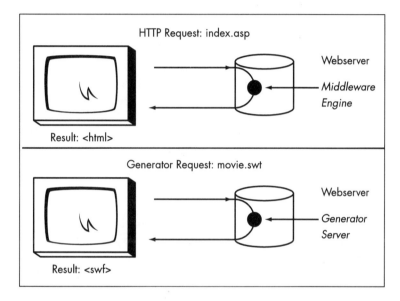

Figure 8.1: Middleware and Generator processes.

This relationship works because Flash uses Generator objects as placeholders to represent content (text, images, and other Flash elements) that will be served when the movie is generated. Before Generator objects can be served, they must be processed at the server or locally on a development platform, as in Flash. Middleware pages will not display correctly without first being translated by the server. If you were to view an ASP page before running it through the webserver, for example, you would see a lot of code and little, if any, content. The situation is similar with Generator: Unless the Generator objects are first processed, a Flash movie built with Generator objects (a Generator movie) will display the Flash movie without any of the dynamic content.

Generator Products

There are three versions of Generator: Authoring, Developer, Enterprise editions. The latter two are designed to be installed and managed from a webserver. (See the documentation at the Macromedia site for a list of existing platform configurations—www.macromedia.com/support/generator).

Both the Enterprise and Developer versions will produce the same result; the main differences between them being their price and the way they implement Generator. The Authoring Edition is probably the most widely used and, unfortunately, the least known. It is included with Flash 5 and enables dynamic movie generation from a development environment. The following sections will describe each product in detail to help you decide which version you need.

Authoring Edition (AE)

The Authoring Edition (AE) of Generator is included with Flash 5 and is thus your least expensive version. AE is a great tool for local development of dynamic Flash movies that will be loaded to the Internet. But, unlike the other versions, AE does not let you perform any backend integration or on-the-fly content insertion—although, with ingenuity, you can simulate some of this functionality locally. When you create a Flash movie that you know will be subject to frequent changes, it makes sense to develop it for easy adjustments, and AE can make this a feasible solution.

Developer Edition (DE)

The Developer Edition (DE) is the scaled-down version of the Enterprise Edition and is sold at approximately a third of the cost. It is geared more for development and backend usage. DE can do almost everything the more robust version is capable of doing, except that it has limited ability to process many movies quickly for realtime Internet use. As such, DE is better suited for backend processing. However, this version can use only one processor on the webserver and is single threaded. Having a single thread means that DE can process only one task at a time, whereas multiple-thread capability allows a server to process several tasks at once without queuing tasks one after another. Thus, if DE is loaded on a multiprocessor server, Generator can use only half of the available processing power.

Enterprise Edition (EE)

The Enterprise Edition (EE) is the solution for high-volume sites that need dynamically created content. In addition to backend processing, EE can use multiprocessors (if available) on the webserver for an even faster result. EE also includes a caching tool, which allocates such content as fonts, images, and other Flash movies to memory for extremely swift retrieval. This caching adds to EE's utility for realtime content delivery.

To determine which version to purchase, ask yourself: "Do we need to process the site content (specifically Flash movies) on the fly, how often will we need to do so, and how much content is there?" If you find that little time is involved and a low number of adjustments will have to be made, consider AE or

DE. As time and adjustments increase, you will move up to a DE or EE solution until the site or application volume reaches a point where EE is the only viable option. See Figure 8.2 for a comparison.

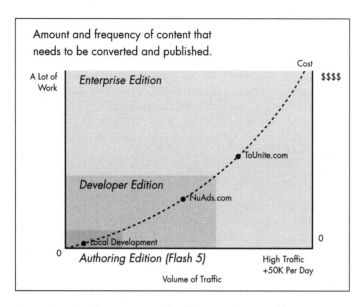

Figure 8.2: Generator matrix work-traffic-cost comparison.

Before we get into the nitty-gritty details of working with Generator to manage content for delivery on PPCs, let's consider a more general real-world situation where Generator would be useful. The greeting card site, like www.ToUnite.com, is a good example of where Generator can be useful, because it has both high volume and constantly changing content, and it uses EE to serve dynamically created Flash greetings.

In lieu of creating a slew of Flash movies, this site uses one base movie to load in all images, sounds, and text. Because it uses EE, this one base movie becomes the pivot to create an array of unique experiences. Consequently, updating and managing the content is simplified because the content—which is seasonal and changeable and constantly needs to be updated—has been separated from the base movie (the FLA).

The site www.NuAds.com is another good example of a Generator implementation. This company offers its clients the opportunity to create Flash-based commercials for use with its parent company's network, the NuWays Network. The challenges here are that the commercials are personalized for each client and must be complete Flash movies, with no Generator placeholders. All of this has to occur on a server so that the client can manage its own commercials, a hands-off operation for the NuWays Flash development department. Given that the movies need to be created on the backend, and site traffic is such that it does not appear to be causing any load problems, DE is the best choice. However, once traffic reaches a certain level and the number of movies created each hour surpasses a predetermined number, an upgrade to EE will be required.

When a server is not available for you to use Generator EE or DE, then AE will be more than adequate. Remember that Generator operates with placeholders, which are replaced with data when processed (published or exported in a local environment). This data is referred to as variable data and can be as simple as a text file with a list of variables to be replaced. This text file can simulate the results of a database record set, and it is possible to copy and paste the results of a middleware file into this text file and replicate the use of middleware in the local authoring environment. Although AE is not a solution for dynamic content that requires constant adjustments, it is a good solution for local development and for practicing with Generator technology.

Generator Alternatives

Generator is not the only software solution for dynamically creating Flash movies. The following is a list of several alternatives:

- Swift-Generator by Swift-Tools (www.swift-tools.com) is an interesting alternative that uses an additional file (Swift Script File [SWS]) for processing the dynamic variables. The Swift-Generator forum on www.flashkit.com offers additional support.

- ASP or PHP Flash Turbine by Blue*Pacific Software (www.blue-pac.com) requires a good understanding of ASP or PHP for effective use. Flashkit.com also maintains a Turbine forum for additional help and questions.

- JGenerator, by Dmitry Skavish (www.flashgap.com), is an open-source project (Apache-style license), built to emulate Macromedia's Generator. With many developers adding to this project, it has the potential to grow quickly.

- Ming by Opaque Industries (http://ming.sourceforge.net) requires PHP and is script intensive. An online forum is available at www.f256.com/forum/?db=ming.

- X-Wave by SAXESS Software Design (www.saxess.com/wave) converts XML into SWF via a proprietary language, SWFML. It requires a Java virtual machine and may not support all versions of Flash.

- StarFish by Andrew Stopford (www.a-coda.com) is not necessarily an alternative to Generator but rather a tool to use Macromedia Generator from a server-side scripting environment. StarFish is a component object model (COM) object, which allows for the server-side generation via a script like ASP.

Why Generator and Dynamic Flash?

What is the most important and most expensive item in business and development? Time! Generator can reduce the time involved in extended development and thereby increase the speed and efficiency of delivery. Granted, the initial development of dynamic Flash movies might take slightly longer, but the time needed to make subsequent changes will be substantially shorter. When using Generator AE, instead of tearing open the Flash movie and adjusting the movie itself, you can open the appropriate variable text file and make the adjustment there. Once you make that edit, you simply republish, or export, the Flash movie to implement the desired change.

Generator is an outstanding tool for making such changes easily and, when DE or EE is used on a webserver, it's even easier to make a change. Flash movies containing Generator objects on the webserver (with the file extension .swt) are known as templates because the Generator server has yet to process them. (Generator movies are typically referred to as SWTs.) The Generator objects point to variables that are usually implemented as data files and are updated from a database. The templates wait until they are requested by a user or a back-end application and are then processed with dynamic content. Flash does not enter the process here at all; the server does all of the work of replacing the placeholders with dynamic content. With this structure in place, you can make changes by updating the database files, either dynamically or manually.

Although developing for the PPC and similar devices is a new arena for developers, it is not that much different from developing Flash in general. Creating dynamic Flash with Generator objects makes development faster and easier, and it leaves more time to research new ways to make this process even better.

Generator for the PPC

Because of the PPC's limited screen size, there are some obvious differences in how a Flash movie is initially created. Limitations on content sizing, colors, playback speed, online interaction, and ActionScripting all factor into how Flash is developed for the PPC. However, Generator can help you overcome some of these limitations when you are developing content for multiple platforms. Too, because Generator is an extension of Flash, there are no additional limitations to be suffered when using Generator to create your Flash movies.

Generator can be particularly valuable to us when developing for the PPC because Generator's use of placeholders allows us to pull from varied databases. Because these placeholders are filled only with Flash elements once the movie is processed, they can be filled with data designed specifically for each device. This gives us greater flexibility, because the data for the PPC will most likely differ from what is used in a normal desktop browser, given the PPC's smaller screen size and limited memory.

Although it may seem difficult to drive the same Flash movie with varied database content and to target those databases according to specific devices, Generator makes it simple. A Flash movie created with a Generator object can be used for both the browser and the PPC, with no need to create two movies. Depending on the device, the placeholder for the content looks for that dynamic content either locally or on the server.

As shown in Figure 8.3, two sets of database records can be used: one to return data for the desktop and another to return data for the PPC or "other" device. Targeting the location of data can be done very easily in Flash and is even possible outside Flash. (The examples that begin on page 212 will explain this concept in greater detail.)

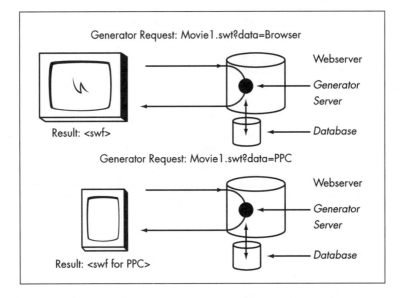

Figure 8.3: The Generator movie's online request from a browser and a PPC.

Using Generator

If you are already familiar with Flash and understand middleware, you probably understand how to use Generator. Developing with Generator for the PPC is surprisingly similar to developing for the desktop.

Regardless of platform, Generator must be told what content to use. This process of sending Generator the needed information for creating dynamic Flash movies can be accomplished with four different modes:

- Online
- Offline
- Online-offline
- Authoring Edition

Let's look at each mode.

Online Mode

Generator can be served by EE or DE only when it is in online mode. Online mode is designed to facilitate the realtime replacement of content without the need to create completely separate Flash movies.

By using the Object and Embed commands in HTML, as with regular Flash movies, only the movie extension changes, as well as a query string, if relevant. The extension of a Generator movie is .swt (Shockwave template), and the query string consists of the name-value pairings that follow the question mark after the extension. For example:

```
<OBJECT classid="clsid:D27CDB6E-AE6D-11cf-96B8-444553540000"
codebase="http://download.macromedia.com/pub/shockwave/cabs/
flash/swflash.cab#version=5,0,0,0"
WIDTH=550
HEIGHT=400>
 <PARAM NAME=movie VALUE="Movie1.swt?x=text+message&day=Monday">
 <PARAM NAME=quality VALUE=high>
 <PARAM NAME=bgcolor VALUE=#FFFFFF>
<EMBED src="Movie1.swt?x=text+message&day=Monday"
quality=high
bgcolor=#FFFFFF
WIDTH=550
HEIGHT=400
TYPE="application/x-shockwave-flash"
PLUGINSPAGE="http://www.macromedia.com/shockwave/download/
index.cgi?P1_Prod_Version=ShockwaveFlash"></EMBED>
</OBJECT>
```

This HTML code requests a Generator movie named Movie1, together with two variables named x and day with respective values of text message and Monday. When the server sees this code, it knows to deliver a Flash movie—but first it must find and process the Generator template named Movie1. The problem is, there is no Flash movie ready on the server to satisfy this request; there is only Movie1.swt.

The Flash movie, Movie1, is the result of this Generator template being processed with variable information, which can be reused for an unlimited amount of time and for an unlimited number of visitors.

Offline Mode

As discussed previously, offline Generator processes templates much like the online mode, although offline use creates an FLA that must be hosted on the server. The code for viewing the offline Generator movie will be the same as for a normal Flash movie; the only difference is how and when the Generator movie is created.

For example, consider a site that uses a Flash-based navigation system that changes every day. A Flash developer could create a Generator template for this navigation system that would use placeholders instead of actual Flash elements. This template would then be loaded to a webserver where Generator DE or EE is also loaded. This navigation template does nothing until a command line is executed, at which point a Flash movie is created: the navigation movie with all of the dynamic content loaded into it.

Although broken up for clarity in this book, an example of this command line is:

```
Generate -swf navigation.swf navigation.swt
-param link_1 "About US" -param link_2 "Products and Services"
-param color1 "#ff8000" -param color2 "#000000"
```

The generate command tells Generator to perform a translation and deliver a result. The next part, -swf, specifies the type of result to be created; in this case, a SWF file. (Images in JPEG, GIF, and PNG format; QuickTime movies; and executable files are also options.) Next is navigation.swf—the name for the new movie Generator is creating; navigation.swt is the template to be used for this process. The last several items (beginning with -param) are variables that the template will need to process for the dynamic content.

Online-Offline Mode

Online-offline processing is a combination of both the previous modes with an online middleware component to initiate the Generator processing. This mode is popular for three reasons: It can deal with a high volume of hits, it guards against overloading a server with the constant online processing of dynamic Flash output, and EE is so costly.

It is inefficient to generate an entire site as a Generator file and have it load anew for every visitor, because doing so would place too much load on the server (that is, demand too much processing power from it). The most efficient use of Generator is to use the unique elements of its dynamic creation for the tasks Flash cannot handle on its own.

For example, some dynamic Flash movies might not change as much as others, so there is no need to process them with every visitor. Instead, a time-based action can be used to generate these files every 30 minutes. This development model lets Flash do what it does best and complement that with the judicious use of Generator. This method has become more popular because it makes simulating some of the robustness of EE feasible by using the DE version.

Using offline-online mode requires a command-line statement to be executed from a server-side process, such as ASP. Execution of this command line creates a new movie just as with the offline method, but this time all of the items can be dynamic and processed almost in realtime. The name of the new file, the template used, and all of the variables are dynamically inserted into this method without requiring a developer to type in the command line. Once again time, speed, and efficiency are all optimized: Flash does not have to be opened nor does a developer have to edit any variable data—the whole process happens live upon request.

Here is a bit of an ASP script using ASPExec to execute a command-line statement for Generator:

```
newMovie = "D:\Web\Movie_9122001.swf "
useTemplate = "D:\Web\Commercials\2.swt "
Params = "-param header ""Test 6.3"" -param nametext ""Name Text""
-param Addr ""Address\rSan Diego\rCA" "-param ADL ""LINK""
-param ADU ""http://www.Google.com""-param Coupon ""THE COUPON
 GOES HERE."" -param img1 ""D:\Web\Images\2_Default1.jpg""
-param img2 ""D:\Web\Images\2_Default2.jpg"""


' ---- Execute command for new SWF
 Set Executor = Server.CreateObject("ASPExec.Execute")
     Executor.Application = "C:\Program Files\Macromedia\
Generator 2\generate.exe"
   Executor.Parameters = "-swf" & newMovie & useTemplate & Params
   Executor.TimeOut = 500
   strResults = Executor.ExecuteDosApp
 Set Executor = nothing
```

NOTE *The use of \r in the Params line (line 3) alerts Flash to a line break within a text field.*

Command-Line Usage for Online-Offline Generator Mode
A server-side process like ASP can process command-line statements for Generator to create new movies, but ASP can't do so alone. Additional components are needed on the server, like these:

- ASPExec by ServerObjects Inc. (www.serverobjects.com) is a popular COM object used to execute a command-line statement from ASP.

- StarFish by Andrew Stopford (available at www.a-coda.com) is another COM object that can be used within ASP to execute the command line. The object was created specifically for Generator, along with another object for assistance with writing proper ODBC statements for Generator.

- exec is a server-side script command (like ASPExec) used in PHP and JSP to execute statements.

- ColdFusion includes the <CFObject> tag, which allows you to use COM objects, like ASPExec, within ColdFusion. ColdFusion also has two other tags available for executing Generator command-line statements: <CFExecute> and a custom tag specific to Generator called <CFX_Generate>.

Authoring Edition Mode

Generator's Authoring Edition (AE), unlike DE or EE, uses the local development environment of Flash 4 or 5 to execute the Generator process instead of a server-side process. With AE, when a Generator template is created, it can be previewed in Flash with the Test Movie command (select Main • Control • Test Movie). This testing environment simulates the command-line execution mode from the offline method and displays the results in the Flash Player. In this way, the template is processed and a complete Flash movie, a SWF, is created. (If you are familiar with using Smart Clips, this use of AE is quite similar, but considerably more powerful.)

Most Generator support material available today talks about the first two modes, online and offline, but you can find a great Generator solution right under your nose. Generator and Flash development for the PPC can take advantage of the power of Generator AE in the same way Flash developers do for the desktop browser.

This brief introduction has described how to use Generator in local development to gain speed, efficiency, and time. Now for a little demonstration.

Practical Applications of Generator

What sorts of content are practical for deploying to the PPC, or what sort of Flash content, facilitated by Generator, should be made available for the PPC? Here are a few ideas:

- City/state map and mass transit guides
- City/state travel resources, as in a restaurant guide
- Foreign currency calculator
- Movie/film promotions or trailers
- News-feed displays
- Portable games (for those long, boring commutes)
- Portable presentations or presentation notes
- Portable product installation/troubleshooting guides

The following examples will demonstrate several ways to make Flash and Generator movies more efficient and to deliver a better experience for the handheld and other device viewer. All examples are available on the accompanying CD-ROM in the Chapter 8 folder.

Portrait-Landscape Movie Adjustment

The common desktop browser interface is based on a variation of 800 × 600 pixels, so its width is greater than its height, like a landscape layout. As discussed in Chapter 2, the PPC's height is greater than its width, resembling a portrait-style layout. As a result of this difference in orientation, most Flash movies created for the desktop browser will not view optimally on the PPC.

NOTE *As of this writing, when developing for the PPC, you must include both the pixel height and width in the HTML <OBJECT> tags, and not as a percentage. (Because PIE is the only browser available for the PPC, there is no need to include the HTML <EMBED> tags; these tags are used for browsers such as Netscape that need plugins to display Flash.)*

To maintain the original landscape aspect of a formatted movie and to avoid scrollbars, you must reduce both the height and width proportionately. But because of the PPC's small screen size, proportionate scaling of the movie will make it even smaller—and potentially unrecognizable or unusable—as seen in Figure 8.4.

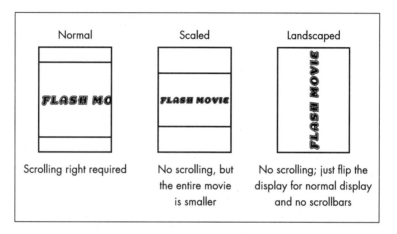

Figure 8.4: Screen proportionate views.

A better solution for many applications is to reformat the Flash movie to rotate 90 degrees. Although doing so will require the viewer to rotate the PPC 90 degrees, and the device menus will no longer be in synch with the content, both the quality and the original aspect ratio will be more true to the designer's intent.

Let's look at how to use Generator to accomplish this in each of its four usage modes: authoring, online, offline, and online-offline. Each mode will produce basically the same result—a movie turned 90 degrees—though in different ways.

Create a Movie

To begin, we'll create a new Flash movie with a stage size that is slightly larger than the PPC's screen, but we'll pretend that this movie is designed for use with desktop browsers as well as the PPC. We'll use the same movie for each of our examples.

1. Create a new movie called LP-swap.fla, with a stage size of 500×375.

2. Place a text box onto the stage using an Arial font face, a point size of 28, and any color. Insert some text into this box, enough to fill several lines.

3. Save this file and, using File • Publish, publish an SWF and an HTML file. Your resulting files will automatically be named LP-swap.htm and LP-swap.swf.

4. Open the LP-swap.htm file, remove the comments, remove the <EMBED> tag, change the width and height (width = 200 and height = 240), and add ID=PPC after the height item in the <OBJECT> tag. Save this file and then copy both the SWF and the HTML file to your PPC.

The HTML page should look like this:

```
<HTML>
<HEAD><TITLE>LP-swap</TITLE></HEAD>
<BODY bgcolor="#FFFFFF">
<OBJECT classid="clsid:D27CDB6E-AE6D-11cf-96B8-444553540000"
codebase="http://download.macromedia.com/pub/shockwave/cabs/
flash/swflash.cab#version=5,0,0,0"
WIDTH=200
HEIGHT=240
ID=PPC>
 <PARAM NAME=movie VALUE="LP-swap.swf">
 <PARAM NAME=menu VALUE=false>
 <PARAM NAME=quality VALUE=high>
 <PARAM NAME=bgcolor VALUE=#CCCCCC>
</OBJECT>
</BODY>
</HTML>
```

When viewing this in PIE, you will see the entire movie, but the text will be smaller than you intended. But notice that there is plenty of room above and below the text. Hmmm . . . what would the movie look like if it were rotated 90 degrees counterclockwise?

Example 1: Authoring

To manipulate this movie locally in the authoring environment:

1. Create a new movie in the same folder as LP-swap.swf and name it Landscape.fla. Use a stage size of 375×500, the opposite of LP-swap.fla.

2. Open the Generator Objects panel from the Generator Objects window, as shown in Figure 8.5, and locate the object called Insert Flash Movie.

Figure 8.5: The Generator Objects panel.

3. Drag this object to the stage.

4. The Generator Inspector panel will open once the object is on the stage. Enter detailed information regarding the placeholder here: LP-swap.swf for File Name, false for Cache, false for Scale To Fit, false for Expand Frames, and Mov for Instance name—as shown in Figure 8.6. This information tells Generator how and what to process.

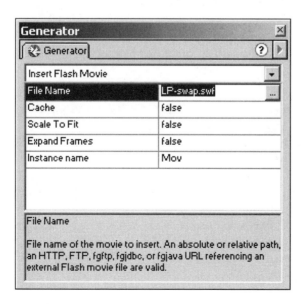

Figure 8.6: The Generator Inspector panel.

5. Close the Generator Inspector panel.

6. Rotate this Generator object 90 degrees counterclockwise by selecting Modify • Transform • Rotate 90° • CCW.

7. Save this file and publish it, using File • Publish, to create SWF, HTML, and SWT (Generator) files. Even though there is no use for the Landscape.swt file with this specific step, it is required for processing the Landscape.swf file. You can delete Landscape.swt once you create Landscape.swf.

8. Open the Landscape.htm file, remove the comments, remove the <EMBED> tag, change the width and height to (width = 200 and height = 240), and add ID=PPC after the height item in the <OBJECT> tag. Save this file and copy both to your PPC.

When Landscape.htm is viewed in PIE, the text is considerably larger and more easily viewable. This process of using a Generator template locally to produce a new Flash movie that has been reformatted from portrait display to landscape display is a prime example of using the authoring environment with Generator to manipulate files easily.

Additional Authoring Mode, Reuse Information

You can reuse the files and process from Example 1 for the portrait-landscape movie. Create the new HTML and SWF files as follows:

1. Open the Landscape.fla.

2. Skip Steps 1 and 2 from Example 1, but repeat Step 4, entering the movie name for the new project.

3. In the Publish settings (File • Publish Settings), change the name of the output files to reflect your new project and then, proceeding from the File menu, use File • Publish to create both SWF and SWT files. Note that you will be publishing only the SWF and the SWT; the HTML will not be necessary.

4. Open LP-swap.htm and change the name of the Flash movie in the <OBJECT> tag to reflect your new movie. Then save this file with a new name: newLP-swap.htm.

By repeating Step 4 of Example 1, you can change the File Name entry in the Generator Inspector panel to the name of the new movie you want to reformat. You will also have to change the name of the output file to avoid overwriting what you have already created.

In the Publish settings, deselect the HTML option as well as the default name settings and then enter a new name for this SWF and select Publish. Once you've created this new movie, you'll need an HTML file (which was not created in the Publish process because one—LP-swap.htm—is already 95 percent complete). Open the LP-swap.htm file in an editor, change the name of the SWF movie in the Object tag, and save this HTML file under a new name. Through a little file manipulation, you are able to reuse elements in lieu of repeating each of the steps above.

Example 2: Online

For those who surf the Internet with PIE, using Generator on the server presents an even easier solution.

Return to Step 4 of the Landscape.swf creation process on page 214. As shown in Figure 8.7, you will replace the entry in File Name with a Generator variable. (This new variable will be replaced on the fly with a query string name-value pairing.) The variable is named x, and the value will equal the name of the Flash movie that is to be displayed in landscape format. The File Name entry for the Generator Inspector panel should now be {x}—the curly braces tell Generator to process the value of the variable x as the name of the movie.

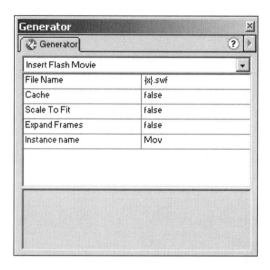

Figure 8.7: The Generator Inspector panel with a dynamic variable.

Here's the step-by-step process:

1. Change the File Name entry to {x}.swf.
2. Save the file as LandscapeTool.fla.
3. Again, from the File menu, use the Publish settings, followed by the Publish command to create just the SWT and load it to the server.
4. Load several test movies (such as LP-swap.swf) to the server to use for testing.
5. Open LP-swap.htm to edit the name of the movie and replace the current entry with the name of the new Generator template (just created in Step 3), as shown here:

```
<PARAM NAME=movie VALUE="LandscapeTool.swt?x=LP%2Dswap">
```

6. Save this file as LandscapeTool.htm and load it to the server.

Occasionally, adjusting the query string?x=LP%2Dswap to match the movie you want to view in a landscape format is only acceptable if the frequency of change is rather low. Otherwise, middleware would make this quite dynamic. ASP, for example, could dynamically create a query string that would allow this file to reformat any movie to landscape view.

Example 3: Offline

Reformatting a movie offline is similar to the Authoring mode because separate movies are created by a developer and not by an automated process. No additional Flash or Generator programming is needed if the online mode has already been completed.

This mode uses the same template, LandscapeTool.swt, created in the last example while the template is on the server. With a slew of templates on the server that need to be reformatted, a developer can execute a command line to Generator that will produce a new Flash movie in landscape view.

This is a great approach for formatting several movies to be used throughout the website (without opening Flash or creating a backend process requiring middleware to initiate the process). Here's an example of what the command line would look like:

```
generate -swf Movie1_Landscape.swf LandscapeTool.swt
-param x "LP-swap"
```

Example 4: Online-Offline

The combination of Online-Offline mode relies heavily on middleware. It uses the Landscape.swt file from Example 2, so you will need to load this file to the server if it is not all ready there. Once again, no Flash programming is needed here—only a middleware process that will initiate the command-line function. The following code presents the ASP version:

```
<%@ LANGUAGE="VBSCRIPT" %>
<%
response.expires = 0
'//-- Grab the name of the movie to be used in the
'//-- Landscape reformatting from the query string
'//-- [ LandscapeTool.asp?x=LP%2Dswap ]
    x = request.querystring("x")

'//-- Create variables to be used within the Generator command line.
    Generator_template = "LandscapeTool.swt"
    newMovie = "NewLandscapedMovie.swf"

'//-- Create a variable to represent the location of this file,
'//-- all new movies and templates will be generated into the same location or
'//-- (folder) as this middleware file.
```

```
      fullPath = request.serverVariables("path_translated")
      PathEnd = InStrRev(fullPath,"\")
      thisPath = Left(fullPath, PathEnd)

 '//-- Execute DOS command for Generator
  Set Executor = Server.CreateObject("ASPExec.Execute")
       Executor.Application = "C:\Program Files\Macromedia\
 Generator 2\generate.exe"
       Executor.Parameters = "-swf " & thispath & newMovie &
 thisPath & Generator_template & " -param x """ & x & """"
       Executor.TimeOut = 500
      strResults = Executor.ExecuteDosApp
  Set Executor = nothing

%>
<HTML>
<HEAD><TITLE>LP-swap</TITLE></HEAD>
<BODY bgcolor="#FFFFFF">
<OBJECT classid="clsid:D27CDB6E-AE6D-11cf-96B8-444553540000"
codebase="http://download.macromedia.com/pub/shockwave/cabs/flash/
swflash.cab#version=5,0,0,0"
WIDTH=200
HEIGHT=240
ID=PPC>
 <PARAM NAME=movie VALUE="<%=newMovie %>">
 <PARAM NAME=menu VALUE=false>
 <PARAM NAME=quality VALUE=high>
 <PARAM NAME=bgcolor VALUE=#CCCCCC>
</OBJECT>
</BODY>
</HTML>
```

The portrait-landscape movie adjustment examples here use the Generator object either to create new movies or to use the Generator template to serve varied content. The original movie will never be overwritten unless you rename the new movie with the same name as the original. In this way, you can change your movie without harming the original, and you can make changes quickly and easily.

Summary

Alone, Flash is a powerful application. With Generator (or any of the Generator alternatives listed in this chapter) and the ability to create dynamic applications, Flash becomes an intelligent, dynamic authoring engine. Even in its simplest implementation, Generator's functionality is extremely valuable for repurposing content for display on the PPC .

Chapter 9 will show you how to streamline advanced Flash development—for deployment on both the desktop and the PPC—with Generator elements built into Flash movies.

PART TWO
FLASH ON VIDEO, DVD, TV, INTERACTIVE TV, AND BEYOND

9

VIDEO PLAYBACK DEVICES AND FORMATS

Bill Williams and Bill Turner

So you have a cool Flash animation that a local television station would like to broadcast, and they're talking in what sounds to you like Martian language about required tape formats. Here we'll explain the various professional videotape formats.

To animators and artists who have worked only in Flash for the Web, choosing the best tape format can be difficult. Everyone is familiar with the home VHS deck and tape format, but VHS is the lowest-quality videotape available; it is intended only for consumer-delivery purposes. The existence of so many different tape formats can lead to confusion, particularly if you've never worked with video output in mind. When you need to output for broadcast or industrial/corporate video, and several copies of your work will be made, VHS is *not* what you choose for the master tape.

Before we launch into recording formats, we'll discuss the criteria and issues that you must consider when researching the right format for a particular application. We'll describe the various formats in detail and recommend how they should be used. Along the way, we'll address connection types. In Chapter 10, you'll learn how to prepare your Flash animations for videotape output.

What's the Right Format for Your Application?

The right format depends largely on the intended use and available formats. For broadcast, you must select a format that television stations will accept. Even though most will use standard Betacam SP, it always makes sense to ask the stations before investing the time and money on an unacceptable format. If the material is to be duplicated, you should choose a format of higher quality than the delivery format. If the desire is to record for archival purposes, the best digital format currently available should be your first choice. Keep in mind that backing up the uncompressed digital video file is always the best choice. If you have to archive the video/animations to tape, make it the best tape you can afford.

You must consider one very significant, often overlooked, factor when selecting a delivery format: whether the delivered video will be compressed again. Compression artifacts can build up after repeated compressions/decompressions. Artifact buildup can occur in distribution or in post-production. To reduce or eliminate this problem, you should use the best tape medium available.

The last few years of the twentieth century witnessed an outpouring of new digital recording formats. All of them are good in their own way, but only a few have received popular acceptance in the professional world. One analog format, Betacam SP, has a continued strong presence in the professional market. At the beginning of this century, all of the formats listed in Table 9.1 were still in use. (In the table, image quality is scored 1 to 10 based on using the optimal input/output [I/O] method of the videotape recorder [VTR]. In this scale, 1 = VHS [poor], and 10 = best available.)

Table 9.1: Tape-format comparison

Format	Dominant Users	Analog/ Digital	Available New in 2001	Image Quality	VTR Cost Range (US)
¾"	Local cable	Analog composite	No	2	
VHS	Consumer	Analog composite	Yes	1	$60–$1,800
1"	Local broadcast	Analog composite	No	5	
8mm	Consumer	Analog composite	No	2	
Betacam	Local broadcast	Analog component	No	6	
¾" SP	Local broadcast and cable	Analog composite	No	4	
Betacam SP	Broadcast, cable, industrial	Analog component	Yes	6	$7,700–$39,000
D1	High-end post-production	Digital component	No	10	
S-VHS	Low budget	Analog composite	Yes	3	$300–$7,000
D2	Broadcast and high-end post-production	Digital composite	No	7	
Hi8	Low budget	Analog composite	Yes	3	

(continued on next page)

Table 9.1: Tape-format comparison (continued)

Format	Dominant Users	Analog/ Digital	Available New in 2001	Image Quality	VTR Cost Range (US)
D3	Broadcast, high-end post-production	Digital composite	No	7	
Digital Betacam	Broadcast, high-end post-production	Digital component	Yes	9	$49,000
D5	Broadcast, high-end post-production	Digital component	Yes	10	$72,000
D9, Digital S	Local cable, broadcast, and industrial	Digital component	Yes	8	$8,000–$20,000
MiniDV	Low budget	Digital component	Yes	6	$1,200–$3,000
DVCam	Local cable, broadcast, and industrial	Digital component	Yes	7	$3,800–$10,000
DVC Pro	Local cable, broadcast, and industrial	Digital component	Yes	7	$4,000–$20,000
Betacam SX	Local cable, broadcast, and industrial	Digital component	Yes	7	$20,000-$27,000
Digital 8	Low budget	Digital component	Yes	6	$1,200-$2,500
DVC Pro-50	Local cable, broadcast, and industrial	Digital component	Yes	8	$10,000-$25,000

Each tape format in Table 9.1 has advantages and disadvantages. Some comparisons between formats are clear and objective, whereas others are more subjective. Objective features include luminance resolution, color resolution, luminance and color noise, dynamic range, and recording method. Subjective factors include the effect of image enhancement used to improve perceived detail, detail in complex images, motion artifacts, and dropout compensation.

Of the most popular formats, the ones shown in Figure 9.1 can deliver a digitally generated image. These popular formats, as well as others listed in Table 9.1, will be described in more detail in the sections that follow.

Figure 9.1: Various tape formats: Digital Betacam 124 (left-most), Digital Betacam 32 (top left), VHS (top, no case), BetaCam SP 60 (right-most), Mini DV (little ones), and Betacam SP 30 (remaining one). The numbers indicate time in minutes.

VHS

VHS was created as a consumer format, primarily for personal recordings and distribution of professionally produced material. This format has gained wide acceptance and is an excellent method to inexpensively distribute video material, including review copies of digitally produced video. Compared with other tape formats, VHS format is of minimum quality, and it should never be used as a master tape for duplication or distribution.

Betacam SP

Betacam SP is an improved bandwidth version of Betacam. The format was created to provide broadcasters with a high-quality portable video acquisition and post-production format. It has evolved into the most ubiquitous professional tape format available. It records component-analog video, which means that separate luminance and two-color signals are recorded. Figure 9.2 shows a Betacam SP deck.

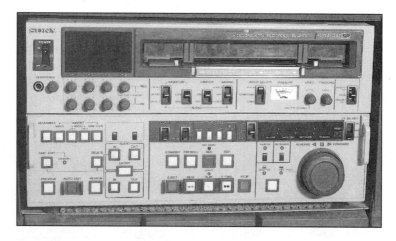

Figure 9.2: Betacam SP deck.

The bandwidth of Betacam SP depends on the type of video equipment used. Broadcast and professional model VTRs deliver a signal exceeding the broadcast resolution standard, and the UVW series VTRs roughly meet the broadcast standard. This format is very commonly used for making duplication masters for distribution to broadcasters and tape duplicators. Though it is an analog format, Betacam SP has proven to be a highly reliable workhorse in the broadcast industry since 1986. If the need is for a high-quality and widely available professional format, Betacam SP is an excellent choice for broadcast and videotape duplication masters.

S-VHS

S-VHS is an enhanced bandwidth version of VHS. It has significantly better luminance resolution but the same color resolution as VHS. It can be used as a master for VHS duplication but, because of its color-resolution limitations, it will produce copies that are of poorer color quality than can be achieved with other formats. Computer-generated material generally has excellent color resolution. S-VHS will not do those images justice and is not recommended for mastering or high-quality distribution.

Hi8

Just as S-VHS is to VHS, Hi8 is an enhanced bandwidth version of 8mm. It suffers from the same limitations as S-VHS but, being a much smaller format, it is less robust than S-VHS. You should not use this format for mastering or distribution. You could use it as a transfer medium only and duplicate it to another format for airing or duplication.

Digital Betacam

Designed as a digital replacement for Betacam SP, this format has gained significant acceptance in the broadcast and post-production community. It records 4:2:2 10-bit component digital using a very mild compression of about 90 megabits per second (Mbps). (See the sidebar below for definitions of these terms.) This results in an advertised "lossless" compression. Analog component and composite, but not S-video, are available on many decks. Because of its wide availability in the high-end production world and the fact that its bandwidth exceeds that of Betacam SP, Digital Betacam should be a top choice for high-quality image distribution or mastering. Figure 9.3 shows a Digital Betacam deck.

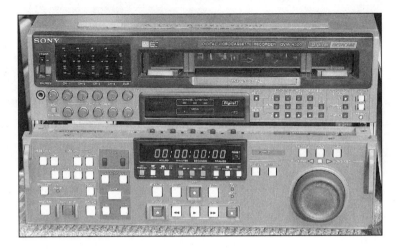

Figure 9.3: Digital Betacam deck.

Terms of the Trade

The term "4:2:2" is technical shorthand for the sampling rate of the three signals of component video. The first component in 4:2:2 is Y, or luminance; the second two components are two color difference signals: R–Y (red minus luminance) and B–Y (blue minus luminance). The 4 (Y) in 4:2:2 is sampled approximately four times a standard reference signal, and the 2:2 (R–Y and B–Y) are each sampled approximately two times the standard signal or half the rate of the Y (luminance) signal. This results in the color video signal having about half the resolution of the luminance video information. In 4:1:1 video, the color resolution is about one-quarter that of the luminance signal.

The term "10-bit sampling" means that each component of the video signal has 10 bits representing its level. This yields four times more video-level information than does 8-bit sampling. Recording at 90Mbps requires the full bandwidth video to be compressed (reduced in size) into a 90Mbps data stream to be recorded.

D5

D5 is technically the best of the best. This format uses uncompressed 4:2:2 10-bit component-digital recording. If you need unquestioned lossless performance, this is the right choice. It has all the advantages of Digital Betacam, but uses uncompressed recording. D5 is not as widely available as Digital Betacam. As with any selected format, be sure those receiving your tape can play it.

D9 (Digital S)

D9, formerly known as Digital S, is a compressed 4:2:2 8-bit component-digital recording system, recording at 50Mbps. The system uses a mild compression, resulting in minimal artifacts. Most digital video workstations produce this video format (4:2:2 8-bit), and the quality is nearly identical to Digital Betacam or D5. Being much less expensive than Digital Betacam or D5, the format is an excellent choice for mastering and high-quality distribution. As with D5, this format is not widely available, so be sure those who receive D9 tapes can play them.

MiniDV

MiniDV is a consumer product that, because of its excellent performance, has made significant inroads in the cost-conscious professional production arena. Today many professional MiniDV products are available. This format uses a compressed 4:1:1 8-bit digital recording scheme at 25Mbps. This is a lower quality than that produced by most digital video workstations, but far better than VHS. For most situations, MiniDV will be compatible with broadcast video quality requirements, provided there is no further video compression. Figure 9.4 shows a Pro MiniDV deck.

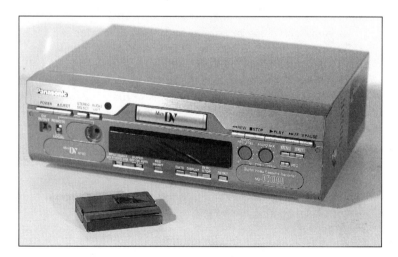

Figure 9.4: MiniDV deck with tape.

The good news is that this format is the least expensive of all those that might be appropriate for mastering for good-quality distribution. The bad news is that there is a modest quality compromise in resolution, as well as possible artifacts on still images (which are generally impossible to detect in motion video). In addition, the tape format, despite digital error correction, is not as robust as its truly professional counterparts, DVCam and DVC Pro. Use this format with caution for mastering and delivery.

DVCam

DVCam was designed to be a professional acquisition format. It uses the same compression scheme as MiniDV, but records to a more robust tape in a more reliable manner. This format is more costly than MiniDV, but is more consistent and therefore better suited for professional use. It suffers from the same compression limitations as MiniDV. Many facilities have the capability to play DVCam. If this format meets the technical requirement, it is a viable low-cost option.

DVC Pro

DVC Pro is a professional acquisition format directly competing with DVCam. It has virtually identical performance specifications and most of the same pros and cons as DVCam. Its installed base is similar to that of DVCam. It uses a different recording technique, and the result is a slightly more reliable system. Of all the 25-bit recording systems, this is the most robust, and it is an excellent low-cost choice.

Betacam SX

Betacam SX is an acquisition and post-production format based on the highly reliable Betacam family line. It uses a 10:1 MPEG2 compression scheme, which is very mild, resulting in an excellent image reproduction. This format might show some artifacts, especially on still images, but should yield excellent results if used as a master for duplication or airing. As with any significantly compressed video, caution should be used if further compression is anticipated. This format performs well and is less expensive than Digital Betacam, but has a limited installed base.

Digital 8

Digital 8 is a format designed for consumer applications. It uses the same basic encoding system as MiniDV, but records to Hi8 tape. The same pros and cons apply to this format as to MiniDV, but Hi8 has a much smaller installed base and is not postured for professional distribution. This is not the best choice for most distribution needs, but it could be an acceptable personal mastering format.

DVC Pro-50

DVC Pro-50 uses a compressed 4:2:2 8-bit sampling system recording at 50Mbps. It has very similar features to D9. It is an excellent choice from both a cost and performance standpoint. Just as with other new or limited availability formats, be sure all those needing the recording can play the format you deliver.

Web Links

Some of the formats not mentioned in Table 9.1 might be suitable for delivery to a client. The installed base for all of the discontinued formats is rapidly diminishing, so if an appropriate alterative format is available, you should use it. Here are some helpful links:

- An abundance of information on tape and delivery formats can be found here at www.high-techproductions.com.
- You can find a listing of nearly every TV station in the United States and the world at www.high-techproductions.com/u_s.htm.
- Yet another link from High-Tech Productions is a comprehensive video glossary found at www.high-techproductions.com/glossary.htm.
- Another helpful link is the Sony website at http://bpgprod.sel.sony.com.

Connections

When using any VTR, you should use the highest quality I/O port (see Figure 9.5). In other words, if it is a digital deck, the first choice should be the digital I/O, then the component analog, then the S-video I/O, and finally, the composite I/O. The performance evaluations in this chapter are all based on evaluations using the best VTR I/O option.

Figure 9.5: Connections (left to right): coaxial cable or RF; RCA (or phono plug); S-VHS; BNC; FireWire 4-pin (usually on a camera); and FireWire 6-pin (usually on computers or drives). Generally, the quality of these connectors improves from left to right, with the exception of FireWire, which is high-quality because it is digital.

Let's take a look at each of these connection types.

Composite Connections

As you might know, most people use the composite output to the TV from the device, tape, or DVD. This connection is the least expensive, but also the lowest quality. It uses one RCA plug for video and another for sound (two when using stereo, for a total of three). Nearly all modern TVs have this connection.

NOTE *When using tape (or standard VCR), you can use radio frequency (RF), an even lower-quality connection than composite. This single cable carries both image and sound and travels via coaxial cable—exactly like the cable that brings channels into your house if you subscribe to cable TV.*

S-Video (or S-VHS)

The next higher-up connection is S-video (S-VHS). The image is carried via a larger round plug containing multiple pin connections, similar in appearance to a musical instrument digital interface (MIDI) plug, though not quite as large. This method requires that the TV itself have the accepting connection. The sound is carried via separate dual RCA jacks (stereo), as in a composite connection. S-VHS yields a much superior picture than composite, but unfortunately only higher-end TVs offer it. In addition, typical VHS tape decks do not take advantage of it in the same way a DVD player could. You'd also need an S-VHS tape deck to see improvement. These tape decks can be difficult to find for home use; they are a dying breed mostly used for industrial tape editing.

RGB

The highest (and rarest in home use) connection is RGB—which stands for red, green, and blue. This configuration is mostly used in video editing and reference monitors. RGB uses three separate cables for the image—one for each R, G, and B signal—and uses BNC connectors (a twist-and-lock gold connector) to the monitor or deck. The reason we mention RGB here is some newer high-end TVs and DVD decks are beginning to use this connection. Even PlayStation2 offers a special RGB cable. Using this connection on a PlayStation2 results in graphics so sharp and clean that prolonged viewing almost hurts your eyes. We'll probably see this connection more and more as high-definition television (HDTV) becomes commonplace.

Audio Connections

If you intend to have sound, you need to connect audio. Usually you'll connect via an RCA (also known as phono plug), which you're probably familiar with if you have a home stereo. Higher-end audio can use XLR connections, which are more robust and suppress noise. These connections are commonly used with microphones and amplification systems, as shown in Figure 9.6. For a glossary of audio terminology, please see http://www.recordingeq.com/reflib.html.

Figure 9.6: The female (left) and male (right) XLR connectors.

Of course, the future (actually, the present) is constantly changing. All the connections to the TV screen we've discussed so far are of the analog sort. Some computers, such as Apple's Cinema Display, now use a purely digital connection. We expect TVs will follow suit, but that's for another day.

Basic Tips

Using higher-quality video equipment than your ultimate delivery media can reproduce ensures that the loss of quality in the recording and playback system will not limit the quality of the aired or duplicated video. Remember, VHS delivers only 230 lines of horizontal resolution, and standard broadcast is 331 lines. It is wise to use formats that exceed these specifications, but only to the extent that the improved quality makes it to the viewer. In other words, don't go from high-quality tape to low-quality and back to high; this practice can only deteriorate the image. Always step down (quality-wise) to the end delivery method.

The best way to select a format is to ask the users who will receive your videotapes what formats they prefer. That way, you can establish one or two formats as the standard delivery options.

DVD Anyone?

Cost-effective DVD creation has arrived. Many facilities today can accept digital animations on CD-ROM or DVD-ROM and incorporate the content into a production. Even if you're asked for a videotape, it doesn't hurt to inquire about delivery on a disk; your client might prefer it. Of course, if you do go this route, be sure to ask the destination (the place that plans to broadcast or duplicate your work) about acceptable formats. Most will be able to accept some form of QuickTime format, but this is not always the case. You might have to convert your files from one format to another. Cleaner Pro 5 can be very useful in these situations. While converting, always try to keep artifacts (recompression) at a minimum by using the lossless compression formats such as QuickTime's Component codec. This will mean larger files but far better end quality.

NOTE *International video standards include NTSC-M (30 FPS in the United States, Canada, and Japan), PAL-I (25 FPS in the U.K.), PAL-B, G, H (25 FPS in continental Europe), PAL-M (30 FPS in Brazil), PAL-N (25 FPS in Argentina), and SECAM-L (25 FPS in France and Russia). With all these formats, international distribution can seem confusing. An important factor when producing video for any application is the frame rate of the distributed video. All of the international formats use one of two frame rates: 30 (actually 29.97) or 25. When producing animations, you should use a frame rate that is easily converted to the delivery format to avoid unexpected stuttering in the motion.*

DVD Players

We'll mention the use of DVD players here not as a method of delivering broadcast material like animation footage to TV stations, but rather as a method of delivering directly to consumers the highest possible quality they can play in their living rooms or computer dens.

   The use of DVD players in the home has expanded quite dramatically in the last few years and is on pace to be everywhere VHS tape is today—which is virtually every home.

NOTE *In an attempt to keep clear what can be a very complicated issue to those new to DVD, this section discusses playable content delivery. You could just as well deliver your animation footage as data on a DVD-ROM disk, such as the raw digital animation file, to a service bureau or broadcaster for transfer to a master tape format. This is assuming the broadcaster has the appropriate equipment to deal with your file.*

Standard Home Players

Standard home players are pretty much that: standard. Some of the earlier players might not cooperate because of piracy protection schemes, but most such problems have largely been ironed out. A world region scheme has been incorporated whereby a disk destined for the United States will not play on a DVD player in China, for example, unless it has been authored with the appropriate region codes to do so. Once the disk is produced, there is little to nothing you can legally do to change it short of modifying the foreign player's hardware (which is usually illegal). Because the DVD signal is so clean (approaching master-tape quality), you can see that it would be very easy indeed to create high-quality bootleg copies onto VHS tape—hence the protection scheme.

Many different kinds of DVD disks exist as well. Most DVD disks are for video only, others are for data, and others can deliver both. A data-only DVD, usually known as a DVD-ROM (such as a PlayStation2 disk), will not play in a home DVD player unless it was mastered as a mixed-mode disk (having both data and MPEG2 video sections). DVD video such as the type you'd normally rent or buy from the local video store usually contain only video but can play on your computer with appropriate player software.

Visit http://sdm.sony.com/services/index.html to learn more about DVD formats as well as packaging and logos you can use in your DVD project.

Computer Players

The fact that most computer DVD players can process mixed-mode disks (data and video) opens up a whole new world for multimedia as well as animator/filmmaker audiences. By using a mixed-mode DVD, you can include Flash games and interactive projects as well as linear video animation or live-action productions. Think of these mixed-mode DVDs as CD-ROMs on steroids with nearly 10 times the potential capacity (9GB on DVD-ROM compared with 650MB on CD-ROM).

Unfortunately, standards for computer DVD players can vary from platform to platform. Even within the same platform, discrepancies and incompatibilities can erupt. If the end user is not up-to-date with the latest software, it could cause problems, such as rendering your disk useless to the end viewer. Because the variables associated with computers and data content can be tremendous, you might have to seek specialized information beyond the scope of this book. A good rule to follow, though, is to obtain permission for your DVD disk to carry any software player installers needed to view the disk—the Flash player, for instance, if you're distributing Flash games. With Flash, you also have the option of creating standalone self-contained Flash games or other interactive projects for both Macintosh and PC platforms that will not need outside software to run.

Summary

You now have some basic information about what can be a confusing flurry of tape formats. A format that's acceptable as a corporate or industrial video might not be suited for network broadcast. Network broadcast formats could be overkill (financially) for a local cable channel or commercial delivery. But here's the good news: Your Flash-authored animation can play from any of them. Picking the proper format for delivery is the key.

Chapter 10 covers the dos and don'ts of creating Flash animations that will look professional when played back on *any* video device such as the ones introduced in this chapter.

10

PREPARING FLASH ANIMATION FOR VIDEO

Bill Turner

The significant differences between a computer monitor and your television screen can affect your Flash animation. This chapter will take a look at the issues involved in preparing your Flash animations for videotape output.

Say you have a really great web animation and you'd like to play it from videotape. It's certainly possible to do so as it is, but the animation will probably look terrible if you simply dump it to videotape without considering certain factors. Because of the extreme differences between your computer monitor and the TV screen, you'll need to prepare your file differently for each device. In fact, some ways of creating animation in Flash itself can stifle output to videotape—such as using movie clips, a real no-no when videotape is the intended destination.

This chapter will show you what to do to port your Flash to professional videotape formats (introduced in Chapter 9) so that your work will look professional on the TV screen. It will also introduce issues you should consider before you even start that next great cartoon or any type of animation.

NOTE *The rules covered in this chapter will also generally apply when you're creating animations for DVD output (discussed in Chapter 11).*

Video Concerns

Because Flash is an excellent tool for creating animation, particularly character animation, chances are you'll have clients who will want to use the animation in a video format. You might even want to create animation for video simply because it's so cool to do so. If you're aware of the various issues beforehand, your endeavors will be more successful.

For one, the differences between computer monitor display and TV display are dramatic—so much so that you should seriously consider these issues before you even start your animation. While some elements can be altered for video after they're produced, your production will be more streamlined if you address them up front.

NOTE *The big plus in doing Flash animation with strictly video in mind is that you can ignore processor and bandwidth constraints on the playback machine. Every video device will play back full-screen at full speed with full fidelity sound. This means you can get a little crazy with the art and sound, pushing it much farther than you would for computer-only playback.*

Briefly, the main issues to consider when designing Flash for video are:

- Computer monitors are non-interlaced; TV sets are interlaced. This can cause unsightly jitters in animations.

- Colorspace, the range of colors and how they're displayed, differs from computer monitor to TV screen.

- The viewable area of a TV screen is often larger and less dense than that of a computer monitor.

- Computers use square pixels; TVs use rectangular ones—which can cause unwanted distortion of art.

- Flash-specific work habits, such as using movie clips or event sounds, can result in mysterious missing content in the final video file.

- To get the best quality video output, you have to know the proper video codecs (compression/decompression algorithms).

Keep in mind that tape and disk are very closely related because both are commonly displayed on a television. DVD, as we all know, has a much higher image and sound quality than does tape, but they both must go through the TV screen. This screen is the common denominator. (Chapter 11 will deal with DVD-specific production and uses this chapter as a foundation.)

The Differences Between Computer Monitors and TV Screens

Have you ever watched a news show, with all the computers in the background? If so, have you ever noticed the dark horizontal bars traveling up or down the computer screens? As you probably know, the news people on the set do not see those lines; what you're seeing is the difference between non-interlaced computer monitors and interlaced TV monitors. The TV cameras catch the gaps in the beginning and end of the cathode ray's cycle on the computer screens.

The computer monitor's (non-interlaced) cathode ray starts at the top of the screen and scans (energizes) each pixel on the screen horizontally, non-stop, until it reaches the bottom. Then, it starts over again from the top. This happens very rapidly, so your eyes never really notice the gaps between start and finish. On a standard TV, this same cathode ray process executes, but every other set of horizontal pixels (or line of resolution) is scanned and energized. This explains why computer monitors, with their higher refresh rate, are easier on your eyes and usually cost more. Figure 10.1 shows the difference between a computer monitor and a TV screen.

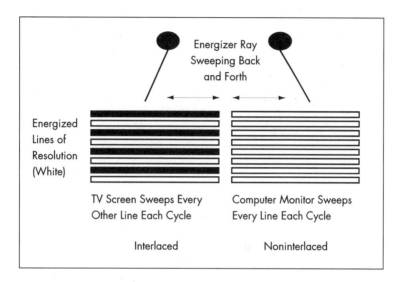

Figure 10.1: Interlaced (TV) versus noninterlaced displays.

Each scan of a standard TV screen is known as a *field*. In North America, this happens 60 times per second (actually 59.94) in order to create 30 (or 29.97) frames of images per second (Source: The National Television Standards Committee [NTSC]). Two fields equal one frame of image. This is generally much slower than a computer monitor's refresh rate, which explains why we can see the gaps when a computer monitor is captured by a TV camera.

This apparently useless esoteric hubbub is not really hubbub at all: The fact that TV is interlaced affects how your animations will look on the screen. The result is the shimmering of patterns and jittering of lines that you will not see on your computer screen but that will scream "Amateur!" when someone views the same animation on a TV via videotape or DVD. Before addressing the solutions to these problems, we'll look at the two types of TVs: common TVs and reference monitors.

Common TVs and Reference Monitors

Unless you're in the business of editing video for TV or other purposes, you're probably unaware that two different types of TV monitors exist.

Common TV

One is the standard TV we are all familiar with. With it, you can receive channels and watch shows broadcast by networks or cable. You can hook up the VCR or DVD player and watch recorded content of all sorts. It's just a TV.

Reference Monitors

On the professional end of things, we find what's commonly called a *reference monitor*. Reference monitors cannot receive channels, because they generally do not have a tuner. They cost a great deal more than standard TV sets: A 19-inch reference monitor can run into the thousands of dollars. These expensive monitors generally look like gray steel boxes with a bunch of mounting holes everywhere.

When properly set up, a reference monitor, as shown in Figure 10.2, gives you the most exact picture possible. The monitor can accept various connections and can even daisy-chain these connections to other monitors or recording devices. Some can show genlocked overlays (an analog method of overlaying video, graphics, or text) or even distinct color channels (isolating the red, green, or blue signals, for instance). Reference monitors can display the image as it will appear on a standard TV, or they can show you the overscan area (the image area hidden by the casing of the standard TV tube) using a built-in underscan method. Some are even capable of splitting the screen so that you can compare different signals.

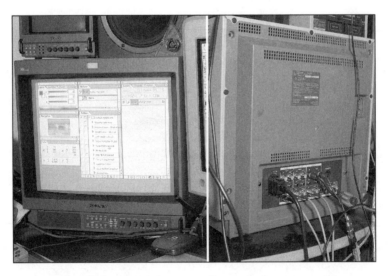

Figure 10.2: A 19-inch Sony reference monitor, front (left) and back (right).

Another important reason to use a reference monitor is color fidelity. The colors shown on a reference monitor are as exact as possible. Usually the reference monitor will have built-in calibration that uses various test patterns. Once calibrated, the colors are the best they can be. The common joke among video pros that NTSC means Never The Same Color exists for a good reason: Every person who's ever fired up the boob tube has most likely fooled around with the color controls—hue, saturation, brightness, or tint. This makes it impossible for you, the designer, to control what an end user will see with respect to color. Your perfect, painstakingly designed green logo might very well look baby blue on someone else's TV. The only thing you can do is to make certain that it is green on a calibrated reference monitor and hope that the color controls of the destination TV haven't been altered too much.

The Budget Approach

Although reference monitors provide the best picture, their cost may put them out of reach for the small independent animator on a budget. Acceptable color can be roughly achieved on a good standard TV, such as one that uses a Trinitron tube. This, along with a test-pattern generator (either borrowed or purchased), can lead to good color rendition. The test-pattern generator outputs a standard known image (such as color bars) to which you can adjust your standard TV using its color controls. You'll need to check and recalibrate every few months. Test-pattern generators hook up to the TV's video in port, and they generally cost between $200 and $500, much less than a reference monitor. You will still lose the other benefits of using a reference monitor, but you do at least ensure the colors' accuracy.

TV Color Issues

How does a designer determine the right colors in the first place? We'll focus on the NTSC (National Television Standards Committee) standard for North America.

Most modern computers display 24-bit color (which supplies millions of colors). This makes it easy to display most colors, with the exception of fluorescent and metallic colors or effects. In contrast, the TV screen is not able to display so many colors. In fact, some colors that it can display have been deemed illegal by the NTSC because certain legitimate colors, when abutting other colors, cause a super contrast that can bleed; some colors can even bleed through to other channels. Bleeding is a very pronounced muddiness between the two colors and can cause a deterioration of the image (a spiking of horizontal lines). A good example would be a very bright red (illegal) next to an extreme yellow (also illegal), which would cause a spiked blur of brown between them—not something you'll want. Figure 10.3 shows the Flash color bar with the NTSC illegal colors removed (this figure is also included in the Chapter 10 folder of the CD-ROM).

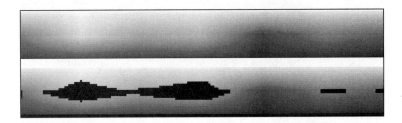

Figure 10.3: The Flash color bar with the NTSC colors removed (black areas).

A standard TV can display any of 16 million colors that a computer can but, because of technical broadcast reasons well beyond the scope of this book, the colors most offensive to the broadcast signal have been deemed illegal and should be avoided.

The equipment itself presents another group of issues you must deal with. In broadcasting, certain levels must be met in order to broadcast the signal over the airwaves (to avoid the channel signal bleed-through). If your animation or graphics are outside this range (illegal as metered by various signal scopes), they must be changed before they can be broadcast. Of course, no police officer will swoop down to throw you in the slammer for using bright red next to yellow, but the technicians at a TV station, in an effort to broadcast quality video, will simply not accept your work.

Two Ways to Keep It Legal

One solution is to simply export your animation out of Flash to QuickTime or any other digital video format that After Effects can read. From there, you might apply the Broadcast Colors filter that comes with After Effects to the entire animation, as shown in Figure 10.4. This filter will force the colors to conform. Unfortunately, the results are not always desirable. Greens, yellows, and some reds suffer dramatically, especially if you've used the standard built-in Flash palette.

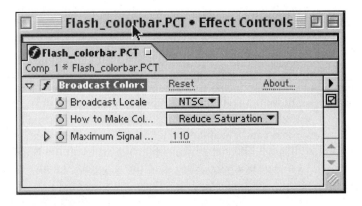

Figure 10.4: The Broadcast Colors filter in After Effects.

However, the best way to avoid the color pitfall is to address this issue when you're creating the art. We realize this is not a very good solution for existing art and animation, but it will save you many headaches in the future. The accompanying CD-ROM provides a PNG file you can import in Flash and use as an onstage color picker. As described in Chapter 2, you'll use the Line or Fill eyedropper. Simply drag the eyedropper to the section of the supplied image that contains the desired color. We recommend that you save frequently used colors in a Flash color set. When you do, you'll notice an absence of colors (illustrated by black) in the middle of the color bar (as shown in Figure 10.3). This is where illegal video colors exist on the built-in Flash Color Picker that you find in the Mixer panel. We've enlarged this PNG for your convenience; you can resize it to make it smaller but you risk blurring the colors via anti-aliasing.

Another very helpful way of choosing colors for your art and animation is to use the TV monitor. If you have a setup (usually via a special video card) whereby you can view the Flash stage on a TV screen while creating the art, you can view the art in realtime as it will appear on the TV. We strongly recommend you create a setup like this if you want to do a lot of Flash animation for video.

If you insist on using illegal colors, they will probably be too bright or overly saturated. The result could be color vibration (an undesirable flickering of color that hurts your eyes to watch) or the bleeding discussed earlier. You can simply leave color to chance if you're a hobbyist, but if you are looking for professional results or you're broadcasting via cable or network television, you'll want to be sure your colors work as you expect.

After Effects: Handy, but Limited

If you are inclined to produce motion graphics—like flying logos and animated type, for example—use an application such as Adobe's After Effects.

The problem with After Effects, however, is that you cannot draw directly in the program as you can in Flash. This hinders character animation to the point of uselessness. The ideal solution is to finish all animation in Flash and reserve After Effects to put the final polish on the work before outputting to video—that is, all the compositing and creating special effects that you cannot do in Flash. Adding a lens flare to a sunset scene leaps to mind as something Flash alone cannot do.

A number of resources are available for learning about the many applications of After Effects. A good starting point is Adobe's website at www.adobe.com.

Macintosh Color Picker

If you're using the Macintosh, you can purchase a software extension that helps remove the color problem while you're creating art for video display. Synthetic Aperture offers a great solution called Echo Fire, which you can find at www.synthetic-ap.com. The Echo Fire package comes with a custom color picker you can access from Flash's color selection palette (when you choose the system Color Picker). If you choose your colors here, the software will inform you of the color's legality in video, and it will give you a chance to click the Legalize button, which takes you to the best color that video can display. The Echo Fire software also comes with a FireWire DV video player and a small application that allows whatever you have on your computer screen (Flash included) to be routed through FireWire and viewed on your TV screen while you create the art. This gives you the ability to see exactly what the colors and art will look like on a standard TV or reference monitor.

Avoiding the Jitters

Drinking way too much coffee or Mountain Dew can be one cause, but the jitters we're talking about are the ones in our animation. Jitters or shimmers (roughly the same thing) are caused by art that does not respect the interlaced TV display (explained on pp. 229–230). Because the TV's cathode ray scans only every other horizontal line per frame cycle, this means that one line is *not* being scanned during each frame. In essence, only half the frame, or field, is being displayed at any given moment.

This technical bottleneck can make certain elements of your art flicker or jitter. The vertical lines are not the problem; the *horizontal* ones will kill the image. Any horizontal line drawn in Flash (at 100 percent) of less than 1.5 points will result in this jittering. Therefore, even when drawing lines going in all directions, including horizontal—such as is usually the case when you're creating cartoons—you should avoid using thin lines.

But what about when you need a thin line for details? You can fix the animation (after exporting to QuickTime or other video-editing format) in our friend After Effects. In After Effects, you can apply the Reduce Interlace Flicker filter to areas of the animation that exhibit this problem. For consistency, you should apply this filter across the entire animation. The filter imposes a slight blurring to the art that causes anti-aliasing to become more pronounced. The more pronounced this effect (the larger the number in the filter setting, as shown in Figure 10.5), the less it will jitter.

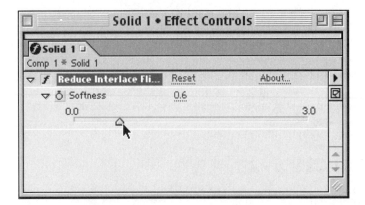

Figure 10.5: The After Effects Reduce Interlace Flicker filter.

Shimmering occurs when you're using certain patterns in your art that result in a slight but annoying flashing in areas where the offending pattern exists. Shimmering is also directly related to the interlaced nature of TV screens. You can avoid shimmering by ensuring that the patterns you use (such as a field of grass) are not too detailed. By applying a little blur to the pattern before using it in Flash, you can dramatically smooth shimmering. If your pattern contains highly contrasting repeating areas of about one or two pixels, it will probably shimmer. The solution that stops jittering animations (the Reduce Interlace Flicker filter) will help stop shimmering as well. As with jittering, you should attempt to stop shimmering while you're creating the art by being aware of the problem during production.

Because the standard TV's resolution simply is not as high as that of a computer monitor, fine details become lost in the transition from computer to TV screen. High-definition television (HDTV) could help alleviate some of these difficulties if stations choose to broadcast at high resolution, but until broadcasters and the Federal Communications Commission (FCC) agree on this issue, we must deal with the limitations.

Framing Composition (Action-Safe/Title-Safe)

Underscan (mentioned in the section "Reference Monitors" on page 228) allows the reference monitor to show the entire picture—which suggests that some of the picture is being hidden, given that we do not watch reference monitors in our living rooms. That's right—a good portion of the picture is completely hidden from your view on every TV produced. Panasonic recently ballyhooed a TV set with 20 percent more picture. How did it achieve such magic? By simply showing you more of the picture that has always been there anyway: the overscanned areas outside the action-safe areas!

Video pros have been keenly aware of what's known as the action-safe and title-safe areas for years. Put something important (such as the last digits of a company's phone number) outside these areas, and chances are you'll be getting a severely agitated phone call from the advertiser once the commercial is broadcast.

These areas (outside action-safe and title-safe) are an odd sort of TV wasteland: You might have an image there, but you must be sure it is unimportant! Applications such as After Effects and video editors like Final Cut Pro and Premiere contain guides to show you exactly where these areas are. Because Flash was designed for the Web, it doesn't have these guides. The accompanying CD-ROM includes NTSCsafeareas.fla, shown in Figure 10.6, which contains the guides you need. To use it, you can either copy the layers of the FLA file containing the guides, or you can use the file as a template whenever you begin creating an animation for video. Simply keep important art inside the bounds and you'll be fine.

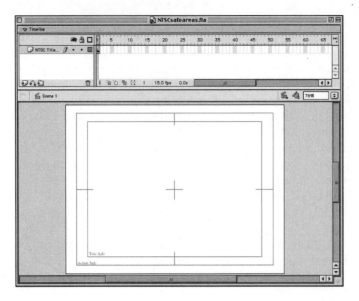

Figure 10.6: Action- and title-safe areas set up in a Flash authoring file for NTSC.

Actions—such as characters, important scenery elements, and the like—should be contained inside the action-safe rectangle. Think of action-safe as the outer boundaries of the view, or the edge of the TV screen. Think of anything outside the action-safe areas as the bleed area.

Text must be contained inside the smaller title-safe rectangle in order to be read. You can cheat a little here, though, by using crawlers (text that runs across the bottom or the top of the screen) or by scrolling text. Just be sure the text spends most of its onscreen life inside this area. At the very least, be sure your text is within the action-safe area, but use the space outside the action-safe area at your peril—it might not be seen on some TVs. This is because each TV set manufacturer has some leeway regarding how to place the tube. The tube may or may not line up perfectly to its casing, which blocks the overscanned area—thus the action-safe area can get sloppy from set to set, even among like models of TVs.

Dealing with Square-to-Rectangular Pixels

The computer produces square pixels, but the TV generates rectangular pixels (really not pixels, but lines of resolution). This can lead to undesirable distortions in any art going from Flash to video or DVD. This problem is easily rectified if you know what to do beforehand.

Frame dimensions for video can vary slightly from format to format, but the standard for computer-generated, square pixels is 640 × 480. These are the dimensions you should use in Flash. Because your computer monitor uses a square-pixel format, this format will scale nicely into the format required for video. Mini DV, for example, uses a format that is 720 × 480 pixels, but this is a rectangular-pixel format, as is all NTSC TV video. You might wonder, "Why not work at 720×480 pixels in the first place?" The answer is that, because the computer deals in square pixels, anything you draw that needs to be circular, such as the tires on a car, will appear squished and distorted on TV. If you work at 640×480 pixels on the computer, the circles will be elongated when they're scaled to the 720×480–pixel video file. The circles will look distorted on a computer monitor, but they'll look perfectly fine on a TV screen. This concept can be confusing if you're new to video; refer to Figure 10.7 for a visual explanation.

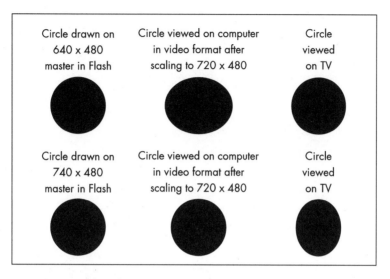

Figure 10.7: The square-to-rectangular pixel problem.

You might be considering scaling your art up from 640×480 to 720×480. In the bitmap world, it's generally taboo to scale up because it introduces unpleasant artifacts. In Flash, with its vector art, no artifacts result. This is the beauty of vector art. Vector art is merely a collection of mathematical calculations describing the lines, which means you can scale up to any size you want and not introduce unwanted artifacts. Even with the use of bitmaps in Flash, you will be scaling up only in the horizontal direction and only by 80 pixels. The artifacts caused are insignificant and very difficult to see on the TV's lower-quality screen. If even the slightest threat of artifacts still causes you discomfort, you can author in Flash at 720×540 and scale down the 540 dimension to 480—but it's really not worth it.

Frame Rates

Videotape and DVD always play at 30fps (frames per second)—actually, 29.97fps, but because Flash cannot specify this rate, we go with 30fps—or an evenly divided segment thereof. The actual playback speed is 29.97fps and, if you were doing video animations longer than about 7 minutes, this frame rate would be an important distinction. In longer animations done at 30fps and played at 29.97fps, a slight drifting of the audio synchronization would occur at around the 6- to 7-minute point. Because most cartoons or other animations will run under this time limit (they end before drifting starts), you need not worry about it. If you have longer animations that require perfect audio synchronization, you should consider doing the animation in segments and piecing it together in an application (such as After Effects) that can deal with the 29.97fps rate.

Most of the time, you will not want to animate at 30fps; in fact, 15fps seems to be ideal for cartoons (compare Figures 10.8 and 10.9). When your animation is created at 15fps, the video will simply show one animation frame for every two video frames, and everybody's happy. The big plus of the lower frame rate is it means you have to create fewer drawings. This can be a huge timesaver, so think twice before attempting 30fps hand-drawn animation. Figures 10.8 and 10.9 shows the difference in the amount of drawing needed. If you were to make your animation at 13fps, 26fps, or some other number not evenly divisible into 30fps, the animation would end up with serious stuttering problems when you played it back from tape because the number of frames drawn cannot be resolved by the playback rate properly. Some frames may be lost and others linger too long, causing stuttering.

NOTE *If you are doing mostly logo moves and motion graphic–style animations in Flash, you are better served by 30fps. If this is your sole purpose for animation, you are better off using an application (such as After Effects) that offers far more sophisticated control over this type of animation. You can, of course, export any art you've created in Flash to After Effects via Illustrator or another bitmap format so you don't have to re-create all new elements.*

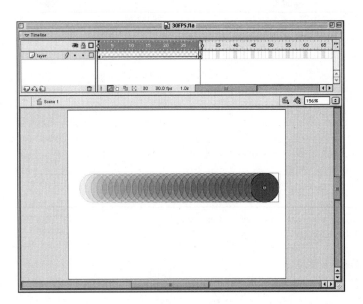

Figure 10.8: Note how many images are needed to animate the circle with the time resolution at 30fps.

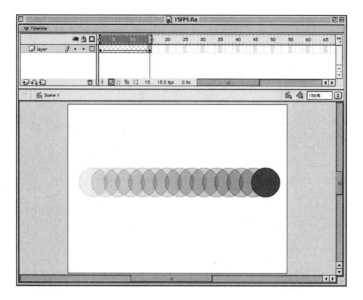

Figure 10.9: The same distance is covered in the same time, but this clip uses fewer images at 15fps.

Field Rendering

The section "The Differences between Computer Monitors and TV Screens" on page 226 explained the fact that TV is interlaced and that each frame is built of two fields (a field being every other line scanned during a frame's duration). This technical fact comes into play with video by allowing a fast-moving object to be smoothly displayed via the camera blurring that occurs naturally.

In computer-generated animation, particularly in Flash, no blurring occurs unless you impose it by creating it in the art. Some high-end 3-D animation applications actually apply motion blur to fast-moving objects at render time. Flash does not. When outputting art from Flash, you get a distinct series of frames—you do not get fields. This is not a serious problem when you're working with character animation. Traditional cell animation quite frankly never used fields in the first place, so why should Flash?

Field rendering is where half frames (the field, or one screen of horizontal scan lines that we spoke of earlier) are used instead of full frames. By weaving these fields together at playback time, you achieve a smoother sense of motion. This can be very important in applications such as high-end logo animation where precision movement is required. In a program like After Effects, field rendering is mostly transparent to the artist as it goes about rendering what is actually 60fps and merging it into 30fps for playback. In Figure 10.10, we see the words "Field Rendering" moving across the screen. Notice the horizontal lines (on a TV screen you would not see them); these lines represent the fields as rendered by After Effects. Flash, unfortunately, cannot do true field rendering.

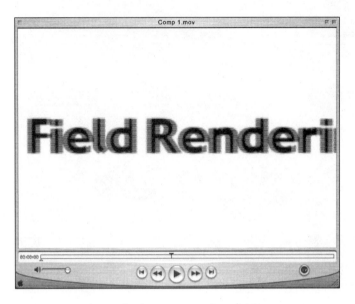

Figure 10.10: A frame of video consisting of two fields.

You could export from Flash at 60fps, bringing your animation into After Effects and creating the proper fields for playback. However, we've found that this adds little to the smoothness of the Flash animation. When you do character work at 15fps (not field rendered or converted to such in After Effects), it is largely a waste of time. We suspect that Flash does not use sub-pixel movement; therefore, field rendering yields no improvement in smoothness.

Graphics Concerns

The sky is the limit when you're creating a Flash animation for video. You can do things that would cause overload during computer/browser playback but not on videotape or DVD, thanks to the 30fps non-stuttering full-screen playback. This means you can use all sorts of bitmaps for backgrounds and even for moving parts of the scene to make your Flash animations look great.

Though it still makes good economic sense to use symbols to save time in the art department, certain cases require that you simply forgo them. Graphic symbols and instances of them on the main timeline stage can sometimes be restricting. Because file size is not a concern, you might want to employ such tricks as duplicating a certain move's symbol and customizing it to suit your needs. For example, with lip-synching you can opt to draw every frame instead of dealing with the restriction imposed by reused symbols.

Unfortunately, the beloved Movie Clip (MC) symbol (the heart of interactivity in a Flash piece) is totally useless for video output. If you use a MC symbol when exporting to QuickTime Video or AVI, the symbol will just sit there on its first frame and do nothing else until it leaves the timeline. If you are converting a web-based animation to video, the solution is to change all MCs to graphic symbols via the Instance panel, as shown in Figure 10.11, and specify the setting

Play Once, Loop, or Still Frame (plus the frame number). Even this process can be fraught with problems, particularly timing issues. If the clip does not play long enough, you will have to re-keyframe or rework it altogether on the main timeline. If you know you're doing animation for video, avoid using MCs.

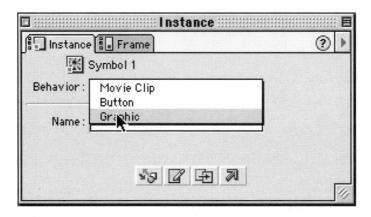

Figure 10.11: Changing movie clips to graphic symbols.

Using large Flash-generated gradient blends can yield undesirable results in video. What happens is not Flash's fault, but the fault of the video compression codec used. If you use uncompressed video as your format, it's not a problem, but you'll need an expensive video board to use uncompressed files; they can become quite large. For example, using MPEG 2 to encode video destined for DVD will give you very distinct and unpleasant horizontal lines in the Flash-generated gradients, particularly the gradients used on a horizontal axis. Other video codecs, such as the QuickTime Animation codec, will yield the same, though perhaps not such pronounced, results. The workaround is to use a bitmap gradient area (created in Photoshop or another bitmap editor) with a slight bit of noise added to it. Import this graphic into Flash to replace the gradient and all will be well. The noise in the gradient interrupts the smooth gradation, causing the compression codec to interpret it as detail you want. The animation will look better on the TV screen.

Sound Concerns

Sound is an art and profession all its own. Certainly an animation would be pretty dull without sound. Following are some major issues pertaining to use of sound in Flash destined for video or DVD.

Those of you who use MC symbols, take note: They do not work for video output, period. Why repeat this information? Most Flash authoring that uses MC symbols also uses event-synched sounds. The event synch method will not work for video output. Nested timelines, such movie clips or even graphic symbols containing sound, will not work. Just as all symbols must be the graphic type, all sound must reside on the main timeline in order to output to a video codec.

This sound must be set to the Streaming option as well (in the Sound panel). You'll know if a sound is set to Streaming by dragging the playback head on the main timeline. If you hear sound, that means it's set to Streaming. If you hear nothing, that means it is most likely set to Event and must be changed, or it will not export to video. If you've output to a video codec such as QuickTime Video (not to be confused with plain QuickTime, which is actually a Flash track in a QT wrapper—see the sidebar on page 241) or AVI and the sound is missing, this is the problem.

Acquiring Sound

Every Macintosh comes with built-in sound. Nearly every PC comes with a soundboard or circuitry of some sort, generally Sound Blaster. If your computer is capable of recording (actually digitizing) 16-bit 44.1KHz stereo sound, you're in business.

However, keep the following in mind when acquiring sound for your video production:

- Use original sound or sound that you have the rights to use, either by purchase or other such contracted means. This means you should not use Napster (or any other) downloaded MP3—it's illegal and unethical. You wouldn't want a recording artist taking your animations for free, right?

- Your sound should be as clean as possible—by this, we mean uncompressed 16-bit 44.1KHz without a ton of noise and other unpleasant nuisances.

- Use a format Flash can accept, such as AIFF or WAV.

- Ensure that the sound fits the time span needed and makes sense for the animation. This can be the tough part. There are no hard and fast rules as to how a sound or music fits an artwork. You just know when it does, so audition several before choosing.

File Formats

Although you could import any type of sound file Flash can accept, we don't recommend using pre-compressed sound files. The reason for this is simple: You will be outputting the sound track at its highest uncompressed quality when the animation goes out to tape or DVD. With an SWF export, you destroy the sound with severe compression (usually MP3); with tape, you will not. You'll want the cleanest sound possible going in and out of Flash.

When you import extremely large sound files (over 15MB, though it's hard to nail down exactly) into Flash, the program can become quite unstable. (This happens frequently with the Macintosh version of Flash.) Keep in mind that Flash will let you import sound files of nearly any size and will allow you to work for hours on this doomed file. Later, when you open the FLA you've worked so hard on, it simply will crash the Mac. If you are lucky enough to get the doomed file to open, be sure to delete sound files from the library and resave the file as a new FLA. Then, you can trim down the file to the size needed. Sometimes, this is not possible, as is the case with a music piece. With voice sound files, you can cut the file into smaller pieces at blank areas of the sound and re-import accordingly. If you do have a large sound file you absolutely must use in the video production, consider applying this music or sound in Final Cut Pro (to the exported Flash animation video) or another video editor in which file size is not an issue.

Outputting to Tape

After you have a good bit of animation, around 15 to 30 seconds worth, it's a very good idea to output to tape to see it play. Think of this step as a test run. You don't want to find the mistakes after doing the entire 5-minute piece—mistakes you could have avoided. If you have not been able to view your art on a TV screen during creation, you might want to test even sooner. In this situation, even a simple still held for 20 seconds can tell you much about what needs to be done.

If you're outputting to VHS (the standard household tape on a common VCR), be prepared for a quality letdown. Color saturation and quality of patterns and lines can suffer quite a bit compared with what you're accustomed to seeing on the computer monitor. The end viewer, not having seen the original on computer, might not notice the difference, but you will. The best you can do in this situation is to use the best-quality tape you can at its highest recording speed (SP). Make sure the heads are clean and operating properly before you start recording. Even with all these precautions, the result will be lower quality than what you see on computer screen.

The plus, however, is in size and scope. It is quite exhilarating to see your work on a big-screen TV with a booming sound system. And you can see it running at full-screen frame rates that would be nearly impossible to achieve on anything less than the most powerful computers. To get these results, we must first export from Flash to a video format that will play to tape.

Choose the Right Command

On the Macintosh, with QuickTime installed, you will be offered two choices via Flash's File • Export Movie command. One is simply QuickTime. This choice is *not* video, but a method that exports a QuickTime Flash track—in essence, a SWF in a QuickTime wrapper. What you want for video is File • Export Movie • QuickTime Video. This selection creates the bitmap video file you'll need for editing in After Effects, Final Cut Pro, and so forth. When in doubt, simply look at the exported file's size: If it's tiny (2MB or less), it's not really video, but a QuickTime Flash track.

You export to video a bit differently than the usual Flash export. For one thing, instead of the Publish dialog box, you select the File • Export Movie command. From here,

PC users choose AVI; it is not possible to export QuickTime video straight out of Flash on the PC. If you want to use QuickTime, you can output to uncompressed AVI and convert to the QuickTime format you desire using an application such as Cleaner Pro 5 (formerly Media Cleaner Pro). By using uncompressed AVI, you do not taint the animation with compression before the conversion, which may taint it even more with compression artifacts.

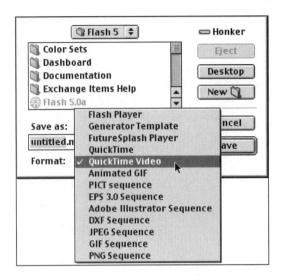

Figure 10.12: Macintosh users choose QuickTime Video from this list.

Mac users select QuickTime Video (see Figure 10.12). After choosing QuickTime Video, you'll be presented with the Export QuickTime dialog box, shown in Figure 10.13. Specify the settings you want—dimensions, format, compressor, quality, and sound format. Figure 10.13 shows the settings for exporting directly to DV NTSC format. After you finish the export, this format could be played directly to Mini DV tape using an appropriate player, such as Final Cut Pro or another compatible DV player.

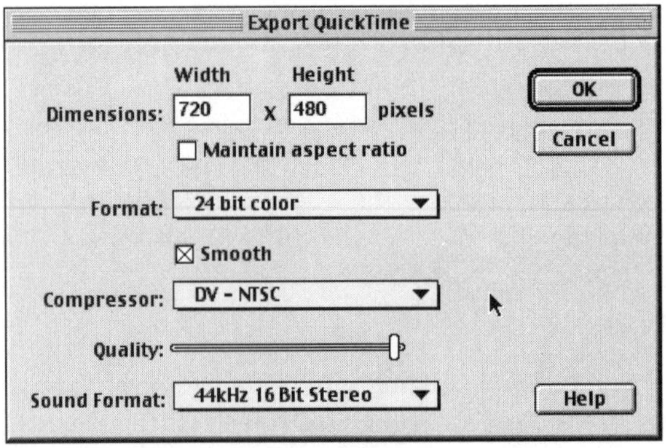

Figure 10.13: The settings for DV output.

FireWire, iLink, IEEE 1394, and Mini DV Tape

Mini DV (or DV for short) is the newest kid on the block and is gaining rapid acceptance because of its low cost and near-Betacam SP quality. Many companies produce DV decks and cameras. Companies such as Sony, Canon, JVC, and Panasonic produce a wide range of equipment compatible with the FireWire (IEEE 1394, or what Sony calls iLink—all the same thing).

FireWire makes it easy to acquire, edit, and output high-quality video. FireWire itself—the interface to these decks, cameras, and even hard drives—has been built into every Macintosh (except the lowest end iMac) for some time now. PC makers are also hopping on the bandwagon with their newer offerings. If your PC does not have FireWire (or 1394), you can install a relatively inexpensive PCI board and software to give your PC an interface to the video decks and cameras that use the high-speed bus.

You can work with DV and Flash animation on a simple consumer DV camera (now priced under $1,000). Of course, if you do lots of editing and shuttle the tape back and forth repeatedly, you risk wearing out the heads prematurely. If you intend to do a large amount of DV work, look into buying a more robust professional DV deck (the price ranges from about $3,000 to $7,000). Figure 10.14 shows a Mini DV recording and playback deck. Unfortunately, a deck lacks the camera functionality, but if your only concern is outputting animation or lots of live-action editing, a dedicated deck makes more sense. Save your camera for what cameras do best: acquiring live-action video content.

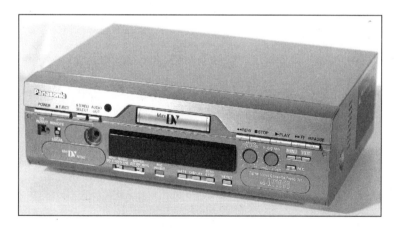

Figure 10.14: A Mini DV recording and playback deck.

The wear on the heads of your camera is limited somewhat by the fact that all editing will go on digitally inside the computer. The deck or camera simply records the results of your work from the computer.

The Benefits of Mini DV

Briefly, Mini DV enables loss-less digitization. Here's why: Analog video cameras and decks record a signal to the tape medium. This signal determines how the picture and sound will look and be heard. DV cameras and decks take a stream of digital information and record this information onto tape in digital format— just a huge slew of 1s and 0s. In the case of a camera, the video is digitized and compressed using hardware compression, and the data written to the tape in realtime. When you bring this data into your computer (via FireWire), you are actually downloading it from the camera or deck, not digitizing as you would be doing with analog tape sources. It's this very technique of downloading the information that makes possible the luxury of loss-less quality. Even if you brought the video from the deck to the computer and back to the deck again, there will be no loss in quality.

This is not possible with analog; it needs to be digitized each time it enters the computer, which results in a degradation of image, or what's known as *generation loss*. If you've ever tried to copy one home VHS tape to another VHS tape and seen how terrible the copy looks, you've experienced generation loss. DV avoids this loss.

The other benefit to using DV is the time-code imprinting the tape affords. Generally this time code is frame-accurate. (We say "generally" because this time code can vary by a frame or two, but it's accurate enough for most purposes.) Even if your VCR has a digital time readout, in most cases it is merely reading the footage of tape that has passed the playback head (much like an audiocassette deck will) and translating it into time. It's a rough estimate at best, and not sufficient if you need to find a precise place on your tape. Even if you remove your DV tape, insert another, and then reinsert the previous tape, the time point of the tape will still be right (usually down to the frame). This is not possible on home VCRs.

The last benefit—but certainly not the least—is the size of the tapes. You can fit about ten DV tapes in the same space as one VHS tape—which leaves room for other toys.

Dedicated Video Boards

Another method of acquiring video and outputting back to video on a professional level is to buy a dedicated digital video board. Once you install the board in your system, you'll have the I/O needed to edit video as well as lay your Flash animations to tape. Professional-level video digitizing boards differ from the consumer-level video digitizers, such as the ones that use the USB port and require no internal circuitry (a PCI board, for example).

Video board manufacturers offer a wide variety of choices. Some will have high-end component I/O; others offer composite; and still others offer everything, including DV (FireWire). As you might expect, the prices can range dramatically as well—from around $100 for a simple FireWire (IEEE 1394) PCI card to many thousands for a full-blown Avid system. The sections that follow look at some current digital video board offerings. Be sure to check manufacturers' websites regularly, because times and technology change rapidly.

Media 100

Media 100 Inc. offers a wide range of solutions and prices. The Media 100i starts at about $3,000 (for uncompressed video playback); the full-blown system, for full-fledged, high-end broadcast design and post-production, costs about $18,000. Media 100 also offers many software products, such as Cleaner Pro (formerly Media Cleaner Pro) that is indispensable for doing lots of video production for broadcast or Web in any format you want—QuickTime, Real, MPEG, or VFW. You can find Media 100 at www.media100.com.

Avid

Avid is not only in the business of moving pictures and video, but audio as well. Its Pro Tools systems (under the DigiDesign name) are the basis of nearly every professional audio production/recording company. Of course, Avid also offers a wide range of video solutions for broadcast. We could fill a book on Avid's offerings for video production and editing, so you might want to do some research at www.avid.com.

Also keep in mind that Avid offers some killer animation software: Soft Image for 3D and Toonz for 2D, as well as Elastic Reality for high-end morphing and transition effects.

Matrox

Matrox offers affordable solutions to PC users on a budget, with offerings such as the Marvel G450-eTV. The company also offers many types of dual-head video cards. With a dual-head graphics card, your computer's desktop space will extend across two monitors (not duplicated, but a larger desktop), which doubles the useable screen. Mac users have long recognized the luxury (and necessity, given today's complicated applications) of having two and even three monitors to spread out those tool palettes. Ah, the breathing space! They may be found at www.matrox.com.

Formac

Most Mac users will be using FireWire (unless you get into the high-end broadcasting realm of Media 100 or Avid), but how do you connect the regular old VCR or S-VHS deck to FireWire? Formac has a nifty little box it calls Studio that can do just that. Studio converts (in realtime) any composite or S-video input to a DV data stream for editing in any digital video editor, such as Final Cut Pro or Premiere. They can be found at www.formac.com.

NOTE *This chapter deals with getting Flash animation out to video. Appendix 1 describes how to get live-action video that will play on a PPC into Flash.*

QuickTime Video Codecs

QuickTime is Apple Computer's longstanding video and audio platform. It also deals with still images, such as TIFF and PICT. QuickTime has been cross-platform since version 3 and now, at version 5, offers all the flexibility you would ever need in editing digital video.

But suppose you want to serve Real Video from your Web site. No problem; any QuickTime clip you've edited can be converted to any other format via the appropriate software. Applications, such as the aforementioned Cleaner Pro, do a fine job of converting any form of QuickTime video and audio to any other format.

You can download the basic QuickTime software for free at www.apple.com/quicktime. The pro version ($29.95) is useful if you want extra capabilities in the QuickTime Player, such as exporting and converting files or special effects authoring, but if you don't need these extra features, you don't have to download or pay for it.

Nearly every Mac has QuickTime right out of the box. Even though most PCs do not come with QuickTime, you can easily download and install it. This gives you flexibility in trading files, not to mention the outstanding range of codecs QuickTime provides for both video and audio.

> **NOTE** *A codec is a compression/decompression algorithm used in video and audio projects. Because uncompressed video can take up tons of storage space, methods have been developed to compress and decompress (codec) in realtime for capture and playback.*

QuickTime Codecs Explained

No matter what platform you're using, you'll find that dealing with digital video is an art of tradeoffs. What is acceptable for one purpose can be totally unacceptable for another. So how to begin? Good question. You can study for many hours, days, and months and still not know the best codec (and settings) for your needs. It is an art indeed.

Some codecs are better at saving quality at the expense of speed; others take the speed route. Here's a good rule of thumb: Better quality codecs, such as Component, might not play back on slower machines; poorer quality codecs, like Video, will play back on nearly any machine. It's really quite simple: Less compression means more data that has to be moved through the processor to display on screen. More compression means an image with less quality but smoother playback.

Following is a brief summary of various QuickTime codecs related to 2-D animation, like the kind you'll be creating with Flash. Not all the codecs shown in Figure 10.15 pertain to animation projects.

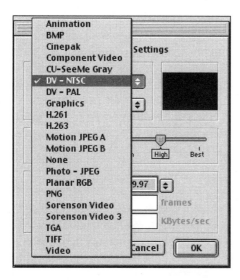

Figure 10.15: Some of the QuickTime codecs.

If you have the QuickTime Player Pro, you can change from one codec to another via the Export option (which is not available in the standard QuickTime download). This option is perfect for a simple conversion, as you can see in Figure 10.16, but if you want more control and batch rendering (converting multiple large videos can be very time-consuming), you might want to use Cleaner Pro (discussed earlier on page 241).

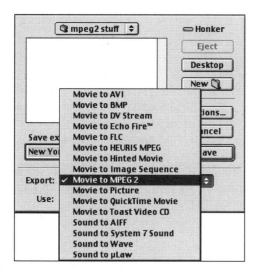

Figure 10.16: Some of the QuickTime Player export options.

Animation Codec

The animation codec is a loss-less form of compression. It's also one of the few codecs that can save the alpha channel of your animation. The alpha channel describes the cutout areas of your animation for compositing on top of other animations or video. When saving with alpha channels in mind, be sure to choose the 32-bit option (24 bits of color, 8 bits of grayscale alpha information).

The disadvantage of using the animation codec is the large file size and slow playback. This codec is best used as an intermediate file format when you want to composite various animation elements in an application such as After Effects.

DV

DV (NTSC or PAL) is the codec used in association with FireWire. When video is taken with a Mini DV camera, the image data is compressed on the fly with hardware using this standard codec. In contrast, when video or animation is compressed on your computer for playback to Mini DV tape, a software codec (supplied with QuickTime) is used.

The biggest advantage of using the DV codec is the high-quality playback to tape in realtime. File sizes are moderate because it takes approximately 3.6Mbps (megabytes per second) to store the information. This figure is also important to the smooth playback of any DV codec video. The rule of thumb here is that you'll need a drive and system that can sustain about twice the rate of the video data; in this case, about 8Mbps. The faster your hard drive and system (with SCSI cards and so on), the more you can avoid stuttering and frame dropping upon playback of DV material.

The disadvantage of using the DV codec is its inability to store an alpha channel for compositing purposes.

None

Mysterious as it seems, the None codec is exactly that: none. This is raw, uncompressed video. It is the cleanest a video or animation can be. It is the largest file a video or animation can be. Be sure to have plenty of storage space when using None. The None codec can store alphas for compositing, but will not play back full-screen in realtime without some serious hardware assistance.

For Flash animation that will be integrated or combined with other footage, this is the choice to make. The animation codec tends to slightly corrupt the integrity of Flash artwork, particularly gradients. So if you have the space and need to integrate your animation with, let's say, live-action à la Roger Rabbit, None is the best choice.

Photo JPEG

Hey, isn't JPEG just for photographs, not animation? Well, yes and no. Because animation is a series of rapidly displayed images (or photographs), the Photo JPEG codec begins to make sense. By using this codec, you'll get much smaller files for storage and, depending on how much of this lossy compression you apply, a decent quality. This is a good codec to use after the project is done, and you want to archive it on CD-ROM or other media.

Be aware that using heavy compression can cause artwork, particularly line artwork, to artifact more noticeably than photo or live-action video imagery. These artifacts are most visible on hard-contrast areas, such as where a flat field of color meets a black line (as in most cartoons). Because you'll be creating mostly line artwork in Flash, you'll want to test a section before committing the entire animation file to this codec for archiving. By keeping the setting at about 80 percent quality, you should be safe. With testing you'll be even safer. There's nothing worse than compressing all that hard work, then archiving and tossing away the original, only to find that the compressed version (the only one left in existence) stinks. Trust us on this: Test.

Of course, using this codec for archiving purposes is great if you have little disk space and only a CD-ROM burner for backup purposes. If you have lots of storage, fast data tape backup (many gigabytes worth), and plenty of patience with progress bars, then archiving the uncompressed versions of everything is best.

Custom Codecs

Your video capture and playback card might supply an assortment of codecs. Some digital video card vendors use custom codecs that take advantage of various hardware (chip) enhancements. These types of codecs are generally used only for video capture and playback, and not compositing (they usually do not save alpha channels). When using this or any codec, you might need to convert (or render) the clips you want to play back into the custom codec compatible with your card.

Miscellaneous Codecs

Many other codecs are available, such as Sorenson, which is extremely popular for web and CD-ROM video and known for its stunning quality at very low data rates. Sorenson, however, is mostly used as a delivery format where low data rates and high quality are a must, such as the web. The Sorenson codec will not play back to tape via FireWire or a video board.

MPEG 1 is also a delivery format and is not recommended as an authoring format for videotape. MPEG 2, however, is ideal for playback and is the codec used in DVD production.

There are many third-party codecs for tasks such as video conferencing and web casting (again, not for authoring and editing).

What About Audio Codecs?

When doing Flash animations for video output, you will not use compression of any type. Though some codecs are fine for audio, such as MP3 and Q Design for music, they are not needed in this type of production. You'll want your audio to remain as untainted as possible throughout the production process.

Summary

This chapter presented major issues to consider if you need to prepare your Flash animations for videotape. The knowledge you have gathered here will apply in other video realms besides broadcast tape. DVD and games such as the PlayStation2 are often played on a television screen, so the basic rules in this chapter apply to them as well. However, there are other things to be considered when preparing Flash animations for DVD. Chapter 11 looks at Flash DVD production.

11

FLASH ANIMATIONS TO DVD
Bill Turner

With the help of the new Apple G4 desktop computers, DVD production is now within the reach of nearly anyone. You may now go from concept to Flash to DVD without ever leaving the desktop. In this chapter, you will learn how to do this by exploring the new Apple G4, along with the needed software.

This chapter will focus on why DVD is beneficial to use, and will exemplify this through use of the new G4 Macintosh—the only platform at this time capable of producing DVD on the desktop for relatively little financial investment. Five years ago, it cost upwards of $500,000 to do what $4,000 can do now. Independent filmmakers rejoice!

Before discussing the equipment, however, you'll want to understand why you'd want to animate DVDs. We discuss this and explain bringing Flash animation to DVD using the G4 Macintosh while acquainting you with the hardware and software needed. We'll point out and clarify certain areas of particular difficulty or confusion. We'll cover preparing Flash content for DVD and, to allow you to gain a hands-on understanding and to show you exactly how to get your Flash animations readied for DVD production, we walk you through an example.

The Best Flash Can Look on TV

We're all very aware of the quality of Flash animations on the Internet, but you may not be aware of Flash's ability to create animations that can be shown on your big-screen TV. As you've read in preceding chapters, transferring Flash animations to videotape is certainly a plausible solution, but one that suffers from the same problems as transferring movies to videotape: reduced picture and sound quality and lack of random access. This makes DVD production of your flash animations a very desirable solution. Few things are cooler in the world of Flash animation than displaying your work at its highest quality on any consumer DVD player in any venue so equipped.

The most remarkable thing about using DVD as the outlet for your Flash animations is the pristine digital quality DVD brings to the table. Unlike a videotape, particularly VHS tape, DVD is nearly an exact digital duplicate of the original (see Figure 12.1). The colors are far more saturated and true, the lines and textures are crisper and clearer, and the sound is as outrageously good as it can be. Add random access, multiple languages, and mixed mode (data and video for computer playback), and you have a very compelling reason to look closely at doing your Flash work with only DVD in mind.

Figure 11.1 The pristine quality of DVD animations.

Another big plus of producing material on DVD is offered by the mixed mode version of the DVD specification. Mixed mode simply means there's both video (including sound) and data—as in PDF or HTML documents, photos, Flash games, and applications most common CD-ROMs have today. Mixed mode will normally work only on computers with DVD playback ability.

The problem with DVD production in the past was the high expenses that the production demanded. Apple Computer's new solutions go a very long way toward drastically reducing the cost of equipment needed to produce professional DVDs right on your very own desktop. This revolution in technology has paved the way for independent animators, and live action filmmakers for that matter, to create incredibly high-quality animations and video to be delivered via the magic disks. We're not saying this cannot be done on Windows PCs—it certainly can—but it requires a patchwork of systems, disk burners, drivers, software applications, and other such equipment. In contrast, Apple's new G4 solutions are elegant and have software integrated in and controlled by Apple for creating top-notch professional DVDs right out of the box, right now, and it works beautifully.

Because of this all-in-one solution for creating DVDs, we will be focusing on that platform, the G4 Macintosh. All the software discussed runs on System 9.1 or above. In the future, Mac OSX will come into play, but for now, 9.1 does just fine and dandy.

Apple's G4 with DVD-R Writer

As of this writing, Apple offers two desktop G4 towers that can perform not only DVD mastering but actually burn the DVD disk, right out of the box and with nothing else to buy. They start at around $2,500, with the top-end machine costing around $3,500. This is a mere pittance of what the *software alone* used to cost just a few years ago.

Although the computers ship with iDVD software bundled (and that alone may be enough for most hobbyists), the software of choice for producing pro-level DVDs can be found in Apple's DVD Studio Pro software that we'll be peeking at shortly. This software may seem a bit pricey at around $1,000, but if you're serious about doing pro-level DVD, it's quite reasonable. In fact, your first paying job could more than cover the expenses of the entire setup (computer and software) by a large margin, making this a very attractive deal.

DVD-R Writer Is the Key

The DVD Reader/Writer is the key ingredient in these new computer systems. With this type of mechanism, you can make complete and usable copies of your animations on DVD. These DVDs can be played back on almost any consumer DVD player; they even play on a Sony Playstation2. How's that for spiffy? Of course, these disks can also play like any other DVD movie on a computer outfitted with DVD playback hardware; since most modern computers (PC or Mac) have this ability, you can see a wide audience stretch out before you.

While the Apple solution is great for making a few DVDs, or what's known as "one-offs," it can also make the data files needed for mastering a DVD. Mastering is what is used when you want to make many copies (as in thousands) of your DVD. The blank DVD disks, though a good deal, are still quite expensive at $10 a pop, so you can see that you don't want too have to many testers or failures. (They make pretty, but expensive, drink coasters.) If you know you'll need many copies of a DVD, sending the data off to a duplication house is the best bet, as we'll discuss later in this chapter.

The cool part is that a fully mastered DVD can hold nearly 10GB, as opposed to only 650MB on a CD-ROM. This vast amount of storage means you could have not only the 30-minute, full-screen, full-sound animated classic of your creation, but all the websites, games, and support material on the same disk, without ever leaving the farm. Think of it as "portable everything" where your content is concerned. DVDs also make for a great backup medium, in case you ever need to find a place to keep that folder of 26 consecutive playing days' worth of MP3s.

Apple's DVD Studio Pro

As we mentioned earlier, every DVD burner-equipped G4 Mac comes with software known as iDVD. This is free software that will enable the owner to create DVDs, but is limited in time allowed (duration of content). iDVD also forces one to conform with pre-made (but somewhat customizable) layouts of your DVD content. It's very nice that they include the software, and for most hobbyists, it may be all you need.

To really get into creating real, fully customizable DVDs, though, you will need to learn the industrial strength software by Apple known as DVD Studio Pro. This is not an application for those easily distracted. Even with Apple's famed ease of use, this puppy gets hairy—so hairy, in fact, that it's a very good thing indeed that they include an "in application" testing function. Without it, you'd be burning up those $10 disks left and right—making a nice set of coasters for your next party.

We know this is a book on Flash, and we do not intend on writing a manual for DVD Studio Pro. But we'd be remiss if we didn't include at least a smattering of what goes on after you leave Flash with content destined for DVD.

A Brief Introduction to a Complex Application

DVD Studio Pro, as we've mentioned, is industrial strength and, as such, has a somewhat longer learning curve than most hobbyists' applications. But once you get the hang of all the jargon, it's not so bad. Because you can do so many things with DVD Studio Pro, the application needs a lot of buttons and options. Though you could get by with a single desktop set up (one monitor), two or even three monitors are very desirable, enabling you to spread out the workspace.

Okay, now you're wondering, "Well, it's just a DVD; it can't be all that complicated." True, if all you're doing is plastering Flash animation on it, it's easy. But if you want to make your DVD have various movies with various key scene markers inside the movies, and you want it to play in English, French, and Spanish, it gets a bit more complicated. Top it off with a DVD that, when played on a computer, can automatically access a website, and you have even more to think about.

Here's an example: Say you have a client who wants to give out an animated show that entertains as it teaches employees about safety. The client has employees that speak in both English and Spanish. The problem is that this info may need to be updated from time to time. The client doesn't want to produce and distribute all new DVDs every time this info changes. So, you make a master DVD (that will be duplicated and handed out to employees) with all non-changing entertainment and whatnot, and have it link to the company's pertinent web page for constantly updated material. Of course, one could put the whole shooting match on the webserver and make everyone download everything, but full screen video can be something of a hindrance to download, to say the least. I think you're getting our drift here. Make it on DVD.

A Look Around the Interface

Now that you can see why the DVD thing is shaping up to be hot, if not already, with all its usefulness, let's take a little walk around some of DVD Studio Pro's main interface and functions.

Once you launch the program, you are presented with a pile of windows; they are neat little piles, but piles just the same, as you can see in Figure 11.2. You can now see the reason behind having multiple monitors.

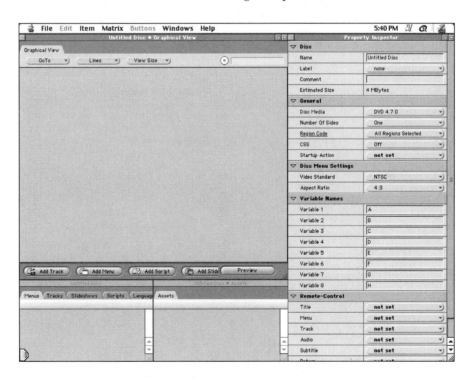

Figure 11.2: The overview of DVD Studio Pro.

The first thing you'll do in a DVD Studio Pro project is to import "assets," or your movie clips, soundtracks, and menu art. You'll import your clips via the standard File • Import and choose the file dialog. Once imported, the content appears in list form in the Assets bin. By selecting an asset, you can find out all the details about that particular clip in the Property Inspector (see Figure 11.3). You'll use this Property Inspector quite a bit because it's the main place to make and change settings.

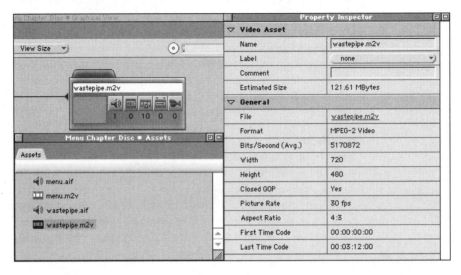

Figure 11.3: The Assets bin with video track selected showing details in the Property Inspector.

You'll notice that the property inspector is mode-sensitive. Depending on which mode you're in, the information and controls there will change to reflect what it is you're working on at the time. For example, while working on a Motion Menu (which we'll explain how to make shortly), the Property Inspector jazzes itself up accordingly, giving you all the settings you need to perform linking and creation of buttons as seen in Figure 11.4.

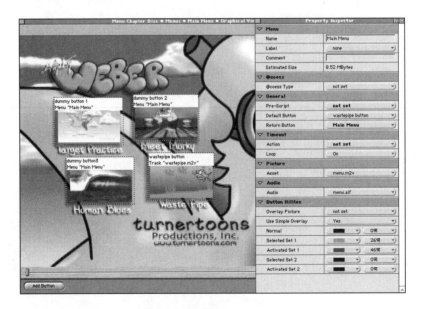

Figure 11.4: The menu mode of DVD Studio.

While the previous screen shots give you quick glimpses of the interface, this next shot (Figure 11.5) shows that actual project that we've made, with the folder motif being used for the content. Note the arrows pointing from one folder to another. This is an overview of the interactivity that will be used to navigate the movies once on DVD. For the sake of simplicity, there's really only one menu which points to one movie. This can get really complicated when having, say, one menu pointing to a submenu pointing to 16 different movies. The arrows become more helpful, but at times can become a gnarled mess. Thankfully, you can show or hide arrows in various levels of detail.

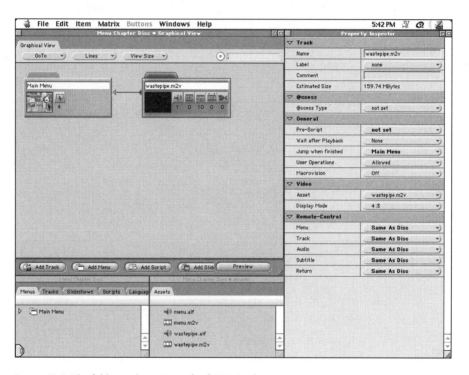

Figure 11.5: The folder and arrow motifs of DVD Studio Pro.

While the program is quite deep, we have touched on the main areas you'll be using. The intention of this book is not a replacement for the fine manual Apple supplies with DVD Studio Pro, but to give you a short preview of what you'll need to work with.

Clearing Up Some Audio Confusion

While the manual is fairly clear, there are a few head scratchers in there as well. We'd like to touch on one of the most important ones you may encounter when first using the application—Remember to designate a language! We'll explain. . .

The very first thing you'll stumble on after importing your assets is the fact that you must re-link the audio track to the video track, using the folder motif we viewed earlier. When you drag a video asset from the assets bin to the disk's graphical view window, you'll see it makes a folder. In the folder, you'll see various buttons for audio, chapters, angles, and so on. Once you have linked an audio track to a video track, you think, "Okay, all done." Not! The audio will not play when tested. Why? Well, because this is a DVD that can be made with many languages on the same disk, you *must* specify which language the audio track is. Okay, *now* it makes sense.

To do this, simply click the audio button on the asset's folder in graphical view window. This opens another window showing you the various audio tracks associated with that video asset. We only have one, in English. Once you select this track, the Property Inspector responds by giving you various options you can carry out on the selected audio track as seen in Figure 11.6, the most important one being the language selection. It defaults to None, so therefore no audio would play. How about that? Simply pop up the language menu and select English (or whatever language you are using) and all will be well with the world.

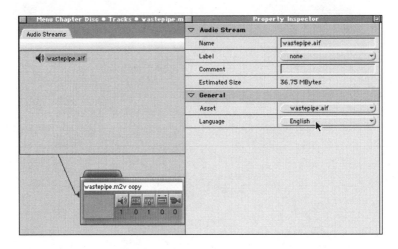

Figure 11.6: Setting the audio track's language.

Fear not, Flash animator, we'll be walking you through the entire process of creating a simple DVD playable on any home DVD player next. We felt that before doing so, it would be wise to have you become a bit familiar with the basics of DVD Studio Pro. We brought extra attention to the audio linkage problem, because it can be quite confusing until you know the solution and reasoning.

Preparing Flash Content for DVD

Preparing your Flash animations for output to DVD is a little different than for video tape. What we'll do in this section is to give you some tips on how to make the files the best they can be before committing to DVD. We'll cover various issues, such as video issues that pertain to both tape and DVD, as well as some coverage and project on creating motion menus (something that's simply not possible on videotape).

Video Rules Still Apply

As we discussed in the previous chapter on making your animations for video-tape, there are certain rules you should adhere to. We will quickly summarize them and comment on any issues that may apply to DVD specifically.

Even though a DVD is far superior in quality to videotape, we're still faced with the common display—the TV set. It is because of the TV's shortcomings, that you must still follow the rules for display.

Title-safe and action-safe areas still apply, so be sure the critical art is within the actual viewing area of the TV screen (see Figure 11.7). The same is true for the interlace flicker. Even with the work playing from a pristine DVD data flow, the TV itself introduces the flicker, not the content. So care must be taken here, as well, with thin horizontal lines as we explained in Chapter 10.

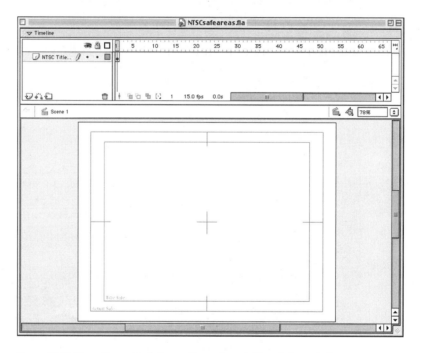

Figure 11.7: You still need to follow action-safe and title-safe boundaries.

Color and Clarity

On the subject of color space, a DVD can handle better color resolution than videotape, and since it's not being broadcast, there's really no need to worry too much here about illegal colors. It will be up to you, the creator as viewer, to judge what looks good and what doesn't. Even with the wider latitude in color rendition, you can still overdo it. Certain super intense colors such as a very bright blue or yellow still have difficulty displaying without bleeding (carrying over offending color into other colors).

The picture's color and clarity is dependent upon how the DVD player is connected to the TV set. If you use composite connections (most common), you will get a fairly good image, but if your player and TV supports it, component (three different connectors, one each for the RGB signal) is the best it can be. If you do have component connections, it will still be of help to use the composite connection for test watching, since this is how most end viewers will see it.

We really just mention this here as a reinforcement of what should be done *before* you get to the point of mastering a DVD. These issues mentioned here and discussed in greater detail in Chapter 10 should be considered during the actual production of the content.

Creating a Motion Menu in Flash

Okay, you have an understanding of what you can do with Flash in the video realm. You've followed all the rules from Chapter 10 and this chapter. You have an Oscar-worthy animation in the can and you want it on DVD. You could simply plop it on the DVD as is and it will work just fine. "But wait, this is a class act, we need a menu just like the big shots use in Hollywood!" Indeed you do—and to be extra fancy, you want a Motion Menu since one that just sits there without motion is kind of boring.

What we'd like to do is to walk you through exactly how we created the one we've used on the CD-ROM that accompanies this book (see Figure 11.8) and why we used Flash instead of After Effects, Final Cut Pro, or other options. Of course, you can simply apply these steps to your own creations. We certainly hope the insight you gather will fuel you to create even more outrageously cool stuff.

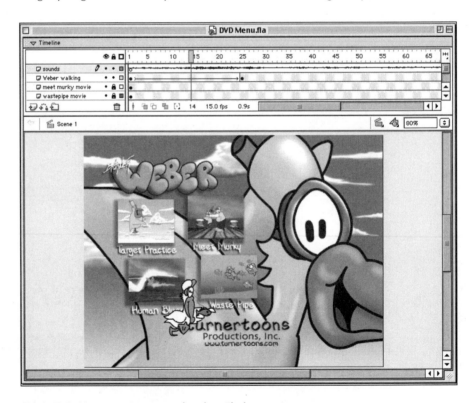

Figure 11.8: Motion menu creation directly in Flash.

So Why Flash?

First we'd like to explain why we did not use After Effects or other such animation programs for our motion menu creation. It's really quite simple. In Flash,
you can draw using Flash's excellent drawing tools, and animate cartoons or anything else while viewing the video clip's frames (assuming you've imported video
clips into Flash's timeline). You simply can't do this in AE. The all-in-one feedback (with onion skinning, or the ability to see past and future frames at same
time) can be critical when trying to draw animation on top of video frames that
you'll be using for the motion menu.

This is a good time to explain exactly what a motion menu is. You've seen
them on the DVDs you may rent, the options and selections buttons are there
with a movie or movies playing, and usually there's some form of background
music. What is really happening here is a seamless video loop. At times, it can
be quite difficult to have video loop seamlessly, because video usually does not
contain a repeating pattern like music does. To combat this fact, you can make
the motion menu last longer, so that when the bump back to the beginning does
happen, it won't happen as often. This makes the video loop back glitch less
annoying. So, in a nutshell, a motion menu is really just a looping video clip
with buttons waiting to be chosen. So now that we know what a motion menu is,
it should make it easier to create one in Flash. Let's try it!

If you look in this chapter's folder, you will find all the content we used. We
would've loved to have given you the entire DVD, but due to CD-ROM space
constraints we can only give you one full cartoon movie (the entire DVD would
take five CDs to hold). However, the motion menu we'll be talking about has the
preview to all four cartoon shows that would comprise the entire DVD product.
For our motion menu walkthrough, this is sufficient.

1. The first thing we did was to take short edits (roughly a bit more than the
   length of the finished menu loop in time duration of about a minute) from
   the finished cartoon shows to be included on the final DVD. These cartoons
   were already in QuickTime format. We simply resized them much smaller to
   120×90 pixels and removed any audio. We then saved them with no
   compression to maintain quality. These clips will be the motion part of our
   menu. The clips will also act as the buttons. They will simply play in a loop
   until one is selected to be viewed.

2. In Flash, we made a new FLA project (we've included the finished one on
   the CD-ROM; see Figure 11.9). In order to keep files small enough to fit on
   CD-ROM, we made this Motion Menu project rather short in duration of
   around 8 seconds. Ideally, you'll want to make your a bit longer—a minute
   or so should do it, depending on your content.

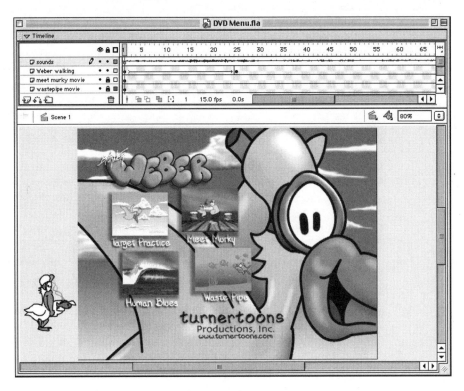

Figure 11.9: The DVD Menu file main screen in Flash.

3. We then imported all our content into Flash in the usual way. We used a background still (which could have been a movie) that takes up the entire screen. This still carries all the text you read. We chose to have the text in a Photoshop-created still, in order to use effects that cannot be done in Flash with text, such as soft drop shadows and airbrushed effects. We also added a background sound of birds at the beach that will loop.

4. Next, we set up the various layers needed in the timeline as seen in Figure 11.10. It's very important to use layers, as this keeps elements separate and easier to deal with. As you can see from the file supplied, we have a background layer with still, a layer for sound, movie clips, and animation of walking pelican.

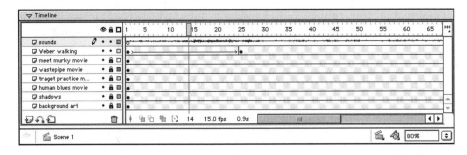

Figure 11.10: The layers set up in Flash.

5. We then went about the task of arranging things in a fashion we found appealing, keeping in mind what we've learned about action-safe and title-safe (see Chapter 10).

6. Next is the magic. We decided we wanted the star of the show to walk out, toss a fish in the air, and eat it (as seen in Figure 11.11). This is the part that would be impossible to do interactively in AE. The short little animation adds appeal, but also functions to inform you to choose a cartoon to watch. Here is where you may get incredibly clever in your DVD production. You could have, let's say, an announcer, or someone who informs you of the various choices that can be made from this menu. This could be quite helpful in a DVD production for a corporation trying to teach employees safety practices, for example. This is what makes Flash a great choice for the animator wanting to make motion menus for DVDs.

Figure 11.11: The added animation hand-drawn to background.

7. Next, we tested all the motions to make sure they were what we wanted. After that step, we were ready to output to a QuickTime Video file for use in DVD Studio Pro.

Keep Your Flash Animation Clean for Better Transfer to DVD

Since the entire purpose of DVD is to be as high of quality as possible, it makes little sense to use severely compressed and otherwise junky stuff. For the source, you want the very cleanest files you can possibly have. This usually means uncompressed video all the way through the editing process.

Though you can use footage with the DV compression used (and you are forced to if you use camera footage [live action] by default it must be compressed), it's not recommended for animation. Particularly with Flash animation, you will generally have lots of flat color areas that meet black lines, such as is common in cartoons. By using the DV compression before going to DVD, you will be compressing it twice (once as DV second as MPEG-2 for DVD). Compressing twice can introduce unwanted artifacts around the high contrast areas of the image, such as where flat color meets black lines.

As long as you know you're going to DVD, the wise choice is to keep all animation movie files uncompressed up to the final MPEG-2 compression that will be actually burned onto the DVD. This is how you achieve the ultimate in quality.

QuickTime 5 and MPEG-2 (The DVD Format)

All the new G4s (actually any Mac and most PCs), will have the new Quicktime 5 video and audio system-level software. With QT5 (and DVD Studio Pro installed), you will have the ability to export any video file to MPEG-2. MPEG-2 is the standard compression algorithm used in DVDs today. It's a very high-quality codec, meant strictly for playback. You will not be doing any editing with the MPG-2 codec, so make sure all that work is done before converting to MPEG-2.

Keep this rule in mind: For best results, edit in uncompressed (or at least DV codec for live action stuff) codec or "None." After all is edited and no more changes are needed, then convert (compress) to MPEG-2.

For sound along this path, you will want to do the same thing: Keep it uncompressed all the way through the editing process, and keep it in stereo if at all possible. In fact, even if you have some mono sound effects or such, convert them to stereo even if only pseudo stereo as its fidelity will be stronger.

One of the strange things you'll notice as you take your animation files to MPEG-2 is the fact that the process extracts and makes into a separate file the audio track of your work. What you end up with after conversion is two files for every one movie file you've created, one for video and one for audio. In the example included on the CD-ROM, they are named wastepipe.aif (sound track) and wastepipe.m2v (video data stream). These two files come together in the DVD as one movie that plays in English.

You may wonder why this separation happens. Good wondering! We knew you'd ask. The reason for separating the sound from the video facilitates multiple languages. Thus, you can have one video data stream (an extremely large file) but four different audio tracks in various languages (much smaller files than duplicating everything). By doing this, your data on the DVD is very economical and you can have four versions of the animation to choose from at playback time. Even though DVDs hold an enormous amout of data, video files are enormous as well.

Processing Movies for DVD

What we'd like to do next is to walk you through a session of converting animation files from Flash to what is needed for use in DVD Studio Pro. We are assuming you have already created all the animation, and are sitting in Flash, wondering what's next.

To do this, you will need the Pro version of QT5, it usually comes with DVD Studio Pro. The reason you'll need the Pro QT5 is the standard free version will not export. This exporting to MPEG-2 is essential to creating a DVD. If you are so inclined and have the software, Cleaner Pro (formerly Media Cleaner Pro) should be capable of doing batch conversions of many various video and animation clips by the time you read this. If you regularly work with many clips, it would be a wise purchase, since you can set it and forget it. The conversion process, depending on length of clip, can be quite time-consuming, even on a dual processor G4. So you can easily see how setting up a batch and going home for the evening while compression takes place is a good plan—beats the heck out of watching and waiting for the proceedings to finish. But, for one clip at a time, QT5 player will work just fine.

Though some of this information concerning Flash to QuickTime Video output is covered in Chapter 10, we'll repeat certain parts here in this walk-through for the sake of continuity.

Project: Get Animations out of Flash and into DVD Studio Pro

You have a completed animation in Flash. You've done all the testing and you're satisfied with the results. The next thing you need to do is to output to Quicktime Video format.

1. In Flash, with the target FLA open, go to File • Export Movie. In the proceeding dialog popup, choose QuickTime Video (recall our discussion earlier about not using plain old QuickTime, as this does not make a video file but rather a Flash track readable by QuickTime; see Figure 11.12) and name the file.

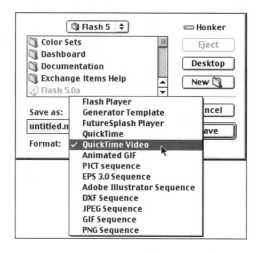

Figure 11.12: The QuickTime Video Export option in Flash.

2. In the next dialog, Figure 11.13, is the Flash version of the Quicktime dialog. You want to choose size 720 × 480 with Maintain Aspect Ratio unchecked. (Recall our past discussion about square to rectangular pixels conversion.) This forces the animation to appear squished a bit on computer screen, but will look fine on TV.

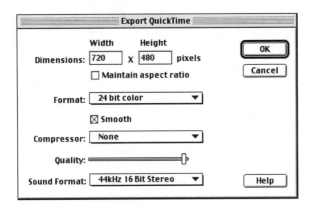

Figure 11.13: The Flash QuickTime options settings preparing for DVD use.

3. For format, choose 24-bit color and check the Smooth box. This will give you the highest color fidelity available and will anti-alias all art.

4. Under compressor, choose None, and crank the slider all the way to best quality. Even though the none compressor means exactly that—no compression—we are still spooked by the quality slider, so for superstition's sake, crank it all the way to best (to the right hand side).

5. For sound, set it to be 44KHz 16-bit stereo. Why settle for less?

6. Click OK and allow this to render to a file. Depending on length and complexity of your animation, this can take some time.

7. Now you can close Flash. All done with it. We will note that for the purpose of this mission, we will not be editing the Flash output in any other application. (If you need to, it is at this point you would take the video file into After Effects, Final Cut Pro, or other to do any special effects or editing of any sort. Just remember after editing in such an application to render the results to an uncompressed video file, just like you did from Flash, and carry on the remaining steps.)

8. Open the resulting movie from above in QT Player Pro.

9. From here use File • Export. In the proceeding dialog, choose Movie to MPEG2 from the Export popup. See Figure 11.14.

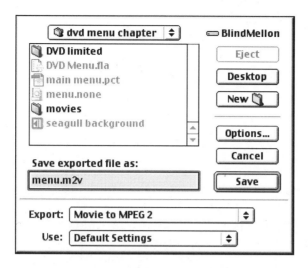

Figure 11.14: QuickTime Player Pro Export dialog.

10. Before going any farther you should check in with the Options button in the QT Export dialog, as seen in Figure 11.15. Here you will find all the settings needed for MPEG-2 Encoder compression. Be sure NTSC is checked, or engaged radio button (if in an NTSC area otherwise PAL). Also engage radio button for 4:3 aspect ratio, as this is the standard ratio for most TVs today (16:9 is for HDTV). If your animation has audio, check the Save Audio box too.

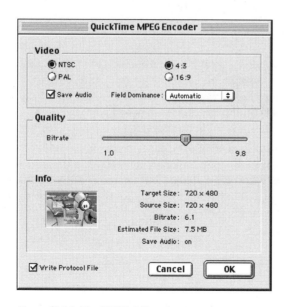

Figure 11.15: The MPEG-2 Encoder options.

11. While still in MPEG Encoder options, set the quality slider to around 7.2 MB per second. Keep in mind this quality slider is for video *only* (audio is output uncompressed). Even though DVDs can manage a sustained throughput of over 9 MB per second, setting it to the full 9.8 will leave no bandwidth for audio and your video will not play. 7.2 MBps seems to be a good quality and playable data stream compromise. You can, of course, experiment with going lower. By going lower, your files will be smaller (thus more time on a disk), but quality will begin to suffer.

12. You may leave Write Protocol File checked.

13. Click OK to dismiss MPEG Encoder options. These options should remain throughout any subsequent compression sessions, but it's always nice to check before committing to it.

14. Back in Export dialog, choose a name and a place to save your file. Click OK to commence the compression process.

15. After it's complete, you should now have two files, an audio track file and a video data stream file, ready for importing into DVD Studio Pro for DVD authoring.

Continuing the Motion Menu

We paused for a bit in our explanation of the motion menu example included on CD-ROM, the reason being that you need to have an understanding of the video formats used before we could get back to it. Now you should have a fair understanding of how to get animations out of Flash and into a video format that you can use in your DVD production.

So in order to complete the motion menu, we'll now walk through the process of hooking it up (wiring it) in DVD Studio Pro.

1. We now have (after conversion to MPEG-2) two files for our menu. One menu.m2v is the video data stream and the audio named menu.aif. We imported these menu files along with that actual cartoon show files that will play, into DVD Studio Pro in the standard way via File • Import and pointing to files in resulting import dialog.

2. After this, we first needed to make a content entry to have the menu point to the cartoon show itself. By dragging the video stream named wastepipe.m2v to the graphical view window, it creates an asset folder as seen in Figure 11.16. The we drag the associated audio track to this folder to link it to the video.

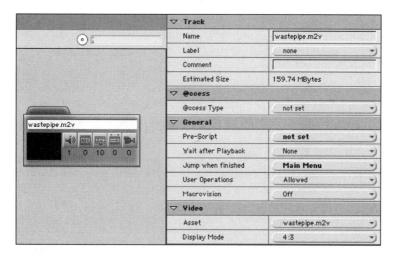

Figure 11.16: The assets of the cartoon show shown as folders in DVD Studio Pro.

3. By clicking the audio icon of the asset folder (looks like a little speaker), you can then select the linked track and assign the all important language to it in the Property Inspector. We chose English for obvious reasons. We now have a basic working asset entry that the menu can point to when used.

4. For creating the menu, you must click the Add Menu button at the bottom of the Graphical View window (see Figure 11.17). This creates a new empty menu folder that we'll add the menu content to (that we previously created in Flash).

Figure 11.17: Adding a menu asset folder.

5. You can add these elements (video and audio tracks) by dragging and dropping them onto menu folder from asset bin. We were sure to do the same language association for this audio as we previously did in step 3.

6. We now have our ducks in a row and it's time to hook up the menu. By double clicking the video icon (in the Menu folder), we enter Menu Mode. Here you can see the entire screen as it will be seen on a TV set.

7. Using Item • New Button command, DVD Studio Pro creates a new untitled button and the Property Inspector changes to reflect the options available. You can either graphically drag the hot area (represented by the dotted lines), or you can be precise by entering the dimensions in the Property Inspector. It's also a very good idea to name the button at this point in the Property Inspector, to avoid confusion that will surely happen once you have more button to deal with as seen in Figure 11.18.

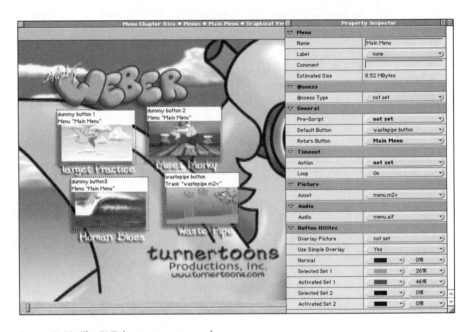

Figure 11.18: The DVD button creation mode.

8. Next drag to place the button where desired. Keep in mind that this area will have a tint of color that you can choose to show it's activated in the finished DVD. Unfortunately, at this time DVD Studio Pro can only use rectangles (or squares of course) to define a button in a motion menu. So design wisely.

9. After the aesthetics are dealt with, it's time to hook this puppy up. With the button still selected and viewing the Property Inspector, you'll see under the Action section the command "Jump To." We use this to jump to the only cartoon we actually have, wastepipe (see Figure 11.19). Since in this abbreviated version, we do not have the other cartoons available, we have set all other buttons to simply jump to Main Menu.

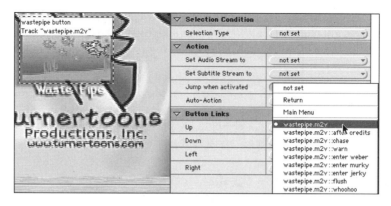

Figure 11.19: The "Jump To" command.

10. You can now close the Menu Mode by closing the window containing the graphics. You should return to the Graphical View window, and the folders there should now have arrows pointing to where the menu will send you when activated.

11. From here it's now a good time to test what we have. Using Item • Preview Disc will send you to a full screen version of the project (see Figure 11.20) with controls that are very similar to the standard controls found on a DVD player remote control. You may now play it as though it was really on a DVD. After checking that we have it just right, we're ready to make a DVD disk.

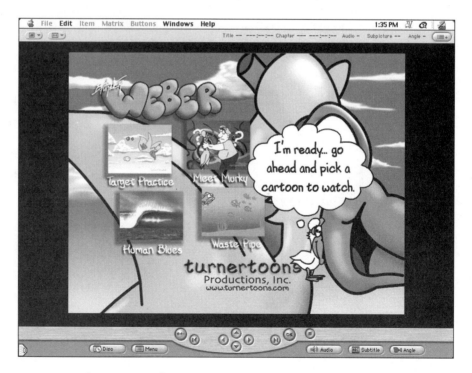

Figure 11.20: The DVD test run function of DVD Studio Pro.

12. Here's the real beauty of this system. Once everything has tested positive you can burn a DVD. Simply insert a blank DVD into the Mac and choose File • Format and Build Disc. Go get a Dew or take a little break; your DVD will be ready shortly.

Of course, this is a very basic but necessary starting point in creating a DVD of your Flash animation. For further depth in the use of DVD Studio Pro, please refer to the manual and Apple's web site at www.Apple.com. All manner of DVD functionality can be achieved such as chapters, web link hotspots, and slide shows.

Mastering a DVD for Mass Duplication

So far we've talked about making a single or just a few one off DVD disks directly from the Mac itself. What if you needed more, like a thousand, or a million? Yikes! It would take roughly 97 years to burn 1 million DVDs (60 minute in duration) constantly burning 24/7. . . .

Mastering, or making the master files for mass duplication, is obviously the only way to go. DVD Studio Pro can do this too, but not from a burned disk. In other words, an Apple machine-burned DVD disk will *not* work as a master for duplication.

The Files You'll Need to Transfer

The process for mastering is actually not much different than making a one-off disk. When we used File • Format and Build Disc in the previous section you may have noticed the File • Build Disc option right underneath it. With this option chosen, DVD Studio Pro compiles (multiplexes) all the video, audio and interactive data in to a folder (that you name) with two subfolders that will automatically be named AUDIO_TS and VIDEO_TS. These folders contain the data necessary to mass-duplicate a DVD production (see Figure 11.21).

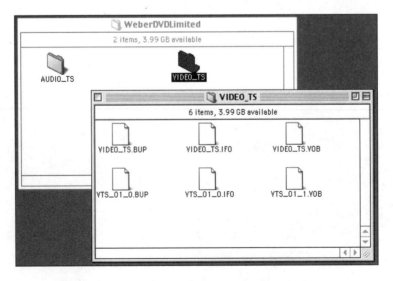

Figure 11.21: The folders and files needed to master a basic DVD.

Keep in mind that these folders can become huge. It's not uncommon that DVD video files run in the multiple gigabytes realm. Not a real big problem, since hard drives today are inexpensive and hold tons of data. The problem crops up in the transferring of this large amount of data reliably. Unless you live with a mass duplicator in your studio, you will need to move this data somehow. Generally, an Exabyte or other form of tape drive is the best option. Actually, if you have a spare hard drive hanging around, that could work as well. The caveat here is there are so many varying data tapes and data formats, that the best thing to do once you find a duplication house you want to deal with is to make double sure of what they can read and then conform to it. Do this research as early in the process as possible if you are on a deadline, so you don't get stuck holding a bag of unusable data at the last minute.

Duplication Houses

Although there are many, many duplication houses—and suppliers of disks, labels, and equipment—we cannot list them all. We suggest that you start with www.diskmakers.com. Of course, you can also check the relevant area of our website, www.flashthefuture/11, for updates and further resources.

Summary

While creating DVDs can be a very complex subject, much beyond the scope of a single chapter, we have given you a good footing on how to use Flash in the content creation of such material. You should now be prepared to get the very best video image possible by using the methods describe here, such as keeping all video uncompressed until final format destination (MPEG2). We have also pointed out why Apple's new G4 product line is the one stop for personal and even professional DVD production. Goodbye VHS tape . . . it's been nice knowing you.

In these last three chapters, you learned how to prepare Flash for delivery to video and TV, as well as how to deliver them with DVD. In our next chapter, we'll look at the opportunities and techniques for the use of Flash in another area of TV: the new frontier of ITV.

12

DEVELOPING FOR
INTERACTIVE TV

Brett Jackson

In Chapter 11 we took a look at how to deliver your Flash animations with DVD. In this chapter we'll discuss interactive television
(ITV)—the technology as well as the industry—and how to recognize, design, and deliver Flash-powered ITV applications. We'll also
take a look at what industry professionals think of the wide world of ITV.
ITV consists of a new class of Internet devices, set-top boxes, that many
believe will revitalize the Net economy and bring the Web into every household. These set-top boxes will let you go online while watching TV, and will
even meld broadcast programming with interactive elements in heretofore-
impossible new ways.

Flash is already being adopted as the authoring tool of choice for ITV
because of its uniform cross-platform appearance, interactive multimedia capability, animation and design possibilities, and its functionality as a time-based
medium. The understanding of ITV that you will glean from this chapter will
give you valuable insight into its wide-ranging implications, as well as the tools
you will need in order to target your preferred ITV application, develop it, and
then demo for your client.

An ITV Primer

Many Flash developers wishing to develop for interactive television may never have seen ITV in action. While it may be easy to imagine ITV's eventual omnipresence, as of this writing it can still be difficult to find demo models in major electronics stores. To better understand ITV's potential let's take a look at the state of the industry, the promise of interactive TV, and the basic steps you'll need to take to develop and deliver Flash content to the ITV viewer.

The ITV Industry

At this writing, the ITV industry is in an awkward infancy. While the technologies needed to create interactivity exist, the ultimate ITV infrastructure is unknown. Too, consumer demand for ITV has yet to develop and ITV itself is fractured by competing proprietary standards that choke widespread development and hurt the chances of popular acceptance.

ITV's Potential

Despite these problems, ITV offers thrilling possibilities. For one, ITV could more than double the number of people using the Internet by bringing the Internet to televisions everywhere. ITV promises to combine the hypnotic power of television with the best-loved computer applications: the Web, email, instant messaging, and networked games.

To better grasp the commercial potential of ITV, imagine all of these elements combined into one personalized data swell. Such a convergence of broadcasting and content control could allow for personalized commercials and compelling, targeted programming: When viewers tune in to their favorite program, they would see a version adapted to their specific tastes.

ITV could lift e-commerce to new, impressive levels. "T-Commerce" merges television's ability to create consumer demand with the Internet's ability to transact sales instantly. Applications using this functionality are already appearing: You see a commercial for deep-dish pizza and, by clicking the icon in the corner of your TV screen, you can order that very pizza with your remote control. It will be delivered to your door, to your specifications, without your having to avert your gaze. Commercials might become like dim sum, a non-stop parade of products, each posing a simple question—yes or no? A nod from you would debit your account and add the item to your Amazon.com grocery list.

What's in the Box?

So what of the technology behind the ITV screen? For the foreseeable future, ITV will be delivered as a coded component inside the signal sent by the viewer's cable or satellite provider, with its hidden information decoded by a set-top box. This box will strip out the interactive content and interpret it as distinct elements, not unlike the way an Internet browser receives HTML from a distant server and displays the information as easy to understand graphical web pages.

ITV ultimately offers four kinds of capability, as shown in Figure 12.1. We'll discuss the scope of each of these capabilities in the following sections.

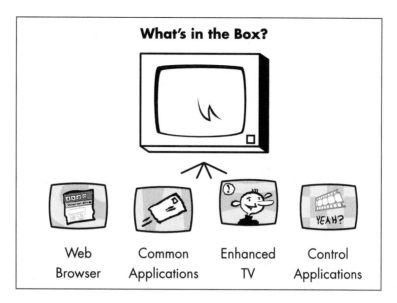

Figure 12.1: Possible ITV components.

The Web Browser

Any set-top box can call itself ITV if it has a Web browser and the ability to connect to the Web. This is both the most common feature across the different ITV platforms and where Flash most commonly appears. Although some ITV info is encoded in the broadcast signal, most current ITV devices require the viewer to go online using their telephone wiring.

Common Applications

Most set-top boxes will offer the ability to browse the Web and send email, as well as the ability to send instant messages, chat in real time, use a picture phone, and read newsgroups. Address books, calendar, calculators, and the like are also becoming more common.

Enhanced TV

Enhanced TV means that broadcasts have added features and content with which the viewer can interact. Sometimes called two-screen TV or synchronized TV, in this model of ITV, the television show being broadcast sends a trigger that is synchronized with the on-screen action, and which allows the viewer to launch additional content. This is already being used for interactive voting (viewers can affect a broadcast or play), as well as interactive game shows. Enhanced TV is also used to present special interactive commercial offers.

Control Applications

Control applications offer services specific to the set-top box. Perhaps the most common example of a control application is the interactive television guide that lets you see what is playing on all the channels and read show descriptions.

Personal video recording (PVR) is another. PVR is like a smart VCR—it's capable of recording many hours of your favorite broadcasts to an internal hard disk, even with the ability to skip the commercials. Some boxes offer only this capability without the ability to web-browse.

Another common control application is *video on demand* (VOD), which allows viewers to rent movies without leaving the house. (Anyone who has ever had to hunt for a purportedly in-stock movie at Blockbuster will appreciate the value of this.) Networked video games could also be considered control applications, given that newer gaming consoles offer substantial browsing and networking capability.

The Technical Details

How does ITV content get to where it needs to go?

Well, at this instant, every TV in your city (and in your home) is receiving ITV content. In addition to the viewable television broadcast, invisible, encoded content is packaged into the television signal, to be decoded by the ITV receiver. The part of the TV signal used to transmit this information is called the *vertical blanking interval* (VBI), and it appears as a black stripe on the top and bottom of your screen. You can sometimes see the VBI when your television loses its vertical hold. Figure 12.2 shows a breakdown of the VBI signal on its way to the box.

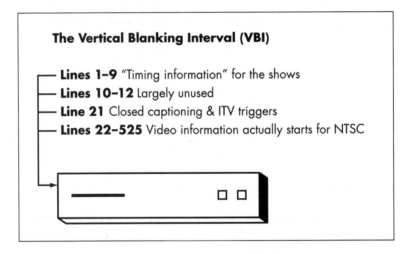

Figure 12.2: The VBI occupies the first 21 lines of the total 525 lines transmitted in every second of NTSC (National Television System Committee, the format for U.S. television) TV airtime.

Line 21 of the VBI contains triggers that alert the set-top box that additional interactive content is available. This trigger will have a URL and can contain, among other things, a limited amount of human-readable text, an expiration date, and ECMA scripting (the syntax familiar to Flash's ActionScript). Although the URL itself is fairly standardized, each receiver will set its own implementation to let viewers choose whether they want to view the enhanced content.

For example, if the target website were UNcom.com, the trigger would begin with a URL in the format www.UNcom.com. Following this, any number of bracket-enclosed attribute/value pairs may be defined. The name attribute usually follows with information about the link (for example, [name:Hire Experts!]).

The expires attribute provides a date after which the link is no longer valid, in the format yyyymmddThhmmss, with a capital T separating the date from the time. For example, [expires:20151105T220401] would expire on the first second of 10:04 PM (AKA 2204 hundred hours) on the 5th of November in the year 2015.

A complete URL (in the ATVEF format discussed below under "What This Means for Flash") would look like this:

```
<http://www.UNcom.com>[name: Hire Experts!][expires:20151105T220401]
```

NOTE *The complete ITV hyperlink encoding format is specified by the Electronic Industries Association specification EIA-746-A, "Transport of Internet Uniform Resource Locator (URL) Information Using Text-2 (T-2) Service," which can be purchased at Global Engineering Documents' website at http://global.ihs.com/.*

Who Is Getting ITV Out There?

Of course, the content for ITV has to come from somewhere, and it is important to understand the levels and functions of each contributor. Figure 12.3 shows how the various agencies are involved in the grand scheme of ITV distribution.

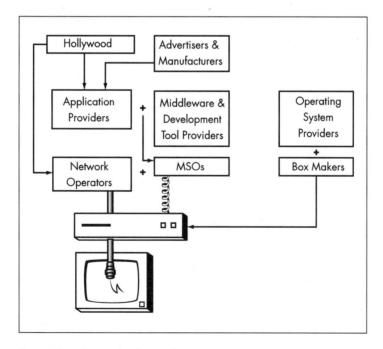

Figure 12.3: The ITV distribution chain.

Multiple Service Operators (MSOs)

The multiple service operator is the ISP of ITV, but, unlike your ISP, the MSO may not offer access strictly to the Internet. More MSOs are likely to offer restricted interactive content fenced off from the rest of the Web in setups known as walled gardens. Subscribers to a walled garden can follow a hyperlink out to the larger Internet, but others can't link in. Frequently these walled gardens are used as personalized portals, offering news, financial information, sports, and various applications.

Network Operators

Network operators are the broadcast, cable, and satellite companies that own the equipment used to deliver the signal to your home. If you have digital cable and a cable box, you may already have a set-top box in your home. Because it is less expensive to install a slightly more advanced cable box and delay offering ITV services than it is to install conventional cable boxes and replace them later, many network operators are using ITV boxes (with their interactive functionality disabled) in place of cable boxes. Obviously, these network operators have decided to invest in ITV in anticipation of offering ITV services sometime soon. Most likely, these network operators will solicit programs and advertisements from Hollywood and may also court application providers to provide branded ITV content for their set-top box interface.

Operating System Providers

An ITV box is essentially a dedicated computer, with its own operating system, that uses your TV as its monitor. As with a personal computer, the hardware and software may both be obtained from multiple suppliers. For example, operating system providers (like Microsoft and Liberate) team up with a technology provider (such as Scientific Atlanta and WebTV) to produce a set-top box for the network operators to distribute. Some ITV operating systems can already run Flash within their interfaces, independent of their browsers.

Application Providers

Flash developers are the application providers. These entities and production houses specialize in producing ITV programming, advertising, and applications to run on set-top boxes, inside walled gardens, and on the Internet. Application providers work with Hollywood, advertisers, and MSOs to produce the interactive content and services that put the I in ITV.

Hollywood

Hollywood, AKA the television show producers, whether in Hollywood or Vancouver, makes the television programs and advertisements that contain our interactive elements. Hollywood is closely involved with network operators and works with advertising agencies and MSOs to produce programs for integration with interactive content.

Advertisers

Along with network operators and MSOs, advertisers commission the bulk of new interactive content. Though historical records may someday identify ITV as the defining technology that sparked an intellectual renaissance, it's the advertisers' determination to sell bottled water or stuffed-crust pizza that will build the infrastructure. Motivated by advertising dollars, some network operators are subsidizing set-top boxes hoping to popularize what may be the greatest selling tool ever invented. And, in addition to further binding viewers to their televisions with interactive content, advertisers may benefit from the viewing data culled from boxes (each with a unique IP address) to target marketing at the neighborhood level—and possibly even to specific households.

What This Means for Flash

The ITV industry has started to lay some interesting groundwork for standardization. The ATVEF (Advanced Television Enhancement Forum) mentioned in our discussion of ITV URLs is the most widely adopted ITV standards document in the United States. (The spec doesn't include Flash because it is meant to outline the *minimum* requirements necessary for consistent industry development and also because Flash is proprietary software beholden to unpredictable business interests.)

As of this writing, WebTV (the receiver that users buy to run MSN TV) has the greatest acceptance of the available ITV boxes. WebTV's winning combo of ATVEF compliance and endorsement of Flash predict a likely model for developing standards.

Flash should play an expanding role in the future of ITV for the following reasons:

- The ATVEF protocols are HTML-based, so the logical next step for box makers is to include the most desirable add-ons.

- Generally, set-top boxes are software-upgradable so that plugins like Flash can be updated.

- Most boxes are processor-limited, which makes Flash's tiny footprint and ascetic bandwidth demand very valuable assets.

In the current incarnation of the ITV box, Flash will be found most commonly in the web browsers. But other platforms are also using Flash as the OS interface because of its stellar motion graphics and ease of updating. If a platform reads Flash natively, then it also offers the opportunity for developers to build applications (like games and hybrid web software) that are easily created and updated.

The PEAR AVENUE Example

For example, PEAR AVENUE, INC. is producing an ITV entertainment system called SEZ ("says"), whose Flash 5 presentation layer takes complete advantage of unbelievable new interface possibilities. Interactions between the viewer and SEZ consist of simple conversational exchanges with characters in a storyline.

Your character of choice might be our Teen Sports Fan, Javen, or our Active Senior, Uncle Tony. Javen likes extreme sports and pop, especially boy bands. Uncle Tony likes to travel, and his only bane in life is that his girlfriends keep dying. You can therefore imagine that Javen and Uncle Tony will present programming information and services that are of interest and relevance to them personally and in a style consistent with their characters. We call this approach *affinity-based categorization.*

"Future Radio" is PEAR AVENUE's concept piece for supplemental entertainment in the form of conversational interfaces. It engages viewers in dialog with a character from a fictional affinity universe. Using text dialog and Flash animation, they add depth to the characters. The characters that make up the interface know each other, have relationships, and interact together. While the "Future Radio" story is a sci-fi comedy, other affinity universes can be created in other styles and storylines that will cross over with normal television production.

The SEZ interface is produced daily at their studio in Mountain View, California, which keeps the interface fresh and exciting. According to PEAR AVENUE's CEO, Steven Ericsson-Zenith, "The successful delivery of interactive consumer services on the next generation of communication and entertainment devices depends on new and entertaining interfaces: interfaces that people will enjoy, that will enable them, and that will compel them to return often. Our interfaces are FUN."

Who Are the Major Players?

The following table lists the most prominent ITV players. All are also early adopters of Flash for ITV.

Table 12.1: Flash player adoption among industry leaders

Platform	Version
Liberate TV Navigator	Flash 5
MSN TV	Flash 4
WebTV	Flash 3
Liberate TV Navigator Analog (used by AOLTV)	Flash 3
ICTV	Flash 3

Despite this encouragement, we still have a long way to go. Although these platforms all support Flash to some degree (and several have committed to future upgrades), their Flash content is playing on assorted set-top boxes, each with different hardware configurations that will affect playback unpredictably.

What Does ITV Have to Offer Flash Developers?

Although we await the day that ITV becomes ubiquitous—and nearly every television show, commercial, and station identification is made entirely in Flash—there are already plenty of places for an entrepreneurial Flash developer to make his mark on the small screen.

WebTV

WebTV has the biggest ITV audience to date and a very substantial following. If you're itching to explore the concepts of ITV development, WebTV has all the basics. The box reads ITV triggers from any VHS tape or DVD, just as though it had come from a satellite, and a response to a trigger can bring up any site on the Internet. Simple HTML tags can allow you to embed a TV window into your web page along with Flash content, and you can even test the content on your PC using a free WebTV emulator called the WebTV Viewer. (You'll find specific instructions for doing so as well as the emulator at the MSN TV Service Developer Support Site, http://developer.msntv.com.) Figure 12.4 briefly compares the two options.

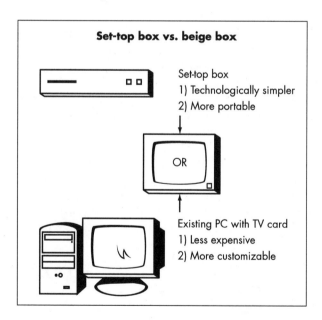

Figure 12.4: Comparison of set-top and desktop ITV.

Desk-Top Boxes

Although it may seem a little like cheating, many people are enjoying ITV on their computers, and for development purposes, that puts us on much more familiar ground. Viewers favor using the PC over the traditional set-top box to view ITV content for many reasons. First, Microsoft Windows 98 and higher comes packaged with a free, proprietary version of WebTV, called WebTV for Windows. Add a TV tuner card and you will be able to view and develop ITV content on the same screen.

Others are watching ITV content on television, but are using a PC with a TV Tuner card as their media entertainment center. In this configuration, the PC acts as a PVR, but with much more memory than either Tivo or Replay TV— and it can edit content. (Sony is releasing the Digital Studio PC expressly for this purpose.) Many buyers think of this not as abstention from buying a set-top box, but as upgrading to add extra functionality to the personal computer that they use more.

Spiderdance

Spiderdance and MTV made history in 1999 with the launch of WebRIOT, the first television show designed from the ground up for interactivity. With tens of millions of games served over two seasons, WebRIOT broke new ground for interactive TV.

Developing with Flash and their proprietary TruSync system (which deploys ITV content synchronized exactly to the television broadcast), they've set out to reach the largest possible ITV audience. Spiderdance conceived the idea of sync-to-broadcast PC/TV convergence as a real-world solution for implementing interactive TV on a wide-scale, producing interactive television that requires no special hardware or hook-ups. As set-top boxes, smart TVs, and wireless devices become viable interactive TV platforms, Spiderdance's backend server system will be able to talk to them through standard Internet protocol, though for the time being users watch TV and participate with the on-screen occurrences using a PC.

"Using two screens keeps the TV display crystal-clear and unmodified. The crowded overlays and postage-stamp size video screens of past ITV convergence de-emphasized the TV product. We believe just the opposite should happen. We believe the TV programming should take center-stage with full-screen unmodified video.

"With the synchronized use of the home PC, the computer provides a platform for in-depth interactivity that complements the TV program, rather than competing with it. Viewers' existing PC knowledge and Internet familiarity means that there is a very low barrier to getting on board with a Spiderdance-enhanced TV show. In fact, it couldn't be easier."

–Tracy Fullerton
Spiderdance President and Founder

Streaming ITV

QuickTime and Real Video both allow you to embed Flash in their media streams, which in turn allows you to make the video plugin's playback dimensions full-screen. The advantage is that the video component occupies only a small area of the screen, leaving the larger area framing the video to your Flash movie. As illustrated in Figure 12.5, the video will appear as if embedded in Flash (although technically speaking it's the other way around).

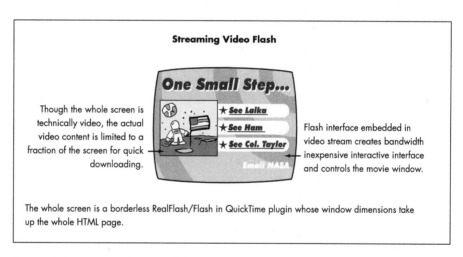

Figure 12.5: A visual explanation of Flash embedded in a streaming video plugin like RealVideo or QuickTime.

One advantage of this scenario is that Flash buttons can be used to control the frame actions in the video, so that the user can navigate the content just as they might move through the chapters on a DVD. Too, given this much control, synchronization is simple.

Whether this content is viewed on a set-top box that supports streaming media or on a regular desktop system, the only limitation to broadcasting your own interactive television station is the bandwidth.

Storyboarding and First Steps

Getting a foothold in ITV development may seem a little daunting; after all you won't be able to experiment by posting your demos on some little-watched channel. To test your demo, you would ideally see your designs come to life on ITV. If you can't get your hands on the specific set-top box you're developing for, substitute another commercially available one.

Every multimedia developer knows that storyboarding is crucial to interactive content design, and ITV is no exception. You will miss entire outcomes if you try to imagine the bifurcating schematic of ITV content in your head.

When storyboarding ITV, you must first choose between two types of ITV elements: constant and synchronous. Your choice will affect every decision that follows.

Constant Elements

Constant elements are enhancements that remain available for the duration of a show. For example, a discrete link may linger in the corner of the screen or a stock ticker may slowly trail by during a financial program.

Synchronous Elements

Synchronous elements are tied to developments in the program. For example, trivia, plot summaries, and sports scores are synchronous elements that can be used to create new entertainment and information experiences. These techniques are already being used to great effect on game shows such as "Who Wants to Be a Millionaire" and "The Weakest Link," but imagine the possibilities for gambling on sporting events, educational children's programming, whodunits, and the depraved new premises of reality TV.

Triggering Elements

Next, you'll need to produce a facsimile of the television broadcast that refers to show-appropriate content to be produced. If you're planning to develop synchronous content, you should watch the program and carefully note the time stamp when synched Flash elements are to be introduced.

Time stamp? Yup. Recall that ITV triggers are embedded in the video signal. Just as closed-captioning can be carried on videotape, triggers can be encoded and stored on that portable medium.

An additional piece of software (or hardware) is necessary to add triggers, both to extract the timing cues and to encode interactive triggers back into the signal. Most any software program for closed captioning will allow you to insert hyperlinks, but here's a list of some manufacturers and organizations that develop and provide triggering capability:

National Captioning Institute, closed captioning service provider
http://www.ncicap.org

Mixed Signals Technologies, Inc., closed captioning software publisher
http://www.mixedsignals.com

Leapfrog Productions, closed captioning software publisher
http://www.leapfrogproductions.com

The Norpak Corporation, data encoder manufacturer
http://www.norpak.ca/

ITV Dos and Don'ts

Now that you've got a general sense of how ITV works and how to get your Flash content into the box, let's take a look at some special technical and usability considerations for making your movie ITV-ready.

Technical Concerns

The golden rule of any media development is to know your audience. Before getting started with your development you should know whether your target audience

- Has a broadband connection,
- Has a fast processor, and
- Is web savvy.

Substantial differences between set-top boxes can cause you to regress an entire version of the application and to lose critical functionality that you may rely on. (For example, you might find that your platform supports nothing past Flash 3!) If you are lucky enough to know which box you're developing for beforehand, get your hands on that hardware before you start designing.

Version Regression

The first place you will see version regression is with ActionScript: Because so few set top boxes use even the Flash 5 player, you cannot design to utilize Flash 5's advanced scripting capability. You can still work in Flash or 6 and retain control over backward-compatible scripting by setting the version number in the Publish Settings (File • Publish Settings • Flash • Version). To clarify what we mean by version regression, refer to Figure 12.6.

As Figure 12.6 demonstrates, if you set your version number to Flash 3, all of the actions in the object actions panel that are off limits to the Flash 3 player will be highlighted (in yellow in the real program). You can even dial back the ActionScript settings to see what was installed in Flash 1.

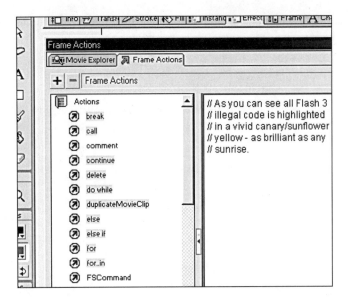

Figure 12.6: The ActionScript panel with restricted code for developing in Flash 3.

Follow these development procedures to save yourself a lot of time and heartache:

1. Start light on your Flash movie. Put down the basic elements first (such as the main timeline animations) with FPO (for placement only) symbols as stand-ins for your final graphics.

2. Test at every stage to make sure that everything runs properly to reduce the likelihood that you will need to tear out random patches of your movie when the inevitable bug creeps up.

3. Add any scripting elements needed for your movie's interactivity. Once you have this core functionality in place, test for compatibility on your target platform. By getting this dry run out of the way you may catch a potential *Titanic* while it's still a *USS Minnow*.

4. Add the heavier items, one at a time, in order of lowest bandwidth and processor load (the lighter the better). Insert your primary concept concern first. Then, if you absolutely must have complex and gigantic artwork, add it next. If your soundtrack is key to understanding the Flash movie, add that next, but beware of overloading the processor. Even though you may be able to cram in all of your swollen artifacts without crashing the ITV browser, economy will benefit you every time.

What Makes Design "Good"?

There is a science to designing interactive displays for ITV. As with any visual medium, good design should consider the focal point and craft the path that the eye will follow throughout. Opinions vary about ITV's responsibility for preserving the sanctity of the television show, but whether you believe the show comes first or you think it's more important to empower the viewer, you will have a flickering, brightly-colored rectangle to consider at all times.

You have two distinct basic interface schemes available to you when designing for ITV: layered and embedded.

Layered Displays

Layered displays are layouts built by laying small semi-transparent, interactive panels on top of the TV viewing area. Layered displays are visually pleasing (kind of futuristic-looking) and can offer an intuitive and unobtrusive way to explain concepts to the viewer. Still, layered displays have their faults which you will need to beware of as you design:

- Because layered displays use only a small area on the screen, they can display only a limited amount of information.

- When creating ITV to be used with live content, be careful not to obscure important parts of the television broadcast. If you have television personalities bouncing all over your screen, it will be very tricky to create a layering scheme that works.

Layering is accomplished in several ways, which vary depending on the platform's specifications. For example, some set top boxes always have an invisible browser window that overlays the television display. For these boxes you would create a Flash movie at the exact size of the on-screen panel. Other systems open the Flash movie at full-screen size, and alternate between making the movie background transparent and applying translucent Alpha gradients on top so that the program is still visible but the background contrasts sharply with the foreground. Figure 12.7 shows the arrangement and relative proportions of elements on the screen.

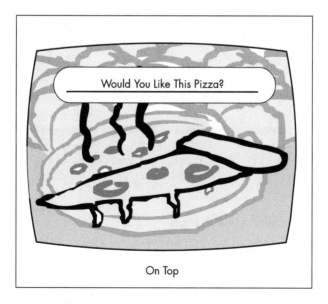

Figure 12.7: A layered interface.

Embedded Displays

Embedded displays are just the opposite of layered displays. Unlike layered displays, the user interface of embedded displays takes up the entire screen, and the television content is relegated to a small *picture-in-picture* (PIP) rectangle. In some ways, this kind of display gives the developer more control over both the show and the interactive content.

While embedded displays shrink the television picture, they offer a great deal in return. For example, Figure 12.8 shows two advantages: The embedded display doesn't obscure the show in any way, and it allows for greater control over the viewer's focus because the television display can be resized dynamically. Too, given the relatively large size of the embedded display, there is more space for text onscreen and greater opportunity to control the visual hierarchy.

Figure 12.8: An embedded interface.

Like layered displays, the way you handle embedded displays will vary depending on the ITV box. Both the ATVEF specification and WebTV allow you to embed your television picture just as you would an image, using a simple tag that declares the type of content and its dimensions. This is fairly consistent across the industry, but with some interesting variation. For example, you may be able to use CSS layers or to embed the picture directly in Flash if the player has strong HTML support.

TV Watchers Sure Are Different

When developing for ITV, you'll find that the standard Web psychology and familiar aspects of usability are turned on their heads. Many TV watchers have become ITV users by happenstance (because their cable company dangled free email in front of them), and they may have little if any experience with conventional web browsing. The familiar elements of interface design that seasoned Flash developers might too easily take for granted (like radio buttons, check boxes, and drop-down lists) cannot be trusted to convey their meaning to this new audience.

While these limitations might choke the HTML developer, Flashers, who have been criticized for not having enough constraint when using familiar elements, should view this as an opportunity. If you design sensibly using the traditional GUI widgets, the add a dash of reasoned pictorial explanation, you have the ability to develop an interface that both novices and experts will appreciate.

Flatland Exports

Flatland Exports is doing work with Flash in the ITV realm. Much of their most complex work has been prototyping advanced set-top box interfaces. One such unique interface is the Onekey Keyboard, which is shown below. Head square Adam Wolff explains the principle behind the keyboard with only one key:

"Most on-screen keyboards for devices such as televisions look exactly like off-screen keyboards. Why? The computer keyboard is itself a metaphor—a carryover from a time when striking a key actually engaged a mechanism that imprinted the page. This keyboard uses time as its organizing principal and tries to help speed input by highlighting likely combinants for the typed sequence.

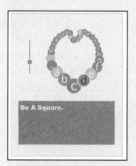

"To operate the keyboard you click once to select a key or click and hold to make the keyboard move quickly among the set of most likely next characters. . . . Double-click to erase your last entry. As you get more adept you can increase the keyboard speed with the slider on the left."

Another challenge for the developer is that the ITV viewer is separated from his TV screen (his monitor) by an average of 10 feet. Too, these net-potatoes are using a remote control (instead of a mouse or a cursor), with four directional buttons to tab through on-screen options.

Our challenge, then, is to design an interface that will work for both inexperienced users and seasoned web surfers who must now surf from a distance with limited controls. As such, avoid designs that require scrolling and that use inlaid scrolling text. For one, some ITV platforms don't support scrolling at all, so expecting users to scroll through content outside the boundaries of the screen is like giving your audience a Chinese finger trap. Alternatively, use an interior panel to flip though smaller screens like a tiny virtual Rolodex consisting of small cue cards of text content.

The TV Screen

Major changes are required in order to prepare the average web page for viewing on a TV. For one, the television picture is not nearly as clear as your monitor's. In addition to offering fairly low resolution, the TV's interlaced display is not ideal for displaying fine detail. (This is such a significant problem that television stations have to be so careful about the outfits of their on-air personalities wear. A checker print fabric or herringbone can pulsate on screen.)

Design faults of this type can be unpredictable so test early and often unless you're willing to resign yourself to using only flat colors and gentle gradients. For the most reliable results and fewest surprises, test all of your artwork during the design stage using a computer-to-video scan converter to connect the computer to a television.

Also, when compared with the TV, computer monitors underscan their display so that the entire picture can be seen. TVs overscans, which causes the edges of the picture to spill outside of the set's physical boundaries: Television producers know this and actually film with the expectation of losing the picture at the screen borders.

The biggest problem you'll face when adjusting for this spillage is that there is no definitive measure of how much picture is lost because the amount varies *widely* from television to television. WebTV and other boxes may suggest that your Flash movie be 560 pixels wide × 420 pixels tall, which is a good starting point, but even this safe center will spill off the screens of many TV sets.

Your best bet will be to approximate the actual picture size by dividing the signal into two regions: action-safe and title-safe. Figure 12.9 will help you to understand the ratio of the two areas.

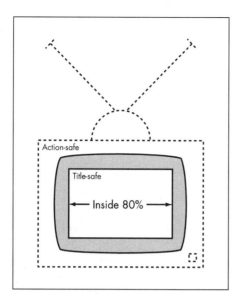

Figure 12.9: The action- and title-safe areas of a TV screen.

The action-safe area is essentially the entire picture; the closer you keep to the middle of it the more assured you'll be that your image will be seen. The action safe area is acceptable for things like car chases that go on- and off-screen constantly.

The title-safe area is for text and other elements, like subtitles, that must have their on-screen borders preserved. The title-safe area is essentially the aspect ratio of the screen (approximately 1.33:1), but it's constrained to the inner 80 percent of the entire viewing area. (For your convenience, the file AspectRatio.FLA in the Chapter 12 folder on the CD-ROM has a reusable background movie at an acceptable aspect ratio, with the action- and title-safe areas clearly marked in a guide layer.)

Millions of Colors and Lots of Issues

The television will display millions of colors with no dithering, but there are about as many rules for their proper use as there are colors. For example, some intense colors can actually interfere with broadcasting (by overdriving the electron guns that create the picture), and are known as "NTSC illegal." Or, a very bright red object on screen can crash through the channel barrier and appear over other broadcasts.

For your convenience, the file NTSC.clr in the Chapter 12 folder of the CD-ROM contains a Flash color table that you can use to approximate the standard Flash color palate in NTSC by choosing Add Colors in the Swatches panel. If you follow some simple guidelines you will minimize the chances of color carnage.

RGB

The RGB color model uses a series of three numbers to represent the levels of red, green, and blue, with levels ranging from 0 (darkest) to 255 (brightest). For example, the most garish, road-flare red is described in RGB as 255, 0, 0, while blindig yellow is 255, 255, 0. To keep RGB colors TV legal, you must treat 225 as the uppermost brightness *for all three primary values*. For instance the brightest allowable yellow is 225, 225, 0. You can approximate the color white (now entirely off limits because it causes the screen to buck and shimmy) as a light gray (225, 225, 225) or beige (225, 225, 100).

HSB

In most cases you will be working entirely in RGB, but occasionally you might import a file or get proprietary box guidelines expressed using the HSB (hue, saturation, brightness) color model. The default settings in Flash's Mixer panel are RGB, but by clicking the options triangle in the upper right corner of the panel you invoke the Options pop-up, which enables you to change to HSB (or another color model).

HSB's danger to NTSC is saturation, and to be safe on all televisions you should set your color saturation below 75 percent. The NTSC display makes all colors look brighter, so don't worry if your color loses some of its bite on the computer monitor after desaturation.

Using Adequate Contrast

Contrast is an important tool for pulling interactive elements up from the background and for creating order in your composition. Inadequate contrast can make your text unreadable, your design flat, and your interface virtually invisible when seen next to the the television screen.

Once you turn a design element into a symbol, the Flash Effects panel presents an option for you to set the element's brightness. In pre-NTSC designing, there was never any reason to use this option, because it has the same functionality as tint but is limited to black and white. On projects that need to meet NTSC standards though, the brightness option is a pretty handy tool because it lets you fine-tune a design element by nudging its contrast to make it a little brighter or a bit darker.

When developing for a proprietary system, the system's creators will likely provide a preferred color palette for use on that specific system. Many different software applications, such as PhotoShop and Debabelizer, can create NTSC-acceptable substitutes for any color you need; WebTV even offers a free web-based tool at their developer's site.

While the available tools make it simple to convert color samples to NTSC-acceptable alternatives, all of these options are worthless if you test these colors only on the computer monitor. Test them on a TV.

The Written Word

Flash and fonts work very well together, and when developing for ITV, you'll need every ounce of Flash's sophistication, control, and finesse with fonts because the list of no-nos for TV use is a long and complicated one.

Contrast

Text is perhaps the most important element we can use to create contrast within the design space, but TV's many color limitations restrict us from falling back on type conventions. For example, using black text on a white background would have major complications because of the NTSC bias against white, so choose a dark background with light-colored text. It can be visually pleasing to couple different shades of the same color on the TV screen, such as using a dark blue background with light blue text.

Size

Font size is a big issue. While a point size of 12 to 14 is a good choice for a computer monitor, choose a point size between 18 and 20 for NTSC TV body text to be readable by most viewers. If smaller type is a must, stay away from the three Flash system fonts (_sans, _serif, and _typewriter) because they don't anti-alias (their horizontal lines are only 1 pixel tall and may disappear on the television's line-based display). Flash anti-aliases text set on its default of high-quality, which is very desirable for ITV design.

Additionally, some ITV platforms automatically increase HTML text by several points on websites designed for viewing in PC browsers. Although Flash 5 can support HTML text, Flash text is not be affected by this conversion; the control and responsibility are in the hands of the developer.

Be Concise

Because text has to be bigger, scrolling is taboo, and because (regardless of your development scheme) you will have less screen real estate than on a PC, you should limit the amount of body text. Be concise to save yourself headaches and your audience eyestrain.

Spacing

Kerning, tracking, and leading are the three different types of letter spacing that can be altered in Flash's Character panel to create optical evenness. Given all of NTSC's problems with fuzziness (and more bleeds than watercolor paper), be extra careful to provide ample negative space around letters, words, and lines. Set the type more loosely than normal and have your colleagues test it to get varied opinions on its readability.

Style

The fonts most commonly used to set body copy are either serif or sans serif. Serifs are the tiny embellishments that hang off of the edges of the characters in some fonts like Times New Roman. Sans serif fonts lack these little embellishments.

The conventional wisdom is that these serifs are visual cues that enhance readability by enhancing the distinction between adjacent letters. However, the opposite is true on television displays; flowery adornments become blurry and make the letters blend together. As such, your best bet is to use sans serif fonts when developing for TV, such as Arial or Helvetica, and to refrain from using all capital letters.

NOTE *A current design trend in Flash movies is to use "pixel" or "bitmap" fonts—tiny fonts that don't anti-alias in Flash because they lay within the pixel grid. These fonts are pure poison to ITV because their small size makes them nearly invisible.*

Summary (I Want My ITV)

This chapter has presented a preview of an exciting new industry and some suggestions about how Flash can be expected grow within it. As of of this writing, your development options have training wheels: ITV is operational, but hardly as exciting now as it will be.

We have a long way to go before we're all enjoying Flash games while sending email from the TV in our den, but most industry estimates suggest that widespread ITV penetration will happen within the next 5 years. (For more information, check www.flashthefuture.com/12 for updates.)

TV is one place where Flash, happily, has already put down some significant roots. The most interesting work in this field is being done now in Flash because it bridges the gap between the conceivable and attainable.

13

AUTHORING FOR THE NOKIA 9200 COMMUNICATOR SERIES

Chris Pelsor, Ian Chia, and Doug Loftus

The Nokia 9200 Communicator series is the first phone to license the Macromedia Flash Player. Although other cellular phones (such as the Microsoft Pocket PC Phone Edition device) also support the Flash Player, the Nokia 9200 series flagship line of phones presents a number of challenges specific to this platform.

Read Me First

As with the Flash Player for Pocket PCs, Macromedia provides a Content Development Kit for the Nokia phone. We highly recommend that you carefully read through the authoring guidelines document first (available at www.macromedia.com/software/flashplayer/resources/devices/nokia/), because it will walk you through the unique platform requirements of this device. Once you've digested the official Content Development Kit and its accompanying samples, this chapter is intended to augment that information with explanations of additional developmental limitations and techniques that the CDK omits.

Screen Size and Color Palette

The Nokia Flash Player is able to present content with two screen sizes, which are switchable using fscommand. The phone renders Flash content at 468×200 in the smaller window setting, zoomable up to a full-screen size at 640×200.

Color Conversion

The official Content Development Kit recommends optimizing color bitmaps to a 16-bit color depth before importing into the Flash authoring environment, because the Nokia Flash Player will render only a subset of this color range because of hardware limitations. The actual conversion is from a 16-bit palette of 32,768 colors to only 4,096 colors using the Communicator's 12-bit color display. (You'll find an in-depth discussion of the color palette used by the Nokia Communicator in Appendix 1, "The Truth About 12-Bit Color Displays.") Think hard about that conversion to 12-bit color from your 16-bit source image, because you'll actually lose 28,672 colors out of the original 32,768. That's a lot of missing colors!

Do Your Own Conversion

To obtain the best visual quality for photographic-type images, which typically rely on a broad range of gradients, it's best to convert the image to a dithered 8-bit (or 256-color) image. Although 4,096 colors sounds preferable compared with only 256 colors, you're relying on the mercy of the Symbian operating system to map your lovely 16-bit gradients to the actual 4,096 colors available on the Nokia screen. This will usually result in ugly visual banding effects. The time-honored technique to avoid this is to dither your image (by mixing up the dots of adjacent colors so that discrete colors blend smoothly into each other, rather than moving abruptly from one area of color into the next). Using a quality image processing tool to dither your image into 8-bit will have better results than allowing the Nokia's operating system to remap the final 4,096 colors.

For example, follow these steps if you are using Macromedia Fireworks to convert your file:

1. Open your original 16-bit or higher color depth image in Fireworks.
2. Switch to the 2-Up view within the image's window.
3. From the main menu bar, select Window • Optimize to open the Optimize palette window. Select GIF as the export file format and choose the WebSnap Adaptive indexed palette.
4. Select the 256 setting in the colors drop-down menu.
5. Leave all the other settings alone except for Dither. By dragging this setting between 0 to 100 percent, you can choose the amount of dithering appropriate for your image. Compare the source image with the dithered version in the Document window to obtain the best compromise.
6. Because of a quirk of Flash, images that are cropped right to the edge will show strange artifacts when overlaid with other visual assets on the stage. The standard workaround is to add a transparent border, a single pixel

wide, around the whole image. To do this, proceed from the main menu, select Modify • Canvas size, and re-enter the new canvas dimensions by adding 2 pixels to the width and 2 pixels to the height. Leave the Anchor settings alone and click OK.

7. Select the Rectangle tool in the toolbox. From the main menu, select Window • Fill to open the Fill palette and select None in order to draw an unfilled box.

8. From the main menu, select Window • Stroke to open the Stroke palette. Select the Pencil category along with 1-Pixel Hard as the category and 1 as the tip size. In the color well, pick a color that's unused in your image. It's important to select a radically different color so that the optimization process won't remap this to a color already used in your image. You will use this border color as an index for the transparency.

9. In the left Original pane of the Document window, drag a rectangle from the top left corner to the bottom right corner so that a single-pixel box outline is placed in the empty border you created in Step 6. Fireworks won't allow you to draw in the right side pane, because this is the optimized GIF image's view.

10. Open the Optimize (Document) palette again via Window • Optimize. In the transparency drop-down menu, select Index Transparency and select the + eyedropper below the menu to add color to your index transparency. Then click your eyedropper in the single-pixel border in the left Original pane of your main Document window. In the right side pane, you'll observe that the border has turned transparent with no other effect to your image.

11. Save the processed image by selecting File • Export in the main menu and then import the resulting GIF into Flash.

12. Open Flash's Library and locate the filename of the image you just imported. Open the Properties window by selecting the Library item and clicking the i icon at the bottom of the Library palette. Uncheck the Allow Smoothing setting and choose Lossless (PNG/GIF) as the compression setting. Click OK. The file can now be used successfully in Flash.

Although the Nokia's color palette values differ slightly from the standard web-safe palette, any remapping of a properly dithered web-safe image will be imperceptible.

To obtain the best visual quality for images that rely on solid colors, it's advisable to design them with the color palette available on the device. If you don't have that luxury, you can either refill the colors using the Nokia's color palette or remap them again using the WebSnap Adaptive palette. Just make sure that you don't dither the image, because this will cause unpleasant artifacts in an image that emphasizes solid blocks of color. The color palette is included in Appendix 1, "The Truth About 12-Bit Color Displays."

UI Conventions on the Communicator

From a UI design standpoint, the two most striking features of the 9200 series Communicator are its display dimensions and the fact that user input is entirely key-based: There is no mouse and no touchscreen. On the bright side, because the Flash Player runs as a standalone on this device, the entire display area—a whopping 128,000 square pixels (!)—is available when movies are run in FullScreen mode. In reality, however, 640×200 is a pretty odd-sized chunk of real estate and, especially when coupled with a keys-only input scheme, it can be a challenge to design a UI that fits within these constraints, yet still performs well for the user.

Check the Style Guide

It can be helpful to see how existing applications for the 9200 series devices attempt to solve some of these design problems. We highly recommend that you also take a look at the *Nokia 9210 Style Guide*, available as a PDF download to developers who register at http://www.forum.nokia.com/. Although this guide is intended for developers creating applications with the Symbian SDK, it estab-lishes guidelines for navigation and layout that, for the most part, can also be applied to Flash content.

We suggest that you study these guidelines because, by developing designs that leverage the language of resident applications and OS utilities, you can avoid re-inventing the wheel and instead create schemes for navigation and task completion that should already be familiar to most Communicator users. The remainder of this section will take a look at a few UI conventions employed on the Communicator.

Navigating a Folder Tree

Navigation on the 9200 series Communicator is carried out primarily using a set of four arrow keys provided on the keyboard. Two distinct types of navigation are possible using these keys, and the Flash Player provides a new key combina-tion, CTRL-P, that allows users to toggle between the two modes. One mode involves the use of an Arrow Manipulated Pointer—which is a cursor that can be moved freely (horizontally and vertically) around the screen using the arrow keys. This technique is intended to be used mostly with web pages where, for example, an image map might be provided for navigation, requiring the use of a pointer. However, controlling a pointer with arrow keys can be tedious, and this is not the preferred method of navigation for applications.

In the other navigation mode, the application controls which screen element has focus in response to the user's press of an arrow key. As the CDK points out, Nokia-compliant applications and Flash content must be navigable using this latter method or using the TAB key to sequentially select UI elements. However, many interfaces require greater navigational flexibility than a straight TAB approach affords and will benefit from implementing arrow key-based input.

As an example, Figure 13.1 shows how arrow keys are employed for folder tree navigation on the Communicator. As shown at the left of Figure 13.1, pressing the down arrow moves the selection rectangle down to the next folder. Then, as shown at the right, arrowing right expands the currently selected folder and moves the selection rectangle to the first item within the expanded folder. Here, arrowing up and down moves the selection rectangle through the items contained in the folder. Arrowing left collapses this folder and returns it to the state shown at the left.

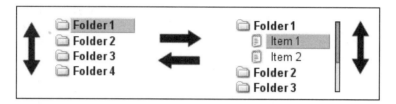

Figure 13.1: Navigating a folder tree on the Nokia Communicator.

Application Layout

Many Communicator applications take advantage of the wide display area by presenting two distinct views of an application at the same time. As shown in Figure 13.2, for example, a contact list might be displayed to a user with a list of names on the right and individual contact info on the right. In the scenario depicted, the left-hand view is active. Names are scrolled using the up and down arrow keys, pressing ENTER displays the expanded information for the person selected, and the TAB key, or right and left arrow presses, are used to toggle between views.

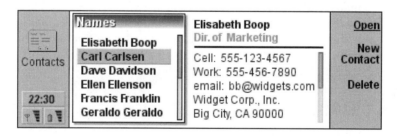

Figure 13.2: A typical application layout on the Nokia Communicator.

Note that an interface of this type is inherently modal—the same input gesture can produce a different response depending on the active application view. (See Chapter 3 for an in-depth discussion of modal interfaces.) For this reason, it's important to provide strong visual cues that allow the user to easily discern which application context is currently active. In the example shown, the active view is given a border and shadow, which is a typical technique used by many Nokia Communicator applications.

The choices seen at far right in Figure 13.2 are activated using a set of hardware keys termed command buttons, not shown here, but arrayed ATM-style down the right side of the screen on the device. Unfortunately, these buttons are not accessible to content running within the Flash Player. Instead, these buttons are mapped to the menu commands of the Player itself. Therefore, Flash developers face additional challenges when designing feature-rich interfaces for the Nokia.

Coding for Key-Based Navigation

It may be obvious from the preceding section that creating an interface that is navigable using only arrow keys will require a bit more coding than is typically necessary in a mouse-driven application. These techniques for coding a key-based interface can readily be applied to the Communicator. See the sections that deal with the Softkeys object in Chapter 3, which explain a strategy for managing application contexts and user input.

Sound Limitations

Although 8Kbps is recommended for MP3 audio, 16Kbps sounds much better and does not appear to tax the system to a significantly greater degree. However, sound quality will also depend on what else is happening in the application while sound is playing. Any navigation via arrow keys while sound is playing will most likely cause pops and clicks in the audio. Furthermore, 16Kbps MP3 audio will create larger files. If you need more memory for other things and can get away with lower-quality audio, use 8Kbps audio.

Because the hardware is limited to one speaker, you can reduce file sizes further by using only mono sounds. The Nokia is able to play several sounds at the same time but is limited by the size of the sounds being played and the number of sounds being played concurrently. There is no hard and fast rule to this, because—as we stated previously—this limitation is with the processor, not with the Flash Player. The key is to test early and test often. Our experience has been you can play about five to seven sounds concurrently before the processor locks, and no sounds are played at all.

Animation Limitations

Although the CDK states that the Nokia is capable of 12 frames/second animation, the player is subject to the limitations of the Nokia's processor: In practice, the Nokia can only produce frame rates between 3–7 frames/second. Consequently, animations are limited, as are any motion-based navigational embellishments. As with other Flash movies, bitmaps do animate better than vectors, but because of the limited processor and memory capacity of the Nokia, you are better off minimizing or severely limiting animation to those elements that gain from being animated, or elements that require animation to function properly.

If you have decided to include animation, should it be a tweened or a scripted animation? We've found that animation with ActionScript will usually yield better results. However, this rule is not absolute: Sometimes, experimenting with tweens in addition to programmatic animation may give better results. Remember that multiple simultaneous tweens can be processor-intensive, and performing any type of animation on an element that has a modified alpha setting will require even more resources.

Contrary to the specifications in the official Content Development Kit, alpha transitions are supported by the Nokia Communicator Flash Player. However, we strongly recommend limited use of alpha in all design elements. Alpha transitions consume considerable CPU cycles, which will be very noticeable because of this device's slow processor.

Memory on a Budget

When working with the Flash Player on the Nokia Communicator, you must be aware of the 2MB limitation. This 2MB memory limitation is all-inclusive, meaning that the player *and* content must fit into this memory space. This is not a limitation of the player, but a "feature" of the Symbian 6.0 operating system that restricts the amount of memory available to each application.

Start Your Calculators

The player itself weighs in at a modest 1.1MB of memory. That leaves you, the developer, with about 900KB to 1MB to work with. But, depending on how many other applications are running along with the Flash Player, this memory space may be further depleted. When calculating the size of your movie, you must include any and all content, including dynamically loaded content, in its full (uncompressed) size. For example, if you want to stream MP3 audio to the phone, you must include the *full* file size in your calculation, otherwise you will try to load in more data than the player can handle, and your users will receive an Out of Memory error. A sample estimate may look like this:

2 MP3s at 100KB:	200KB
1 Interface at 50KB:	50KB
2 JPEGs at 50KB:	100KB
Combined file size:	350KB

As well as calculating file sizes, you need to consider the actual memory consumption that decompressed visual and audio assets require. For example, a heavily compressed JPEG will still decompress to use the amount of memory required to draw the image in an offscreen memory buffer before rendering to the stage. A 640 × 200–pixel image compressed at 100 percent quality will decompress to fill the same amount of memory as a version compressed at 25 percent, even though the compressed file sizes and image quality will be radically different. Try to avoid overlaying many large bitmap images onscreen, because each image will require its own sizeable buffer.

Execution Demands

In addition to multimedia, ActionScript will consume memory during execution. The two main contributing factors to excessive memory consumption are:

- Excessive use of variables, whether extensive arrays or instantiated objects
- Parsing large XML documents

Just as a bitmap requires some storage memory managed by the Flash Player, ActionScript variables need a space to store the object or variable during execution. Although a single-integer variable will consume only a few bytes, an array with ten thousand elements will require considerably more. If your project demands use of large arrays or a large number of objects, you should think long and hard about the memory requirements and architecture of your code.

Parsing XML also requires a large buffer during the conversion from the string representation of data into a tree of nodes. The Player will free up the memory after the initial parsing process, but if the XML document requires more memory than is available within your 2MB allocation, your Flash application can cause the Nokia Communicator to hang.

Working with the XML object in practice can be tricky: Because the XML object creates an elaborate system of arrays, your 9KB XML document can be enough to bring the Flash player to its knees. This is not, however, necessarily due to the XML file's size, but to its complexity. For example, consider an XML document that had 94 nodes, with 2 nodes nested below each, like this node:

```
<person>
    <firstName>Chris</firstName>
    <lastName>Pelsor</lastName>
</person>
```

Although the XML object was able to handle this, adding just one more node set caused the player to run out of memory. The natural tendency is to compact this structure so that the subnodes become attributes:

```
<person firstName="Chris" lastName="Pelsor">
```

Using this method, the Flash Player was able to handle 154 nodes, yet still pass in the same information. Obviously, your results will vary slightly based on node name lengths, the amount of data in a node or attribute, the level of complexity (nesting nodes becomes more and more expensive, in terms of memory, with each level that you add to the hierarchy). Keep in mind as well that the numbers given are the absolute limits, with no other elements or actions occurring. If your data structure is flat and large, you may want to consider loadVariables, because, with this method, the data is passed into the application and handled differently than in XML. Consequently, if you use loadVariables, you will probably be able to include more information. Sometimes, using SAX-style parsing instead of Flash's DOM-style XML will be more efficient in memory use. (For more information about the SAX XML technique, refer to the XML section of Chapter 5.)

Working with Dynamic Data

When using dynamic data via loadVariables or XML, keep in mind the size of the content being sent down. A useful method for testing the file size is to access the server-side data source outside of Flash (usually through a web browser) and save the data file to disk. Next, look at the size of the file. This will help you to estimate the amount of memory you need to set aside for dynamic data. (Doing this early in the project will provide you with a standalone data source, which can be handy if you are developing using a live data feed and that feed suddenly dies.)

Estimating Shortcut

A key feature of the Flash 5 player on the Nokia is a shortcut key combination, CTRL-SHIFT-M, that allows you to see how much memory is currently available. Using this while running other apps that come with the phone will help you predict real-world usage and, in turn, estimate how much data or content you can load into your movie at any given time. As you can see, a little planning will go a long way toward preventing out-of-memory errors.

Estimating memory usage during the design phase of your project can save you a lot of time when you're building and testing your application. As always, test early and test often and test on your target machine to prevent any sort of surprises when you deliver your application.

ActionScript Speed

To illustrate the differences in speed between devices, we ran some simple benchmarks on desktop PCs, a Pocket PC with a 206 MHx processor, and a Nokia Communicator. The first benchmark, which is a prime number sifter, clearly illustrates the differences in speed.

Finding highest prime below 5,000, averaged over 5 calculations (using the pseudo-thread prime finder code discussed in Chapter 5) produced the following:

Windows 2000/Pentium III 500MHz with Flash 6 Player	0.889 seconds
Windows 2000/Pentium III 500MHz with Flash 5 Player	0.934 seconds
Pocket PC 2002/StrongArm SA-1110 with Flash 5 Player	17.479 seconds
Symbian 6.0/Nokia Communicator 9210 with Flash 5 Player	72.422 seconds

The XML object behaves differently in the Nokia player than it does in other Flash 5 Players. The Nokia is the only Flash 5 Player where the XML parsing code object is native, and not written as ActionScript bytecode under the hood. As a result, it is optimized for the best performance possible. Because the XML object is native, you actually *hurt* performance by trying to use Branden Hall's

XMLNitro prototype. All of the programmatic functionality available in XMLNitro, most notably ignoreWhite, is available in the Player, so you don't have to worry about any missing features—as you do with the other Flash 5 players.

With this said, another bugbear of ActionScript is the String.split() method. Enterprising developers have created replacement prototypes that greatly improve performance. These improvements were not made native like the XML parser and therefore should be used if you are doing any sort of work on the Nokia with strings. You can investigate these methods at I-Technica (http://i-technica.com/flashlist/index.php?n=1475).

Optimizing Your Online Access

When working with XML, keep in mind that light documents lead to fast processing for two reasons. First, a lighter document is, obviously, downloaded more quickly. Second, and more important, a lighter document means less information, which in turn leads to faster parsing.

When working with XML, you can improve performance in several ways, including abbreviating node names, attributes, and values to their smallest possible value. For example, the following node

```
<person firstName="Chris" lastName="Pelsor" isMarried="true">
```

could be condensed to

```
<p fn="Chris" ln="Pelsor" im="1">
```

The improvements to the first two attributes (firstName and lastName) are obvious; we simply abbreviated the attribute name. The third attribute was improved in two ways: First, we abbreviated the attribute, and second, the string simulates a binary Boolean by changing true to 1. (Strictly speaking, 1 is not binary. It's a string representing a binary value.) To save yourself future problems with these abbreviated names, you can document the data format in the Flash source file, and if possible, in the server-side script generating the XML.

One final thing to keep in mind is that when developing Flash applications for the Web, designers tend to send down whatever information they may think the movie needs and then write ActionScript to do mathematical calculations, string conversions, and other light work. When working with the Nokia and wireless content in general, let the server do any sort of data manipulation and send only the final content to the device. This strategy utilizes the significant CPU power available on the server and lightens the processing load on the slow wireless devices' CPUs.

If you proceed by concentrating first on thoughtful creation of a data format and then make sure to send preprocessed data to the device, you will save users time and money and improve the overall performance of the application that you develop for these devices.

Testing Networked Content in a Staging Environment

Developing Communicator content that requests online data via http:// or XMLSocket poses some issues. You could test infrequently and be willing to make connections to the Web over your slow wireless connection, but in addition to incurring call costs during a continual QA and development cycle, this approach is not efficient.

Fortunately, Intuwave is currently developing the m-Router application, which allows the Nokia Communicator to connect to a desktop machine via the serial cable. Using this approach, your Flash content can access a staging server on your local desktop or share the Internet connection of your desktop PC. More information about the m-Router product can be found at www.intuwave.com.

Extending Flash Applications on the Nokia Communicator

Because the standalone Flash Player does not run within a browser environment, it has no access to JavaScript. Also, getURL is not supported and fscommand is only supported in a very limited form.

How are we able to perform simple application tasks, such as reading and writing to a local text file to save preferences, or perform more complex tasks requiring access to system APIs normally locked off from Flash?

The solution lies in an approach that is similar to that discussed in Chapter 7, where a solution to connect Flash to device applications was built using Microsoft's eMbedded Visual Basic and eMbedded Visual C++. By developing a custom socket server that can communicate with Flash via XMLSocket, you can achieve a high degree of interactivity between Flash and the host application. The socket server can be part of a general utility application that works with your Flash content. In this manner, requests to read and write data to the local file system as well as to access other system APIs are readily available.

The operating system for the Nokia Communicator is currently the Symbian OS Version 6.0. The Symbian OS Version 6.x Java runtime implements the PersonalJava 3.0 environment and JavaPhone 1.0, an API for telephony and user customization developed by Symbian, Sun, and others. The Java implementation supports raw sockets, and a Java-based socket server can be developed to communicate with the Flash movie, all on the local device. More information about the Symbian implementation can be found in their detailed operating system overview document, available from www.symbian.com/technology/symbos-v6x-det.html.

Summary

This chapter covered the core concepts in developing Flash content for the Nokia 9200 series cell phone.

Although the Flash Player for the Nokia 9200 series phones may appear to be a limiting platform, it allows you to develop true wireless applications that begin to transform the way people interact with their world. The advantage of developing in Flash for the Nokia 9200 is that, by thoughtful use of dynamic data, visual effects, and key-based navigation, developers can quickly create applications and content that are truly engaging and that will allow users to become more connected.

Chapter 14 will look at ways in which developers can optimize their workflow in order to leverage their Flash applications to run on multiple devices.

14

AUTHORING FLASH CONTENT
FOR UBIQUITY

Ian Chia

As Macromedia Flash continues to proliferate, it may become as ubiquitous on handheld devices and set-tops as it is on desktop browsers. For the first time, content developers would have the opportunity to create work that is deployed not only to desktop browsers, but also simultaneously to other devices across many platforms. Consequently, it's time to consider how to best manage such complex development within a context of ubiquity.

Previous chapters have discussed the unique aspects of different Flash-equipped platforms. This chapter will consider the numerous activities that are required to author complex Flash content for simultaneous deployment across multiple platforms. We'll also show you how, by following a detailed roadmap for development, the numerous phases of content and application development can be carried out more successfully. This map will provide strategies for managing the development of complex projects, from initial planning to final deployment, while remaining mindful of the opportunities for ubiquity.

Flash for the Future

Throughout this book, you've seen examples of Macromedia Flash applications on different devices and hardware platforms. Each of these platforms have unique strengths and weakness, and we've examined authoring techniques catering to each platform's specific strengths and constraints. But what we haven't considered so far is the case for ubiquity. *Ubiquity* (which is derived from the Latin word "ubique," meaning "everywhere") is used in the realm of software development to describe an application that can be deployed on multiple platforms simultaneously. Flash is celebrated by developers for giving them an authoring environment that includes, among its many other benefits, the convenience of creating content that runs on many platforms, using common assets and a common code base and fulfilling part of Java's promise to "write once, run anywhere."

Macromedia has committed to selling what they term the "Flash platform" as a solution to developing content for many consumer device. Because we expect Macromedia to continue to deliver on their promise, we are confident that we'll see new and novel uses of Flash in the future (Flash on your car dashboard, refrigerator, or microwave oven, anyone?). With the continual announcement of new licensing agreements between Macromedia and a growing host of partners—that includes Microsoft, Nokia, Liberate, Motorola, OpenTV, Moxi, Samsung, and many other consumer device manufacturers—it becomes ever more likely that we'll begin to see significant penetration of Flash content in consumer items.

Consequently, savvy Flash developers are mindful that their Flash content has the opportunity to be delivered to multiple platforms, each of which has its own unique constraints, as well as respective advantages and headaches. But to achieve this goal successfully, we need to have a clear development process in place, with detailed strategies that will enable us to cope effectively with the range of Flash content that is destined to be delivered to multiple devices and in varied contexts.

Imagine, If You Will . . .

This chapter considers a hypothetical end-user Flash application: a SWF that stores a few user preferences that are used, on a regular basis, to retrieve small samples of music sent from an extensive audio database. Imagine that this SWF will be deployed on a desktop browser, on an interactive TV set-top box, and also on Pocket PCs. This example will illustrate the many critical junctures that must be drawn on our development map if we want to successfully navigate such a complex development journey.

More Platforms, More Planning

If our content is destined to ship on more than one particular hardware/ software configuration, then we will need to understand how successfully the various Flash Players will run different aspects of the content. You are probably familiar with this concept, given that Flash content creators often have to deliver content on Windows, Macintosh, and Unix operating systems, and in a wide range of web browsers—each with their respective quirks.

Seasoned as you might think you are, Flash developers have thus far been sheltered, to a great extent, from this gamut of quirks by the Flash Player's excellent playback fidelity. Although you may have had to fix some HTML tags or adjust the frame rate of your movie for better comparison between Windows and Macintosh, overall, Flash content tends to work identically across the major browsers on different platforms of desktop computers. However, this breadth of fidelity is about to change. That's because this multitude of new device platforms comes with a multitude of new issues. Planning is the solution. If we want to keep all of these exciting opportunities under control, we need to plan.

Plan? Me?

The idealist notion of planning up front is all well and good, but many developers' first instinct is to dive in with some rough code straight away. Even you, the deliberate developer, may be tempted to rough out a working prototype and then adjust it to fit as you go along. There are many temptations, particularly because the beginning is often an exciting time when your enthusiasm for a project is at a peak. The noble ideal of a "good plan" is often dismissed at this stage, because the plan can be vague and undefined in many developers' minds. What we aim to do in this chapter is to outline a plan—a tour map if you like— that will guide you through the production process. You can choose to navigate your project however you wish, but this map will outline the major destinations and set markers at the possible pitfalls that await you along the way. Ultimately, knowing the landscape will enrich your journey. And if you've traveled this road many times already but keep tripping up in the same spots, hopefully our map will show you new directions to routes that you've previously missed.

Typical Activities

Traditional software development has many phases. Researchers have identified a number of these activities, which are listed below along with our own insights about each. We'll also include steps relating to asset collection and production, because multimedia development includes the gathering and reworking of content, which is a challenge that's alien to traditional software development. By ordering these development phases into a production timeline, milestones for a typical Flash development project would include the following, ordered in four major phases: design, development, testing, and deployment.

A. Project Design
1. System specification
2. Outcomes: Identifying requirements and problem analysis
3. Design of a solution

B. Development: Production, Coding, and Debugging
4. Asset gathering, pre-production, and management
5. Multimedia design and production
6. Coding development
7. Debugging
8. Documentation

C. Testing (aka Quality Assurance Cycle)
9. Unit testing
10. System integration
11. System testing/regression testing/usability testing

D. Deployment and Maintenance
12. Deployment
13. Maintenance

When creating your development plan for a rollout on multiple devices and platforms, consider each of these phases with ubiquity in mind. You want your software to run everywhere. By keeping this goal in mind your plan will naturally integrate many common parts as you move ahead toward final delivery of the product.

We won't talk about scheduling, because this chapter is focused on the tasks necessary to build a product. For an excellent and entertaining article on "Painless Software Schedules," visit http://www.joelonsoftware.com/stories/storyReader$31.

Project Design

System Specification

This is the place to list where we expect our content to appear. Be as specific as possible, listing exact details. In the system specification, you'll need to make a detailed list of information pertinent to the project, such as upon what browser or device specific player the content will appear on each platform. Ask as many questions as possible and question each detail to ferret out subpoints. Ideally, your questions could form a diagram in the pattern of a tree. Some of the questions we would ask for our hypothetical project would include these: "What type of network bandwidth will you have to deliver the Flash movie? Is there local storage for your preferences? If so, where is the storage and what—if any—are the limitations to access and retrieval? If there is no local storage, is there networked storage available? What is the screen size? What are valid colors we can use? How does the device connect online to retrieve the music samples?"

Middleware and Backend Details

Besides the hardware specifications of the device that your Flash will be delivered on, it's important to detail any related middleware and backend databases that will be connected to this device. For example, the interactive TV set-top might have a persistent connection to an extensive backend system, given that it's always switched on. Such information might suggest benefits to be exploited on this particular device. For example, the downloading of the audio assets to the set-top could be scheduled to happen very late at night when other usage is typically lowest. In contrast, the same application deployed upon the Pocket PC must contend with the fact the connection to the backend server is most likely to be intermittent and will be usually initiated by the end user. Although the same database is shared by the Pocket PC and set-top applications, the middleware to connect them are different, because the set-top resides on a proprietary cable TV network, whereas the Pocket PC connects via the Internet.

Similarly, the colors used in designing the set-top interface must be limited to those that are TV-safe (to avoid unfortunate moire effects), but the palette used in the PPC interface is a less-restrictive 12- to 16-bit color palette.

Here's the bottom line for the early stages of authoring for ubiquity: At this point of your journey, you need to make sure you know what your delivery device is capable of, and you also need to make sure that you understand how the device will connect to the whole system.

Having exact specifications from the very beginning will inform every other step of your plan. If you were building a house, before you draw up the house plans or hammer a single nail, you need to know where your house is going to be situated, what materials are available, and the type of access that both you and the final residents will have to the home site. Now imagine if you are planning to build a number of houses in a range of locations, all based on a principle template. That's the situation you face if you're planning a ubiquitous rollout of Flash content.

To further clarify the issues and concerns that you need to take into account at this initial phase of the planning, Table 14.1 lists an overview of Flash deployment on many platforms. For your convenience, the table is also provided as an Excel file in the "Flash_deployment_overview" directory in the Chapter 14 folder of the CD-ROM. Go ahead and edit and adjust it for your projects.

Table 14.1: Flash Deployment Overview

Feature	Handheld	Phones	Personal Computers	TV Set-Top (Liberate, WebTV, AOL TV OpenTV)	DVD	Other Network Devices (Kiosks, ATMs, etc.)
Processor Speed	Slower processor	Slower processor	Fast processor with Flash visuals rendered in software	None	Rendered video	Generally slow
Network Connectivity	May or may not have network connectivity	Always connected	Generally connected. Typical connection at 56K modem with minority at broadband	Generally active for the television content, uses dial-up for interactive content	None	Always connected
Screen Size	Small (120 x 160 to 240 x 320)	Small (around 180x80) to large (Nokia 600 x 200)	Generally 800 × 600 pixels or more	648 x 486 or 720 x 540 to match aspect ratio	648 x 486 or 720 x 540 to match aspect ratio	Very small
Screen Type	LCD (Color 12- to 16-bit)	LCD (Color 12- to 16-bit)	Monitors (CRT or LCD), non-interlaced	TV (NTSC/PAL/SECAM resolutions and color apply) Interlaced	TV (NTSC/PAL/SECAM resolutions and color apply) Interlaced	LCD (Color or B/W)
Keyboard/ Keypad	Virtual	Alpha-numeric keypad	Full keyboard	Virtual and limited remote control	None	Varies
Cursor Control	Stylus	Cursor key on alpha-numeric keypad	Typically two-button (Windows) or one-button (Macintosh) mouse	Cursor keys on remote control	Cursor keys on remote control	Alphanumeric keypad

(continued on next page)

Table 14.1: Flash Deployment Overview (continued)

Feature	Handheld	Phones	Personal Computers	TV Set-Top (Liberate, WebTV, AOL TV OpenTV)	DVD	Other Network Devices (Kiosks, ATMs, etc.)
Storage Capacity (Persistent HD or Card)	Limited: 32–512MB memory card/ 1–2 gigabyte Microdrive/ Iomega Clik	Storage is usually via network	Hard drive with multiple gigabyte capacity	Most store information locally	None	Storage is via network
RAM	32/64 MB	Low	Typically 32 to 128 MB RAM	Varies from box to box	None	Limited
Interaction with Browser	Limited interaction with browser scripting	Usually not equipped with browser	Comprehensive (No JavaScript to player under Mac Internet Explorer up to Flash 4. Two-way communication between JavaScript and Flash Player on all other browsers.)	Set-top browser (expect Gecko to be AOL TV's standardized browser eventually)	None	None
Access to File System	Cookies under browser. Standalone solutions available.	Networked file system	Cookies under browser. Standalone solutions available.	No filesystem generally, though some allow a networked filesystem	None	None
Network Bandwidth	56K Modem/ Wireless/ Broadband	2G to 2.5 Networks	56K Modem/ Wireless/ Broadband	Broadband	None	Proprietary networks
Player Upgradable	Yes	Downloaded and upgradable	Yes	Varies from box to box	None	None
Printing Capability	No	No	Yes	Some	No	Depends on application

Outcomes: Identifying Requirements and Problem Analysis

Once you've determined what technologies will deliver your content, you should examine what project outcomes have to be met. Returning to our hypothetical Flash music application, one key requirement might be that the range of artists or styles of music (or both) that are offered to users will be changed quarterly. Knowing this requirement at the project design stage means that the architecture for the visual and coding components can be designed appropriately. Discovering this requirement *after* the design stage means that costly changes to the architecture, which will affect both visual design and underlying code, will be needed.

If you try to incorporate new additions to the project down the track, they may not be accommodated successfully. Properly drawing out all of the components in the early design stage will help to isolate or expose many of the later "what if" questions and will also help to avoid "feature creep," the dread phase where successive additions are cobbled onto the project. Aside from the madness that it engenders among developers, feature creep usually complicates development, hinders delivery, and compromises quality.

Benefits of Client Input

Another advantage of good project design documents is that they can spur the client to envisage what the final product will be like. From the client's perspective, the investment of a good deal of thought in answering your design questions will usually help the client to have a better picture of the software product. (This is good because they are, after all, paying you vast sums to build it.) Even if they can't hold it in their hand or see it on a screen, assisting the developers in answering specifications, approving the storyboards and flowcharts, and marking the delivery milestones on their calendars will help to create a definable product. Then, after all this specification is done, all that's left is to collect your progress payment and then build it!

Although it's easy to make fun of the business side of this process, there is an absolute truth here: Strong design documents are an incentive for both the client and the developer, because completion of this phase should be a tangible, billable milestone. If you, the developer, adhere to this process of project planning, clients can be assured that the product they invest money in will have a strong fidelity to the design document, which is something that they can hold in their hands.

Through the planning process, the development company has engaged the client's assistance in defining the end product, thereby building confidence in the client-developer relationship. Furthermore, they have jointly arrived at a clear vision of the product—a vision that addresses both the client's concerns about how the end product will solve their problems as well as the developer's concerns regarding how the product will achieve the intended outcome(s) in a technically efficient manner.

Design of a Solution

The design stage of a software product involves the creation of documents that describe the implementation of a solution. These documents together provide a range of detailed perspectives to view the solution, ranging from a general specifications document to technical flowcharts, storyboards, technical specifications, data models to the milestones document. Investing time into the design phase enables thoughtful planning of the many inter-related aspects of a software product, rather than over-focus on any one aspect to the detriment of the whole.

Specifications Document

The specifications document outlines all of the critical features and elements of your application, in plain English. It will both include and be substantially based upon the findings of the first two steps that have been discussed so far: systems specification and outcomes.

An introductory, overall executive summary section should provide an explanation of the project. Another key component of this document is an estimate of the time required for each feature, and each feature will have a detailed description that is as specific as possible. This document serves as the outline for the final outcome(s) of the project, so it's important that the client's expectations clearly match the specifications listed. If not, then the document will need to be revised subject to the client's input, prior to proceeding to the step.

Flowcharts and Storyboards

Flowcharts and storyboards each serve different purposes. Often, flowcharts are used to illustrate the navigation path through an application or the logic of an application unit or system. Storyboards, on the other hand, outline features such as user interfaces or animations. Both are extremely useful for both development planning and documentation for the client. Although it's possible to have beautifully drawn flowcharts and storyboards, it's perfectly acceptable to have simple pencil and paper versions as well. Use whatever's appropriate for you and your client. Just remember that these are excellent tools in the project design stage and that they should serve the needs of both the developer and the client.

Technical Specification Documents

The technical specifications documents detail programmatic aspects that aren't easily conveyed by flowcharting logical processes. These include the analysis of data objects and the data modeling of database designs, detailing the planning process from conceptual model, to a logical model to the schema used to represent the final data structures. Design of the application programming interfaces (APIs) may also be established at this stage as part of the target specifications.

Milestones Document

The milestones document establishes concrete outcomes during the lifespan of a project. Depending on the complexity of the project, the milestones may range from two to five or more phases. A milestone usually comprises of a group of features reached by a certain stage of development, such as the initial proof of concept, a beta stage, or the final deliverable. They're useful because a client can see satisfactory checkpoints reached as the project progresses, and the developer has some protection—because the client should be required to sign off as each milestone is achieved. Milestones can also serve as a billable outcome, ensuring the client and developer have reached an agreed-upon point, and therefore should plan upon a progress payment for the work done so far.

Development: Production, Coding, and Debugging

After completing the initial design phase of a project, the logical move is to begin development. Compared with the other major phases, the development phase is usually the most intensive, occupying most of the overall life of the project. Although developers sometimes have the mistaken notion that development "is" building the product (because this is when they're busiest), the truth is that successful development requires adequate attention to be given to all four major phases: design, development, testing, and deployment.

If we have done our job in the initial phase, our product has been precisely thought out and described—which means that development is now a matter of turning these documented concepts into reality. Development tasks can be focused and will follow the clear roadmap that detailed in the specifications document. Of course, actual development is often far from being so methodical and precise. "Code cutting" can be a messy process. But the fact that the overall systems have been specified, the flow of the product has been clearly planned out, and the design of screens has been storyboarded means that we are building to a reasonable plan. This major phase of the development of a multimedia project will encompass the gathering, creation, and production of multimedia assets—it is also the period where we create, document, and debug code.

Asset Gathering, Pre-Production, and Management

The need to gather raw assets for delivery is sometimes alien to those who are more familiar with a formal software engineering model. But for multimedia development, it's vital to have this procedure in place, because multimedia projects can involve literally hundreds of assets, which may include logos, text documents, images, and videos. If you've done your work in phase one, you will already know whether these will be provided by the client or sourced by research within your own team. Most likely, these assets will arrive over a period of time and in many different file formats. These raw multimedia assets will go through many iterations during the pre-production and creative design process before arriving in their final, usable form.

Imagine if you were asked to recrop a particular image and change the color scheme at a late beta stage. What if the current image is a low-resolution SWF with a sepia color scheme, and the client requests a high-quality, full-color version instead? What if that image is just one of 300 80MB images that were provided by the client over a period of 6 weeks? Clearly, you'll need a well-organized archival system to receive and log raw assets so that you can quickly track down the original without having to sort through the entire collection. Different schemes have been developed to organize the multimedia gathering process, and it's only necessary to find the model that works for you. To get you started, here are a few useful resources that cover asset management within a multimedia production process:

- Firstborn Media's FlashForward 2001 presentation on the topic "Concept to Product: Project Management." The speaker's notes are downloadable from http://www.flashforward2001.com/nyc_notes/ferdman/.
- The authoritative book *Web Project Management: Delivering Successful Commercial Web Sites*, by Ashley Friedlein (Morgan Kaufmann Publishers, 2000; ISBN: 1558606785), covers every aspect of large-scale web projects, with most sections equally applicable to Flash projects.
- The book *Web ReDesign: Workflow that Works*, by Kelly Goto and Emily Cotler (New Riders, 2001; ISBN: 0735710627), also has techniques applicable to Flash web-based applications as well as HTML websites (http://www.web-redesign.com).

As the raw media assets arrive, a pre-production process should be in place to transform and archive both the original file and edited file. For example, the client might supply a 80MB 300dpi CMYK Photoshop file that will be used as a banner ad within the final application. The pre-production team member would alter this to a 72dpi RGB PNG image suitable for the design and development teams to work with and then archive both the original Photoshop file and the production PNG according to the previously established, formal management process. The desired result will be that, should it be needed again, the original can be found easily—thereby liberating the developer to focus on the task of software development, instead of being continually distracted by the need to locate and convert Photoshop files. Cost saving advantages are also obvious. Instead of paying a software developer to convert image files, an intern with basic Photoshop skills will happily undertake this role.

Now, let's return to our hypothetical Flash music application for a moment. It's likely that some, if not all, of our target visuals will have to be delivered in three different formats: desktop, Pocket PC, and ITV. A project that targets a single platform may have 100 final visual assets, but an application destined for ubiquitous deployment might require 300 final visuals. It's not hard to imagine that, as the project scales, the complexity and number of assets will grow quickly, which re-emphasizes the critical need for a formal, quality asset management system. An ad hoc system can easily doom such a project.

Multimedia Design and Production

Flash software projects most often feature strong multimedia content, because this is one of the main attractions for developing in this environment. Although a traditional software engineering project may involve some graphic design and production, a Flash-based product will usually involve heavy amounts of resources in multimedia design, alongside a parallel engineering effort. By separating the code aspects and the presentation aspects (that is, the multimedia visuals and audio), developers and designers are able to focus on completing their tasks in parallel, reducing the need to wait for each other's assets. Flash projects also tend to require more time spent in usability design, and this is an area where front-end presentation experts should hold sway.

Development and Staging Environments

When you're creating applications for multiple platforms, it's important to set up the development environment correctly. If an application is targeted for a Pocket PC as well as a desktop browser, then provision for testing on a Pocket PC needs to be part of the development environment, rather than relying on testing and tweaking at the end of the production process. For applications that will be distributed over networks such as intranets and the Internet, the application should be tested on the whole system as much as possible. To clarify:

- The development environment is the client and server software that you'll be building the application on, and meeting this requirement might be as simple as installing the webserver, application server, and database server all on your local desktop.

- The staging environment is where your clients can visit to review progress and what the Q/A people will use to test the application.

The advantage of having separate development and staging environments is that you can continue to develop without holding up either client review or the Q/A cycle.

The section "Testing (aka Quality Assurance Cycle)" on page 302 will discuss testing in detail, but for now it is important to remember that accurate development and staging environments will reveal specific platform issues during the coding, debugging, and Q/A processes. These issues may include processor speed, screen size, audio capabilities, and usability. Remember this valuable advice that we'll emphasize until it's a mantra in your mind:

> "Test early, test often, test on all of your target machines."
> –John Dowdell, Macromedia Technical Support

For example, building our demo music application within the Flash authoring environment on our desktops is fine, but unless we check how the visuals appear on 12-bit Pocket PC devices or on the ITV screens of our set-top boxes, we may not be aware of potential dithering or other color issues until long after the visual design process is complete. If the problem doesn't surface until the final Q/A cycle, we'll have to bring back the designers to alter the graphics and remake assets—a scenario to be avoided because it vastly complicates final delivery.

Coding Development and Debugging

The emphasis on careful management so far extends to the engineering efforts as well. Investing time into best practices during the coding development process ensures that as the project scales in complexity and across platforms and multiple tiers, the code remains manageable. This next section discusses strategies to manage this, discussing ActionScript best practices, version control, debugging and documentation strategies.

ActionScript Best Practices

Because Flash was originally an animation tool and its scripting capabilities have been added with each successive release, the continual development of ActionScript has meant that a Flash application can be coded in any number of ways. This flexibility allows for many solutions to a problem, but it also makes it difficult for a group of developers to collaborate on a project. Consequently, complex projects such as cross-platform ubiquitous content need clear coding standards to be established so that team collaboration, version checking, and integration will proceed as smoothly as possible. By structuring your Flash movie along the following guidelines, your code will be more portable and will follow Macromedia's suggested best practices for developing advanced Flash applications:

- Keep as much code as possible in one location within the movie. By separating as much data as possible from presentation, the task of editing and maintaining the code will be made easier.

- Use #include .as files to simplify file versioning and differencing. (For more about #include, refer to Chapter 5's section on using ActionScript includes entitled "Don't use a semicolon!" on page 118.)

- Use frames and layers to maintain application states.

- Discourage the practice of attaching complex code to movie clips and buttons. If logic is required, try to call a function located back in a root-level frame, because this approach ensures that the code will then be centralized.

- Try to initialize your movie in a central script rather than distribute code in different layers or frames.

- Scope variables so that local and global variables are carefully established.

- Document/comment clearly whenever code diverges to account for differences in platforms.

- Use a combination of server-side detection and ActionScript's getVersion() to deliver customized content for web applications on multiple platforms.

With the release of Flash MX, Macromedia has signaled a serious intent to provide quality developer documentation to aid its promotion of Flash as a front end to complex web applications. Macromedia provides extensive resources in their Flash MX Application Development Center, available at www.macromedia.com/desdev/mx/flash. You can also check the relevant area of our site, www.flashthefuture.com/14, for updates.

Version Control

Although you're probably familiar with the major versions of the Flash authoring software, such as Flash 4 and 5, you may not understand why the Flash Player has seemingly arbitrary numbers like 5.0.30.0 or 5.0.41.0 or 6.0.0.25. Why hasn't Macromedia released players in a more logical numbering scheme like 5.1, 5.2, and 6.0? The reason lies in version control, which is a valuable strategy used to manage software development. Version control is appropriate for all development groups, ranging from the lone coder to larger teams, such as Macromedia's Flash development crew.

Developers who are not using version control software will develop their own file renaming and backup strategies, usually as a life-saving strategy. This can mean repeatedly saving the file with incrementally different filenames to preserve a traceable record of the development history, just in case the need arises to revert to an earlier version. It might also mean that the source files will be routinely backed up to a different location. What it usually doesn't mean is a commented history and a way to quickly check the differences between versions (known as a "diff" in the coder community).

Dedicated version control software offers all of the above and, with complex systems, also accommodates multiple developers working on separate components of a system so that the overall progress of a complex software product can be clearly defined by each component's version. There is nothing wrong with using a simple filename system as version control, but it can be expensive from the viewpoint of time investment and offers fewer features and benefits than when we get the computer to do the job with version control software.

Let the Software Do It

In its simplest implementation, version control software will archive your file with a couple of mouse clicks—it will automatically track the prior versions and automatically increment the build number for you. You can add comments to the archive that will be displayed in a comprehensive revision history. Click OK, and the version control software will automatically backup your file, and archive its history. When you want to review an earlier file, version control will let you easily retrieve the correct version, seamlessly, without the filename ever changing. Figure 14.1 shows the revision history of a Flash project and a comment (in the Description field) related to the interim 1.5 build.

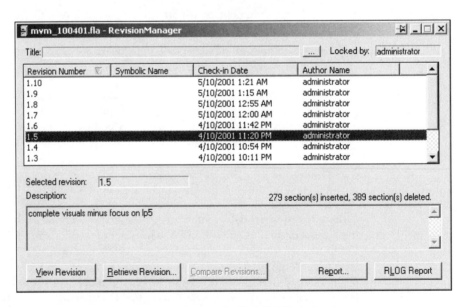

Figure 14.1: Comprehensive revision history of a Flash FLA file in development.

If it's not clear already, we advocate that version control should be used throughout the development, beta testing, and deployment phases of a project. During development, you can use version control as personal insurance. Having access to simple version control at your fingertips enables you to archive code with each significant change and, once it becomes a regular habit, you'll never worry again about losing changes. Complex version control empowers the whole team to work together, without spreading confusion when code components of different versions are distributed throughout the team. During beta cycles, as bugs are discovered and fixes implemented, version control is necessary to document the continued improvement of the product. Finally in release, it's important that software retains the development numbering scheme, so that bugs found in the marketplace can be tracked back to the final version of the code for fixes.

A range of both free and commercial version control software is available. An excellent product for the single Windows-based developer is Component Software's RCS product, which is freely available at http://www.componentsoftware.com/csrcs. A commercial version for multiple developers is also available. The popular and free (and open-source) CVS system (http://www.cvshome.org/) is available from the Linux community. This package is powerful but requires a Linux server and Linux knowledge to set up. Many development companies have Linux boxes set up as web and file servers, so implementing CVS may be possible. CVS has version control clients for Macintosh, Windows, and many other platforms, which offers the advantage that you can integrate with the server from your development desktop.

Returning to our initial discussion about the Flash Player's version history, the reason why the builds are numbered like 5.0.41.0 and 5.0.82.0 is because the public versions of the Player match the internal Macromedia development versions. For example, when the second public revision of the Flash 5 Player was released, the Netscape plugin was numbered 5.0.40.0, and the Internet Explorer ActiveX control was numbered 5.0.41.0. These specific build numbers matched Macromedia's internal efforts up to that point. The Pocket PC Flash 5 Player was numbered 5.0.88.0 for the device manufacturers' reference build, with various internal builds using a range of numbers between 41 and 88. Using this methodical approach, if improvements or fixes are required, makes it easy to return to the archive of any version and track exactly what changes have been made.

Debugging: Not Full Q/A

When you're building your code, you'll often test a component to make sure it's performing as expected. As you fix bugs, it's sometimes tempting to think that a final quality assurance cycle is excessive, because you're already testing the product. This is a fatal mistake. Debugging (that is, the act of diagnosing and exorcising bugs during code development) is not a full quality assurance cycle. Many bugs are found by testers who are unfamiliar with the product, simply because they'll perform steps that you've never anticipated. A rigorous Q/A cycle will in fact cover many aspects of the software that may not be the responsibility of the programmer, because it should also test the performance of a whole system (including a network system) as well as usability—which relates back to the visual, aural, and logical design of a product. Debugging is the programmer's means of analyzing errors and fixing the causes. In contrast, Q/A testing is the activity of revealing software errors. We'll cover Q/A in a moment, but please realize— debugging is *not* full Q/A.

For cross-platform products, a useful strategy is to deliberately structure your code in smaller units. That way, it's easy to test parts on multiple platforms during development. You can isolate performance and compatibility issues quickly when you're checking an isolated section on each device, compared with running a complicated project and wondering from the outside why it's not working. For example, our Flash music application might use a large XML file to select the song preferences. The application runs perfectly on the desktop but grinds to a halt on the Pocket PC. Looking specifically at the XML parser component, you can see that memory usage grows to an unacceptable size within the handheld's limited memory, and the Pocket PC's processor isn't fast enough to chew through the sizeable XML document.

Documentation

Documentation can be an area of heated debate. Programmers have different styles of commenting code, and the number and location of comments and formal documentation vary from person to person. Regardless, it's important that any documentation does the following jobs:

- It helps you remember why you originally wrote the code the way that it is written.
- For someone unfamiliar with the project, it helps them to pick up the pieces.
- When you revise an older piece of code, adding comments to the original helps to track the changes that are being made.
- In a team environment, it tracks the changes made by different individuals and when/why they introduced new code.
- For projects with ubiquitous deployment, clear documentation of areas where code differs because of platform differences will help to clarify which sections are common and which sections diverge for platform-specific reasons.

Testing (aka Quality Assurance Cycle)

A structured testing regime means improved quality of software. Understanding different techniques of testing your application within the quality assurance (that is, Q/A) cycle means that, as the software grows in size and complexity, its reliability will be maintained. Done well, testing will encompass these phases:

- Unit testing
- System integration
- System testing

- Regression testing
- Usability testing

These activities are a vital part of our roadmap toward final deployment of the ubiquitous software product. Stopping at each point along the way will actually speed up the travel toward our final destination of product release, rather than slow us down. Good testing is not a sidetrack before deployment, but really the means to help us build software faster. As we've noted, ubiquitous deployment can mean a corresponding growth in complexity. All the advantages offered by good testing will translate into an easier development process for these more complex projects.

Unit Testing

Testing is often seen as a black-box process, where checks to reveal the accuracy of the software are done by someone unfamiliar with the innards of the software component. But unit testing is the opposite. It's a white-box or glass-box approach performed by the programmer of that unit as someone wholly familiar with the code. As you develop each component, it makes sense to thoroughly test the unit before moving on to the next one. Having a systematic approach to unit testing makes the job of debugging much easier. Not only do you avoid future problems as you integrate units of software together, but when/if you find an error, you'll also know that errors are in the current routine rather than "somewhere" in the larger system. For unit testing to fulfill its mission, it's important to make sure each requirement and design concern for the unit has been satisfied. An ideal time to plan unit test cases is at the design phase of each unit, since this is also a time when you're creating the logical processes. Ideally, the test cases for each unit should stress test your implementation—hence planning for them at the outset will better catch possible flaws within your design.

System Integration

System integration is the process of developing software so that each unit connects to other units and so that the whole structure can be tested as it grows. An incremental approach to integration means that you code and test the program in small units and then combine the units one at a time. Because the resulting system grows at a manageable pace, this process enables you to test the structure incrementally, and you avoid the flaw of building all the units and then combining them at the end. Testing a large completed structure without the earlier integration of smaller units means that the new bugs that inevitably arise will be harder to track, because you won't have a clear idea of their origin.

System Testing

As the system is gradually integrated, test the system through a platform grid. Returning to our demo music application, as each build or milestone is completed, you'll need to make sure that the system for each platform—desktop, Pocket PC, and ITV set-top—functions correctly. Avoid the occasional temptation to skip this step because it feels painful to run through all those targeted platforms again. It's easier to find and fix bugs earlier than later. Remember our mantra: "Test early, test often, test on all of your target machines."

Regression Testing

Regression testing means selectively testing the software system after new code modifications to make sure that any bugs have been fixed and that the previous functionality hasn't been broken by the latest changes.

Regression testing ensures that the same results continue to occur in a systematic way. Because you're trying to ensure identical results through repeated testing, regression testing is far better if executed via automation than by people. Running an application repeatedly to achieve the same test results can rapidly become a boring activity and, consequently, it's much harder for people to spot the bad results. By writing some code to test your system, you will ensure that the regression tests occur reliably and quickly.

Usability Testing

To test usability means testing whether your target audience can use the software. This seems an obvious fact, but the point is that much software goes through a Q/A cycle without the concern of usability being addressed. Concern has appeared in the marketplace about Flash usability, because bad Flash can be a common problem on the Internet (as detailed by Nielsen's infamous "Flash 99% bad" article at http://useit.com/alertbox/20001029.html). This is not to say that we agree that Flash is 99 percent bad, but rather that it deserves strong usability testing, like any application written in any other language. Macromedia provides a range of Flash usability resources at their site (www.macromedia.com/software/flash/productinfo/usability/), and usability testing resources for the Web, such as CNet's "Guerrilla Usability" article (http://builder.cnet.com/web-building/0-7705-8-6861748-1.html), will offer tips equally relevant to Flash Web applications.

Design a Bugbase

Now that we've collected bugs along the way, how do we keep track of them? One solution is a database designed for bug tracking, known as a bugbase. A large range of these bugbases are offered both freely and commercially on the Internet. Knowing how to customize a bugbase and use it is half the problem. If a tester finds a bug, enough relevant information has to be provided in order for the programmer to reproduced the bug and track down the underlying cause. "Painless Bug Tracking" (http://www.joelonsoftware.com/stories/storyReader$245) is an excellent article that trails the process, beginning with a tester's submission of a bug report to its eventual fix by the programmer. A good bug report must have three parts:

1. Steps to reproduce
2. What you expected to see
3. What you saw instead

A programmer must be able to reproduce the bug before that bug can be diagnosed. Even the roughest list of steps to reproduce a bug will make it more likely that the same problem will be observed. Explaining the expected result will help the programmer understand why the tester thinks this is a bug. Explaining what you saw instead means describing the actual buggy result. Obviously, if the steps to reproduce don't end up generating the actual bug, the bug report won't be useful.

When you're creating software for ubiquitous delivery, make sure you include every possible platform combination in the bugbase. If a tester submits a bug but finds that the bugbase doesn't offer that platform as a listed option, that tester will be forced to enter the details into a different field, making tracking difficult. Good bugbases balance efficient bug entry by testers with information that is detailed enough for debugging.

Deployment and Maintenance

When the software is finally completed, it's tempting to think that our job is over. Good software production, however, includes deployment and eventual maintenance as part of the plan. Deployment may be as simple as uploading assets to the production server, or—in the case of ubiquitous deployment— activities such as making different installers for each platform as well as production server setup and uploading. It's important to consider these activities early, when planning the entire project.

The maintenance activities of a released project should also be part of the initial design. Anticipating how updates will be deployed in the product will enable this system to be designed in advance. It's far harder to insert new data or features into a completed and deployed product when the system doesn't allow this. The design of maintenance features also goes hand in hand when developing the security properties of a product.

Learning More About the Process

Many of the strategies touched on in this chapter come from the formal software development world, where programmers and researchers over many decades have encountered these issues and developed best practices to tackle the problems. If you're interested in investigating these solutions on a deeper level, the book *Code Complete: A Practical Handbook of Software Construction*, by Steve McConnell (Microsoft Press; ISBN: 1556154844), is highly recommended. Much of this chapter's themes owe their inspiration to McConnell's work.

Summary

Flash application development can be a complex affair, and the effort to create content that is appropriate for ubiquitous delivery magnifies the complexity. By carefully managing the software development process, the numerous phases of content and application development can be accomplished in an efficient manner. The opportunity for deployment across many platforms also means increased opportunity for errors, so it's important to have a rigorous development scheme in place when creating Flash applications. Carefully considering the many aspects of detailed software development allows you, the developer, to take advantage of the basic "write once, run anywhere" nature of Flash, without dangerously underestimating the effort that's actually involved.

Now that we've shown you the fundamentals (and many very technical details) of authoring Flash content for a wide range of devices—including PPCs, games, video, DVD, and ITV—it's time to put all of this technical stuff into perspective. Chapter 16 will look at some of the most current applications of this technology and share a bit of what we are hearing within the industry. We'll also do a little blue-sky thinking in an attempt to look into our crystal PPC and answer the question, "Where will Flash go next?"

15

EPILOGUE: FUTURE FLASH

Jon Warren Lentz

This chapter is about the future. In order to write it, I peered into my proprietary Flash-driven Crystal Ball, which runs on my PPC, and this chapter is about what I found. As with any crystal ball prediction, one runs the risk of being wrong. The future is fraught with uncertainty. However, I'm pretty confident that while I may err on the minutiae, I think the bigger picture is pretty clear. With a little help from a few of my friends, I hope to outline that picture for you here, now.

Statistics

In addition to the Nokia Communicator Phones and the newly emerging Smart Phones and PPC Phones, the Flash Player already runs on millions of Pocket PCs. Increasingly, more and more Pocket PCs are shipping with the Flash player pre-installed. There are already well over a billion cell phones. What about the future? Experts predict that there will be 167 million devices will be sold in 2005. According to industry buzz, Microsoft has said that they expect to sell 250 million devices—Smart Phones and PPC Phones. Experts also predict that, in these next few years, nearly all cell phones will evolve into devices with features like Pocket PCs—and we are confident that all these will support the Flash Player. At the time of this writing, nearly all major carriers have begun to push a variant of the PPC Phone. One of these, the O2 xpda, is shown in Figure 15.1. So there is ample cause for excitement!

Figure 15.1: The O2 xpda, which is probably the most appealing of any of the initial offerings of PPC Phones.

As my friend Phillip Torrone exhorts, "The best way to predict the future is to invent it." Talking about Flash on devices has become Phillip's obsession. Like a man possessed, he travels the globe to showcase the advances that are being made by Flash developers in the expanding realm of devices. With his classic visionary stance, Phil explained, "If there's a screen that can become a vessel of creativity, we'll get on it. In the short period of time in which rich media could exist on devices, we've moved the needle towards something really amazing. How often can you really do 'new things'—I mean, developed and delivered ideas and concepts that no one has accomplished before? We are the new pioneers. Sure, some of us will get arrows in our backs as we explore this great new frontier, some of us won't make it, some will eat their young . . . but I tell ya, it's all worth it, 'cause there's gold in them thar' hills, folks. Saddle up."

Wireless

The safest bet is not to bet, but if you want to lay down your Flash, I'd encourage you to look at applications targeted at the convergence of the PPC with wireless and telephony. With the recent release of the Toshiba e740, the HP 928 (shown in Figure 15.2), and other wireless offerings, it is reasonable to predict that in the very near future, nearly all PPCs will ship with some form of wireless access. In fact, the PPCs that ship without wireless will most likely be targeted at narrow niche markets while the mainstream PPCs will be untethered. The emergence of these devices signals a broad new opportunity for Flash developers.

Figure 15.2: The new HP 928 is one of many new wireless PPCs that are entering the market in the second half of 2002.

For example, Eric Dolecki developed the *FlashForward 2002 New York City Event Guide*, which was, as the name might suggest, a conference program for FlashForward. It was authored in Flash for the PPC and included wireless updates and a feature that enabled attendees to rate the conference presentations. Still available at www.ericd.net/guide, this application (shown in Figure 15.3) exhibits the range of the features that can be delivered and the design control that can be maintained when authoring with Flash for the PPC.

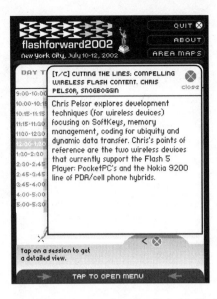

Figure 15.3: A screen from Eric Dolecki's FlashForward 2002 New York City Event Guide, *showing the synopsis for Chris Pelsor's session.*

Eric shared his vision of the future: "Until now, the web and interactive mediums have been suited for those tied to a connection or a hard-wired network. (Now) . . . the web is becoming available to those on the move: those with wireless PPCs, cell phones, tablet PCs, and the growing list of Flash-enabled devices. The Flash development movement is quickly producing a better way to interact with this new wireless medium. With Flash, you can develop powerful applications that deliver robust solutions to users mobile needs, while providing the best in interactivity, user interfacing, audio cues, and maintaining client branding. Flash application developers have the tools to open up the world to new experiences, and offer those experiences to a growing horde of mobile players. We are changing how the world interacts with itself. We chart our own course. We influence the influencers. We lead the charge into a bright, new world—high above the clouds of imagination."

Here are a few clues that may help to indicate the predicted wireless future at both the public and enterprise levels:

- Wireless is coming. For example, British Telephone plans to launch the UK's first public wireless LAN (WLAN) with 400 nodes at key locations such as hotels, service stations, railway stations, airports, and coffee shops. In a separate effort, HP has launched a worldwide initiative to provide WLAN nodes in public places, providing secure high-speed access to email and other applications using virtually any wireless protocol and device. According to the experts, such nodes are expected to grow to 41,000 and reach 21 million users in the U.S. by 2007. In a similar but unrelated effort, according to the *New York Times,* AT&T Wireless, Verizon, Cingular, and other companies would collaborate on Project Rainbow, which is a scheme to build WLAN nodes in public places. Similarly, at TecXNY Expo in New York in June 2002, PC makers convened to discuss, among other things, plans to create the necessary infrastructure to build a wireless utopia.

- Warchalking. As I understand it, the idea was launched over lunch. Jonesing for more wireless access points, these British guys decided to create a language to mark wireless access points with the intent that when they found a node, they would, "leave a chalk symbol for others to find the node with a minimum of all that tiresome netstumbler business." This is relevant to Flash on devices because it provides a indication of the appeal of a wireless network, and the inevitable advent of it. For more about warchalking, please refer to www.blackbeltjones.com/warchalking/index2.html. As shown in Figure 15.4, the warchalking symbols can be downloaded from the site and printed out. This is also available as a Flash asset for the PPC, from www.flashthefuture.com/warchalk.

- Potential wireless applications include businesses, restaurants, hospitals,

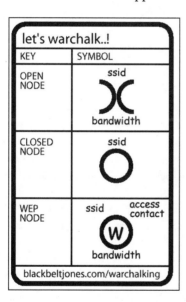

Figure 15.4: The warchalking symbols as originally developed by blackbeltjones.com.

museums, sports venues and stadiums, theme parks, and many others that will find ways to use wireless devices to improve their services.

Consumer Applications

An example of this trend is apparent in the Garfield Animated Today, which is shown in Figure 15.5. This and similar new themes are featured at www.flashen-abled.com/at/. According to Phillip Torrone (the ubiquitous), "This is a big 'first': Business models and industries are forming around Macromedia Flash and mobile devices . . . It's the first time content like this has been licensed to be sold, as Flash movies, for mobile devices. Since there's going to be a billion or more mobile devices . . . (this) seems like a great step in a great direction."

Figure 15.5: One of several Garfield Animated Today screens, which are indicative of a new consumer market for PPC applications—authored and delivered in Flash.

As more and more devices are put into use, there will be a broader market for consumer applications that target specific tasks or offer users the option to customize their devices, or both. Such applications can leverage wireless capabilities or simply enhance the owner's ability to use the device. Flash is an ideal platform for the development of these applications—just add insight and creativity and go for it!

PPC Camera Phones

Right now in Japan, the big thing is sending photos on camera-equipped cell phones. According to Robin Debreuil of Debreuil Digital Works (www.debreuil.com), "It is a big money maker, too." Some PPCs already have cameras, or camera options, and when these cameras become more common, Robin believes, "Flash needs to be able to handle things like capture, upload, and display easily." An enterprising Flash developer could build such an application. For more about this topic, refer to http://story.news.yahoo.com/ news?tmpl=story2&cid=569&ncid=738&e=2&u=/ nm/20020716/tc_nm/telecoms_japan_cameraphones_dc_1.

Games

According to John Romero, co-creator of Wolfenstein, Doom, and Quake, the next frontier for gaming is devices, including wireless and PPCs. His new venture, Monkeystone Games (www.monkeystone.com), is aimed at this frontier—and he is using Flash to hit the target. This view of the gaming future is seconded by Andy Riedel of Xadra, provider of Fortress, a multiplayer gaming engine (www.xadra.com): "Things get really interesting when you hook up with wireless Flash devices!" Figure 15.6 shows the Lobby of Fortress, as displayed on the PPC.

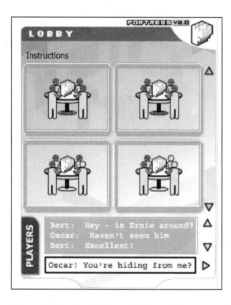

Figure 15.6: A multiplayer Lobby of Fortress on the PPC.

At the other end of the gaming spectrum, it was recently announced that the Flash Player will be integrated into the Nokia Mediaterminal, which is an infotainment device that combines gaming with digital video broadcast (DVB), full Internet access, and personal video recorder (PVR) technology. The Mediaterminal is one of several devices (including the PlayStation and Xbox) that are aimed at transforming the family TV into a multifunctional entertainment center. In the future, we predict that all of these devices will support Flash. For more information, refer to www.macromedia.com/macromedia/proom/pr/2002/nokia_mediaterminal.html.

Presentations

On the mundane and familiar terrestrial level, PPCs are being used to deliver presentations—both one-on-one and to large audiences. Such uses are facilitated by hardware advances such as the Voyager VGA CF Card, which supports a broad range of PPC devices and delivers presentations by connecting to the MARGI Systems 1024 x 768 projector.

Fine Art

In addition to the obvious use of PPCs to display an artist's portfolio, the PPC also offers great potential to artists as the delivery method for an art piece. One such example is an installation titled "Kiss Off," by Peter Strohmeyer and Wil Bown, which is shown in Figure 15.7.

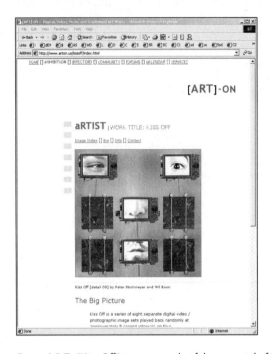

Figure 15.7: "Kiss Off" is an example of the potential of Flash on the PPC as a fine art medium.

The artists explain: "'Kiss Off' is a series of eight separate digital video/photographic image sets played back randomly at approximately five-second intervals on four unsynchronized Pocket PCs. Through composition and proximity, the viewer is encouraged to mentally recombine the separate elements into a completed recognizable form and extract its significance." For more, visit www.arton.us.

Wearable Computers

While we don't have droids or cyborg-enhanced humans (yet), it's now possible for a civilian to dress up in close approximation of one. In fact, there are a number of off-the-rack solutions for such aspirations . . . and they all support Flash.

- Leveraging technology patented by Xybernaut, Hitachi has been working on the world's first commercial Wearable Internet Appliance—WIA, which will run Windows CE 3.0 on a Hitachi SH-4 32-bit RISC processor. According to reports, WIA provides users with instant on/off Internet access and an SVGA (800 x 600) head mount display, which will provide a desktop-like viewing experience. The hands-free WIA PC can be worn while on public transportation, in the office, shopping, or relaxing at home. Services that WIA will target include distance learning, GPS, cellular voice communications and paging, interactive banking, shopping, stock market trading, and entertainment in the form of music, video, and games. Word on the street is that there may be a player in development for this processor. For more information, see www.hitachi.com/products/ information/multimedia/ wia/index.html.

- Perhaps a little less fabulous than the WIA, clothing manufacturers have begun to design and deliver clothing that is suited to the needs of mobile computing. One of the first such efforts is the Scott eVest, which has special channels in the vest to route wires and adapters to and from a plethora of devices. For more about this, visit www.scottevest.com.

- Similarly, a full page ad for Robinsons May Department Store, in the Sunday *L.A. Times*, showed an X-ray insight to the contents of a man's conservative beige trousers. The copy read, "Introducing Dockers ® Recode ™ Mobile ™ Pants . . . Stowaway seam pockets on each side. Designed for your Compaq© iPAQ Pocket PC . . . " As shown in Figure 15.8, the campaign (done in Flash, of course!) is still on the Web at www.dockers.com/mobilesitelet/flash/ mobilePantFlashTest.html.

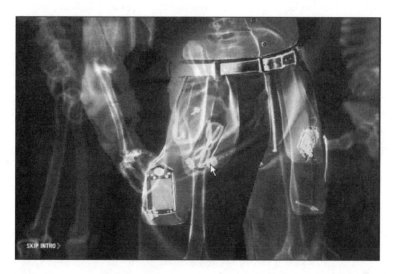

Figure 15.8: A frame from an online ad for Recode Mobile Pants, seen at the Dockers site which is, fittingly, a Flash animation.

- Finally, for those who still think that *Flashing* requires a trenchcoat, there's the Sanyo NY Palm Coat, which can be readily adapted to PPC use. Refer to www.sanyofashionhouse.com/pocketsystem.html.

Conclusion

When I muse about the relevance of PPCs and related devices, I'm inevitably drawn back to an anecdote about the United States Space Program. Apparently, NASA spent millions of dollars in an attempt to develop a ballpoint pen that would work in space. Finally, they gave up and began to send the astronauts up equipped with, yup, a pencil!

Before I owned a PPC, I used to keep a Word document on my desktop, which I updated every evening. Across the top, I kept phone numbers for current contacts, and beneath that, in neatly organized areas, I kept my appointments, errands, and shopping lists. Once I'd updated it I would print it out, fold it into quarters, and then put it in my back pocket. Because I live in Acronym City, I considered this my DPP (Daily Piece of Paper). It was the acme of convenience. During the course of the day, I could pull it out and write notes upon it, cross off items that had been accomplished, and scribble. I never had to wait for it to start up, nor did I need to worry about recharging it. It never crashed.

I preferred this method over a bulky calendar, because there was nothing to lose. The price and the convenience were ideal. And as I used to point out, with my DPP I was free to dash into the ocean to rescue a sinking swimmer (which is something I've done more than once)—without hesitating to empty my pockets. At most, I might lose the jottings from one day.

So to play the devil's advocate, I have to ask: In what ways does my PPC surpass the paper and pen that I formerly carried in my pocket? I'm afraid that I don't have the right answer. The answer is waiting in the future and you, the Flash developers, may be largely responsible for that answer. Right now, the relative inconvenience of my PPC is outweighed by the features that are not available from a sheet of paper. But in order for devices such as the PPC or the PPC Phone to appeal to a broader market, they *must* make more sense to the daily life of the user—not just to users who spend most of their lives shuttling from meetings to airports and back again, but to the people who live more normal lives. (For example, when I am working with saws and wood and concrete while remodeling my house, I do not have the least use for my PPC—it sits in my office.)

I think that the key to this question lies in something that one of my friends (who contributed greatly to this book) said to me in an email. Chris Pelsor observed: "I guess what is most important about developing applications targeted for wireless devices is that it's not as much about doing something that hasn't been done before, as it is about using the applications to change the context of the interaction people have with the world so that they experience things in a way that they wouldn't have experienced them before. Context is king." I humbly concur.

Now that you have read this book, I encourage you to turn the glass around and consider the stark wisdom of Chris' observation. In the meanwhile, I'll be doing the same thing. And when I find applications that meet this criteria and that are worthy of explication, I'll be writing them up and posting them at www.flashthefuture.com/15. See you there.

APPENDICES

A1

THE TRUTH ABOUT
12-BIT COLOR DISPLAYS

Ian Chia and Doug Loftus

Strangely unfamiliar to many designers and developers, the 3600/3700 series iPAQ, the Nokia 9200 Communicator series, and the forthcoming mm02 XDA/VoiceStream Pocket PC Phone Edition devices have 12-bit color displays. Our desktop machines typically use 8-, 16-, or 24-bit color, resulting in 256 colors, 32,768 colors, or millions of colors in the display palette. However, 12-bit color is an unusual beast, and particularly so on the Compaq iPAQ because of the interactions between the device's hardware design and Windows CE.

Knowing the valid colorspace is important when you are designing graphics that rely on solid colors. If your design is based on an unsafe 12-bit color, the hardware will automatically downsample the image for you, resulting in unpleasant banding visual artifacts. Although the maximum 4,096 colors are a far cry from the bad ol' days of the 216-color web-safe palette, it still pays to design with these limitations in mind if you want to make the maximum visual impact on your audience.

Photographic images will usually use millions of colors, resulting in images that look banded on the iPAQ or Nokia display because of its hardware reduction to 4,096 colors. Chapter 2 provides useful Photoshop strategies to dither 24-bit images down to 12-bit, while keeping maximum image fidelity for your Flash projects. However, for designs that rely on solid colors, you'll want to know *exactly* which colors are valid in the 12-bit colorspace. The following sections explain how that colorspace is defined, based on our own considerable research and experimentation aimed at unraveling the mysteries of 12-bit color on the iPAQ.

iPAQ Screen-Safe Colors

On the desktop, the limited colorspace of 8-bit (256-color) displays gave rise to the familiar web-safe 216-color palette, used by designers to ensure that browser-rendered graphics are not dithered on an 8-bit display. Although a 12-bit display is also limited in the number of colors it can faithfully reproduce, the scheme employed by 3600/3700 series iPAQs and Nokia 9200 series Communicators equals a palette of 4,096 solid colors—not nearly as limiting as the web-safe model.

NOTE *It might seem perverse to limit the iPAQ display to only 4,096 colors, when competing Pocket PCs such as the HP Jornada have 32,768 colors, but the limitation is due to Compaq's choice of the ACX704AKM active matrix LCD panel from Sony, which has this color range as a hardware limitation.*

Screen display colorspace is defined using RGB values—a triplet of numbers that specifies the levels of red, green, and blue that are combined to color an individual pixel on the screen (for example, the RGB triplet "125, 0, 125" specifies a medium shade of purple). Because we have only 12 bits of information to deliver the full color value, each component (R, G, or B) must be specified with 4 bits, meaning that each component can only have 16 possible values. Multiplying the R, G, and B together ($16 \times 16 \times 16$), we arrive at 4,096 possible color values. (If you're unfamiliar with binary jargon, a bit is a "binary digit"—meaning it can only take the value 0 or 1. A unit of information conveyed with some number n bits can take 2^n possible values—so, 4 bits can convey one of $2 \times 2 \times 2 \times 2$ [= 16] possible values.)

It can be confusing enough counting in binary for the uninitiated, but in addition, colors are usually specified using hexadecimal notation when authoring for the Web. If you've authored web pages or Flash movies, you may be familiar with using hexadecimal color specifications such as #FF0000 for red in HTML, or 0xFFFFFF to mean white in ActionScript. If you work with the web-safe palette frequently, you may be aware of a pattern among the values: They are all combinations of a finite set of allowed hex values for each red, green, and blue component (specifically 00, 33, 66, 99, CC, and FF).

Obviously, it's much easier to remember a short list of values (00, 33, and so on) than it is to remember hundreds, let alone thousands, of individual colors. Although it's undocumented on the iPAQ, after much research and experimentation, we've identified a similar scheme of "magic numbers" that allows us to derive hex values for all 4,096 non-dithered colors. We find that these hexadecimal R, G, or B values are:

```
00, 10, 20, 30, 40, 50, 60, 70, 80, 90, A0, B0, C0, D0, E0, F0.
```

These 16 possible hexadecimal numbers, each representing an allowed value for the red, blue, or green color component, can be combined to create the 4,096 solid colors displayed on the iPAQ. For example, 0x000000 is black on the iPAQ screen, and 0xF0F0F0 is the brightest white color possible, because it's the sum of the maximum red, green, and blue values. The astute web designer will immediately notice that white on the iPAQ is different than web-safe white, which is normally 0xFFFFFF. As additional examples, the following are also non-dithering colors using this model: 0xE03090, 0x101010, 0x90D0D0, 0x10F070.

Nokia 9200 Communicator Series Screen-Safe Colors

Based on the official *Nokia 9210 Communicator WWW Browser Style Guide* document provided by Nokia, the 12-bit color display for the Communicator phone functions much like that for the iPAQ. The Communicator also uses the most significant 4 bits of each RGB component, and all other colors outside the 4,096-color palette are dithered or mapped to the closest color available. Returning to our hexadecimal numbering scheme, the three darkest shades of red can be listed in ActionScript hex notation as 0x100000, 0x200000, 0x300000. Our list of magic numbers for the Nokia Communicator that allows us to derive hex values for all 4,096 non-dithered colors is exactly the same as the iPAQs:

```
00, 10, 20, 30, 40, 50, 60, 70, 80, 90, A0, B0, C0, D0, E0, F0.
```

What Does It Look Like?

Given that the only way you can view the differences between 8-bit, 12-bit, 16-bit and 24-bit color palettes is on a 24-bit monitor, examples showing these differences are best seen online at www.flashthefuture.com/a1.

At our online resource, you'll also find a range of 4,096 palettes to use when designing with Photoshop, Flash, or Fireworks. Demo FLA files to generate specific 12-bit palettes for both the iPAQ and Communicator can also be downloaded.

As always, if you're considering accessibility in your visual designs, remember to take the requirements of color-blind users into account.

iPAQ Hardcore Colorspace: A Brief Look Under the Hood

The 3600 series iPAQ's actual hardware specification is provided by Compaq for their public Linux implementation at www.handhelds.org/Compaq/iPAQH3600/iPAQ_H3600.html.

That document sheds light on a few confusing ideas. The iPAQ LCD has a 70Hz refresh rate, and the Intel StrongARM SA-1110 CPU is programmed in its 16-bit TFT mode. Color information from the StrongARM CPU is passed to the Sony CXD3508TQ LCD controller as 16 bits, but 4 bits of information are discarded *in hardware*, with the Sony ACX704AKM LCD panel using only the 4 most significant bits for each RGB color.

Because the 16-bit color information is converted to 12-bit color on the fly in hardware, the Windows CE operating system will report color information that is at odds with the actual color display of the LCD. In software, screen capture utilities such as PocketShot or IA ScreenShot will report the number of non-dithered colors to be twice the number of colors displayed on the screen, with the possible R, G, or B values being:

```
00, 08, 10, 18, 20, 28, 30, 38, 40, 48, 50, 58, 60, 68, 70, 78,
80, 88, 90, 98, A0, A8, B0, B8, C0, C8, D0, D8, E0, E8, F0, F8
```

However, visually comparing a color spectrum of these values on the iPAQ screen with a 16-bit desktop computer monitor will reveal that the iPAQ is only capable of displaying the original 12-bit colorspace discussed.

The other confusing trap that the unwary developer can fall into is that Microsoft provides a free Remote Display Control application as part of the Pocket PC PowerToys series. This enables the host desktop computer to display a window mirroring the actual iPAQ display in semi-realtime. However, the colors rendered in this so-called mirror are often inexact approximations of the actual iPAQ display, and screen captures of the host machine's iPAQ window will provide incorrect RGB values. Therefore, you won't want to rely on this method to give you actual RGB values of the iPAQ screen.

A2

XML OR LOADVARIABLES? FROM THE PERSPECTIVE OF A WIRELESS DEVELOPER

Chris Pelsor

When developing a data-driven solution for a wireless device like Pocket PC or the Nokia 92xx line of phones, you have several options. The most commonly used methods are XML documents and loadVariables. Each has obvious advantages and disadvantages, and the one you choose will depend heavily on several factors, including but not limited to:

- The amount of data being loaded at any given time
- Development time/ease of development
- Speed
- Connectivity (that is, will you be connected when you view the content?)

We will focus on the first three factors in particular: file size, development time/ease of development, and speed. For further developments and examples, please check the relevant area of our website, www.flashthefuture.com/a2, for updates and examples.

loadVariables

Most Flash developers are familiar with loadVariables. In Flash 4, it was the method of choice for getting data into and out of Flash. Furthermore, it was flexible enough to allow the use of either static text files or dynamic content. In Flash 5 this functionality was improved with addition of the ability to load data into specific clips and to test for the reception data using the onClipEvent(data) event. (Flash MX further improved and stabilized the implementation.) In both Flash 5 and Flash MX, data formatted for use with this method also tends to be smaller than comparable data formatted in XML documents.

The downside of using loadVariables is that it is very difficult to manage large sets of data manually, especially if that data involves repeated sets of information, such as address lists. There were many workarounds, most notably the use of pseudo-arrays and heavy reliance on variable naming conventions. This approach is very time-consuming to program, and the data is very difficult to work with by hand. It is this type of data that XML was made for.

XML

New to Flash 5, the XML object is a welcome addition to the data access developer's toolbox. Furthermore, with the introduction of XMLnitro (developed by Branden Hall and available at http://chattyfig.figleaf.com/~bhall/code/xmlnitro.as), we have a fast, efficient way to handle large sets of data. XML is also a human-readable format, which makes it simple to use and edit as either a static or dynamic data distribution method.

The downside of using XML is that, because it is text-based, the functionality required to convert a document is very expensive with regards to system resources. String manipulation in any programming language is very processor-intensive, and Flash 5 is no exception. Therefore, if you need your program to work with the data very quickly once it has been received, then XML may not be the best choice.

Another point to keep in mind is that the XML object may be implemented differently on different devices. For example, there are significant differences in the implementation of the XML object in the Flash Player on the Pocket PC and the Nokia 92xx. On the Pocket PC, the XML object is written in ActionScript, so the use of XMLnitro will be beneficial to your app. On the Nokia 92xx phones, the XML parser was made native to the player. Thus using XMLnitro actually *decreases* performance by forcing the player to use an ActionScript version of the parser.

Benchmarks

We can talk all day about personal preferences for one format or another and the reasons for them; but when you get down to it, performance always plays a huge part in deciding what data access method to use. We will be looking at performance results for both creating data for upload and processing time for downloads.

Download Benchmarks

For our download benchmark, we compared two files with identical data structures and two files with near-identical sizes (the two files were off by three bytes). The device used in the tests was a Compaq iPAQ 3630 with 21.34 MB of RAM allocated to programs. The benchmark utility can be found on the CD-ROM included with this book in the Chapter 5 folder under data_driven_benchmarks.

At the time of this writing, the loadVariables loaded an identical data structure approximately 54 times faster than the XML object, as follows:

Time to Download Same-Structure Files (in milliseconds)

Run #	XML File Size: 6.97 KB	loadVariables File Size: 2.82 KB
1	8,237	122
2	8,897	125
3	9,137	125
4	9,302	126
5	9,259	125

As for identical file sizes, the numbers did not change drastically:

Time to Download Same-Size Files (in milliseconds)

Run #	XML File Size: 6.97 KB	loadVariables File Size: 6.99 KB
1	8,984	173
2	9,415	170
3	9,351	175
4	9,408	170
5	9,494	178

Although the times may appear to make it obvious which data format to use, there are, as previously stated, many factors to consider. If it makes coding simpler and more maintainable, or if you will be updating the data by hand as opposed to using a server-side scripting solution, XML may be much more appealing in the end for downloading data.

Upload Benchmarks

Upload statistics simply measure the amount of time to construct from scratch the same documents used in the download benchmarks, using the same device and settings as before. First, we will look at the numbers for identical data structures:

Time to Upload Same-Structure Files (in milliseconds)

Run #	XML File Size: 6.97 KB	loadVariables File Size: 2.82 KB
1	6,361	400
2	7,101	410
3	7,135	411
4	6,995	390
5	7,213	404

And identical file sizes:

Time to Upload Same-Size Files (in milliseconds)

Run #	XML File Size: 6.97 KB	loadVariables File Size: 6.99 KB
1	6,499	1664
2	7,289	1647
3	7,077	1607
4	7,253	1574
5	7,057	1557

Once again, these numbers only illustrate raw processing speeds, and they are only one factor in the many involved in deciding on a data format.

Summary

Because so many factors are involved in deciding which data format to use, we don't believe that one method is better than the other. Instead, we can offer these points to consider when thinking about data on wireless devices:

LoadVariables

- Excellent for use in asynchronous forms
- Good for use with small, manageable, repeated data sets
- Not good for large, repeated data sets like mailing lists, because it can be very difficult to maintain the data if done by hand

XML

- Excellent for repeated data sets of any kind
- Excellent for off-line viewing
- Much easier to program and maintain
- Data is human-readable

As XML for the device space evolves, please check the relevant area of our website, www.flashthefuture.com/a2, for updates or further information.

A3

FLASH FOR C++ DEVELOPERS— AN OVERVIEW

by Jeroen Steenbeek

Developing applications on Pocket PCs usually requires the skills of a C++ or Visual Basic programmer, because these languages have the capabilities required to build content of any sophistication. However, with the introduction of an advanced scripting language in Flash 5, Flash ActionScript–based applications have certain advantages over the normal choices available from Microsoft's eMbedded Visual Tools. Extensive rich media support and a rapid application development environment, like that offered by Flash, can make some projects more viable than they might be in another language.

One of the main strengths of Flash is its virtual machine, which allows content fidelity with great accuracy on a wide range of operating systems and hardware platforms. Coming from the C++ world, you'll be relieved to know that Flash handles common application issues—such as distributing correct Dynamic Link Libraries, rendering graphics, embedding fonts, playing audio, and accessing network services—all within the self-contained Flash Player. The metaphors for these technologies are covered in other chapters within this book—but if you're a C++ developer investigating the feasibility of Flash as an application development platform for your next project, this appendix will provide you with concepts of how to translate main C++ principles into the Flash ActionScript model and examine main limitations of object-oriented programming (OOP) in Flash.

Let's begin our look at the object-oriented model of Flash ActionScript.

OOP in Flash

Although Flash ActionScript uses objects, it does not support formal declarations of classes. C++ requires a strongly typed class definition at compile time, whereas classes and objects in Flash are defined, constructed, inherited, and modified at runtime. The main difference between the object models of C++ and ActionScript is that C++ supports Class-based inheritance, whereas ActionScript supports Prototype-based inheritance. What does that mean?

Prototype-Based Inheritance

An object in Flash is a compound data type with its own variables and methods, derived form the base class Object. A constructor function defines a class of objects, and constructor functions are invoked to create object instances. Each constructor function has a prototype property, which contains constants and methods that are passed on to objects created with that constructor function.

Prototypes are the key to inheritance, function overloading, and other typical OOP practices in Flash.

When invoking a constructor function, the resulting object instance is provided with a __proto__ property, which refers back to the prototype property of the constructor function. Via this __proto__ property, each object inherits all properties of the prototype of its constructor function. By extending the prototype of a constructor function with methods and variables a class can be customized. Thus all object instances created with the same constructor function inherit the same properties.

The __proto__ property defines which prototype a class instance is derived from. Inheritance is implemented by assigning the __proto__ property of a constructor function prototype to the prototype of another constructor function.

Summarized, a prototype can thus contain the following properties:

- Functions
- Constants
- A reference to another prototype

All object instances created with the same constructor inherit all properties of their mutual prototype property.

Each object instance in turn can additionally have:

- Instance functions
- Instance variables
- A reference to the prototype used to create the instance

These functions and variables are local to the object.

Using ActionScript to Simulate C++ Structures

Even though ActionScript is not a class-based object oriented programming language, it allows for many different ways to simulate many class-based programming features.

ActionScript has its limitations, though. For example, the following typical C++ structures are *not* supported in ActionScript:

- Multiple inheritance
- Class destructors
- Access control of class members
- Abstract methods and classes
- Templates
- Exception handling
- Operator overloading

Examples

This section will provide examples of how standard C++ issues can be implemented in ActionScript. Remember, there is not one single right way to implement class-based programming practices in ActionScript. These samples merely serve as an illustration of possible implementations of C++ structures in Flash.

The ActionScript examples in this appendix use the Flash MX notation. Some Flash MX object inheritance structures will not work in Flash 5. Examples for both Flash 5 and Flash MX can be found in the A3 folder of the CD that accompanies this book.

For sake of brevity, C++ code is displayed inline where possible.

Constructing and Working with a Simple Class

This example shows how to define a class and to instantiate, use, and destroy an instance of this class in both C++ and ActionScript.

Listing A3.1: Creating a class in C++.

```
#include <stdio.h>

///////////////////////////////////////////////////////////////////////////
// CFirst class

class CFirst
{
public:
// Construction
    CFirst(int m_value) : m_value(m_value) {};
```

(continued on next page)

```
        // Method
        virtual int GetValue() { return m_value; };

// Attributes
private:
    int m_value;

};

main()
{
CFirst* pfirst = new CFirst(42);
out << pfirst->GetValue();
delete pfirst;
pfirst = null;
}
```

Listing A3.2: Creating a class in ActionScript.

```
//////////////////////////////////////////////////////////////////
// First class

// Define constructor
function First(value) {
    this.m_value = value;
}

// Add method First::getValue()
First.prototype.getValue = function() {
    return this.m_value;
}

// Usage
var f = new First(42);
trace(f.getValue());
delete f;
```

Although both examples achieve the same results, the differences between C++ and ActionScript in these examples are plentiful:

- ActionScript does not need include files to be able to execute specific functionality. All ActionScript capabilities are available any time.
- ActionScript has no program entry point like C/C++'s main() function. Flash program execution starts at the first frame of the main timeline, from where the execution flow is determined by the composition of the movie. ActionScript code is executed either when the Flash playhead hits a keyframe containing ActionScript or when a predefined event is fired for which handler code is implemented.
- ActionScript uses function declarations as constructors to instantiate objects using the new operator.
- Class methods are defined by declaring a function, which must be assigned to the class's prototype property.
- Although it is beyond the scope of this appendix to go into much greater detail, it is worth mentioning that functions in ActionScript in fact have a prototype property themselves.
- ActionScript is non-typed. Each data type in Flash is invisibly encapsulated by one of the standard Flash classes (like Boolean, Number, String, or Object), which enable the programmer to invoke class methods on variables without having to type cast first. Type casting is a process that happens the moment a variable is used in an operator of another class. For instance, the result of the getValue call may be added to a string or may be used in arithmetic operations. Depending on the usage of a variable, Flash type casts automatically.
- Flash does not support access control of class members. The function getValue and the member variable m_value can be accessed, modified, and deleted by anyone, anytime.
- Lastly, like Java, Flash does not support pointers. Flash handles all garbage collection for you; object instances exist as long as there are references to that object. This method of garbage collection is often referred to as garbage collection by reference counting. In the example, the variable *f* increases the number of references to the instance or object of the class First. Deleting *f* is enough to lower the reference count of the instance by one to zero, effectively marking the memory occupied by the instance for deletion by garbage collection.

Inheritance

In this example, the previous code samples will each be extended with a second class, CSecond, which inherits from CFirst. The second class will additionally override a method of its base-class.

Listing A3.4: Inheritance in C++.

```
///////////////////////////////////////////////////////////////////////
// CSecond class

class CSecond : public CFirst
{
public:
    // Construction: call base-class constructor
    CSecond(int value) : CFirst(value) {};

    // Method: override base-class method
    int GetValue() { return -1; }; // Still virtual
};
```
Listing A3.5 Inheritance in ActionScript
```
///////////////////////////////////////////////////////////////////////
// Second class

// Constructor
function Second(value) {
        // Call baseclass constructor
        super(value);
}

// Inherit class Second from class First. Note that the method
// used here is new to Flash MX and will not work in Flash 5.
Second.prototype = new First();

// Overwrite getValue
Second.prototype.getValue = function() {
    return (this.m_value * -1);
}
```

As stated before, ActionScript uses prototype-based inheritance, and here you see it in full action. First, a constructor function is defined. The implementation of this constructor function is rather uneventful; it merely invokes its superclass constructor function. Once the constructor function is defined, inheritance is established by forcing the prototype of the Second constructor function to be an instance of First. This effectively ensures that subsequent instances of Second inherit all methods from the prototype of First!

Lastly, a new method is added to the prototype of the Second constructor function. The method First::getValue() is replaced in execution by the method Second::getValue(). Note, however, that the reference to First::getValue() in the prototype of First still exists. We will use that facility when overloading methods from base classes. But first, you'll need to know about another powerful feature of Flash.

Extending Flash Base Classes

Another feature of Flash that I deliberately failed to mention earlier is that any newly defined class in Flash already has a base class. All newly defined classes automatically inherit from the class Object unless specified otherwise. In the ActionScript examples so far, First is inherited from Object and Second is inherited from First.

Flash allows modifications to any class at runtime without having to inherit from that class. Even the Flash standard classes like Object, Boolean, Number, String, and so forth can be extended—or, as some may say, polluted—with prototyped methods. Listing A3.6 illustrates how the classes First and Second inherit modifications made to the Flash's base class Object.

Listing A3.6: Extending Flash classes

```
Object.prototype.ping = function() {
    trace("I'm here");
}

// Usage
var s = Second();
s.ping();
delete s;
```

When executed, this instance of Second will invoke the ping function, indicating that Second inherited this method from Object via First.

Overloading Methods

Because of its interpreted nature, ActionScript uses dynamic binding exclusively. Listing A3.7 shows that via some tricks, Flash classes are capable of overloading base-class methods while preserving—and calling—the overloaded method.

Listing A3.7: Overloading a method in C++.

```
/////////////////////////////////////////////////////////////////////////
// CThird class

class CThird : public CFirst
{
public:
    // Construction
    CThird(int value, int factor) : CFirst(value), m_factor(factor) {};

    // Overloaded method, still virtual
    int GetValue() { return CFirst::GetValue() * m_factor; };
```

(continued on next page)

```
// Attributes
private:
    int m_factor;
};
```

Listing A3.8: Inheritance in ActionScript.

```
///////////////////////////////////////////////////////////////////////
// Third class

// Constructor
function Third(value, factor) {
    this.m_factor = factor;
    super(value);
}

// Implement inheritance
Third.prototype = new First();

// Overload and extend getValue
Third.prototype.getValue = function() {
    // Call superclass version of this method, and multiply
    // result by m_factor
    return (super.getValue() * this.m_factor);
}

// Usage
var t = new Third(6, 3)
trace(t.getValue()); // Returns 18
delete t;
```

In Listing A3.8, the implementation of Third::getValue uses the method super() to invoke the superclass version of the method getValue. Note that super, in case of multiple levels of inheritance, does not allow you to perform the typical C++ practice to specify which superclass implementation of a method to call. The ActionScript interpreter will merely walk the inheritance chain and invoke the next available implementation of getValue.

By combining the prototype chain and the method-overloading scheme, plenty of C++ features can be simulated. For inspiration, consider the next example that implements Copy Constructors in Flash.

Copy Constructors

Flash is an untyped language. Internally, the primitive data types in Flash are encapsulated by wrapper objects that are created transiently when necessary, allowing for flexible data conversions. If, for instance, you add a number to a string, the number is automatically—and invisibly—converted to a string so the addition can be made.

The fact that variables are dynamically translated between types can sometimes be counterproductive; the actual conversion is controlled by Flash, which may produce unwanted results. Flash base classes therefore provide a series of methods that can be used to perform type conversions manually.

Flash, however, lacks the equivalent of the Copy Constructor in C++. Constructing copies of Object instances in Flash entails a lot of effort but, with a bit of smart programming, you can develop a Copy Constructor yourself.

Listing A3.9: Copy Constructor in C++.

```
//////////////////////////////////////////////////////////////////////////
// CCopyConstrFirst class

class CCopyConstrFirst
{
public:
    // Normal constructor
    CCopyConstrFirst (int value) : m_value(value) {};

    // Default constructor
    CCopyConstrFirst() : m_value(0) {};

    // Copy constructor
    CCopyConstrFirst (CCopyConstrFirst& ssf) { m_value = ssf.m_value; };

    // Method: override base-class method
    virtual int GetValue() { return m_value; };

private:
    int m_value;
};


//////////////////////////////////////////////////////////////////////////
// CCopyConstrSecond class

class CCopyConstrSecond : public CCopyConstrFirst
{
public:
    // Normal constructor
    CCopyConstrSecond(int value, int factor) :
```

(continued on next page)

```
        CCopyConstrFirst(value), m_factor(factor) {};

    // Default constructor
    CCopyConstrSecond() :
        CCopyConstrFirst::CcopyConstrFirst(),
        m_factor(0) {};

    // Copy constructor
    CCopyConstrSecond(CCopyConstrSecond& ccs) {
        CCopyConstrFirst::CCopyConstrFirst((CFirst&) ccs);
        m_value = ccs.m_value;
    };

    // Overloaded method
    int GetValue() { return CCopyConstrFirst::GetValue() * m_factor; };

// Attributes
private:
    int m_factor;
};
```

Listing A3.10: Copy Constructor in ActionScript.

```
/////////////////////////////////////////////////////////////////////
// CopyConstrFirst Class: base class with copy constructor

// Constructor
function CopyConstrFirst(value) {
    // Check if value is an object of type CopyConstrFirst that
    // needs to be copied
    if (value instanceof CopyConstrFirst)
    {
        // Copy constructor
        this.m_value = value.m_value;
    }
    else
    {
        // Normal constructor
        this.m_value = value;
    }
}

CopyConstrFirst.prototype.getValue = function() {
    return this.m_value;
}
```

```
///////////////////////////////////////////////////////////////////////
// CopyConstrSecond: CopyConstrFirst inherited class with copy constructor

// Constructor
function CopyConstrSecond(value, factor) {
    if (value instanceof CopyConstrSecond)
    {
        // Copy constructor
        this.m_factor = value.m_factor;
    }
    else
    {
        // Normal constructor
        this.m_factor = factor;
    }
    super(value);
}

// Define inheritance
CopyConstrSecond.prototype = new CopyConstrFirst();

// Overload and extend getValue
CopyConstrSecond.prototype.getValue = function() {
    return (super.getValue() * this.m_factor);
}

// Usage

// Create a CopyConstrFirst instance using the normal constructor
var f1 = new CopyConstrFirst(42);
trace(f1.getValue()); // Returns 42

// Create a CopyConstrFirst instance using the copy constructor
var f2 = new CopyConstrFirst(f1);
trace(f2.getValue()); // Returns 42

// Create a CopyConstrSecond instance using the normal constructor
var f3 = new CopyConstrSecond(6, 3);
trace(f3.getValue()); // Returns 18

// Create a CopyConstrSecond instance using the copy constructor
var f4 = new CopyConstrSecond(f3);
trace(f4.getValue()); // Returns 18
```

In Listing A3.9 and A3.10, the constructor of a class determines whether the first passed argument is of the same type as the class that is being constructed. If so, the class copies all properties of the argument into its own address space, performing like a typical copy constructor. If not so, the class initializes its properties from the passed arguments.

This example uses the fact that ActionScript variables are non-typed, together with a feature of Flash that has not been mentioned before: A function can be called with less parameters than it was declared with. Flash simply assigns the value undefined to missing function parameters, which is a valid value just like any other value in Flash.

Summary

We hope we have given C++ programmers considering Flash as an alternative an idea of its object-oriented programming capabilities. The topics that potentially can be discussed are countless, and this book is not about programming C++ in Flash.

Because of the flexibility of ActionScript, the possibilities to simulate structures are endless. For example, it was stated earlier that Flash does not support template classes. But is that really true? It may be just a matter of time before some ingenious mind comes up with a full-fledged template structure for ActionScript. Who knows, that mind may be yours. . . .

Concluding, in comparison to C++, Flash ActionScript is a primitive object oriented programming language. Considering the difference in applications of Flash and C++, this primitivism is not necessary good or bad. Large-scale projects require strong typed and thoroughly structured languages like C++, which impose rigorous design and programming practices, allowing for optimal reuse, easier maintenance, and high complexity. Smaller-scale projects may benefit from a more relaxed development environment like Flash. What Flash lacks in powerful OO structures can partially be made up for by the fact that ActionScript can be molded to simulate features of more advanced languages.

Readers who are interested in further information should check the relevant area of our website, www.flashthefuture.com/a3, where—in addition to updates—there will be a listing of relevant URLs.

INDEX

THE ART OF INTERACTIVE DESIGN
A Euphonious and Illuminating Guide to Building Successful Software

by CHRIS CRAWFORD

Renowned author Chris Crawford demonstrates what interactivity is, why it's important, and how to design interactive software, games, and websites that work. Crawford's mellifluous style makes for fascinating and idea-inspiring reading that encourages you to think about design in new ways.

2002, 256 PP., $29.95 ($44.95 CDN)
ISBN 1-886411-84-0

THE BOOK OF JAVASCRIPT
A Practical Guide to Interactive Web Pages

by THAU!

This tutorial/reference teaches JavaScript with real-world examples so you can learn how to work with image swaps, functions, frames, cookies, alarms, and more.

"Of all the JavaScript tutorials out there, *The Book of JavaScript* is one of the more engaging and truly effective."—*Amazon.com*

2002, 304 PP., $29.95 ($44.95 CDN)
ISBN 1-886411-76-X

THE SOUND BLASTER LIVE!™ BOOK
A Complete Guide to the World's Most Popular Sound Card

by LARS AHLZEN *and* CLARENCE SONG

Configure your hardware; watch DVDs in surround sound; record and organize digital audio MP3s; and use sequencers, MIDI, and SoundFonts to compose music. The CD-ROM includes music and audio examples, sample sound clips, SoundFonts, and audio software.

2002, 504 PP., $49.95 ($74.95 CDN)
ISBN 1-886411-73-5

HOW NOT TO PROGRAM IN C++

III Broken Programs and 3 Working Ones, or Why 2+2=5986

by STEVE OUALLINE

Find the bugs in these broken programs and become a better programmer. Based on real-world errors, the puzzles range from easy (one wrong character) to mind twisting (errors with multiple threads). Match your wits against the author's and polish your language skills as you try to fix broken programs. Clues help along the way, and answers are provided at the back of the book.

2002, 304 PP., $24.95 ($37.95 CDN)
ISBN 1-886411-95-6

THE BOOK OF 802.11

Install, Configure and Use Wireless Networking

by JOHN ROSS

This plain English guide to the 802.11b wireless networking standard teaches readers how to use wireless networks at home, work, or in their neighborhood. Includes detailed, practical information on access points, network interface cards, cables and antennas, and wireless software. Readers learn how to protect their wireless access point from unwanted intruders with encryption, password protection, and virtual private networks (VPNs), and how to configure wireless connections for Windows, Macintosh, Linux, Unix, and PDAs.

2003, 504 PP., $39.95 ($59.95 CDN)
ISBN 1-886411-45-X

Phone:

1 (800) 420-7240 OR
(415) 863-9900
MONDAY THROUGH FRIDAY,
9 A.M. TO 5 P.M. (PST)

Fax:

(415) 863-9950
24 HOURS A DAY,
7 DAYS A WEEK

Email:

SALES@NOSTARCH.COM

Web:

HTTP://WWW.NOSTARCH.COM

Mail:

NO STARCH PRESS, INC.
555 DE HARO STREET, SUITE 250
SAN FRANCISCO, CA 94107
USA

Distributed in the U.S. by Publishers Group West

UPDATES

Visit **http://www.flashthefuture.com** for updates, errata, and other information.

FLASH MX REQUIREMENTS FROM MACROMEDIA

Authoring

Windows

200 MHz Pentium processor

Windows 98 SE / Me / NT4 / 2000 / XP

64 MB of free available system RAM (128 MB recommended)

85 MB of available disk space

1024 x 768, 16-bit (thousands of colors) color display or better

CD-ROM drive

Macintosh

Mac OS 9.1 and higher, or OS X 10.1 and higher

64 MB of free available system RAM (128 MB recommended)

85 MB of available disk space

1024 x 768, 16-bit (thousands of colors) color display or better

CD-ROM drive

Playback

Windows

Windows 95 / 98 / ME: Internet Explorer 4.0 or later, Netscape Navigator 4 or later, Netscape 6.2 or later, with standard install defaults, AOL 7 and Opera 6

Windows NT / 2000 / XP or later: Internet Explorer 4.0 or later, Netscape Navigator 4 or later, Netscape 6.2 or later, with standard install defaults, Compuserve 7 (2000 & XP only), AOL 7, and Opera 6

Macintosh

System 8.6 / 9.0 / 9.1 / 9.2: Netscape plug-in works with Netscape 4.5 or later, Netscape 6.2 or later, Microsoft Internet Explorer 5.0 or later, and Opera 5

OS X 10.1 or later: Netscape plug-in works with Netscape 6.2 or later, Microsoft Internet Explorer 5.1 or later, and Opera 5

CD-ROM LICENSE AGREEMENT FOR *FLASH*™: *THE FUTURE*

Read this Agreement before opening the CD package. By opening this package, you agree to be bound by the terms and conditions of this Agreement.

This CD-ROM (the "CD") contains programs and associated documentation and other materials and is distributed with the book entitled *Flash™: The Future* to purchasers of the book for their own personal use only. Such programs, documentation, and other materials and their compilation (collectively, the "Collection") are licensed to you subject to the terms and conditions of this Agreement by No Starch Press, Inc., having a place of business at 555 De Haro Street, Suite 250, San Francisco, CA 94107 USA ("Licensor"). In addition to being governed by the terms and conditions of this Agreement, your rights to use the programs and other materials included on the CD may also be governed by separate agreements distributed with those programs and materials (the "Other Agreements"). In the event of any inconsistency between this Agreement and any of the Other Agreements, those Other Agreements shall govern insofar as those programs and materials are concerned. By using the Collection, in whole or in part, you agree to be bound by the terms and conditions of this Agreement. Licensor owns the copyright to the Collection, except insofar as it contains materials that are proprietary to third-party suppliers. All rights to the Collection except those expressly granted to you in this Agreement are reserved to Licensor and such suppliers as their respective interests may appear.

1. Limited License. Licensor grants you a limited, nonexclusive, nontransferable license to use the Collection on a single dedicated computer (excluding network servers). This Agreement and your rights hereunder shall automatically terminate if you fail to comply with any provision of this Agreement or the Other Agreements. Upon such termination, you agree to destroy the CD and all copies of the CD, whether lawful or not, that are in your possession or under your control. Licensor and its suppliers retain all rights not expressly granted herein as their respective interests may appear.

2. Additional Restrictions. (A) You shall not (and shall not permit other person or entities to) directly or indirectly, by electronic or other means, reproduce (except for archival purposes as permitted by law), publish, distribute, rent, lease, sell, sublicense, assign, or otherwise transfer the Collection or any part thereof of this Agreement. Any attempt to do so shall be void and of no effect. (B) You shall not (and shall not permit other person or entities to) reverse-engineer, decompile, disassemble, merge, modify, create derivative works of, or translate the Collection or use the Collection or any part thereof for any commercial purpose. (C) You shall not (and shall not permit other person or entities to) remove or obscure Licensor's or its suppliers' or licensors' copyright, trademark, or other proprietary notices or legends from any portion of the Collection or any related materials. (D) You agree and certify that the Collection will not be exported outside the United States except as authorized or permitted by the laws and regulations of the United States. If the Collection has been rightfully obtained outside of the United States, you agree that you will not reexport the Collection, except as permitted by the laws and regulations of the jurisdiction in which you obtained the Collection.

3. Disclaimer of Warranty. (A) The Collection and the CD are provided "as is" without warranty of any kind, either expressed or implied, including, without limitation, any warranty of merchantability and fitness for a particular purpose. The entire risk as to the results and performance of the CD and the software and other materials that are part of the Collection is assumed by you, and Licensor and its suppliers and distributors shall have no responsibilityfor defects in the CD or the accuracy or application of or errors or omissions in the Collection, and do not warrant that the functions contained in the Collection will meet your requirements, or that the operation of the CD or the Collection will be uninterrupted or error-free, or that any defects in the CD or the Collection will be corrected. In no event shall Licensor or its suppliers or distributors be liable for any direct, indirect, special, incidental, or consequential damages arising out of the use of or inability to use the Collection or the CD, even if Licensor or its suppliers or distributors have been advised of the likelihood of such damages occurring. Licensor and its suppliers and distributors shall not be liable for any loss, damages, or costs arising out of, but not limited to, lost profits and revenue; loss of use of the Collection or the CD; loss of data or equipment; costs of recovering software, data, or materials in the collection; cost of substitute software, data, or materials in the Collection; claims by third parties, or similar costs. (B) In no event shall Licensor or its suppliers' or distributors' total liability to you for all damages, losses, and causes of action (whether in contract, tort, or otherwise) exceed the amount paid by you for the collection. (C) Some states do not allow exclusion or limitation of implied warranties or limitation of liability for incidental or consequential damages, so the above limitations or exclusions may not apply to you.

4. U.S. Government Restricted Rights. The Collection is licensed subject to RESTRICTED RIGHTS. Use, duplication, or disclosure by the U.S. Government or any person or entity acting on its behalf is subject to restrictions as set forth in subdivision (c)(1)(ii) of the Rights in the Technical Data and Computer Software Clause at DFARS (48 CFR 252.227-7013) for DoD contracts, in paragraphs (c)(1) and (2) of the Commercial Computer Software Restricted Rights clause in the FAR (48 CFR 52.227-19) for civilian agencies, or, in the case of NASA, in clause 18-52.227-86(d) of the NASA Supplement to the FAR, or in other comparable agency clauses. The contractor/manufacturer is No Starch Press, Inc., 555 De Haro Street, Suite 250, San Francisco, CA 94107 USA.

5. General Provisions. Nothing in this Agreement constitutes a waiver of Licensor's or its suppliers' or licensors' rights under U.S. copyright laws or any other federal, state, local, or foreign law. You are responsible for installation, management, and operation of the Collection. This Agreement shall be construed, interpreted, and governed under California law. Copyright © 2002 No Starch Press, Inc. All rights reserved. Reproduction in whole or in part without permission is prohibited.